Comparative Perspectives on Refugee Youth Education

This volume explores the shared expectations that education is a cure-all for the difficulties that refugees and their receiving countries face. Rather than focusing on pedagogy and language, as other volumes on refugee education have done, this book investigates the ways in which education is both a dream solution as well as a contested landscape for refugee families and students. Using comparative, cross-national perspectives across five continents, the editors and contributors critically analyze the educational structures, policies, and practices intended to support refugee youth transition from conflict and post-conflict zones to mainstream classrooms and schools in their receiving countries.

Alexander W. Wiseman is professor of Educational Leadership Policy at Texas Tech University, USA.

Lisa Damaschke-Deitrick is professor of Comparative & International Education at Lehigh University, USA.

Ericka Galegher is independent researcher affiliated with Lehigh University, USA.

Maureen F. Park is PhD candidate in Comparative & International Education at Lehigh University, USA.

Routledge Research in International and Comparative Education

This is a series that offers a global platform to engage scholars in continuous academic debate on key challenges and the latest thinking on issues in the fast-growing field of International and Comparative Education.

Titles in the Series Include

Actionable Research for Educational Equity and Social Justice
Higher Education Reform in China and Beyond
Edited by Wang Chen, Edward P. St. John, Xu Li, and Cliona Hannont

Cooperative and Work-Integrated Education in Asia
History, Present and Future Issues
Edited by Yasushi Tanaka and Karsten E. Zegwaard

Reforming Education in Developing Countries
From Neoliberalism to Communitarianism
Izhar Oplatka

Social Justice Education in European Multi-ethnic Schools
Addressing the Goals of Intercultural Education
Cinzia Pica-Smith, Rina Manuela Contini, and Carmen N. Veloria

Education and the Public Sphere
Exploring the Structures of Mediation in Post-Colonial India
Edited by Suresh Babu G. S.

Comparative Perspectives on Refugee Youth Education
Dreams and Realities in Educational Systems Worldwide
Edited by Alexander W. Wiseman, Lisa Damaschke-Deitrick, Ericka Galegher, and Maureen F. Park

For more information about this series, please visit: www.routledge.com/Routledge-Research-in-International-and-Comparative-Education/book-series/RRICE

Comparative Perspectives on Refugee Youth Education
Dreams and Realities in Educational Systems Worldwide

Edited by Alexander W. Wiseman,
Lisa Damaschke-Deitrick,
Ericka Galegher, and
Maureen F. Park

NEW YORK AND LONDON

First published 2019
by Routledge
52 Vanderbilt Avenue, New York, NY 10017

and by Routledge
2 Park Square, Milton Park, Abingdon, Oxon, OX14 4RN

Routledge is an imprint of the Taylor & Francis Group, an informa business

© 2019 Taylor & Francis

The right of Alexander W. Wiseman, Lisa Damaschke-Deitrick, Ericka Galegher, and Maureen F. Park to be identified as editors of this work has been asserted in accordance with sections 77 and 78 of the Copyright, Designs and Patents Act 1988.

All rights reserved. No part of this book may be reprinted or reproduced or utilised in any form or by any electronic, mechanical, or other means, now known or hereafter invented, including photocopying and recording, or in any information storage or retrieval system, without permission in writing from the publishers.

Trademark notice: Product or corporate names may be trademarks or registered trademarks, and are used only for identification and explanation without intent to infringe.

Library of Congress Cataloguing-in-Publication Data
A catalog record for this book has been requested

ISBN: 978-1-138-35949-9 (hbk)
ISBN: 978-0-429-43371-9 (ebk)

Typeset in Sabon
by Apex CoVantage, LLC

Contents

Acknowledgments   vii

Introduction: The Contested Expectations of Education as a Panacea for Refugee Transitions   1
ALEXANDER W. WISEMAN, LISA DAMASCHKE-DEITRICK, ERICKA GALEGHER AND MAUREEN F. PARK

PART 1
Global Policy Expectations for Refugees' Educational Transitions   25

1 Education as a Panacea for Refugee Integration? Evidence From Germany and the United States   27
LISA DAMASCHKE-DEITRICK AND ELIZABETH R. BRUCE

2 The Educational Response to Syrian Displacement: A Professionalizing Field in a Politicized Environment   53
ELIZABETH BUCKNER AND MOZYNAH NOFAL

3 Teacher Preparation, Classroom Pedagogy, and the Refugee Crisis in National Education Systems   75
ALEXANDER W. WISEMAN AND ERICKA GALEGHER

4 Creating a Refugee Space in the Canadian School Context: The Approach of an Inclusive Society   102
RATNA GHOSH, DOMENIQUE SHERAB, MAIHEMUTI DILIMULATI AND NARJES HASHEMI

Contents

5   A Comparative Policy Analysis of the Comprehensive
    Refugee Response Framework in Uganda and Kenya   131
    TSHEGOFATSO D. THULARE, CHRISTIN SPOOLSTRA, EILEEN
    DOMBROWSKI, RACHEL JORDAN, AND REHEMAH NABACWA

PART 2
Local Adaptations for Refugees' Educational Transitions   155

6   Female Refugees' Transitions Into Higher Education:
    Comparative Perspectives From Germany, Egypt, and
    Kyrgyzstan   157
    LISA DAMASCHKE-DEITRICK, ERICKA GALEGHER, AND
    MAUREEN F. PARK

7   Emergency Education for Rohingya Refugee Children in
    Bangladesh: An Analysis of the Policies, Practices, and
    Limitations   191
    MAHBUB ALAM PRODIP AND JOHANNA GARNETT

8   Immigrant Latina Youth and Their Education Experiences
    in the United States   220
    GABRIELLE OLIVEIRA AND MARIANA LIMA BECKER

9   Teacher Professional Development in Crisis Contexts:
    Teachers' Reflections and Stories of Change in
    Kakuma Refugee Camp   245
    MARY MENDENHALL, ARIANNA PACIFICO AND SHENSHEN HU

10 "Whose Knowledge?" Putting Politics Back Into
    Curriculum Choices for Refugees   271
    JO KELCEY

    List of Contributors   292
    Index   300

Acknowledgments

The editors are grateful to many colleagues and friends who have encouraged us to pursue this fruitful and important work on refugee education. We are especially grateful to those who have also provided the professional opportunities, well-needed resources, and rigorous, challenging conversations necessary to do research that not only adds to the scholarly research on the topic of refugees and education, but makes an impact to improve conditions, provide opportunities, and create compassion in educational contexts.

First and foremost, we would like to thank Prof. Dr. Karin Amos at the University of Tübingen. Her professionalism and scholarship serve as a firm foundation for her support and encouragement of Alexander W. Wiseman and Lisa Damaschke-Deitrick. Collaboration with Prof. Dr. Amos has made this and many other projects both intensely meaningful and highly productive over many years. Dr. Annika Wilmers and Dr. Sieglinde Jornitz at DIPF Leibniz Institute for Research and Information in Education have inspired and supported our work on refugee and migrant education through their critical insights and backing for professional meetings on the topic. Dr. Christine Rubas at the University of Tübingen has provided opportunities for our colleagues and students to engage directly with programs and people who are on the front line of education for refugees and has been a friend and colleague throughout. Finally, none of this would be possible without the years of inspirational ideas, long hours of hard work, and dedication to both the team and the dream of creating better education for all that Dr. Petrina Davidson contributed to this and related projects. Dr. Davidson has been a spark of light during the conceptual development upfront, a supremely organized planner, insightful thinker and researcher, and a genuine educator and consummate professional throughout every project we've worked on together. Thank you all for making this volume possible, and for your support and collaboration from the beginning.

Finally, we would like to thank our families for always being there, giving us the leeway to meet after hours and over holidays and weekends, and for believing in what we were doing even when we sometimes doubted ourselves. No major work like this is possible without your support, and we cannot thank you enough.

Introduction
The Contested Expectations of Education as a Panacea for Refugee Transitions

Alexander W. Wiseman, Lisa Damaschke-Deitrick, Ericka Galegher and Maureen F. Park

Researchers and policymakers alike share the expectation that education is a tool to either resolve or address the difficulties refugees and their receiving countries face (Sinclair, 2001; Burde, Kapit, Wahl, Guven, & Skarpeteig, 2017). Most research on refugee education focuses on the role that either pedagogy or language plays in facilitating the education of refugees or erecting barriers to their formal education, which is either explicitly or implicitly suggested to be a way to transition refugee and asylum-seeking youth to more productive, healthy, and adjusted lives (Bartlett & Ghaffar-Kucher, 2013; Brown & Krasteva, 2013; Culbertson & Constant, 2015; McCarthy & Vickers, 2012).

While previous refugee education related studies follow a fruitful path, they universally ignored the ways in which education is often presented as a dreamlike solution to refugees' challenges while in reality also being a contested landscape for refugee families and students. The conundrum of expecting education to act as a panacea for refugees is that although it is neither a consistent nor necessarily effective mechanism for transitioning refugee youth into receiving countries and new communities, it still provides legitimacy for the faith in education to create emotional stability, intellectual curiosity, academic achievement, employable skill development, and social integration for refugee youth and their families. This critique neither ignores nor minimizes the positive and productive impact that formal education has had on refugee, asylum-seeking, and forced migrant youth (Peterson, Meehan, Ali, & Durrant, 2017), but instead highlights the need for a balanced, research-to-practice examination of the ways that expectations about "education as a panacea" either are or are not supported by empirical evidence of the actual impact education has on refugee youth and their communities.

A breadth of approaches is necessary to provide both a foundation of conceptual frameworks for understanding the phenomenon of "education as a panacea" within the refugee context, but also to dialectically analyze the various approaches to refugee education that international organizations, national governments, universities, and local schools and communities take. This pluralism of perspectives allows for diverse approaches (1) to the critical analysis of educational expectations by and for refugees as well as (2) to the measurable impact of educational structures, policies, and practices intended to support refugee youths' transitions from conflict and post-conflict zones to mainstream classrooms and schools in their receiving countries (Johnson & Onwuegbuzie, 2004). In doing so, the voices of refugee students and their families, as well as those of educators, aid workers, and practitioners working with them may be heard (Eisner, 2017).

Who Is a Refugee?

In a small Jewish journal in 1943, Hannah Arendt expressed what it feels like to be a refugee, which provides an insight into what the refugee experience, and thus what a refugee is. Arendt (1943) said,

> We lost our home, which means the familiarity of daily life. We lost our occupation, which means the confidence that we are of some use in this world. We lost our language, which means the naturalness of reactions, the simplicity of gestures, the unaffected expression of feelings. We left our relatives in the Polish ghettos and our best friends have been killed in concentration camps, and that means the rupture of our private lives.

The United Nations High Commissioner for Refugees (UNHCR), which serves as the "guardian" of the 1951 Geneva Refugee Convention and 1967 Protocol, defines a refugee as "someone who has been forced to flee his or her country because of persecution, war, or violence" with "a well-founded fear of persecution for reasons of race, religion, nationality, political opinion or membership in a particular social group" (para. 1). As a result of "war, ethnic, tribal, and religious violence" (UNHCR, n.d., para. 1), refugees cannot return home. As such, they are afforded special legal status and protections (Buckner, Spencer, & Cha, 2017) unavailable to other categories of migrants. Haddad (2004) further delineates the term refugees as "political construction[s]" (p. 24) affected by countries' foreign policy strategies that dictate who is provided assistance and the timing of this assistance (Haddad, 2004). This distinction serves to further address the differences in the terms *refugees* and *migrants*, and is thoroughly discussed by Joly (2002). While a definitive definition remains elusive, Joly (2002) identifies two particular factors differentiating refugees from (economic) migrants. First, she points to changed conditions, largely unrelated to these individuals' economic situations, that "jeopardiz[e]" their current lives (p. 7). Second, she notes that these individuals do not leave out of optimism for their future elsewhere, and that they would have remained in their present places had change not occurred (Joly, 2002).

Displacement occurs for a variety of contextual reasons, and the distinction between documented and undocumented refugee and asylum-seeker is often the result of politics (Bartlett & Ghaffar-Kucher, 2013). Not yet afforded the legal protection of refugee status, asylum-seekers are defined as "someone whose request for sanctuary has yet to be processed," (UNHCR, 2017). By the end of 2017, more than 3 million people were awaiting decision on their asylum claims. The United States received the largest number of asylum claims in 2017, with 331,700 (UNHCR, 2017). These growing numbers are largely due to increasing claims from people from the north of Central America (NCA) (UNHCR, 2017). Until recently persons from NCA seeking asylum in the United States due to gang violence and domestic abuse were generally granted asylum. However, recent changes in political discourse have contributed to a hostile environment to migrants and refugees (Oliveira & Becker, 2019), and, as Oliveira and Becker note, the public perception of migrants varies significantly depending on legal status, with unauthorized immigrants viewed as a greater threat (2019). In the United States, largely due to these changing political attitudes, the number of resettled refugees has decreased significantly since 2016, and the refugee admission ceiling has been set for the lowest level since the resettlement program began in the United States in 1980 (Fratzke, 2017).

Migrants and forced migration are notably absent from the official UNHCR definition of refugees. The International Organization for Migration (IOM) (n.d.) defines forced migration as "migratory movement in which an element of coercion exists, including threats to life and livelihood, whether arising from natural or man-made causes." Another category of migrants not officially classified as refugees include internally displaced persons (IDPs). According to the Internal Displacement Monitoring Centre (IDMC), in 2017, there were more than 40 million IDPs as a result of "armed conflict, generalized violence or human rights violations" (UNHCR, n.d.). Although they remain within the borders of their own country and under the protection of their own government, they are often the most vulnerable people; access to humanitarian aid and education is frequently denied.

While the legal definition of refugee is static, it becomes apparent through listening to the experiences of those seeking refuge that refugee identity is fluid, and contextually dependent. Hannah Arendt (1943), describing her experience as a German refugee in the 1940s wrote,

> In the first place, we don't like to be called "refugees." We ourselves call each other "newcomers," or "immigrants." A refugee used to be a person driven to seek refuge because of some act committed or some political opinion held. Well, it is true we have had to seek refuge;

but we committed no acts and most of us never dreamt of having any radical opinion. With us the meaning of the term "refugee" has changed. Now "refugees" are those of us who have been so unfortunate as to arrive in a new country without means and have to be helped.

Arendt's description of her refugee experience represents both the agency to choose how to accept this label as well as the lack of agency in her journey through forced displacement. For the country of reception, refugee is often a means of categorization, but for the individual, this categorization can carry multiple wanted or unwanted labels (Burnett, 2013). For some, the label *refugee* carries significant stigma, largely the result of misconceptions in the country of reception (Burnett, 2013; Zetter, 2007). For example, many of the female refugees in Egyptian universities hid the fact that they were refugees because of the assumed stigma attached to the label and often relished in their newfound identity as students (Damaschke-Deitrick, Galegher, & Park, 2019). For others (see Damaschke-Deitrick & Bruce, 2019; Oliveira & Becker, 2019), the services and support attached to legal recognition of either refugee or asylum-seeker represents reprieve from the vulnerability and instability of displacement. Yet, legal documentation cannot dictate the experiences and identity of those forced to flee and seek refuge elsewhere.

Within this context, this volume adopts an inclusive definition of refugees and asylum-seeking youth. The research and experiences of participants in the following studies echo the complexities of current mass refugee crises, which arguably differ significantly from conditions of former refugee migration (see Zetter, 2007). The authors in this volume discuss individuals and populations that are labeled refugees and/or asylum-seekers through the political definition as well as figurative meaning "that changes based upon the individual, society and place: ranging from those in camp situations to someone awaiting an asylum decision to a refugee successfully integrated into his/her new host society" (Burnett, 2013, p. 2).

As a result of the macro-level policy focus and national level education systems, authors in Part 1 approach refugees and asylum-seekers through the political definition often based on the traditional UNHCR definition filtered through the politicization and public opinions of the countries and regions under study. Still many of the refugee populations in these studies vary greatly from protracted refugee camps in Uganda and Kenya (Thulare et al.), documented refugees and asylum-seekers and those awaiting a decision in the United States and Germany (Damaschke-Deitrick & Bruce), those on their journey through integration in the OECD (Wiseman & Galegher) and Canada (Ghosh et al.), and documented and undocumented Syrian refugees in the Middle East (Buckner & Nofal).

Authors in Part 2 approach the definition through more diverse and figurative meanings related to the undocumented individual in the United States (Oliveira & Becker) and stateless ethnic groups, like the Rohingya seeking refuge in Bangladesh (Prodip & Garnett). Many are documented, some hesitantly, such as the women refugees and asylum-seekers from Afghanistan, Yemen, and Syria in universities in Germany, Egypt, and Kyrgyzstan (Damaschke-Deitrick, Galegher, & Park). Others, such as the Palestinian refugees across multiple national borders (Kelcey) and refugee teachers in Kenya's Kakuma refugee camp from across Africa (Mendenhall et al.), are in a protracted state of displacement receiving support and educational services through a parallel education system under the auspices of UNWRA and UNHCR, respectively.

Although it is important to highlight as outlined in the preceding paragraphs the heterogeneity of these individuals, groups, contexts, and experiences, there are shared characteristics. Significant overlap exists in the experiences and journeys through forced displacement the individuals and populations in this volume face as a result of war, persecution, and violence. For all, they were unwilling victims to the perpetration of these injustices, and as a result, suffered significant trauma on their journey through forced displacement. All must navigate the complexities associated with their documented or undocumented status in their host communities and the loss of their home communities with significant implications on identity reformation. Yet, all managed to participate in some form of schooling in their location of displacement.

Education as a Panacea

Policymakers, the public, and individuals assume that education is a panacea for problems far beyond the scope of schools or academic teaching and learning. This assumption about education has become a solutionist's tool for not only society overall, but all types of issues and populations. Depending on the context, education may be useful for solving issues of health, conflict, the environment, and poverty, among others. Additionally, it is seen as a solution to problems facing the general population as well as more specific groups. With a broader notion of individual rights and abilities (Drori & Meyer, 2006), education is seen as a cure-all for males, females, the disabled, and indigenous groups, among others. The optimism surrounding education is just a segment of the optimism in human abilities to scientifically solve problems at large.

Policymakers' reliance on schooling as the panacea for social, political, and economic problems has been especially transparent since the early 20th century. Evidence that policymakers have used education as a scapegoat for non-education-related national concerns is provided by the many policy documents, mini-conferences, and academic papers that have used international achievement data to blame schools and teachers for these problems.

Although education is often considered a cure for social ills (Amos, Wiseman, & Rohstock, 2014; Wiseman, Damaschke-Deitrick, Bruce, Davidson, & Taylor, 2016), outcomes may not align with solutionist expectations. Additional research is needed to trace policy regarding education for transmitting socio-cultural norms to incoming refugee youth from international, national, and state levels to classroom enactment. Examining how policy is enacted can fill the information gap between the assumed promises of education and resulting practices (see Damaschke-Deitrick & Bruce, 2019). Although contexts vary, these issues have the potential to inform policy and practice and guide leaders and policymakers in various countries beyond the specific focus of translating refugee education policy to practice.

Educators, including principals and teachers, transmit socio-cultural norms and values through formal and informal interactions with students. Although socialization may be taken for granted by the general population, it is important for recently resettled immigrant refugee youth who are potentially unfamiliar with socio-cultural norms for their new contexts as well as host communities who are potentially unfamiliar with socio-cultural norms of refugee and asylum-seeking families. The Syrian Refugee Crisis, for example, resulting in the displacement of more than 12 million people, half of whom are children (Sirin & Rogers-Sirin, 2015), provides an opportunity to examine educational policy and practices to facilitate refugee youths' participation in education and the ability of education to resolve refugee youths' personal and community problems. Education provides access to improved social opportunities by integrating immigrant refugee youth into communities in developed countries (Beirens et al., 2007; Kia-Keating & Ellis, 2007). While there is significant literature on education for stabilizing poor and marginalized refugee communities, especially in immediate conflict and post-conflict locations, limited research exists on education as a solution for integrating highly educated refugees within developed country contexts, as is the case with many Syrian refugees coming into Europe (Sasnal, 2015).

Previous work investigated educational policy to examine how education serves as a solution for social issues and populations (see Wiseman et al.). Regarding refugee education, discourse frequently focuses on solutions and avoiding further escalation in emergency, (post-)conflict, or fragile contexts (Smith, 2009). However, the Syrian refugee crisis led to resettlement in areas outside the conflict. Refugee children often find themselves in unfamiliar places, with little knowledge of their new locations (Strekalova & Hoot, 2008). Educators are instrumental in the process of socialization (Mickan et al., 2007), defined as the "process of acquiring the norms to which all the members of a society conform" (Arnstine, 1995, p. 5). Classrooms become microcosms of society, giving refugee youth opportunities to experience socio-cultural norms and values before being immersed in the larger society (Mickan et al., 2007). Educators in these classrooms are themselves guided by educational policies filtered through their own experiences (Schmidt & Datnow, 2005), presenting individualized interpretations and enactments of international or national policies to their students (Spillane et al., 2002). For example, German teachers may engage in planned or impromptu "social pedagogy" to create intercultural identity awareness, teach socio-cultural norms and values, or emphasize communication in the receiving country's language (Schneider, 2018). Sullivan and Simonson's (2016) review of social-emotional interventions for refugee youth summarizes existing measures related to teachers' social pedagogy, which include intercultural pedagogical practices, teaching of socio-cultural norms and values, and teaching the receiving country's language.

Historically, refugees have low levels of education, poor vocational skills, and few financial resources (Strekalova & Hoot, 2008); however, documentation on Syrian refugees relocating to Europe indicates they are often wealthier, more skilled, and more educated than average Syrians (Sasnal, 2015). These demographics have the potential to create challenges for socialization and integration in new societies, as families may be moving from higher to lower social status in a very different context. Although policies may aim to equalize opportunities, previous research found inequalities may be exacerbated (Wiseman et al., 2016). Finally, the rapid increase in the inclusion of refugees in national education systems (see Dryden-Peterson et al., 2018) and the significant rise in university-qualified refugees from Syria present additional burdens on all levels of national education systems as well as donors to meet the aspirations of these youth to continue their education amidst increasing calls for the prevention of a "lost generation" (Barakat & Milton, 2015).

Schooling as a National Project

As a universally institutionalized system, education is embedded in every nation around the world. Even refugee youth, who are among the most vulnerable and marginalized, are typically enrolled in and attending formal school until they are forced to flee or are engaged in conflict at home. The journey of a refugee youth is difficult and often dangerous and fraught with both hope and dread. At each segment of a refugee youth's journey, education—usually in the form of some sort of schooling—is often present. Not surprisingly, education is both seen and used as a tool to ameliorate the problems and obstacles that children face in conflict and post-conflict situations.

During the 20th century, countries everywhere made large investments in public education to expand and increase the human, social, and political capital of youth attending school (Psacharopoulos, 1994). The rationale behind these investments in education was to make youths more economically productive by making schooling accessible to all youth, thus increasing their levels of educational attainment and providing them with "appropriate" citizenship education, values, and identity. However, an increase in the accessibility of education or in youths' educational attainment alone has neither ensured future economic productivity, social literacy, nor productive citizenship (Carnoy & Levin, 1985). Some of the blame for this failure of mass schooling to create model citizens or societies has been attributed to the rapid changes in technology and information systems that have dramatically altered world labor markets and communication during the 20th century (Carnoy, Castells, Cohen, & Cardoso, 1993). During the latter part of the 20th century schools increasingly shifted their formal curriculum and programs to meet employers' perceived needs rather than offering youth a steady diet of social and political education (Kanter & Lowe, 2000). Some have speculated that this overemphasis on economic productivity and deemphasis in values and citizenship education led in part to the social and political divisions which have resulted in national conflicts and forced the mass migration of refugees in the early 21st century (Khalilzad & Lesser, 1998).

The socio-political development of youth poses severe challenges to government-sponsored school systems because of the often impersonal, mass elements of public schooling (Meyer, Ramirez, Rubinson, & Boli-Bennett, 1977; Meyer, Ramirez, & Soysal, 1992). As a result, the rapid 20th century massification of education has often had dire consequences for youth both in and out of schools (e.g., Akiba, LeTendre, Baker, & Goesling, 2002).

Within the massification of education, access to education for refugees has slowly become embedded within international and national discourse, and subsequently national education systems worldwide. Rather than an institution geared toward human capital production, the role of education has expanded to include access as a universal human right. As Buckner and Nofal (2019) chronicle, the initial codification of this right in the Universal Declaration of Human Rights in 1948 and subsequent international declarations led to a slow normative shift toward the perception of the right to education for all, regardless of citizenship, as well as its role in crisis situations. This shift has potentially significant implications for national education systems.

In particular, questions remain concerning what extent national education systems are capable of providing quality education for all (see Thulare et al., 2019) and to what extent can and should non-citizens access all levels of education, and subsequently, labor markets in resource-limited countries (see Damaschke-Deitrick, Galegher, & Park, 2019). Nevertheless, eight out of the top ten refugee-hosting countries include refugees in their national education systems (Dryden-Peterson et al., 2018). Even when host country governments are unable or unwilling to provide refugees with formal education, governments still recognize the right to education and delegate the provision of education to non-governmental organizations (see Prodip & Garnett, 2019). Inclusion into national education systems is intended to shift the focus from short-term education for emergency relief to long-term education for development to address the increasingly protracted displacement refugees today experience (UNHCR, 2012).

Schools as Development Institutions

Education in developed nations, which are not experiencing conflict nor are in the throes of post-conflict reconstruction, is geared more toward developing high-achieving, productive citizens through formal education. The education that may be most needed by refugee youth and that is often provided in conflict and immediate post-conflict communities, however, is more humanitarian in nature. Education in stable economies and political systems is part of a national project to educate and socialize youth into the mainstream system, whereas education in unstable economies and fractured political systems may be part of the national institution but is supplemented by international relief organizations or subject to breakdowns in teacher provision, curriculum delivery, and infrastructure development.

Sociological research on the institutional environment of schooling emphasizes contextual effects on educational aspirations or achievement (e.g., Buchmann & Dalton, 2002), but there is little specifically on the association between the institutional context of schools and the interrelationship between the social and civic development of youth (Wiseman et al, 2011). There is also a body of literature related to the economic development of youth specifically concerning school-to-work transition (Entwisle, Alexander, & Olson, 2000) and gender stratification (Ramirez, Soysal, & Shanahan, 1997). Other research suggests that in spite of sociopolitical development both within and between nations, traditional values and ethnic identity persist (Inglehart & Baker, 2000), in spite of the influence of globalization cited by so many as the harbinger of cultural and ethnic transformation, if not annihilation.

Indeed, the socio-political development of youth is a function of schooling and a product of nation-building (Meyer, Boli, Thomas, & Ramirez, 1997). Institutionalized school models often focus on individuals' schooling as key to national economic security and competitiveness (Carnoy, 1985). The Western "myth of the individual," where the source of value and change in societies emphasizing school reform is the individual, provides the model framework for schooling around the world (Ramirez & Boli, 1987). Likewise, schooling contributes to the building of individuals as citizens in a nation-state. This argument has been extended to global citizenship, peace education in particular, as access to formal citizenship for many displaced refugees is unobtainable. Nevertheless, schooling is still seen as the vehicle through which development of the skills and knowledge needed as citizens in local refugee camp communities or for repatriation and resettlement.

Researchers are increasingly calling for financial and policy support for expanding the education continuum to include increased access to higher education for refugees (Dryden-Peterson, 2010). Not only is schooling, from primary to the tertiary level, expected to contribute to the realization of individual capabilities but also to be a key component to nation-building and reconciliation in post-conflict societies. To assist with this process and ensure there is no "lost generation" (Barakat & Milton, 2015), supra-national organizations and the professionalization of the field of education in emergencies has developed (see Buckner & Nofal, 2019). These developments highlight the increasing importance placed on schooling as a key development institution to rebuild societies, institutions, and economies.

The importance of schooling as a development institution is embedded within the international development framework. For example, Tikly (2016) argues that the Education for All movement, which again reaffirms the right to education for all, including refugees, is a by-product of similar education and development regimes such as those surrounding the Millennium Development Goals. Within the international development agenda, education for all was seen as a means to alleviate poverty and promote economic growth (Mundy, 2006; Tikly, 2016).

However, supra-national governance at the level of implementation for refugees has largely remained rhetorical and confined to parallel systems of education for refugees in contexts where formal access to schooling is still limited, as is the case for many newly displaced Rohingya refugees in Bangladesh and refugee camps (see Mendenhall et al., 2019; Prodip & Garnett, 2019). Additionally, previous insistence on meeting development goals in education and the persistent focus on primary education has attributed to the inadequate short-term rather than a long-term approach to providing education for refugees in ways that meaningfully contribute to the individual and collective development of their communities whether in urban settings or protracted refugee camps. Despite the increased response by governments to include refugees in national education systems largely through negotiations with individual ministries led by UNHCR (Dryden-Peterson et al., 2018), many barriers remain, such as restricted access to formal labor markets reflecting the limitations of schooling as a development institution for refugees in particular.

Transmission of Identity, Values, and Ideology to Refugee Youth

Research on the transmission of citizenship and ideology to youth suggests that youth are largely influenced by the dominant social institutions in their lives (Youniss et al., 2002). One of the most prevalent of these social institutions in the lives of youth around the world is the school.

The intent to develop youth into socio-political citizens has historically been a part of formal public schooling (Tyack & Cuban, 1995). Over time, however, as educational and technological needs have changed and as democratic states have increasingly replaced authoritarian regimes, the emphasis placed on these needs has shifted. Many nations, especially developed, post-industrial nations, recognize the importance of schooling as a means to provide social mobility for citizens within a nation while establishing national dominance, or at least competitiveness, on the world scene (LeTendre & Baker, 1999). For example, providing refugees with access to education in order to encourage economic and social integration is often a policy priority (see Damaschke-Deitrick & Bruce, 2019). This has historically encouraged policymakers and other "rational" thinkers to make the effort to reform and develop their nations' school systems in order to establish a place in the dominant world order. Increasingly, these legitimacy-seeking strategies include expanding access to public schooling to refugees.

Research suggests that inclusion of refugees in national education systems is more successful in providing access to institutions and services or "structural integration" (Dryden-Peterson et al., 2018, p. 5). More challenging, however, is "relational integration" or access to inclusive identities and connectedness (Dryden-Peterson et al., 2018, p. 5). Relational integration is a contentious dimension of national education systems as it relates to the transmission of the incorporation and transmission of ideas that are shaped by conceptions of national, cultural, and ethnic identity and ideology (Abowitz, 2002). Control over this transmission is traditionally viewed as the responsibility of the national education system. However, contestations over control of curriculum and integration within national educational contexts, particularly in protracted refugee situations, remain (see Kelcey, 2019). Politicization over content and knowledge is connected to the perceived role of education to the development of youth and citizenship, and nation-states' claims to sovereignty over this dimension of education.

As Kelcey (2019) examines, the UNHCR's shift from home country curricula to host country curricula in 2012 had significant implications for Palestinian refugees. Despite UNHCR's intention to facilitate inclusion of refugees in protracted displacement and their access to education, this policy shift does not reflect the complex realities of refugees. The lived experiences of refugees in protracted displacement are often drastically different from the representations in host country curriculum, and they are socialized in schools through a curriculum that often represents a society in which they are unable to fully participate. Nevertheless, the importance of developing values and citizenship remains a cornerstone of schooling. Even when the provision of education is relegated to non-governmental agencies like UNHCR, as is often the case in refugee camps, citizenship education, specifically peace education, is viewed as a necessity to prepare refugees for future repatriation or resettlement (Solem, 2017).

Finally, there is some question as to whether formal public schooling is a dominant venue for the transmission of culture and values versus whether and to what extent youths are instructed in values and ideologies from other less-regulated institutions (e.g., family, religious, and social groups) (e.g., Qadir, 2001). For example, Prodip and Garnett (2019) detail the significant challenges education providers in Bangladesh's makeshift settlements around Cox's Bazar face while trying to encourage Rohingya refugee families to send their children, specifically girls, to learning centers rather than madrasahs. Additionally, there are others who focus on the staunch persistence of traditional cultural values and ethnic identity at the local level even when national school systems are cloaking themselves in the legitimacy of internationally institutionalized schooling models. Some argue that legitimate school structures and processes have been institutionalized based on models of schooling from socially, politically, and economically dominant nations or multinational organizations (Meyer, Ramirez, & Soysal, 1992).

In particular, it has been suggested that there may be institutionalized support for the transmission of separatist ideologies to youth in some schools and nations instead of institutionalized support for global citizenship (Wiseman et al., 2011). Even global citizenship is often criticized as "it privileges Western normative notions about the relationship between the individual and the state" (Bajaj & Bartlett, 2017,p. 3). Bajaj and Bartlett argue that the framework of global citizenship fails to account for the lack of choices, safety, and need for survival in forced displacement. While Koyama (2016) argues that the idealization of global citizenship "only pushes these notions further out of reach for the majority of the world's population, rendering such ideas not only elusive, but also dangerous" (p. 17).

The increasingly "Western" institutionalization of cultural values and ideology in school programs and processes (Haidar, 2002) presents further challenges to the goal of inclusion and societal cohesion through national education systems, which raise issues concerning the development of identity and connectedness between refugees and host communities. For example, implicit and explicit bias in schools and among educators which negatively influence refugee and asylum-seeking youth in the classroom include perpetuation of the ideology of meritocracy (Roxas & Roy, 2012), underestimation of abilities and competencies (Kaplan, Stolk, Valibhoy, Tucker, & Baker, 2016), victimization which leads to marginalization in the classroom (Taylor & Sidhu, 2012), "othering" (Koyama & Chang, 2019), and valorization of native English speakers (Solano-Campos, 2014). Oliveira and Becker (2019) explore the influence of familial expectations and traditional gender ideologies for documented and undocumented Latina immigrant youth to succeed academically in the US education system. However, as their chapter highlights, these traditional cultural values and means of identification within this vulnerable population compound the challenges they face once enrolled in school. Yet, like the stories from the refugee women in universities in Germany, Kyrgyzstan, and Egypt (Damaschke-Deitrick, Galegher, & Park), education provides a "space" to create meaning and an identity outside their documented or undocumented status.

Teachers are vital components to schools (Mendenhall, Pacifico, & Hu, 2019; Wiseman & Galegher, 2019), and in particular, the sociocultural processes at the root of transmission of values and identity (Çelik & İçduygu, 2018). However, as the chapters in this volume show, both data as well as teacher preparation and professional development for teachers working in refugee education contexts are sparse both in protracted refugee camps (Mendenhall, Pacifico, & Hu) as well as in national educational systems (Wiseman & Galegher). The inability to meet the unique and often complex needs of refugees through traditional teacher professional development and preparation approaches is arguably connected to the diffusion of institutionalized models of schooling and subsequent teacher preparation programs. Thus, teachers are often ill-prepared, even through national education systems, to address unique academic and non-academic needs of refugee and asylum-seeking youth. Additionally, lack of teacher supply and national level barriers related to the regulation of teacher qualifications and recruitment (see Mendenhall, Gomez, & Varni, 2018) suggest a serious crisis exists in providing quality education through national education systems worldwide.

Despite recent progress regarding inclusion of refugees in national education systems at the policy level, overcoming the often culturally embedded dimensions of the institution of education, which influence who teaches, what is taught, who is taught, and how it's taught, are a serious challenge, particularly to refugee and asylum-seeking youth. Despite these potential limitations, the chapters which follow also exemplify the ways in which education continues to provide hope and support for both individuals and societies. For example, Ghosh et al. (2019) identify the ways in which Canada's historically inclusive society is the catalyst for the country's successful inclusion of refugees in their national education system.

The goal of this volume is not only to identify the limitations associated with the institutionalization of "education as a panacea" for refugee and asylum-seeking youth and host communities, but also to highlight the myriad ways in which education can continue to support the inclusion of refugees more sustainably and effectively through the recognition of the strengths and limitations of these expectations through empirical evidence presented in the following chapters.

Introduction to the Volume

The volume, *Comparative Perspectives on Refugee Youth Education: Dreams and Realities in Educational Systems Worldwide*, comprises two Parts, which reflect the two institutional levels at which expectations about education as a panacea for refugee students and families are both conceptualized and implemented. Part 1 examines the shared expectations of education at the macro-policy level (e.g., Dryden-Peterson, 2017; Landau & Amit, 2014; Mendenhall, Russell, & Buckner, 2017). Chapters focus on the role of international non-governmental, and governmental organizations, such as the UNHCR, as well as national level education systems in supporting refugees and providing either support or "solutions" through education during times of transition. Cross-country comparisons and single country case studies explain and operationalize global goals and objectives for refugee integration as they transition to receiving countries and the expected as well as implemented role of formal education in this process.

In Chapter 1, Damaschke-Deitrick and Bruce compare the education policies and practices of Germany and the United States to achieve their differing objectives concerning the integration of refugees. Using qualitative data analysis of policies in each country, they compare and contrast policies according to social, economic, political, and cultural factors. Contextualizing these factors within the history and development of integration within each country context, their findings elaborate on the conceptualization of education as a panacea by identifying education policies and practices which reflect this shared institutionalized idea. Nevertheless, their analysis finds that the implementation of such policies still reflects the unique national goals of social integration in Germany and economic integration the United States.

Through a World Culture framework, Buckner and Nofal examine the regional response to the Syrian crisis in Chapter 2 and the ideological shift in the global education movement toward education as a human right in humanitarian crises. Despite the institutionalization of education as a human right in education in emergencies (EiE) at the international level, analyzing the regional response of the Middle East to the Syria crisis through the 3RP, regional cooperation remains largely rhetorical. Additionally, national and local level challenges as well as lack of financial support significantly restrict the actual implementation of this regional partnership.

Through hierarchical linear modeling using PISA 2015 data, Wiseman and Galegher in Chapter 3 investigate the influence of teacher preparation and professional development programs on the academic and non-academic needs of refugee and asylum-seeking youth in the OECD. Their findings suggest that there is a mismatch between current teacher preparation and development programs in national education systems, which often focus on multilingual and multicultural education and individualized learning, and the multifaceted academic and non-academic needs of these youth. Despite the persistent difficulty in influencing the non-academic needs of refugee and asylum-seeking youth, Wiseman and Galegher find aspects of teacher background and teacher training as well as professional interactions and behavior that positively influence academic outcomes.

In Chapter 4, Ghosh, Sherab, Dilimulati, and Hashemi examine Canadian policies toward refugees at the national as well as local level through this single country case study. The recent influx of Syrian refugees forced Canadian provinces to rapidly adjust and develop policies and best practices. This chapter argues that these new policies were influenced by a composite set of humanitarian, political, economic, and demographic, as well as strategic concerns, based on the foundations of an inclusive society in Canada. Their findings identify the importance of the legal, cultural, and historical development of host country societies to the reception and inclusion of refugees and asylum-seeking youth.

Thulare, Spoolstra, Dombrowski, Jordan, and Nabacwa analyze the implementation of the Comprehensive Refugee Response Framework (CCRF) in Uganda and Kenya from the perspective of education experts, policymakers, and practitioners in Chapter 5. Their findings indicate that context matters both at a global scale but also in implementation at the national and local levels. Results suggest that the aspirational paradigm shift to integrate refugees into national societal structures through the CRRF may not be the durable solution policymakers intended, particularly in resource-limited host countries with little financial support or commitment from the international community.

Part 2 examines local district, community, and school-level adaptations of education as an often assumed cure-all for the challenges that refugee youths and local educators experience during this transition process (e.g., Block, Cross, Riggs, & Gibbs, 2014; DeCapua, 2016; Dryden-Peterson, 2015; Mendenhall, Bartlett, & Ghaffar-Kucher, 2017). Chapters focus on understanding diverse variations in refugee education based on the contexts of reception, cultural community, refugee groups, and individual refugee students.

Through the voices of female refugees in higher education, Damaschke-Deitrick, Galegher, and Park undertook a comparative study of refugee women enrolled in universities in Kyrgyzstan, Germany, and Egypt. Chapter 6 fills a research gap in female refugees in higher education, and provides vital information for institutions to better address the diverse and complex needs of female refugee students. Focus is most often placed on preparing refugees for integration into educational settings and communities. However, their findings emphasize the importance of preparation of both female refugees and, more importantly, host communities inside and outside the university context.

Through a series of case studies conducted in Cox's Bazar, in Chapter 7 Prodip and Garnett examine the largely overlooked provision of non-formal education to refugee children in registered camps and makeshift settlements in Bangladesh. Their work explores the limitations of emergency education (EE) for Rohingya refugee children through an analysis of non-formal education policies and practices, which follow the guidelines set forth by the INEE. Despite persistent challenges regarding out-of-school Rohingya refugee children, Prodip and Garnett find that those who do access learning centers experience significant support and gains through the safe learning spaces which provide psychosocial support for many Rohingya children who have experienced immense trauma. However, the lack of formal inclusion in the national education system or even certification of schooling by the Bangladesh government highlights national level obstacles to providing quality and sustainable education in crisis situations.

Through their work exploring the link between gender and schooling within the context of undocumented immigrant Latina youth in the United States, Oliveira and Becker establish the connection between experiences and hardships faced by refugee and asylum-seeking youth and undocumented immigrant youth. Like other refugee and asylum-seeking youth, the story of Stella centers around the high aspirations and expectations she and her family have of schooling and the hardships that follow in US formal education. The findings in Chapter 8 echo existing research on the transmission of familial expectations and culture as well as ideology through schooling and suggest that more attention should be paid to Latina immigrant youth's narratives on schooling and the parallel experiences and challenges faced by undocumented vulnerable and marginalized groups.

In Chapter 9, Mendenhall, Pacifico, and Hu focus on the role of professional development for teachers in refugee camps. Centering the experiences of teachers in the Kakuma refugee camp in Kenya, their results point to the need for higher quality, longer-term support for teachers in displacement contexts, as well as the critical role teachers play in informing policies and practices in contexts of displacement. Their findings suggest that if sustainable gains in student learning outcomes are to be made, significant changes must be made to the teacher management and support framework.

Finally in Chapter 10, Kelcey critically reflects on the 2012 UNHCR policy shift that advocated for refugee students to be taught the host state curriculum of their country of asylum. Her work analyzes the curriculum policies of the United Nations Relief and Works Agency for Palestine Refugees in the Near East (UNRWA), and argues that important political dimensions of curriculum have been overlooked, marginalizing refugee perspectives in policy making. The findings suggest the need for a more nuanced approach to curriculum policies that can help enhance education's protective role.

Despite the diversity of regions and countries present in the following case studies, they are united by the shared assumption of education's vital role in refugee transitions, yet demonstrate conflict in implementing education in ways that universally "solve" refugee youth and family challenges. Many chapters allude to the tension that develops between the normative acceptance of education as a panacea for refugees and host communities and the deeply embedded national values, culture, and identity at the root of national education systems (Buckner & Nofal; Damacschke-Dietrick & Bruce; Ghosh et al.; Wiseman & Galegher). Even government refusal to include refugees in national education systems despite displacement within their borders (Mendenhall et al.) reflects the primacy of protecting the sovereignty of national institutions (Damaschke-Deitrick et al.; Prodip & Garnett; Thulare et al.) and the political nature of refugee education (Dryden-Peterson, 2011; Kelcey, 2019; Oliveira & Becker, 2019). Yet woven within these studies are three key components to better address the needs of refugee and asylum-seeking youth, their families, and host communities. From protracted refugee camps to urban refugees and resettlement, evidence from this volume suggests educational stakeholders must focus on the ways in which education can both mitigate and perpetuate problems associated with the intersection of refugee identity, language, and trauma.

References

Abowitz, K. K. (2002). From public education to educational publics. *The Clearing House, 76*(1), 34–38.

Akiba, M., LeTendre, G. K., Baker, D. P., & Goesling, B. (2002). Student victimization: National and school system effects on school violence in 37 nations. *American Educational Research Journal, 39*(4), 829–853.

Amos, K., Wiseman, A., & Rohstock, A. (2014). *EKSS-Change: Education and scientization as the dynamic forces of late modern 'knowledge societies'. A new order of things?: The scientization of late modern societies.* (Unpublished Manuscript). Institute of Educational Sciences, University of Tuebingen, Tuebingen, Germany & College of Education, Lehigh University, Bethlehem, Pennsylvania, United States.

Arendt, H. (1943). We refugees. *Menorah Journal, 31*(1), 69–77.

Arnstine, D. (1995). *Democracy and the arts of schooling.* Albany, NY: SUNY Press.

Bajaj, M., & Bartlett, L. (2017). Critical transnational curriculum for immigrant and refugee students. *Curriculum Inquiry, 47*(1), 25–35.

Barakat, S., & Milton, S. (2015). *Houses of wisdom matter: The responsibility to protect and rebuild higher education in the Arab world.* Doha, Qatar: Brookings Doha Center.

Bartlett, L., & Ghaffar-Kucher, A. (Eds.). (2013). *Refugees, immigrants and education in the global south: Lives in motion.* New York, NY: Routledge.

Beirens, H., Hughes, N., Hek, R., & Spicer, N. (2007). Preventing social exclusion of refugee and asylum seeking children: building new networks. *Social Policy and Society, 6*(2), 219–229.

Block, K., Cross, S., Riggs, E., & Gibbs, L. (2014). Supporting schools to create an inclusive environment for refugee students. *International Journal of Inclusive Education*, 18(12), 1337–1355.

Boli, J., & Thomas, G. M. (1999). INGOs and the organization of world culture. In J. Boli & G. M. Thomas (Eds.), *Constructing World Culture: International nongovernmental organizations since 1875* (pp. 13–49). Stanford, CA: Stanford University Press.

Brown, E. L., & Krasteva, A. (Eds.). (2013). *Migrants and refugees: Equitable education for displaced populations*. Charlotte, NC: Information Age Publishing.

Buchmann, C., & Dalton, B. (2002). Interpersonal influences and educational aspirations in 12 countries: The importance of institutional context. *Sociology of Education*, 75(2), 99–122.

Buckner, E., & Nofal, M. (2019). The educational response to Syrian displacement: A professionalizing field in a politicized environment. In A. W. Wiseman, L. Damaschke-Deitrick, E. Galegher, & M. Park (Eds.), *Comparative perspectives on Refugee Youth Education: Dreams and realities in educational systems worldwide*. New York, NY: Routledge.

Buckner, E., Spencer, D., & Cha, J. (2017). Between policy and practice: The education of Syrian refugees in Lebanon. *Journal of Refugee Studies*, 31(4), 444–465.

Burde, D., Kapit, A., Wahl, R. L., Guven, O., & Skarpeteig, M. I. (2017). Education in emergencies: A review of theory and research. *Review of Educational Research*, 87(3).

Burnett, K. (2013). Feeling like an outsider: A case study of refugee identity in the Czech Republic. *New issues in refugee research*. Research paper no. 251. Geneva, Switzerland: United Nations High Commission for Refugees.

Carnoy, M. (1985). The political economy of education. *International Social Science Journal*, 37(2), 157–173.

Carnoy, M., Castells, M., Cohen, S., & Cardoso, F. H. (1993). *The new global economy in the information age*. University Park, PA: Penn State University Press.

Carnoy, M., & Levin, H. (1985). *Schooling and work in the democratic state*. Stanford, CA: Stanford University Press.

Çelik, Ç., & İçduygu, A. (2018). Schools and refugee children: The case of Syrians in Turkey. *International Migration*. Volume and pages numbers forthcoming. https://doi.org/10.1111/imig.12488

Culbertson, S., & Constant, L. (2015). *Education of Syrian refugee children: Managing the crisis in Turkey, Lebanon, and Jordan*. Santa Monica, CA: Rand Corporation.

Damaschke-Deitrick, L., & Bruce, E. (2019). Education as a panacea for refugee integration? Evidence from Germany and the United States. In A. W. Wiseman, L. Damaschke-Deitrick, E. Galegher, & M. Park (Eds.), *Comparative perspectives on Refugee Youth Education: Dreams and realities in educational systems worldwide*. New York: Routledge.

Damaschke-Deitrick, L., Galegher, E., & Park, M. F. (2019). Female refugees' transitions into higher education: Comparative perspectives from Germany, Egypt, and Kyrgyzstan. In A. W. Wiseman, L. Damaschke-Deitrick, E. Galegher, & M. Park (Eds.), *Comparative perspectives on Refugee Youth Education: Dreams and realities in educational systems worldwide*. New York: Routledge.

DeCapua, A. (2016). Reaching students with limited or interrupted formal education through culturally responsive teaching. *Language and Linguistics Compass*, *10*(5), 225–237.
Drori, G. S., & Meyer, J. W. (2006). Scientization: Making a world safe for organizing. In M.-L. Djelic & K. Sahlin-Andersson (Eds.), *Transnational governance: Institutional dynamics of regulation* (pp. 32–52). Cambridge, UK: Cambridge University Press.
Dryden-Peterson, S. (2010). The politics of higher education for refugees in a global movement for primary education. *Refuge: Canada's Journal on Refugees*, *27*(2), 10–18.
Dryden-Peterson, S. (2011). *Refugee education: A global review*. New York: United Nations High Commission for Refugees.
Dryden-Peterson, S. (2015). *The educational experiences of refugee children in countries of first asylum*. Washington, DC: Migration Policy Institute.
Dryden-Peterson, S. (2017). Refugee education: Education for an unknowable future. *Curriculum Inquiry*, *47*(1), 14–24.
Dryden-Peterson, S., Adelman, E., Alvarada, S., Anderson, K., Bellino, M. J., et al. (2018). *Inclusion of refugees in national education systems*. Paper commissioned for the 2019 Global Education Monitoring Report Migration, displacement and education: Building bridges, not walls, UNESCO, Paris, France.
Eisner, E. W. (2017). *The enlightened eye: Qualitative inquiry and the enhancement of educational practice*. New York: Teachers College Press.
Entwisle, D. R., Alexander, K. L., & Olson, L. S. (2000). Early work histories of urban youth. *American Sociological Review*, 279–297.
Fratzke, S. (2017). *Engaging communities in refugee protection: The potential of private sponsorship in Europe*. Brussels: Migration Policy Institute Europe.
Ghosh, R., Sherab, D., Dilimulati, M., & Hashemi, N. (2019). Creating a refugee space in the Canadian school context: The approach of an inclusive society, in A. W. Wiseman, L. Damaschke-Deitrick, E. Galegher, & M. Park (Eds.), *Comparative perspectives on Refugee Youth Education: Dreams and realities in educational systems worldwide*. New York: Routledge.
Haddad, E. (2004). *Who is (not) a refugee?* EUI Working Paper SPS No. 2004/6. San Domenico, Italy: European University Institute Badia Fiesolana.
Haidar, A. H. (2002). Emirates secondary school science teachers' perspectives on the nexus between modern science and Arab culture. *International Journal of Science Education*, *24*(6), 611–626.
Inglehart, R., & Baker, W. E. (2000). Modernization, cultural change, and the persistence of traditional values. *American Sociological Review*, *65*(1), 19–51.
International Organization for Migration (IOM). (n.d.). Key Migration Terms. Retrieved from https://www.iom.int/key-migration-terms.
Johnson, R. B., & Onwuegbuzie, A. J. (2004). Mixed methods research: A research paradigm whose time has come. *Educational Researcher*, *33*(7), 14–26.
Joly, D. (2002). Odyssean and rubicon refugees: Toward a typology of refugees in the land of exile. *International Migration*, *40*(6), 3–23.
Kanter, H., & Lowe, R. (2000). Vocationalism reconsidered. *American Journal of Education*, *109*(1), 125.
Kaplan, I., Stolk, Y., Valibhoy, M., Tucker, A., & Baker, J. (2016). Cognitive assessment of refugee children: Effects of trauma and new language acquisition. *Transcultural Psychiatry*, *53*(1), 81–109.

Kelcey, J. (2019). "Whose knowledge?" Putting politics back into curriculum choices for refugees. In A. W. Wiseman, L. Damaschke-Deitrick, E. Galegher, & M. Park (Eds.), *Comparative perspectives on Refugee Youth Education: Dreams and realities in educational systems worldwide*. New York: Routledge.

Khalilzad, Z., & Lesser, I. O. (Eds.). (1998). *Sources of conflict in the 21st century: Regional futures and U.S. strategy*. Washington, DC: Rand Corporation.

Kia-Keating, M., & Ellis, B. H. (2007). Belonging and connection to school in resettlement: Young refugees, school belonging, and psychosocial adjustment. *Clinical Child Psychology and Psychiatry, 12*(1), 29–43.

Koyama, J. (2016). *The elusive and exclusive global citizen*. Working Paper. New Delhi: Mahatma Gandhi Institute of Education for Peace and Sustainable Development/UNESCO.

Koyama, J., & Chang, E. (2019). Schools as refuge? The politics and policy of educating refugees in Arizona. *Educational Policy, 33*(1), 136–157.

Landau, L. B., & Amit, R. (2014). Wither policy? Southern African perspectives on understanding law, "refugee" policy and protection. *Journal of Refugee Studies, 27*(4), 534–552.

LeTendre, G. K., & Baker, D. P. (1999). International comparisons and educational research policy. In G. K. LeTendre (Ed.), *Competitor or ally? Japan's role in American Educational Debates* (pp. 123–140). New York: Falmer Press.

McCarthy, F. E., & Vickers, M. H. (Eds.). (2012). *Refugee and immigrant students: Achieving equity in education*. Charlotte, NC: Information Age Publishing.

Mendenhall, M., Bartlett, L., & Ghaffar-Kucher, A. (2017). "If you need help, they are always there for us": Education for refugees in an international high school in NYC. *The Urban Review, 49*(1), 1–25.

Mendenhall, M., Gomez, S., & Varni, E. (2018). *Teaching amidst conflict and displacement: Persistent challenges and promising practices for refugee, internally displaced and national teachers*. Background Paper for Global Education Monitoring Report 2019.

Mendenhall, M., Pacifico, A., & Hu, S. (2019). Teacher professional development in crisis contexts: Teachers' reflections and stories of change in Kakuma Refugee Camp. In A. W. Wiseman, L. Damaschke-Deitrick, E. Galegher, & M. Park (Eds.), *Comparative perspectives on Refugee Youth Education: Dreams and realities in educational systems worldwide*. New York: Routledge.

Mendenhall, M., Russell, S. G., & Buckner, E. (2017). *Urban refugee education: Strengthening policies and practices for access, quality, and inclusion: Insights and recommendations from a 16-country global survey and case studies in Beirut, Nairobi, and Quito*. Unpublished study funded by the US State Department, Bureau of Population, Refugees and Migration, Washington, DC.

Meyer, J. W., Boli, J., Thomas, G. M., & Ramirez, F. O. (1997). World society and the nation-state. *American Journal of Sociology, 103*(1), 144–181.

Meyer, J. W., Ramirez, F. O., Rubinson, R., & Boli-Bennett, J. (1977). The world educational revolution, 1950–1970. *Sociology of Education, 50*(4), 242–258.

Meyer, J. W., Ramirez, F. O., & Soysal, Y. N. (1992). World expansion of mass education, 1870–1980. *Sociology of Education, 65*(2), 128–149.

Mickan, P., Lucas, K., Davies, B., Lim, M.-O. (2007). Socialisation and contestation in an ESL class of adolescent African refugees. *Prospect, 22*(2), 4–24.

Mundy, K. (2006). Education for all and the new development compact. *Review of Education*, 52, 23–48.

Oliveira, G., & Becker, M. L. (2019). Immigrant Latina youth and their education experience in the United States. In A. W. Wiseman, L. Damaschke-Deitrick, E. Galegher, & M. Park (Eds.), *Comparative perspectives on Refugee Youth Education: Dreams and realities in educational systems worldwide*. New York: Routledge.

Peterson, A., Meehan, C., Ali, Z., & Durrant, I. (2017). *What are the educational needs and experiences of asylum-seeking and refugee children, including those who are unaccompanied, with a particular focus on inclusion? A literature review*. Canterbury, UK: Canterbury Christ Church University, Faculty of Education. Retrieved from https://www.canterbury.ac.uk/education/our-work/research-knowledge-exchange/themes/education-for-social-justice/docs/literature-review.pdf

Prodip, M. A., & Garnett, J. (2019). Emergency education for Rohingya refugee children in Bangladesh: An analysis of the policies, practices, and limitations., In A. W. Wiseman, L. Damaschke-Deitrick, E. Galegher, & M. Park (Eds.), *Comparative perspectives on Refugee Youth Education: Dreams and realities in educational systems worldwide*. New York: Routledge.

Psacharopoulos, G. (1994). Returns to investment in education: A global update. *World Development*, 22(9), 1325–1343.

Qadir, S. (2001). The concept of international terrorism: An interim study of South Asia. *The Round Table*, 90(360), 333–343.

Ramirez, F. O., & Boli, J. (1987). The political construction of mass schooling: European origins and worldwide institutionalization. *Sociology of Education*, 60(1), 2–17.

Ramirez, F. O., Soysal, Y., & Shanahan, S. (1997). The changing logic of political citizenship: Cross-national acquisition of women's suffrage rights, 1890 to 1990. *American Sociological Review*, 65(5), 735–745.

Roxas, K., & Roy, L. (2012). "That's how we roll": A case study of a recently arrived refugee student in an urban high school. *The Urban Review*, 44(4), 468–486.

Sasnal, P. (2015). *Who are they? Two profiles of Syrian refugees*. Warsaw: Polski Instytut Spraw Międzynarodowyc.

Schmidt, M., & Datnow, A. (2005). Teachers' sense-making about comprehensive school reform: The influence of emotions. *Teaching and Teacher Education*, 21(8), 949–965.

Schneider, B. (2018). Methodological nationalism in linguistics. *Language Sciences*. Retrieved from 10.1016/j.langsci.2018.05.006

Sinclair, M. (2001). Education in emergencies. In J. Crisp, C. Talbot, & D. B. Cipollone (Eds.), *Learning for a future: Refugee education in developing countries* (pp. 1–84). Geneva, Switzerland: United Nations High Commissioner for Refugees.

Sirin, S. R., & Rogers-Sirin, L. (2015). *The educational and mental health needs of Syrian refugee children*. Washington, DC: Migration Policy Institute.

Smith, A. 2009. *Education and conflict: Think piece prepared for the Education for All Global Monitoring Report 2011*. Paris: UNESCO.

Solano-Campos, A. (2014). The making of an international educator: Transnationalism and nonnativeness in English teaching and learning. *TESOL Journal*, 5(3), 412–443.

Solem, E. (2017). Where am I a citizen? Exploring peace education as citizenship education in refugee camps: An analysis in Dadaab. *Reconsidering Development*, *5*(1). Retrieved from https://pubs.lib.umn.edu/index.php/reconsidering/article/view/905

Spillane, J., Diamond, J. B., & Burch, P. (2002). Managing in the middle: School leaders and the enactment of accountability policy. *Educational Policy*, *16*, 731–762.

Strekalova, E., & Hoot, J. L. (2008). What is special about special needs of refugee children?: Guidelines for teachers. *Multicultural Education*, *16*(1), 21–24.

Sullivan, A. L., & Simonson, G. R. (2016). A systematic review of school-based social-emotional interventions for refugee and war-traumatized youth. *Review of Educational Research*, *86*(2), 503–530.

Taylor, S., & Sidhu, R. K. (2012). Supporting refugee students in schools: What constitutes inclusive education? *International Journal of Inclusive Education*, *16*(1), 39–56.

Thulare, T., Spoolstra, C., Dombrowski, E., Jordan, R., & Nabacwa, R. (2019). A comparative policy analysis of the comprehensive refugee response framework in Uganda and Kenya. In A. W. Wiseman, L. Damaschke-Deitrick, E. Galegher, & M. Park (Eds.), *Comparative perspectives on Refugee Youth Education: Dreams and realities in educational systems worldwide*. New York: Routledge.

Tikly, L. (2016). Education for all as a global regime of educational governance: Issues and Tensions. In S. Yamada (Ed.), *Post-education for all and sustainable development paradigm: Structural changes with diversifying actors and norms* (International Perspectives on Education and Society, Vol. 29, pp. 37–65). Bingley, UK: Emerald Group Publishing Limited.

Tyack, D. B., & Cuban, L. (1995). *Tinkering toward Utopia*. Cambridge, MA: Harvard University Press.

UNHCR. (n.d.). What is a refugee? Retrieved from https://www.unrefugees.org/refugee-facts/what-is-a-refugee/

UNHCR. (2012). *Education strategy 2012–2016*. Retrieved from www.unhcr.org/protection/operations/5149ba349/unhcr-education-strategy-2012-2016.html

UNHCR. (2017). *2017 global trends: Forced displacement in 2017*. Retrieved from www.unhcr.org/5b27be547.pdf

Wiseman, A. W., Astiz, M. F., Fabrega, R., & Baker, D. P. (2011). Making citizens of the world: The political socialization of youth in formal mass education systems. *Compare: A Journal of Comparative and International Education*, *41*(5), 561–577.

Wiseman, A. W., Damaschke-Deitrick, L., Bruce, E., Davidson, P., & Taylor, C. S. (2016). Transnational scientized education discourse: A cross-national comparison. In J. Schmid, K. S. Amos, J. Schrader, & A. Thiel (Eds.), *Internationalisierte Welten der Bildung—Bildung und Bildungspolitik im globalen Vergleich (Internationalized worlds of education: Education and training policies in global comparison)* (pp. 121–146). Baden-Baden: Nomos.

Wiseman, A. W., & Galegher, G. (2019). Teacher preparation, classroom pedagogy, and the refugee crisis in national education systems. In A. W. Wiseman, L. Damaschke-Deitrick, E. Galegher, & M. Park (Eds.), *Comparative perspectives on Refugee Youth Education: Dreams and realities in educational systems worldwide*. New York: Routledge.

Youniss, J., Bales, S., Christmas-Best, V., Diversi, M., Mclaughlin, M., & Silbereisen, R. (2002). Youth civic engagement in the twenty-first century. *Journal of Research on Adolescence*, *12*(1), 121–148.

Zetter, R. (2007). More labels, fewer refugees: Remaking the refugee label in an era of globalization. *Journal of Refugee Studies*, *20*(2), 172–192.

Part 1

Global Policy Expectations for Refugees' Educational Transitions

1 Education as a Panacea for Refugee Integration? Evidence From Germany and the United States

Lisa Damaschke-Deitrick and Elizabeth R. Bruce

Introduction

As a result of war in Syria as well as conflict and unstable circumstances elsewhere, including Afghanistan, Kosovo, the Democratic Republic of Congo, and Eritrea, Europe and North America have experienced a higher influx of refugees in recent years (Organisation for Economic Co-operation and Development [OECD], 2015; United Nations High Commissioner for Refugees [UNHCR], 2017). Looking across data from 2006 to 2017, asylum applications peaked in 2015 with a slight decrease in 2016 before decreasing by almost half in 2017 across European Union member states (Eurostat, 2018). In Germany, the Bundesamt für Migration und Flüchtlinge (BAMF; Federal Office for Migration and Refugees) registered about 477,000 refugees in 2015, even though arrivals actually numbered approximately 890,000 (Beauftragte der Bundesregierung für Migration, Flüchtlinge und Integration [BBMFI], 2016). Despite recent declines, the United States has historically been the leading country for resettlement worldwide (Mossaad & Baugh, 2018). Notably, large numbers of those received overall have been children and adolescents, both unaccompanied and separated, alongside individuals with special needs stemming from violence and maltreatment (UNHCR, 2016).

This influx of refugees poses challenges to the economic, social, political, and cultural contexts of the receiving countries, particularly regarding the integration of newcomers. Different challenges also arise as arrivals to Europe come from more varied countries than in the past and have more diverse reasons for leaving their homes (OECD, 2015). To aid in coping, international organizations, and the United Nations High Commissioner for Refugees (UNHCR) in particular, advocate using education as a panacea or solution to integrate newcomers when they arrive. Education is expected to provide the necessary skills and knowledge to participate in society. It has been argued that the idea of education as a solution or panacea for integration has become ubiquitous, accepted as a shared idea, and promoted on the international level (Wiseman, Damaschke-Deitrick, Bruce, Davidson, & Taylor, 2016). This belief in education's role is exemplified in the following quote from the UNHCR Division of International Protections:

> Education provides knowledge and skill development that strengthens the capacity of refugees to be agents of social transformation, and is essential to understanding and promoting gender equality and sustainable peaceful coexistence. The future security of individuals and societies is inextricably connected to the transferrable skills, knowledge, and capacities that are developed through education.
> (2012, p. 3)

Though aligning with international expectations of integrating newcomers with the help of education, countries have pursued education policies and practices for refugees differently, just as they have pursued varying goals for integration overall. For example, some Western countries mainly focus on social and cultural integration regarding language proficiency, residential inclusion, and even religious and ethnic inclusion, while others focus primarily on achieving economic integration through the employment and eventual self-sufficiency of newcomers (Portes & Rumbaut, 1996, 2001; Van Tubergen, 2006). Differences in the main objectives for integration appear related to the history and development of integration in a particular country and on that country's current economic, social, political, and cultural contexts. The influence of national integration objectives on education policies and practices to place refugees on a path to achieve these objectives has not been researched. This study addresses this gap.

The focus of this study is on the integration of refugee children and adolescents through education in Germany and the United States. The reason these particular countries were chosen is threefold. First, the countries are similar in that they have federal systems of education. However, variations in their handling of integration over time are evident. Finally, objectives of what integration is meant to achieve economically, socially, politically, and/or culturally in each context differ as well. Thus, it is possible to compare how different integration objectives become evident in education policies and practices in the two countries.

This study contends that German education policies and practices have been established to prepare refugees for social integration, and particularly for German language acquisition. German language knowledge is often considered key to education and labor market access and to integration overall. A report published by the German government highlights: "Anyone learning our language today, starting an apprenticeship, or undertaking training will be more likely able to find their place in our society tomorrow"[1] (BBMFI, 2016). For the United States, this chapter maintains that education policies and practices have been primarily focused on preparing refugee students to enter the labor market and achieve economic integration. Exemplifying this, the OECD (2015) describes the US resettlement approach as "front-loaded with the expectation that refugees will, where possible, rapidly enter the labour market" (p. 13).

With these contentions in mind, this research addresses the following question:

> How do differences in integration objectives become evident in education policies and practices for refugees in Germany and the United States?

Influenced by international organizations and scripts framing education as a solution to achieve integration, the two cases of Germany and the United States are studied qualitatively through detailed content analysis examining national policy documents and representative evidence of practices. The investigation allows for a critical comparison of these two cases to identify where differences in refugee education for integration occur.

We begin by giving an overview of integration and operationalizing the term. Then we present the conceptual framework guiding this chapter: sociological neo-institutionalism leading to the widely held belief in education as the solution for integration. A description of the methodology follows before demonstrating how integration is understood in the two countries. Policies and practices for refugee education in Germany and the United States are then presented according to whether they address economic, social, political, or cultural aspects. In particular, we analyze the ways in which Germany and the United States apply education as a key solution for refugee integration within their borders.

Conceptualizing Integration

In the literature, integration has different meanings and is often subject to debate. In the US context, integration is often used as an "antonym of segregation" (Alba, Sloan, & Sperling, 2011, p. 397; Anderson, 2001), while in many countries in Europe, integration is seen as a substitute for assimilation. Alba and Nee (2003) discuss how assimilation relates to integration, presenting assimilation trends in the United States since the mid-1960s and arguing that these continue to shape immigrant experiences today.[2] This article follows the broader definition of integration offered by Alba et al. (2011) who define it as preparation of "newcomers for a robust membership in the host country, corresponding with the ability to participate in various institutional sectors as fully entitled members" (p. 397). This chapter argues that education is deemed *the* solution to enabling "the ability to participate" through integration.

The research on integration is delineated further with work on "sociocultural integration" (Alba & Nee, 2003; Van Tubergen, 2006, p. 7) and economic integration (Van Tubergen, 2006). Socio-cultural integration research can be further broken down into its individual components, social integration and cultural integration. Social integration references "the extent to which immigrants interact socially with natives" and cultural integration concerns "the degree to which cultural values and patterns are shared among immigrants and natives" (Van Tubergen, 2006, p. 7). According to Van Tubergen (2006), "economic integration indicates the degree of economic equality between immigrants and natives" connecting its strength to lower unemployment, better jobs, and increased income (p. 7).

Research on integration, or rather assimilation at that time, started with the first great US immigration wave in the late 19th and early 20th centuries. The assumption was that over time, immigrants would assimilate into the new host society. However, as Van Tubergen (2006) highlights, these researchers underestimated the impact of macro-level factors on newcomers' abilities to achieve assimilation, including "the role of the immigrant group and the influence of the receiving context" (p. 8). Immigrant groups show, for example, variation regarding their language proficiency. In addition, regional differences also exist: depending on their destination, newcomers have different chances to integrate. These "contexts of reception" can be differentiated by government policies, status of the labor market conditions, and community characteristics (Portes & Rumbaut, 1996, 2001; Van Tubergen, 2006, p. 13). For example, Alba (2005) investigated the assimilation of second-generation immigrants in France, Germany, and the United States, identifying citizenship, religion, language, and race as key factors for assimilation.

Existing research has mainly focused on either economic and political integration or on socio-cultural integration (Van Tubergen, 2006). In this chapter, our approach is to look across economic, social, political, and cultural factors relevant for the integration of refugees.

Conceptual Framework: Education as a Panacea for Refugee Integration

The conceptual framework employed is based on sociological neo-institutionalism as an overarching theory. Sociological neo-institutionalism provides explanations for ways education systems in different countries enact universally taken-for-granted scripts with institutional actors engaging in legitimacy seeking (Jepperson, 2001; Meyer, Boli, Thomas, & Ramirez, 1997). Uniform approaches to enactment are neither expected nor guaranteed by sociological neo-institutionalists, and decoupling between global norms and local enactment is often evident (Jepperson, 2001; Meyer et al., 1997).

Education has become a solutionist tool employed worldwide not only for society as a whole but also for distinct issues and specific populations or groups (Wiseman et al., 2016). This study investigates the way in which the global script of education is used as a key solution or panacea for the integration of refugees. International organizations like the UNHCR promote the global understanding of the central role of education as a solution to integrate newcomers into a country (see UNHCR Division of International Protection, 2012). The belief in education as a panacea to transition refugees to a new host country is understood to occur through improving language aptitude, enhancing social inclusion, and learning key skills necessary for the labor market, among others (see Koehler, 2017; OECD, 2015).

This study builds on work offering evidence of an inclusion approach to refugee education, which has begun to replace the parallel education for refugees that was previously widespread (Dryden-Peterson, 2015, 2016; Dryden-Peterson et al., 2018; Dryden-Peterson, Adelman, Bellino, & Chopra, Under review). Dryden-Peterson et al. (2018) define inclusion as "the process of coming together through refugee learners' access to government schools and/or the curriculum followed by the governments of the host countries" (p. 7). The evidence presented here gives insights into what constitutes this access and curriculum for refugee students in the educational systems of Germany and the United States.

Allemann-Ghionda (2009) noted how comparative analysis of individual European countries' educational policies demonstrates differences of interpretation as a result of different situations and politics in these countries at a certain point in time. Countries, including Germany and the United States, considered here, exhibit a spectrum of differences in enactment despite sharing similar global views regarding norms and beliefs about education (Wiseman et al., 2016). The differences arise as each country makes choices based on its own society, culture, and history (Fernanda Astiz, 2006). Education policymakers and educators filter scripts through their own frameworks, including their understanding of integration and the education system's institutional structure. Using the lens of sociological neo-institutionalism, this study examines how the script of education as a key solution for refugee integration is decoupled and adapted in these different national contexts. The analysis allows for comparisons to assess similarities and differences for education policies and practices connected to the integration of refugee children and adolescents in Germany and the United States.

Methodology

Research Design

For this chapter, we used a comparative qualitative case study to consider the two chosen countries in depth. Qualitative case studies allow for a detailed, thorough analysis (Kaarbo & Beasley, 1999).

Materials Selection and Qualitative Content Analysis

This study was conducted between January 2017 and January 2019. To begin, we gathered materials outlining the integration of refugees and immigrants, as well as materials outlining transition policies for them, to understand the situation in Germany and the United States. We also gathered materials outlining educational policies and practices used for refugee students. While the initial goal was to focus on documents from the government level, it soon became clear supplementary materials from entities outside of the government, including think tanks, professional organizations, and advocacy groups, among others, needed to be included for a more complete picture of education for refugees across all of the factors under investigation. To further augment the analysis, we included secondary literature, including journal articles and books, especially for those factors for which policy documents were unavailable. We chose to look for materials published or accessible between 2010 to 2018. This allowed us to capture policies and practices in place during the recent high influx of refugees, particularly in Germany and particularly as a result of war in Syria. Since numbers peaked in Europe in 2015 (Eurostat, 2018), this time frame allowed time for policy to be presented and practices to emerge.

Through the literature review done in preparation for qualitative content analysis, we identified four factors as crucial for refugee integration:

1. economic factors
2. social factors
3. political factors
4. cultural factors

To operationalize these so that they could guide the analysis, deductive and inductive category construction was used (Kuckartz, 2014): subcategories were derived both deductively from reviewed literature on integration and inductively from the analyzed documents (see Table 1.1).

Table 1.1 Factors influencing integration

Economic Factors	Social Factors	Political Factors	Cultural Factors
• Commodification of knowledge and skill building • Labor market access	• Language • Supplementary services, including mental health	• Citizenship • Civics	• Conceptions of race and ethnicity • Religion and value systems

Note. The literature reviewed to develop these subcategories included: Ait-Mehdi, 2012; Alba, 2005; Alba & Nee, 2003; Allemann-Ghionda, 2009; Meer, Pala, Modood, & Simon, 2009; Portes & Rumbaut, 1996, 2001; Wiseman et al., 2016; UNESCO, 2012; UNHCR, 2016; U.S. Department of State Office of the Spokesperson, 2016; Van Tubergen, 2006.

Country Contexts

As stated in the introduction, differences in the main objectives of integration are related to the history and development of integration in a country alongside that country's current conditions. Thus, this section gives an overview situating integration and education for refugees in Germany and the United States.

Germany

The right of asylum is recognized in Germany's constitution. Nevertheless, since the 1970s, politics in Germany have primarily prevented reception of more immigrants, refugees, and asylum-seekers (Bundeszentrale für politische Bildung [BpB] & Institut für Migrationsforschung und Interkulturelle Studien [IMIS], 2017). Germany only began to recognize its status as an "Einwanderungsland" (country of immigration) after 2005 and only then was integration formally recognized as a government task. For instance, an integration program on the federal level was implemented and a National Integration Plan was set in place (Bendel, 2014; BpB & IMIS, 2017). The sudden high influx of refugees in 2015 led to a restriction of the asylum laws in Germany with the passing of the Integration Act in 2016. For example, it contained the measure that a permanent residence permit is only issued after five years instead of three (BpB & IMIS, 2017).

The asylum process in Germany is governed by the Asylum Procedure Act. Asylum applications are processed by the BAMF in local reception centers, including initial data collection, processing, and administration of lodging and social services. Policies addressing integration for asylum-seekers and refugees are framed across all levels, from the EU to the national to the local. Also, implementation involves numerous actors: politicians, professionals (legal, health, education, pastoral), foundations, companies and enterprises, and volunteers. Germany's decentralized system leads to the situation that education policies and practices for newcomers vary by state (UNESCO, 2018).

Due to the sudden high influx of refugees in 2015, German policies, administrative practices, infrastructure, and education system were not prepared for the high number of newcomers entering the country in such a short amount of time. This often led to long waiting times to register and find appropriate accommodations (BBMFI, 2016). Additionally, refugee children did not always immediately arrive in public schools. German first reception centers, in some cases, housed refugees for up to six months, and access to education was not guaranteed during this period. For example, 45 of 180 children from one Berlin reception center attended school in November 2015 (Koehler, 2016). This time was perceived as a "refugee crisis" in German society and politics.

The United States

In 1948, the US Congress passed the first legislation dedicated to refugees[3] (Office of Refugee Resettlement [ORR], n.d.b). While initially concerned with resettling Europeans, subsequent laws were focused on resettling those fleeing Communist control in many countries (ORR, n.d.b). Stirred by issues surrounding an onslaught of refugees to the United States at the end of the Vietnam War, the Refugee Act of 1980 was inaugurated and with it the Federal Refugee Resettlement Program (ORR, n.d.b). This program aids the refugee resettlement process "to assist [refugees] to achieve economic self-sufficiency as quickly as possible after arrival in the United States" (ORR, 2012, para. 1). Agencies assisting refugee resettlement exist at both federal and state levels. At the federal level, the Office of Refugee Resettlement (ORR) works in cooperation with the Department of State to place refugees in geographical locations with services that can enable them to "become active, contributing participants" in their new communities (ORR, n.d.c). ORR also works across sectors to connect with other organizations, further strengthening programs offered (ORR, n.d.c). At the state level, refugee assistance is administered primarily by state governments but also through public-private partnerships and the Wilson-Fish Alternative Program (ORR, n.d.a).

In the United States, on average, it takes 18 to 24 months for the entire refugee resettlement process to be completed (Felter & McBride, 2018). This process begins, in general, when an individual registers with UNHCR (Felter & McBride, 2018). The UNHCR, or possibly a US embassy or non-governmental organization, refers these individuals to the network of US State Department Resettlement Support Centers (Felter & McBride, 2018). From there, an extensive vetting process takes place. If nothing concerning emerges during this process, the individual is cleared to come into the United States (Felter & McBride, 2018).

For education, federal actions and funding guidelines lead state and local education systems to develop and implement programs adhering to these criteria but with a degree of flexibility, impacting students including refugees, as explained in the sections that follow. The length of the resettlement process can create a lag in schools' reception of refugee students and discovery of needs to be addressed. Adding further complications, refugees tend to be scattered around the country and, therefore, dispersed across schools (Zong & Batalova, 2017).

Since taking office in 2016, US president Donald J. Trump has decreased the ceiling on the number of refugees that can be resettled as well as implemented more stringent guidelines for entry, greatly increasing workloads for those conducting security checks (Davis, 2018). In addition, under his administration, a number of agencies serving as part of the resettlement process are projected to be shuttered, a loss of support expected to hinder resettlement into future administrations (Alvarez, 2018). These changes have been accompanied by rhetoric frequently framing refugees from certain countries as national security concerns and focusing on cultural differences (Davis, 2018; Weinstein & Ferwerda, 2018).

Results

This section details the results of the qualitative analysis of integration efforts found in education policies and practices for each country, presented according to economic, social, political, and cultural factors and the subcategories for each presented in Table 1.1.

Germany

Economic Factors

Especially on the state and municipality levels, measures, including professional orientation, career counseling, and interventions for early school leavers, have been implemented for the needs of young people with regard to labor market access, often with a special focus on immigrant or refugee students (Bendel, 2014). The 2019 Global Education Monitoring (GEM) Report highlights the importance of vocational training to refugees' future employment opportunities. The report refers to a program, "Willkommenslotsen" (Welcome Guides), which successfully helped recruit and place 3,441 refugee students into vocational training in 2016 (UNESCO, 2018).

Other efforts and measures for labor market integration for refugee youth often vary between the different states. For example, in the state of Baden-Württemberg, the "Cooperative Career Orientation for New Immigrants" is offered for students aged 10 to 20 during preparation classes. In a group of 12 to 15 participants, the students learn, develop, and enhance their competences and skills for future careers. The emphasis is on practical learning, and the students get to know vocational training pathways, gain insights into different professions through company visits and receive help with applications for internships (Ministerium für Kultus, Jugend und Sport Baden-Württemberg, n.d.a).

Despite these efforts, Germany continues to have difficulties integrating refugees into the labor market and tailoring support for students. The 2019 GEM Report criticizes that refugees were often placed into less academic schools after their arrival and almost 85% of those over age 16 were placed in special classes separate from mainstream education, making the entrance into university difficult afterward (UNESCO, 2018). A governmental report highlights goals regarding improved access to the labor market for immigrants and refugees that include increasing access to vocational training for migrant and refugee adolescents, increasing intercultural awareness at workplaces, and fighting against discrimination in education, among others (BBMFI, 2016). Koehler and Schneider (Forthcoming cited in Koehler, 2017) found that, overall, some schools struggle to bridge refugee students' previous education with that received in German classrooms and to offer support on an individual basis. Teaching modifications are not always available, and even switching to a language other than German to assist students is often not practiced (Koehler, 2017).

Social Factors

Since the high influx of refugees in summer 2015, the general consensus in German politics and society has been that education is the key to integration and particularly, the earliest possible access to German language support should be provided in the interests of a rapid integration of refugees (Bundesamt für Migration und Flüchtlinge [BAMF], 2015b, 2015c; Kultusministerkonferenz [KMK], 2016). This investment in language is effective: newcomers who demonstrate a strong German language proficiency have a higher chance of employment and better paid jobs, as well as better access to education and legal and medical services (UNESCO, 2018).

Measures have been adopted to encourage refugees to take integration classes, mainly focusing on German language and orientation in Germany. The influx of refugees led to an increase of participants in integration courses of about 70% from 2013 to 2015 with Syrians being the biggest group for the first time (BBMFI, 2016). The proof of a particular language level is a requirement for starting vocational training or for access to university.

Since school attendance is compulsory in Germany, refugee children have to attend a school within their first six months of arrival in Germany until they are 18 years old. In schools, "welcome classes" have been installed which offer separate language-intensive lessons for refugee students (UNESCO, 2018). These welcome classes are also called Vorbereitungsklassen (preparation classes) at regular schools and Vorqualifizierungsjahr Arbeit/Beruf ohne Deutschkenntnisse (VABO; pre-qualification year for work without knowledge of German) at vocational schools for students over 16 years. In the beginning of 2016, about 23,900 students were enrolled in preparation classes and around 5,800 in pre-qualification classes in the state of Baden-Württemberg (Ministerium für Kultus, Jugend und Sport Baden-Württemberg, n.d.b). In these classes, the main goal has been to introduce and teach German language to refugee children and adolescents, so they are able to participate in regular classes afterward (KMK, 2016). Refugee students tend to stay in the preparation classes (depending on individual progress) up to one year. From 2014 to 2015, 562 new teachers were hired just for these preparation classes in Baden-Württemberg, and about 600 more new teachers were hired in 2016 (Ministerium für Kultus, Jugend und Sport Baden-Württemberg, n.d.b; Shah, 2015).

Disagreements exist around the best approaches to structuring newly arrived students' schooldays: should they remain in preparation classes longer, though this keeps them apart from their fellow students? Should they be integrated earlier into regular classrooms? Or is a mixed approach advised where refugee students attend classes in certain subjects that require less language proficiency? (Koehler, 2017). Also due to the high influx of refugees, there has been a shortage of German as a Second Language teachers in particular (Hanke, 2015). According to the 2019 GEM Report, Germany needs significantly more teachers and other educational specialists for the education of refugees (UNESCO, 2018).

Supplementary services, including counseling and mental health support, are offered for free by the federal as well as the state levels for newcomers. These services focus on education, the labor market, and German language learning, but also on personal situations, health, family, and living situations (BAMF, 2015a; Bundesministerium für Familie, Senioren, Frauen, und Jugend, 2017). School-based mental health provision varies across Germany as each state is responsible for health education (Dadaczynski & Paulus, 2015). As a result, school counselors may include counseling teachers and school psychologists assigned to certain public schools, districts, or private schools (Strasser, 2013). These individuals' responsibilities can include career advising, work with students having learning and behavioral issues, and strategies for teachers and parents (Strasser, 2013). In Baden-Württemberg, training for teachers who deal with traumatized children and adolescents at school is offered. Contents of the training include stress reactions and traumas, pedagogical-psychological and stabilizing options for dealing with stressed students, and self-care in school life. Also individual counseling of teachers is offered (Ministerium für Kultus, Jugend und Sport Baden-Württemberg, n.d.b).

Political Factors

Historically, Germany has been reluctant toward naturalization as seen in the Federal Naturalization Guidelines of 1977: "the Federal Republic is not a country of immigration [and] does not strive to increase the number of citizens through naturalization" (cited in Gathmann & Keller, 2014, p. 7). German Citizenship Law underwent a reform in 1999 and allowed for German citizenship through naturalization after eight years of residence and "the assurance of earning a living for oneself and family members entitled to maintenance, impunity as well as sufficient German skills. In addition, knowledge of the legal and social structure, and the living conditions in Germany must be verified" (BpB & IMIS, 2017).

Beyond the issue of naturalization, refugee families with children are frequently in a place of immediate uncertainty in terms of knowing their options within the unfamiliar German school system and the status of their applications for asylum (Koehler, 2016). In most cases, refugees under the age of 18 cannot be deported and have the right of schooling. However, parents are not always positioned to advocate for their children because of too few translators to assist them in navigating their choices (Koehler, 2016). Delays in hearing outcomes from asylum requests can be months or years, distracting and discouraging parents and students as they consider their futures (Koehler, 2016).

Despite uncertainties, newcomers receive intensive classes on German history, culture, and values as part of integration courses. The courses cover topics on rights, duties, and social values like religious freedom, tolerance, and equal rights for women and men, which are important in Germany (BAMF, 2017). In welcome classes at school, refugee children and adolescents study geography of Germany and social and civic studies, with a focus on democracy education.

Cultural Factors

When Germans themselves speak of ethnicity, they often talk of someone who has a "migrant background" or who is "bio-deutsch" meaning "organic German" (The Economist, 2016). This is similarly reflected in the official language of micro-census questionnaires which in 2005 added questions designed to indicate whether "migrant background" labeling was applicable or not (The Economist, 2016). This label is defined by the Statistisches Bundesamt (n.d.) as any person immigrating into "the territory of today's Federal Republic of Germany after 1949," German-born foreigners, and "persons born in Germany who have at least one parent who immigrated into the country or was born as a foreigner in Germany" (para. 3). This labeling has consequences for schooling. Students are often divided by whether they have an "immigrant background" or not and are also divided into different immigrant groups depending on their country of origin and their socioeconomic status. Some of these immigrant and refugee students are being placed more often into less academic school streams, making it more difficult to access university afterward (UNESCO, 2018).

As to religion, a lack of separation between religion and the state is evident in the tax system, whereby taxpayers may offer monetary support to a religion of their choosing. In public schools, religions are taught by government-employed teachers, although Islam is often not included. This is just one example of what Alba (2005) calls the "deep institutional and cultural embedding" of Christian religions in the country (p. 33). Prominent physical displays (e.g., crucifixes in Bavaria's schools and omnipresent Christmas markets), cultural activities (e.g., Fasching), and holidays (e.g., Heilige Drei Könige Feiertag [Three Kings Holiday] in some states) are just a few examples of the ubiquity of Christianity in German daily life (Alba, 2005). Employing cultural mediators to work with students dealing with conflicts, including how to navigate religious practices alongside school requirements and how to balance the German value system within the framework of values and laws of which students are already familiar, is advocated to ease transitions (Koehler, 2016).

The United States

Economic Factors

In the United States, the most recent federal education law puts economic factors front and center, including for refugee students, building from previous laws that committed the nation's school system to offering additional educational supports to students who could benefit from them (Elementary and Secondary Education Act of 1965) and enacting accountability measures to ensure student achievement across the board (No Child Left Behind Act, signed into law in 2002) (Brenchley, 2015). The Every Student Succeeds Act, signed into law in 2015, is in essence a culmination of these previous laws, "requir[ing] states and districts to ensure that all students . . . graduate high school ready for college or a career" (U.S. Department of Education, 2017). In line with this, states are required to assess students in reading/language arts and mathematics in grades 3 through 8 as well as once during high school. Additionally, during each grade span all students must be assessed in science, and each year English learners in grades K–12 must be assessed on English language proficiency (U.S. Department of Education, 2017).

Thus, knowledge acquisition, so that students, even if they are English learners, can increase their exposure to and knowledge across multiple subjects at once, is evident across practices. Schools in some locations use sheltered instruction with refugee students (Bridging Refugee Youth & Children's Services, n.d.a, n.d.b). In this approach, English instruction takes place while also building knowledge in other subjects like social studies, mathematics, and science (Echevarria, Short, & Powers, 2006; Genesee, 1999). Schools are also tailoring this type of programming for newcomers according to individual students' needs and their current proficiency (Bridging Refugee Youth & Children's Services, n.d.a). In some cases, subject-area classes are taught with an English as a Second Language teacher and general education teacher certified in the subject area working side by side (Sugarman, 2017).

With an eye to future access, whether for training, education, or employment, documenting qualifications is a part of discussions regarding response to refugee students at the secondary level. As part of a series to support the White House Task Force on New Americans, Deborah

Short stressed the importance of clarifying diploma requirements for high school refugee and immigrant students upon their arrival (White House Task Force on New Americans, 2015a). In terms of measuring proficiencies, Short highlighted assessing students, not only in language, but also in mathematics (White House Task Force on New Americans, 2015a). Looking beyond high school graduation, some refugee students like those at LEAP High School in St. Paul, Minnesota, have received career education and advanced writing training with an eye toward moving on to postsecondary education (www.spps.org/).

Related to individuals' self-sufficiency, ascertaining students' own aspirations for their futures has also been advocated, alongside parental encouragement of college education (White House Task Force on New Americans, 2015a). The Parent Institute for Quality Education in California, subsequently replicated across 10 additional US states, encourages parents even early on to instill aspirations of higher education by making a college campus visit annually (White House Task Force on New Americans, 2015b).

Social Factors

The Equal Educational Opportunities Act of 1974 requires that English learner students be able to "participate meaningfully and equally in educational programs" (p. 1) without "unnecessary segregation" (p. 2) (U.S. Department of Justice & U.S. Department of Education, n.d.a). Federal funding guidelines lead state and local education systems to develop and implement programs, including for English language learning, that adhere to their criteria (McHugh & Sugarman, 2015). States also offer school guidelines to determine if students are eligible for additional funding or monitoring (California Department of Education, 2018 and Oregon Department of Education, 2018 cited in UNESCO, 2018), though in some cases this is needed to offset local funding shortfalls and not specific student needs (Farrie, Luhm, & Johnson, 2015 cited in UNESCO, 2018).

As far as building language skills, school districts have leeway to choose from various English learner instructional programs, including ones utilizing separate instructional periods, as long as the program is conducted in "the least segregative manner consistent with achieving the program's stated educational goals" (U.S. Department of Justice & U.S. Department of Education, n.d.a, p. 2). Sheltered instruction (previously described in the "Economic Context" section above) is another approach to language, which enables students to continue to build these skills while simultaneously learning other subject matter (Echevarria et al., 2006; Genesee, 1999; Shriberg, Frost, Melgoza, & Wolfe, 2010). Bilingual and multilingual language instruction has, on the other hand, met noticeable resistance (Kim & Slapac, 2015 cited in UNESCO, 2018).

Data on learning outcomes, across all academic areas, including English, is a driver of US language policy. State and local accountability is ensured by reporting this data at the federal level (Shriberg et al., 2010). The United States no longer focuses merely on basic language proficiency, instead looking to ensure proficiency in academic English. This has been especially beneficial to refugee students who often have limited or interrupted schooling, as it has led to increased attention on spoken English, basic literacy, and subjects covered in prior grade levels (Shriberg et al., 2010). Reliance on data from literacy tests not written in students' home languages, however, can lead to a special needs misdiagnosis, inadequately serving student needs (Adair, 2015 as cited in UNESCO, 2018).

Turning to school-based mental health support, from 1975 to 2005, the United States expanded the overall number of students served (Flaherty & Osher, 2003; Paternite, 2005). Within schools, school psychologists, social workers, counselors, teachers with specialties in behavior issues, and school nurses contribute in this area. These individuals work to provide mental health supports alongside tools for achieving success in school (Paternite, 2005).

The National Association of School Psychologists (NASP) advocates a number of mental health supports for children that are especially relevant for refugees. First, the group encourages recognition of trauma as it contributes to feelings and behaviors including anxiety, depression, aggression, and disciplinary issues (National Association of School Psychologists [NASP], 2015). Frequent communication between parents and teachers, as well as additional referral avenues, are also advocated to get extra counseling to those in need. However, evidence from some US middle schools warns against "over-reliance on PTSD-related explanations for the behavior of refugee students" (p. 9) which can lead teachers and school leaders to overlook other possible roots for behavioral issues like poverty, substance abuse, and domestic violence (Shriberg et al., 2010). Other issues such as cultural considerations with regard to mental health, bullying and harassment, and staff focused on increasing parental involvement are advocated to support the mental health of refugees within the education system (NASP, 2015).

Political Factors

A multi-step process for citizenship exists for both adults and children. Adults must be naturalized to gain citizenship and, in many cases, their children may then "derive" citizenship once this occurs (Nolo, n.d.). The naturalization process for adults, averaging five years, includes passing English language and civics tests (Nolo, n.d.). If children are enrolled in school during these five years, one could see how the child's education could offer potential for parents to progress in English and gain exposure to civic engagement.

For example, Hmong refugee students strived to engage their fellow high school students who were of voting age by holding a debate at school, welcoming elected officials and candidates to visit, and by compiling educational resources related to voting (Catholic Legal Immigration Network, Inc., n.d.). Parent-teacher associations across the United States are another example targeted at parents (Catholic Legal Immigration Network, Inc., n.d.). Vietnamese refugee parents took initiatives to fill gaps in their high schoolers' understanding of financial aid, higher education, and employment by building a network of individuals with expertise into these areas (Catholic Legal Immigration Network, Inc., n.d.).

US schools have found value in not just improving communication but in cultivating leaders among parents of immigrant and refugee students through specific leadership training and education on the way the school district itself is run (White House Task Force on New Americans, 2015b). This leadership can also be an important long-term safeguard for refugee children, as parents become empowered with the knowledge of their student's rights, including, for example, the right to learn in a school in which bias and discrimination do not exist (Council on American-Islamic Relations-California [CAIR-California], n.d.). Despite encouraging parental involvement in practice, teachers' lack of understanding students' families/social networks and disparate views on the roles of teachers can create obstacles in education (see Gichiru, 2016). Training dedicated to familiarizing teachers with family structures of their students and educating them on ways they might potentially interact with families are among gaps identified (Gichiru, 2016).

Cultural Factors

Education systems across the country collect a variety of data, and federal and state obligations require school districts to provide data on race and ethnicity (U.S. Department of Justice & U.S. Department of Education, n.d.b). This mirrors the country-wide census, as well as other data collection measures, that inquires about race and ancestry, with multiple ancestries possible (Coleman, 2013). Race also continues to remain a prominent topic in the country's politics (Lieberman, 2005). Multiple federal actions, such as Titles IV and VI of the Civil Rights Act of 1964 and the US Supreme Court decision in *Plyler v. Doe* (457 U.S. 202 [1982]), bar discrimination by public elementary and secondary schools and school districts on the basis of race, color, or national origin, whether directly or indirectly, including for non-citizen students (Lhamon, Rosenfelt, & Samuels, 2014).

Beyond data, recognizing race and ethnicity within schools is recommended as important in creating an inviting school environment, particularly for refugees. Examples of US schools' strategies to ensure this include highlighting the diversity of the student body through the school's decor and displays (White House Task Force on New Americans, 2015a). An inviting environment is also noted to be created by a school's bilingual staff or the availability of interpreters (White House Task Force on New Americans, 2015a) and school leadership that welcomes a diverse student body is shown more willing to embrace multicultural education (Pica-Smith & Poynton, 2014 cited in UNESCO, 2018). Despite efforts, however, prejudice and discrimination continue to be obstacles, and UNESCO's 2019 GEM Report points out that students from non-English-speaking homes are often mistakenly misdiagnosed as having special needs.

For religion, the United States affirmed separation of church and state including for government employees like teachers in the US Constitution, and consequently, public school teachers may not lead or advocate religious practices when acting as educators (The Boisi Center for Religion and American Public Life, 2007). Despite this separation, religion remains a source of bullying and discrimination in schools, especially for Muslim students (see, for example, CAIR-California, n.d.). For example, in its survey of students in public and private non-Muslim schools across California published in 2015, 55% of US Muslim students said they had been bullied in some way based on their religion (CAIR-California, n.d.). Just 67% of these individuals felt that religious accommodations were made available to them by teachers and school administrators (CAIR-California, n.d.). School-wide training emerges as a thread throughout the documents for this and other factors to strengthen positive approaches and stem negative interactions (CAIR-California, n.d.).

Discussion and Conclusion

The global script of education as a key solution or panacea for refugee integration is disseminated by international organizations. However, decoupling is observed as this script is adapted to different integration contexts. Using the lens of sociological neo-institutionalism and building from literature offering evidence of an inclusion approach to refugee education, the focus of this study was to investigate how differences in integration objectives become evident in education policies and practices for refugees in Germany and the United States. While both have federal systems of education where responsibility lies primarily with the states, qualitative analysis of education policies and practices provides evidence of similarities and differences.

As for economic factors, Germany has increased measures to teach skills especially for practical jobs and vocational training for refugee adolescents. However, following the high refugee influx in 2015, refugee students were often placed in special classes separate from mainstream. By contrast, US education laws have culminated with requirements for *all* students, meant to position them for college and/or careers. Precipitating from these, practices in US schools are focused on knowledge exposure and acquisition broadly and expectations for future success, both in terms of education and/or employment. These laws and practices, however, draw attention to one of the limitations of this study: these are prescriptions and descriptions not perfectly or universally implemented. Further research is needed to investigate their enactment and results yielded.

Considering social factors, results for Germany demonstrate that refugees receive support through integration courses and the priority is language learning. Also, efforts have been implemented at schools to recruit teachers to deal with higher demand for German classes for children and adolescents. These measures show understanding that the German language is seen as key to participation in German society and as a precondition for achieving integration in other spheres of life. The acquisition of a particular language level is a prerequisite for starting vocational training or for access to university. Contrast this with the United States, where skills acquisition across all subjects and remediation if necessary is indicated to be the focus, above English language acquisition alone. In both contexts, school-based supplementary services with focus on mental health are offered to some extent, demonstrating education's role in this area and particularly for dealing with trauma.

Political factors as they relate to citizenship are quite different between Germany and the United States. Germany is not expecting every refugee to receive German citizenship in the future. Nevertheless, attending orientation courses as part of the integration courses and learning democracy education at school are seen as necessary steps toward understanding and participating in German society. In the United States, policy and practice focus on engaging *all* students and parents in decision making and advocacy both inside and outside school, though there is evidence that this is not always the case. These practices align with the opportunity for refugees to naturalize, despite a multi-year wait, at which time they are granted US citizenship.

As far as cultural factors, the analysis shows that having an "immigrant background" is used as a label in Germany. Some immigrant groups and refugees are being placed more often into less academic school streams compared to German students, creating obstacles for them to access university afterwards. Cultural factors, like race and ethnicity, are recognized and documented in US schools. Though federal guidelines bar discrimination in schools, attention to cultural factors, whether systemically or individually, yield mixed results. Sometimes it is beneficial to refugee students (e.g., hiring bilingual staff and interpreters) and sometimes it is detrimental (e.g., poor understanding of students' religious practices, bullying, and discrimination). School-wide training emerges as a thread throughout the documents to strengthen positive approaches and stem negative interactions.

In conclusion, the analysis shows that the understanding of education as a solution or panacea for integration has become ubiquitous and accepted as a shared idea in Germany and the United States. The results also indicate that integration contexts of each country influence education policies and practices found in them. As stated in the introduction, the starting point for this research was the contention that German education policies and practices have been established to prepare refugees for social integration, especially German language acquisition, while for the United States, education policies and practices are primarily focused on preparing refugee students for economic integration. Thus, though adoption of the international script of education as a panacea for refugee integration is evident, education policies and practices in each country emerge as different to align with national approaches to integration.

In Germany, German language acquisition is seen as a precondition for participating in German society and for accessing the labor market and other spheres of society. In the United States, English language is not prioritized. Instead, it is placed on equal footing with all subjects. This can work because individual modifications and accommodations are possible both for students and parents. These practices stem from broad guidelines barring discrimination and requiring student readiness for college or the labor market.

Looking more broadly, in Germany, despite its federal system, numerous documents on policies and practices related to refugee education came directly from the government and its ministries as well as from the Standing Conference of Ministers of Education and Cultural Affairs in a top-down approach. By contrast, we found that documents describing the practices for the United States emerged primarily from the bottom up.

The histories of migration to the countries are impossible to ignore in considering the differences, even though this was not the focus of this study. Germany only started recognizing its status as a country of immigration recently, and schools were not prepared for the high refugee influx in 2015. The federal government had to spread resources and expertise immediately available to begin addressing these newcomers. In contrast, the United States was formed through the displacement of indigenous people by immigrants centuries ago and has a long history of resettling refugees (Castles, 2011; Mossaad & Baugh, 2018). Also, differing attitudes toward individuals' responsibility for their success may contribute. In the German welfare state, government responsibility for supporting citizens is practiced to a greater extent than in the United States. In the United States, individual self-sufficiency is prioritized from the beginning and is an expected outcome.

The global script of education as a panacea for the integration of refugees has been adopted by countries worldwide. The recent influx of refugees has drawn attention to the ways and extent to which this script is enacted. Looking anecdotally, certain patterns may seem evident, but the influence of national integration objectives on education policies and practices has not been assessed broadly and extensively. By looking at two countries with differing objectives, the influence of these is clarified.

Notes

1. Author's translation.
2. Another related term used in this context is *incorporation*. Incorporation is often referred to as political incorporation of groups and organizations on an institutional level and is differentiated from the more individual-focused term *assimilation* (Ramakrishnan, 2013).
3. Asylum-seekers are a separate category from refugees as defined by the Office of Refugee Resettlement (ORR, n.d.c). Throughout this chapter, only refugees are referenced for the US context. While refugees are brought to the United States by the US Department of State, asylees arrive in the United States on their own and must apply for and be granted asylum, which can potentially take many years, at which time most become eligible for Office of Refugee Resettlement services (Myslinska, n.d.; ORR, n.d.c).

References

Adair, J. K. (2015). *The impact of discrimination on the early schooling experiences of children from immigrant families*. Washington, DC: Migration Policy Institute.

Ait-Mehdi, H. (2012). Teaching the history of colonization and decolonization in France: A shared history or to each their own? *Prospects, 42*(2), 191–203. https://doi.org.10.1007/s11125-012-9232-z

Alba, R. (2005). Bright vs. blurred boundaries: Second-generation assimilation and exclusion in France, Germany, and the United States. *Ethnic and Racial Studies, 28*(1), 20–49. https://doi.org/10.1080/0141987042000280003

Alba, R., & Nee, V. (2003). *Remaking the American mainstream: Assimilation and contemporary integration*. Cambridge, MA: Harvard University Press.

Alba, R., Sloan, J., & Sperling, J. (2011). The integration imperative: The children of low-status immigrants in the schools of wealthy societies. *Annual Review of Sociology, 37*, 395–415. https://doi.org/10.1146/annurev-soc-081309-150219

Allemann-Ghionda, C. (2009). From intercultural education to the inclusion of diversity: Theories and policies in Europe. In J. A. Banks (Ed.), *The Routledge international companion to multicultural education* (pp. 134–145). New York, NY: Routledge.

Alvarez, P. (2018, September 9). America's system for resettling refugees is collapsing. *The Atlantic*. Retrieved from www.theatlantic.com/politics/archive/2018/09/refugee-admissions-trump/569641/

Anderson, P. (2001). You don't belong here in Germany: On the social situation of refugee children in Germany. *Journal of Refugee Studies, 14*(2), 187–199.

BAMF. (2015a, October 28). *Beratung für Erwachsene* [Guidance for adults]. Retrieved from www.bamf.de/DE/Willkommen/InformationBeratung/ErwachseneBeratung/erwachseneberatung-node.html

BAMF. (2015b, September 30). *Bildung ist der Schlüssel* [Education is key]. Retrieved from www.bmbf.de/de/bildung-ist-der-schluessel-1596.html

BAMF. (2015c, September 30). *Flüchtlinge durch Bildung integrieren* [Integrate refugees with the help of education]. Retrieved from www.bmbf.de/de/fluechtlinge-durch-bildung-integrieren-1615.html
BAMF. (2017, July 12). *Integrationskurse. Inhalt und Ablauf* [Integration courses: Content and procedure]. Retrieved from www.bamf.de/DE/Willkommen/DeutschLernen/Integrationskurse/InhaltAblauf/inhaltablauf-node.html
Beauftragte der Bundesregierung für Migration, Flüchtlinge und Integration. (2016, December). *11. Bericht der Beauftragten der Bundesregierung für Migration, Flüchtlinge und Integration. Teilhabe, Chancengleichheit und Rechtsentwicklung in der Einwanderungsgesellschaft Deutschland* [11th report of the commissioner of the federal government for migration, refugees and integration: Participation, equal opportunities and legal developments in the immigration society Germany]. Berlin, Germany. Retrieved from www.bundesregierung.de/breg-de/suche/11-bericht-der-beauftragten-der-bundesregierung-fuer-migration-fluechtlinge-und-integration-teilhabe-chancengleichheit-und-rechtsentwicklung-in-der-einwanderungsgesellschaft-deutschland-729972
Bendel, P. (2014, August). *Coordinating immigrant integration in Germany: Mainstreaming at the federal and local levels.* Brussels, Belgium: Migration Policy Institute Europe. Retrieved from www.migrationpolicy.org/article/syrian-refugees-united-states
The Boisi Center for Religion and American Public Life. (2007). *Separation of church and state.* Chestnut Hill, MA: Author. Retrieved from www.bc.edu/content/dam/files/centers/boisi/pdf/bc_papers/BCP-ChurchState.pdf
Brenchley, C. (2015, April 8). *What is ESEA?* [Blog post]. Retrieved from https://blog.ed.gov/2015/04/what-is-esea/
Bridging Refugee Youth & Children's Services. (n.d.a). Serving refugees in the Columbus City Schools, Columbus, OH. Retrieved from www.brycs.org/promisingpractices/promising-practices-program.cfm?docnum=0101
Bridging Refugee Youth & Children's Services. (n.d.b). *Serving refugees in the Lewiston Schools.* Retrieved from www.brycs.org/promisingpractices/promising-practices-program.cfm?docnum=0103
Bundesministerium für Familie, Senioren, Frauen, und Jugend. (2017, January 26). *Künftig begleiten alle Jugendmigrationsdienste junge Flüchtlinge* [Going forward, all youth migration services will support young refugees]. Retrieved from www.bmfsfj.de/bmfsfj/aktuelles/alle-meldungen/kuenftig-begleiten-alle-jugendmigrationsdienste-junge-fluechtlinge/113740
Bundeszentrale für politische Bildung, & Institut für Migrationsforschung und Interkulturelle Studien. (2017). *Focus migration: Country profile: Germany.* Bonn and Osnabrück, Germany. Retrieved from www.bpb.de/gesellschaft/migration/laenderprofile/58349/germany
California Department of Education. (2018). Migrant education program funding. Retrieved September 17, 2018 from www.cde.ca.gov/sp/me/mt/funding.asp
Castles, S. (2011). World population movements, diversity, and education. In J. Banks (Ed.), *The Routledge international companion to multicultural education* (pp. 49–60). New York, NY: Routledge.
Catholic Legal Immigration Network, Inc. (n.d.). *Increasing refugee civic participation: A guide to getting started.* Silver Spring, MD: Author. Retrieved from https://cliniclegal.org/sites/default/files/civic_participation_tool_kit_final_2.pdf

Coleman, D. (2013). *Immigration, population, and ethnicity: The UK in international perspective*. Oxford, UK: COMPAS and The University of Oxford. Retrieved from www.migrationobservatory.ox.ac.uk/wp-content/uploads/2016/04/Briefing-Immigration_Population_and_Ethnicity.pdf

Council on American-Islamic Relations-California. (n.d.). *Mislabeled: The impact of school bullying and discrimination on California Muslim students*. Anaheim, CA: Author. Retrieved from https://ca.cair.com/sfba/wp-content/uploads/2015/10/CAIR-CA-2015-Bullying-Report-Web.pdf

Dadaczynski, K., & Paulus, P. (2015). *International survey of principals concerning emotional and mental health and well-being: Country report: Germany*. Newton, MA: Education Development Center. Retrieved from http://intercamhs.edc.org/files/Principals%20Survey%20-%20Germany%20(09-28-10).pdf

Davis, J. H. (2018, September 17). Trump to cap refugees allowed into the U.S. at 30,000, a record low. *The New York Times*. Retrieved from www.nytimes.com/2018/09/17/us/politics/trump-refugees-historic-cuts.html

Dryden-Peterson, S. (2015). Refugee education in countries of first asylum: Breaking open the black box of pre-resettlement experiences. *Theory and Research in Education*, 14(2), 131–148. https://doi.org/10.1177%2F1477878515622703

Dryden-Peterson, S. (2016). Refugee education: The crossroads of globalization. *Educational Researcher*, 45(9), 473–482. Retrieved from http://nrs.harvard.edu/urn-3:HUL.InstRepos:30194044

Dryden-Peterson, S., Adelman, E., Alvarado, S., Anderson, K., Bellino, M. J., Brooks, R., . . . Suzuki, E. (2018). *Background paper prepared for the 2019 Global Education Monitoring Report: Migration, displacement and education: Building bridges, not walls: Inclusion of refugees in national education systems*. Paris, France: UNESCO. Retrieved from https://unesdoc.unesco.org/ark:/48223/pf0000266054/PDF/266054eng.pdf.multi

Dryden-Peterson, S., Adelman, E., Bellino, M., & Chopra, V. (Under review). The purposes of refugee education: Policy and practice of integrating refugees into national education systems.

Echevarria, J., Short, D., & Powers, K. (2006). School-reform and standards-based education: A model for English language learners. *Journal of Education Research*, 99(4). https://doi.org/10.3200/JOER.99.4.195-211

The Economist. (2016, May 26). Name, date of birth, migration background. Retrieved from www.economist.com/europe/2016/05/26/name-date-of-birth-migration-background

Eurostat. (2018). *Asylum statistics*. Retrieved January 16, 2019 from www.unrefugees.org/refugee-facts/what-is-a-refugee/

Farrie, D., Luhm, T., & Johnson, E. M. (2015). *Understanding New Jersey's school funding formula: the role of adjustment aid*. Pittsburgh, PA: Education Law Center.

Felter, C., & McBride, J. (2018, October 10). *How does the U.S. refugee system work?* Retrieved from www.cfr.org/backgrounder/how-does-us-refugee-system-work

Fernanda Astiz, M. (2006). Policy enactment and adaptation of community participation in education: The case of Argentina. In D. P. Baker & A. W. Wiseman

(Eds.), *The impact of comparative education research on institutional theory* (Vol. 7, pp. 305–334). Bingley, UK: Emerald Group Publishing Limited.

Flaherty, L. T., & Osher, D. (2003). History of school-based mental health services in the United States. In M. D. Weist, S. W. Evans, & N. A. Lever (Eds.), *Handbook of school mental health advancing practice and research* (pp. 11–22). Boston, MA: Springer.

Gathmann, C., & Keller, N. (2014). *Returns to citizenship? Evidence from Germany's recent immigration reforms* (IZA DP No. 8064). Bonn, Germany: Institute for the Study of Labor. Retrieved from http://ftp.iza.org/dp8064.pdf

Genesee, F. (1999). *Program alternatives for linguistically diverse students* (Educational Practice Report 1). Santa Cruz, CA: Center for Research on Education, Diversity and Excellence. Retrieved from http://files.eric.ed.gov/fulltext/ED428569.pdf

Gichiru, W. (2016). An examination of Somali parents' interaction with public schools: Complicating family diversity in educational contexts. *Journal of Family Diversity in Education*, 2(1). Retrieved from http://familydiversityeducation.org/index.php/fdec/article/view/77

Hanke, K. (2015). *Teachers need to be trained in German as a second language* (C. Cave, Trans.). Munich, Germany: Goethe-Insitut, e. V.

Jepperson, R. L. (2001). *The development and application of sociological neoinstitutionalism*. Working Paper 2001/5. Florence, Italy: Robert Schuman Centre, European University Institute. Retrieved from https://worldpolity.files.wordpress.com/2010/05/jepperson-sociological-institutionalism-eui-5-2001.pdf

Kaarbo, J., & Beasley, R. K. (1999). A practical guide to the comparative case study method in political psychology. *Political Psychology*, 20(2), 369–391.

Kim, S., & Slapac, A. (2015). Culturally responsive, transformative pedagogy in the transnational era: Critical perspectives. *Educational Studies*, 51(1), 17–27.

Koehler, C. (2016). *Education, mobility, uncertainty: Refugees in receiving countries' education centers*. Proceedings of the South African International Conference on Education. Towards Excellence in Educational Practices. Retrieved from http://aa-rf.org/wp-content/uploads/2016/09/SAICEd2016-Proceedings.pdf#page=277

Koehler, C. (2017). *Continuity of learning for newly arrived refugee children in Europe* (NESET II ad hoc question No. 1/2017). Vilnius, Lithuania: NESET II. Retrieved from http://nesetweb.eu/wp-content/uploads/2016/02/Refugee-children.pdf

Koehler, C., & Schneider, J. (Forthcoming). *Multi-country partnership to enhance the education of refugee and asylum-seeking youth in Europe – National report Germany*. Bamberg and Hamburg, Germany: European Forum for Migration Studies, Verikom, and SIRIUS—Policy Network on Migrant Education.

Kuckartz, U. (2014). *Qualitative text analysis: A guide to methods, practice and using software*. London, UK: Sage.

Kultusministerkonferenz (KMK). (2016). *Bericht der Kultusministerkonferenz zur Integration von jungen Geflüchteten durch Bildung* [Report of the Standing Conference of Ministers of Education and Cultural Affairs on Integration of young refugees through education]. Retrieved from www.kmk.org/themen/allgemeinbildende-schulen/integration.html

Lhamon, C., Rosenfelt, P. H., & Samuels, J. (2014, May 8). *Dear colleague letter: School enrollment procedures.* Retrieved from www2.ed.gov/about/offices/list/ocr/letters/colleague-201405.pdf

Lieberman, R. C. (2005). Configurations of race and state: The politics of racial incorporation. In R. C. Lieberman (Ed.), *Shaping race policy: The United States in comparative perspective* (pp. 1–26). Princeton, NJ: Princeton University Press. Retrieved from www.jstor.org/stable/j.ctt7rmws

McHugh, M., & Sugarman, J. (2015). *Transatlantic Symposium report: Improving instruction for immigrant and refugee students in secondary schools.* Washington, DC: Migration Policy Institute. Retrieved from www.migrationpolicy.org/research/transatlantic-symposium-report-improving-instruction-immigrant-and-refugee-students

Meer, N., Pala, V. S., Modood, T., & Simon, P. (2009). Cultural diversity, Muslims, and education in France and England. In J. A. Banks (Ed.), *The Routledge international companion to multicultural education* (pp. 413–424). New York, NY: Routledge.

Meyer, J. W., Boli, J., Thomas, G. M., & Ramirez, F. O. (1997). World society and the nation-state. *American Journal of Sociology, 103*(1), 144–181.

Ministerium für Kultus, Jugend und Sport Baden-Württemberg. (n.d.a). *Bildungsangebote für Flüchtlinge und Zuwanderer* [Educational offers for refugees and immigrants]. Retrieved from https://km-bw.de/,Lde/Startseite/Schule/Fluechtlingsintegration

Ministerium für Kultus, Jugend und Sport Baden-Württemberg. (n.d.b). *Fragen und Antworten zur Integration von jungen Flüchtlingen in baden-württembergischen Schulen* [Questions and answers on the integration of young refugees in schools in Baden-Württemberg]. Retrieved from https://km-bw.de/,Lde/Startseite/Schule/FAQs

Mossaad, N., & Baugh, R. (2018, January). *Refugees and asylees: 2016.* Washington, DC: Department of Homeland Security Office of Immigration Statistics. Retrieved from www.dhs.gov/sites/default/files/publications/Refugees_Asylees_2016_0.pdf

Myslinska, D. R. (n.d.). *Timing of the affirmative asylum application process.* Retrieved January 22, 2019 from www.nolo.com/legal-encyclopedia/timing-the-affirmative-asylum-application-process.html

National Association of School Psychologists. (2015). *Supporting refugee children & youth: Tips for educators.* Retrieved from www.nasponline.org/resources-and-publications/resources/school-safety-and-crisis/war-and-terrorism/supporting-refugee-students

Nolo. (n.d.). *Refugees: Apply for citizenship soon, so your children under 18 become automatic U.S. citizens.* Retrieved January 17, 2019 from www.nolo.com/legal-encyclopedia/when-refugee-children-can-become-us-citizens.html

Office of Refugee Resettlement. (2012, August 29). *The Refugee Act.* Retrieved from www.acf.hhs.gov/orr/resource/the-refugee-act

Office of Refugee Resettlement. (n.d.a). *Find resources and contacts in your state.* Retrieved January 16, 2019 from www.acf.hhs.gov/orr/state-programs-annual-overview

Office of Refugee Resettlement. (n.d.b). *History.* Retrieved from www.acf.hhs.gov/orr/about/history

Office of Refugee Resettlement. (n.d.c). *What we do.* Retrieved January 16, 2019 from www.acf.hhs.gov/orr/about/what-we-do

Oregon Department of Education. (2018). *Title I-C Migrant Education*. Salem, OR: Department of Education.
Organisation for Economic Co-operation and Development. (2015, September). *Is this humanitarian migration crisis different?* (Migration Policy Debates No. 4). Paris, France: Author. Retrieved from www.oecd.org/migration/Is-this-refugee-crisis-different.pdf
Paternite, C. E. (2005). School-based mental health programs and services: Overview and introduction to the special issue. *Journal of Abnormal Child Psychology*, 33(6), 657–663.
Pica-Smith, C., & Poynton, T. (2014). Supporting interethnic and interracial friendships among youth to reduce prejudice and racism in schools: The role of the school counselor. *Professional School Counseling*, 18(1), 82–89.
Portes, A., & Rumbaut, R. G. (1996). *Immigrant America: A portrait*. Berkeley, CA: University of California Press.
Portes, A., & Rumbaut, R. G. (2001). *Legacies: The story of the immigrant second generation*. Berkeley, CA: University of California Press.
Ramakrishnan, S. K. (2013). Incorporation versus assimilation: The need for conceptual differentiation. In J. Hochschild, J. Chattopadhyay, C. Gay, & M. Jones-Correa (Eds.), *Outsiders no more? Models of immigrant political incorporation* (pp. 27–42). Oxford, UK: Oxford University Press.
Shah, H. (2015). *Flüchtlingskinder und jugendliche Flüchtlinge in der Schule* [Refugee children and adolescent refugees at school]. Stuttgart, Germany: Ministerium für Kultus, Jugend und Sport Baden-Württemberg. Retrieved from https://km-bw.de/site/pbs-bw-new/get/documents/KULTUS.Dachmandant/KULTUS/kultusportal-bw/Publikationen%20ab%202015/2015-10-21-Fluechtlingskinder-Screen.pdf
Shriberg, J., Frost, K., Melgoza, A., & Wolfe, A. (2010). *Advancing teacher development in Colorado refugee education programs*. Retrieved from www.springinstitute.org/wp-content/uploads/2016/04/executivereporttdrproject.pdf
Statistisches Bundesamt. (n.d.). *Persons with a migrant background*. Retrieved January 28, 2019 from ww.destatis.de/EN/FactsFigures/SocietyState/Population/MigrationIntegration/Methods/MigrationBackground.html
Strasser, J. (2013). Counseling in Germany. In T. H. Hohenshil, N. E. Amundson, & S. G. Niles (Eds.), *Counseling around the world: An international handbook*. Alexandria, VA: American Counseling Association.
Sugarman, J. (2017, November). *Beyond teaching English: Supporting high school completion by immigrant and refugee students*. Washington, DC: Migration Policy Institute. Retrieved from www.migrationpolicy.org/research/beyond-teaching-english-supporting-high-school-completion-immigrant-and-refugee-students
UNESCO. (2012). *Education for all Global Monitoring Report 2012: Youth and skills: Putting education to work*. Paris, France: Author. Retrieved from http://unesdoc.unesco.org/images/0021/002180/218003e.pdf
UNESCO. (2018). *Global Education Monitoring Report 2019: Migration, displacement, and education: Building bridges, not walls*. Paris, France: Author. Retrieved from https://en.unesco.org/gem-report/report/2019/migration
UNHCR. (2016, December). *Regional refugee and migrant response plan for Europe: January to December 2017*. Geneva, Switzerland: Author. Retrieved from http://reporting.unhcr.org/sites/default/files/2017%20Regional%20Refugee%

20&%20Migrant%20Response%20Plan%20for%20Europe%20-%20Jan-Dec%202017%20(December%202016).pdf
UNHCR. (2017). Europe. In *About us: Where we work*. Retrieved from www.unhcr.org/europe.htm
UNHCR Division of International Protection. (2012). *2012–2016 Education strategy summary*. Geneva, Switzerland: United Nations High Commissioner for Refugees. Retrieved from www.unhcr.org/4af7e71d9.pdf
U.S. Department of Education. (2017, December 7). *Every Student Succeeds Act: Assessments under Title I, Part A & Title I, Part B: Summary of final regulations*. Retrieved from www2.ed.gov/policy/elsec/leg/essa/essaassessmentfactsheet1207.pdf
U.S. Department of Justice, & U.S. Department of Education. (n.d.a). *Ensuring English language learner students can participate meaningfully and equally in educational programs* (Fact sheet). Retrieved from www2.ed.gov/about/offices/list/ocr/docs/dcl-factsheet-el-students-201501.pdf
U.S. Department of Justice, & U.S. Department of Education. (n.d.b). *Fact sheet: Information on rights of all children to enroll in school*. Washington, DC: Author. Retrieved from www2.ed.gov/policy/elsec/leg/essa/essaassessmentfactsheet1207.pdf
U.S. Department of State Office of the Spokesperson. (2016, October 4). *Fact sheet: Fiscal year 2016 refugee admissions*. Retrieved from https://2009-2017.state.gov/r/pa/prs/ps/2016/10/262776.htm
Van Tubergen, F. (2006). *Immigrant integration: A cross-national study*. El Paso, TX: LFB Scholarly Publishing.
Weinstein, J., & Ferwerda, J. (2018, February 12). Trump has undercut U.S. refugee resettlement. Here's one way to restore it. *Foreign Policy*. Retrieved from https://foreignpolicy.com/2018/02/12/trump-has-undercut-u-s-refugee-resettlement-heres-one-way-to-restore-it/
White House Task Force on New Americans. (2015a, July 16). *Webinar #2: Creating welcoming schools* [Transcript]. Retrieved from www2.ed.gov/about/offices/list/oela/webinars/new-americans/index.html
White House Task Force on New Americans. (2015b, August 27). *Webinar #3: Engaging immigrant parents and families* [Transcript]. Retrieved from www2.ed.gov/about/offices/list/oela/webinars/new-americans/index.html
Wiseman, A. W., Damaschke-Deitrick, L., Bruce, E., Davidson, P., & Taylor, C. S. (2016). Transnational scientized education discourse: A cross-national comparison. In J. Schmid, K. Amos, J. Schrader, & A. Thiel (Eds.), *Internationalisierte Welten der Bildung* (pp. 121–146). Baden-Baden, Germany: Nomos Publishing.
Zong, J., & Batalova, J. (2017). *Syrian refugees in the United States*. Retrieved from www.migrationpolicy.org/article/syrian-refugees-united-states

2 The Educational Response to Syrian Displacement
A Professionalizing Field in a Politicized Environment

Elizabeth Buckner and Mozynah Nofal

The Story of Three Conflicts

In 1948, 700,000 Palestinian civilians were displaced throughout neighboring countries, including Jordan, Syria, and Lebanon, where they were largely denied citizenship rights, including the right to free public education. In 1949, a wholly distinct United Nations (UN) Agency, the United Nations Refugee Works Association (UNRWA), was founded to provide emergency relief and implement public works programs (Bocco, 2009). Seventy years later, the descendants of these original Palestinian refugees still lack the right to access public schools in some countries, namely Lebanon (Knudsen, 2009).

Between 2004 and 2007, after the US invasion, an estimated 2 million Iraqis were displaced to neighboring countries in Jordan, Syria, Egypt, and Lebanon, generating global attention. In Jordan, unregistered refugees were not permitted to enroll in public schools until 2007, when King Abdullah II took direct action allowing unregistered refugees to enroll in public schools. Joint funding appeals were the extent of regional coordination. At the time, a joint UNHCR-UNICEF appeal encouraged donors to support Iraqi refugees throughout the region, but there was little regional coordination. At a 2007 donor conference, UNHCR gave Jordan $21 million, considered a disproportionately high figure, at 60% of its entire operating budget, and donors pledged $60 million to support refugee-hosting countries with the provision of health and education services (Seeley, 2010).

Less than a decade later, in response to the massive displacement of Syrian refugees (5.6 officially registered refugees), the 2016 Supporting Syria and the Region Donor conference garnered pledges of $12.1 billion dollars for 2016–2020, with an estimated $6 billion for 2016 alone and $6.1 billion for the 2017–2020 period, tied to strong commitments for increasing access to education (Lenner, 2016). In addition to this exponential increase in funding, the massive displacement of Syrians throughout the region has resulted in an unprecedented and coordinated response by the international humanitarian sector, donors, and national governments to create an expansive, professionalized, and regionally coordinated response to ensure that Syrian refugees have access to public schools in all neighboring countries.

The story of these three successive waves of refugee displacement in the Middle East tells us that the large-scale and regionally coordinated response to Syrian displacement, where refugees' right to education is largely unquestioned, is not the historical norm. It was not even the norm at the beginning of the Syrian civil war in 2011. It is unprecedented. It is also surprising, given the fact that no country in the region is party to the 1951 Refugee Convention that guarantees refugees' basic rights, including education.[1] What explains the massive educational response to the Syrian refugee crisis?

This chapter examines the evolving policies and coordination mechanisms of the educational response to the Syrian conflict in the region. It highlights national, regional, and global initiatives that have supported refugees' access to education, through planning, advocacy, and funding. Drawing on the world society theory tradition in comparative education, it argues that the unprecedented educational response must be understood in light of fundamental shifts in global humanitarian and development discourses and the intensification of supra-national governance. First, the long-term shift in global norms that have institutionalized the idea that education is a human right has resulted in its incorporation into humanitarian response plans and the articulation of a global development regime that has set ever more aspirational goals regarding education for all, including refugees. Secondly, largely in response to these new commitments to education for all, a dense network of organizations has developed to monitor and support the right to education, creating new initiatives and accountability mechanisms at the regional and global levels. Combined, this study argues that these normative and policy shifts explain both "why" and "how" the global community has come together to address Syrian refugee education. Nonetheless, we recognize that the reality for many Syrian refugee children is still dire; the study points out the predictable side effects of global normative commitments, including the decoupling between ambitious goals from the highly politicized realities on the ground.

The Syrian Conflict, 2011–2018

The Syrian civil war began in the wake of the Arab Spring in March 2011, as thousands of Syrians participated in pro-democracy protests. Bashar Al-Assad's government cracked down on the protests, and civilians began to form local oppositional brigades in response. By 2012, fighting reached the major urban centers and has continued ever since, with varying periods of regional de-escalation during cease-fires. By 2013, the conflict erupted into a proxy war drawing in regional and international powers including the United States, Russia, Iran, Saudi Arabia, Turkey, and Lebanon's Hezbollah. The rise of the Islamic State in 2013 and 2014 magnified the complexity of the conflict, as swaths of land in Northern Syria came under Islamic State in Iraq and Syria (ISIS) control. As of 2018, nearing its eighth year, the conflict is deeply divided along sectarian lines, with the Sunni majority fighting against the president's Shia Alawite sect (BBC, 2018).

The conflict has had devastating effects on the country and Syrian families. As of December 2018, UNHCR estimates that more than 6.2 million Syrians are internally displaced (UNHCR, 2018a), and 5.6 million are officially registered as refugees with UNHCR, having fled to neighboring countries, including Turkey, Jordan, Iraq, and Lebanon, with Iraq and Egypt also hosting a significant number of refugees. The overwhelming majority of Syrian refugees are hosted in these five neighboring countries, although others have also fled to the Gulf states, North Africa, and beyond.

In terms of sheer numbers, Turkey hosts the most Syrian refugees. In December 2018, there were an estimated 3.6 million refugees in Turkey (UNHCR, 2018a), of whom 800,000 are of school-age and 8% are living in camps (McCarthy, 2018). Access to education varies significantly between those living in camps, where roughly 75% of children attend school, and self-settled refugees living in urban areas, where it is estimated that only 25% are enrolled (Dorman, 2014). To meet demand, Temporary Educational Centers (TEC) emerged and are being operated by non-state actors. As of 2018, the Turkish government has committed to transitioning Syrian refugees out of TECs and into the public education system by 2020–2021 (UNESCO, 2018a).

Lebanon is currently hosting an estimated 1.5 million Syrian refugees, of whom 950,000 are officially registered with UNHCR (UNHCR, 2018a). With a pre-crisis population of 4.2 million, the country has one of the highest per-capita concentrations of refugees worldwide. However, accurate numbers on refugees are hard to access because in May 2015, the Lebanese government demanded that UNHCR stop registering refugees. International and local organizations estimate that the rate of Syrians without legal residency in Lebanon could be as high as 90%, although the Lebanese authorities have not released this data (Khawaja, 2016).

In Jordan, as of December 2018, there were 671,074 Syrian refugees registered with UNHCR, of whom 126,103 resided in two large refugee camps (UNHCR, 2018d). However, it is estimated that almost half of Syrian refugees are unregistered, and there may be as many as 1.3 million Syrians currently in Jordan. Over half of all refugees in Jordan are under age 15 (Krafft, Sieverding, Salemi, & Keo, 2018).

In response to the scale of displacement, a diverse coalition of actors has come together to support refugees' access to education, including host governments, UN agencies, donors, and humanitarian and development organizations. At the global level, the major actors working in education include UNHCR, UNICEF, and UNRWA. Major donors include the European Union and USAID, as well as nontraditional donor nations, including Qatar, Kuwait, the United Arab Emirates, and other Arab Gulf countries. The national governments of refugee-hosting countries, including Jordan, Turkey, and Lebanon, have been active in shaping the terms in which refugees are permitted to enter and permitted to access public schools, and a whole spectrum of humanitarian and development organizations have provided a wide variety of programming, from remedial education, psychosocial programming, early childhood education and development, and transportation. Although Syrian refugees face many barriers to quality education, the scale of the global response presents a model of coordination for supporting refugee education. The next section of this study discusses the ideological foundations upon which this new model is based.

The Shifting Global Landscape

Changing global norms and the growth of supra-national governance structures have resulted in unprecedented action in addressing the educational needs of Syrian refugees. In this section, we summarize these shifts in two parts. First, we examine the normative and ideological shifts that have established education as a human right and infused it into the global development agenda, articulating urgent attention to the issue of education in emergencies (EiE). Second, we summarize the literature from comparative education that documents how global normative commitments have been translated into specific structures at the supra-national level to realize normative commitments through supra-national policy coordination and professionalizing networks.

Establishing Education as a Human Right

This study draws on the world society tradition (WST) in comparative education to make sense of the changing nature of refugee education, including the globally coordinated and well-funded response to Syrian displacement. It argues that the global response to the Syrian refugee crisis is rooted in broader global normative shifts that have occurred over the past few decades, the most fundamental has been the encoding of education as a human right in global development, and the creation of global policies and a professional development community oriented toward protecting that right. In contrast to purely functional accounts of human action, world society scholars argue that nation-states, organizations, individuals, and other actors are embedded in a larger cultural environment that creates and legitimizes actors, roles, and norms of behavior (Meyer, Boli, Thomas, & Ramirez, 1997). The contemporary broader cultural environment is characterized by a belief in individual and collective progress, human rights, justice, and equality.

The spread and entrenchment of human rights in the global imagination, and the particular inclusion of education as a human right in global discourses, have had important effects on education. The Universal Declaration of Human Rights (UDHR), adopted in 1948, states that access to a basic education is a human right. Not long after, in 1951, the United Nations Convention Relating to the Status of Refugees and its 1967 protocol both affirmed refugees' right to education. In total, 145 parties have signed the Convention and 146 have signed the protocol, committing to providing refugees with "the same treatment as is accorded to nationals with respect to elementary education" (UNESCO, 2018a, p. 7). In addition to these two foundational instruments, a series of subsequent international conventions reaffirmed the right to education. In 1976, the Convention of Economic, Social, and Cultural Rights affirmed education as a fundamental right. And in 1990, the Convention on the Rights of the Child (CRC), included the right to basic education.

Nonetheless, the right to education was not a global concern in the postwar era (Lerch, 2017). In most countries, education was not universal, even at the primary level. Moreover, given its acculturating and nation-building roles, public education was considered the domain of the nation-state. International development actors typically left educational policy and funding decisions up to national actors. In other words, despite certain global documents that established education as a universal human right for refugees and citizens alike, the reality is that for most of the 20th century, refugees' right to education was rarely enforced in any meaningful way.

Over the past two decades, however, both the educational development community and the field of refugee studies have witnessed parallel trends that increasingly ground the education of refugees within broader discussions of human rights. In 1990, the global development community coalesced around the idea of education as a human right and began to construct a global agenda and community to ensure all children had access to quality education (Chabbott, 2003). This global vision was laid out at the World Conference on Education for All in 1990 in Jomtien, Thailand, which set an ambitious vision of Education for All (EFA). Although little progress was made in the 1990s, in the 2000s, EFA was reaffirmed at the World Education Forum in Dakar, and the global development community began to take significant and coordinated action (Mundy, 2006). The Millennium Development Goals (MDGs), which were established in 2000, and set out a global development agenda that included ensuring all children completed primary school (Goal 2: Universal Primary Education) provided a further global framework for protecting the right to education.

Over the same period, refugee rights were increasingly grounded within the broader framework of human rights (Fiddian-Qasmiyeh, Loescher, Long, & Sigona, 2014). States' international human rights obligations have been used to advocate for protection for refugees, even in countries that are not party to the 1951 Convention on Refugees. This shift has been particularly important in the case of Syria, as neither Lebanon nor Jordan is party to the 1951 Convention, and Turkey limits its definition of refugee to a person fleeing Europe.

Since the outbreak of the Syrian conflict, the global commitment to education as a fundamental right has been further reaffirmed and elaborated. In 2015, United Nations adopted the Sustainable Development Goals (SDGs), an ambitious global development agenda that follows the MDGs. The SDGs include 17 goals, and SDG 4 commits all countries to quality primary and secondary schooling for all by 2030. Conflict is considered to be one of the major barriers to reaching SDG 4, putting a renewed global attention on refugee education.

Additionally, in September 2016 at the World Humanitarian Summit (WHS) in New York, all 193 members of the United Nations signed the New York Declaration for Refugees and Migrants, which recognized the need for an updating and reconsideration of the 1951 Convention in light of current displacement trends. The WHS has been described as "a turning point" that "helped draw attention to education in emergencies, including for refugees" (UNESCO, 2018a, p. 254), and the Global Compact on Refugees specifically devoted two clauses to refugees' right for education, in which signatories committed to transitioning refugees into public education systems as soon as possible, ideally within three months (UNESCO, 2018a, p. 8).

In short, over the past five decades, the right to education has been consistently and increasingly enshrined and elaborated in global discourses, both humanitarian and development. These ideological shifts, in which education is viewed as a human right, even in times of conflict or instability, and even for refugees who are outside their national borders, have resulted in a sense of growing global responsibility for the education of refugees (Lerch & Buckner, 2018). In the next section, we discuss this parallel trend: the increasing number of organizations and individuals working to realize this right by institutionalizing it in official policy, professional practice, advocacy campaigns, and accountability mechanisms.

The Rise of Supra-National Governance Structures

Over the past five decades, there has been a dramatic increase in the role of supra-national actors in shaping national educational policies. Scholars in comparative education point out that despite the fact there is no global state, there has been an intensification of multilateral governance (Mundy, 2006). This "globalization of educational policy" occurs through the structuration of a transnational organizational field (Ramirez, Meyer, & Lerch, 2016). One important factor in the rise of supra-national structures is the proliferation of international organizations, who collaborate and interact in dense networks. This dense system has been successful in diffusing educational policy commitments around the world (Mundy & Murphy, 2001). A second, related mechanism is the professionalization of the field of educational development, which draws on the increasing rationalization of organizational behavior. EiE has become an increasingly professionalized and technical domain of expertise. Prior research has documented how the field of educational development, once framed as a form of charity, has become increasingly professionalized, with expanding number of journals, degree programs, and professional associations (Bromley, 2010). A similar professionalization has occurred in the sub-field of Education in Emergencies, where professional networks and scientific knowledge in the form of journals and conferences have all proliferated in recent years (Lerch, 2017).

With regards to refugee education, there has been a dramatic increase in global organizations and structures. The 2018 "Global Education Monitoring Report" (GEMR), which focuses on migration and displacement, reports that until only a few years ago "education was long absent from humanitarian needs assessments" (p. 254). However, in 2007, the Global Education Cluster was established by the United Nations Office for the Coordination of Humanitarian Assistance (OCHA) to be a coordinating mechanism for education. The Global Cluster established new guidelines for joint needs assessments, and since then, "education is becoming a standard element in humanitarian response plans: 89% of appeals included an educational component in 2017," according to Education Cannot Wait (UNESCO, 2018a, p. 254). Many other new initiatives have also been founded in recent years to monitor and advocate for education, including the Global Coalition to Protect Education from Attack and Education Cannot Wait, a multilateral fund for education in conflict-affected areas.

Various political and geopolitical motivations also certainly played a role in determining the scale and scope of the response to the Syrian conflict. These include the role of politically powerful backers, including European leaders who were early advocates for education. In addition, the proximity of Syria to Europe invokes both cynical political calculations and a sense of familiarity that has sparked sincere humanitarian concern. It is not surprising that the European Union is the largest funder of the Syrian humanitarian crisis, and Turkey, viewed as a key conduit of migration to Europe receives the most aid, including recent commitments of €3 billion specifically to Turkey to support Syrian refugees (UNHCR, 2018b; UNESCO, 2018a). Nonetheless, advocacy organizations, government officials, and local actors also routinely cite normative rationales as providing a framework for supporting children's right to education (Buckner, Spencer, & Cha, 2018). Ramirez et al. (2016) argue that countries are more likely to "endorse educational reforms that enjoy professional legitimacy" (p. 43). As a result, the global community has significant influence: it is able to both articulate desired reforms and increasingly, enact them by providing policy models, technical support, and funding.

In this study, we argue that both the normative framework and supra-national governance structures have been important factors in understanding the global educational response to the Syrian conflict. In the subsequent sections, we examine how these shifts have played out at various levels. At the national level, we show how education has become a part of the humanitarian response in refugee-hosting countries and national policies have permitted refugees unprecedented access to public schools. At the regional level, we point to a number of regional coordination networks and mechanisms have been effective in coordinating priorities throughout the region. Finally, at the global level, we point to the growing professionalization of EiE and the importance of donor coordination in facilitating these policy shifts through advocacy, technical expertise, and funding. Figure 2.1 visualizes these levels.

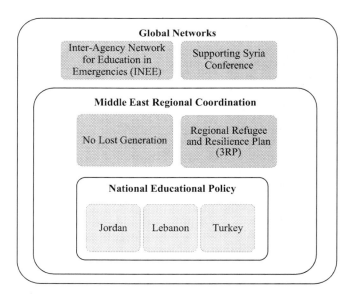

Figure 2.1 The educational response to Syrian displacement, global, regional, and national levels

National Educational Policy: From Exclusion to Inclusion

Syrian refugees began fleeing into Turkey, Lebanon, and Jordan as refugees in 2011. At this time, policymakers in host countries did not anticipate the eventual scale or length of the conflict. Moreover, Jordan and Lebanon's history with Palestinian refugees made discussions of refugee rights a contentious issue. Policy approaches for educational provision adopted in host countries can be characterized as exclusionary, in the case of Turkey and Lebanon, and in the case of Jordan, piecemeal. The rise of coordinated, multi-year, and multi-sector strategies that permit refugees' access to free public schooling has been a dramatic shift, as we outline below.

Turkey

The initial response to Syrian children arriving to Turkey was the establishment of what is known as Temporary Education Centers (TECs). These centers were created by non-state actors to meet the education needs of these children. Initially these TECs were considered illegal, in light of Turkey's strict national education policy that prohibits schooling in any foreign language except by cabinet decree. However, in June 2011, the Ministry of National Education (MONE) passed a policy to permit educational services to refugee children in camps; however, the policy was limited to refugees in camps and there was no education in Turkish (McCarthy, 2018). Moreover, despite large numbers of Syrians settling outside official camps, official education policies only concerned those refugees in camps. The decision to not provide education to refugees outside of camps was an intentional decision on the part of policymakers. McCarthy (2018) explains: "the provision of education for the non-camp refugees was seen as an unjustifiable service that would affect the decision of the refugees to stay or return rather than as a human right" (p. 229).

In 2013, educational providers operating outside refugee camps were first recognized. This policy officially permitted education for Syrians outside of camps, provided by civil society actors. During the same year, in September 2013, another regulation—Education Services for the Syrians Under Temporary Protection—was passed to regulate, standardize, and coordinate educational provision for Syrian refugee children in and out of the camps. More importantly, the ministry began an official cooperation with Syrian National Coalition, which was acting as the Syrian Interim Government. As a result, the ministry permitted schools operated by Syrians to teach the Syrian curriculum and in Arabic, despite provisions in the Turkish Constitution and the National Education Law that mandate the Turkish curriculum and language.

Over time, it became clear that the policy of official exclusion was increasingly untenable. In April 2014, a new immigration law (Foreigners and International Protection Act no. 6458) was passed, which provided a legal basis for refugee education for the first time. In October 2014, the MONE issued a circular that changed the official stance on education of refugees. This circular referenced both international treaties, including the Convention on the Rights of the Child and International Covenant on Economic, Social, and Cultural Rights, as well as Turkey's existing law on primary education on national education, which guarantees access to national education. The new circulars and policies explicitly sought to ease Syrians' access to education. The MONE's 2014 circular "decreed that a 'foreigner identification document'—not a residency permit—was sufficient for registration in the Turkish public school system" (p. 229). At the same time, the government mandated that all students in TECs study 15 hours of Turkish a week, to facilitate their transfer to public schools, and Turkish authorities clearly committed to increasing the number of Syrian refugees enrolled in public schools.

By 2015, more than 100 public schools in the provinces of Adana, Ankara, Diyarbakir, Gaziantep, Hatay, and Kayseri were designated second shift schools for Syrians. And in early 2016 almost 80,000 Syrian children were studying in Turkish public schools. In 2017, the number of Syrian students in public schools was 170,000 compared to 300,000 students in TECs (McCarthy, 2018). Moreover, Turkey's current policy is to eliminate the need for TECs by the 2020–2021 school year (UNESCO, 2018a, p. 62). This transition has been supported by significant funding from the European Union, including €300 million for Promoting Integration of Syrian Children into the Turkish Education System, part of the EU's €3 billion in aid to Turkey for refugees (UNESCO, 2018a, p. 62).

Lebanon

The policy time line in Lebanon follows a similar trajectory from an official policy of exclusion to one of government-led response and inclusion into the public system based on discourses of human and child rights. Syrian refugees began fleeing to Lebanon in 2011 and at the time, the two countries shared an open border. Throughout 2012, the Lebanese government and its Ministry of Education and Higher Education (MEHE) allowed international and local NGOs to step in to provide informal educational programing.

However, in 2013, there was an abrupt policy shift when the Lebanese government decided to take the lead in the educational response. In May 2014, the Lebanese Ministry of Education and Higher Education, together with the World Bank and the Center for Educational Research and Development (CERD), launched Reaching All Children with Education (RACE), an official policy framework to the Syrian refugee crisis focusing on three pillars: access, quality, and systems strengthening (MEHE, 2014). RACE's objectives focused on reaching vulnerable school-aged children (3–18 years) affected by the Syrian crisis to ensure they have access to quality formal and non-formal learning opportunities in safe and protective environments. The three major objectives were: (1) promote equitable access to education services; (2) enhance the quality of student learning; and, (3) strength the education systems in Lebanon's education sector. The policy included opening second shift schools and targeting roughly 400,000 out-of-school children (MEHE, 2014).

Buckner et al. (2018) argue that this policy shift occurred due to transnational actors exerting leverage through both normative pressures and financial incentives. Although Lebanon is not a signatory to the 1951 Convention on Refugees or its 1967 Protocol, it ratified the CRC in 1991, and the Lebanese Constitution states that Lebanese law must be consistent with its international obligations. Buckner et al. (2018) report that in interviews, ministry officials explained how Lebanon's commitments under the UDHR, along with its compulsory education laws, compelled education for refugee children. In their interviews, NGO respondents also mentioned that they use either the CRC or UDHR in their advocacy efforts for refugee children's rights, including education and valid residency documents upon birth.

In addition to this normative pressure, international actors provided direct financial support to encourage Lebanon to open public schools to Syrian refugees. RACE is supported by both international donors such as UNICEF, UNHCR, and bilateral donors. Lebanon has received significant donor assistance to cover the costs of educating Syrians and provide non-formal education in public schools (MEHE, 2014). In 2014–2015, donors also began covering the annual parents' fee for Lebanese children. Building on the success of the first plan, Lebanon recently initiated the second phase of the policy, known as RACE II.

Jordan

Educational policy for Syrian refugees in Jordan was more accommodating initially than either Lebanon or Turkey, and aligned to a 1998 Memorandum of Understanding between the government of Jordan and UNHCR that detailed rights for non-Palestinian refugees in Jordan. Jordan's history with educating Iraqi refugees likely also set a precedent for welcoming Syrians into public schools.

Starting as early as 2012, Syrian refugees were permitted into public schools in Jordan through a UNICEF-led program called Emergency Education Relief (EER); however, as in the other countries, initial approaches were short-term and piecemeal. A key shift happened around 2014, when Jordan changed its approach from one of emergency humanitarian relief to adopting a longer-term government-led, development-oriented approach that also prioritized expanding Syrians' access to public schools. This approach was institutionalized as a resilience-focused and multi-year approach through the Jordanian Response Plans for the Syria Crisis (JRPs). There are currently 340 double shift schools in Jordan (Double Shift, 2019). The current JRP outlines a multi-year approach spanning 2018–2020 (Ministry of Planning and International Cooperation (MPIC), 2018).

From the WST perspective, the policy shifts in Turkey and Lebanon are striking; at the national level, it seems that normative commitments to global conventions played some role in facilitating more inclusive educational policies for refugees in all three countries. At the same time, it is also worth pointing out the striking difference between Turkey and Lebanon, and Jordan's initially more inclusive policy. National politics certainly play a role; however, it is also important to recognize that when Syrian refugees began to arrive in Jordan, the Jordanian government already had in place explicit policies for emergency education, and normative commitments to refugees' right to education were already codified in Jordanian policy. This suggests that inclusive policy models may outlast particular conflicts once they become institutionalized.

As national governments in Turkey, Jordan, and Lebanon began to incorporate Syrian refugees into their public school systems, regional initiatives developed to coordinate, support, and strengthen these national efforts through the creation of official region-wide advocacy and coordinating initiatives. In fact, one of the most striking differences between the response to Iraqi displacement and Syrian displacement less than a decade later is the extent to which regional coordination is evident. This is the topic to which we now turn.

The Structuration of a Region-Wide Educational Response

At the regional level, refugee crises caused by the massive displacement of Syrians has led to a diverse coalition of actors coming together in new ways, and the emergence of a new model of regional coordination. In this section, we profile the development of two regional initiatives: No Lost Generation, and the series of Regional Refugee and Resilience Frameworks (3RPs).

No Lost Generation (2013)

The No Lost Generation (NLG) initiative is a regional coordination mechanism that focuses on children and youth affected by both the Syrian and Iraq conflicts. NLG serves as a vehicle for advocacy and funding. It intentionally focuses on aspects of humanitarian assistance that are often overlooked or underfunded when other priorities such as shelter, food, and health seem more immediate: education, child protection, and adolescents and youth.

Launched in 2013, at the World Bank and International Monetary Fund annual meeting, NLG is embedded within other international humanitarian response plans. It comprises over 30 members, including UNICEF,

Mercy Corps, Save the Children, World Vision, and governments. NLG works to provide a regional framework for the humanitarian responses in Syria and Iraq, and serves as a platform for advocacy through involvement in key international conferences. Initially focused on the Syrian conflict, in 2016, NLG was expanded to include Iraq as well. It also extended NLG's work from two pillars: Education and Protection, to include Opportunities for Youth and Adolescents (NLG, 2018).

NLG does not implement specific programs, fund organizations, or directly impact policy. However, as part of its advocacy, it set ambitious targets to enroll 2.1 million Syrians out of school in Syria, and the roughly 700,000 out-of-school children in neighboring countries (500,000 in Turkey, 135,000 in Lebanon, 35,000 in Jordan, 25,000 in Iraq, and 5,000 in Egypt) (NLG, 2018). To meet these ambitious goals, it set the following goals in education: increasing school enrollment, keeping children learning; improving quality of education; expanding vocational and remedial secondary education and alternative ways of delivering education; and strengthening education systems to better support learning for refugees and vulnerable host communities.

It also seeks to link efforts in sectors that are difficult to address independently such as child labor and child marriage. By 2017 NLG had launched newsletters and a Tech Task force and had coordinated the first NLG EdTech Summit, an innovative forum to discuss technology and education which involved young people impacted by the conflict in Syria and Iraq. Because NLG is an advocacy and coordination initiative, its goals and activities are closely aligned to other regional efforts, such as the Regional Refugee and Resilience Plan (3RP), to which we now turn.

The Regional Refugee and Resilience Framework (2015)

In 2015, the UN system and over 270 NGOs came together to create the Regional Refugee and Resilience Framework, or 3RP, to coordinate the humanitarian response across the multiple national borders of Iraq, Syria, Lebanon, and Jordan. Under the 3RP Framework, humanitarian responses to the influx of Syrian refugees are nationally led processes, with each government in the region in charge of a national plan. This is described as "a nationally owned, but regionally coherent plan" (UNHCR, 2018c, p. 8) with the goal of integrating humanitarian assistance, resilience, and development approaches. The 2018–2019 3RP highlights "the importance of national ownership in securing a more effective and sustainable response" (UNHCR, 2018c, p. 8).

The 3RP model includes a number of innovations, including an explicit intention to ensure responses benefit both refugees and vulnerable host communities, in light of the multiple and overlapping vulnerabilities each community faces. In addition, the 3RPs focus on integrating humanitarian and development sectors through harmonized funding. The 3RP sets longer-term goals for education and encourages donors to provide multi-year funding (UNHCR, 2018c, p. 5). The integrated regional approach has also been successful in incorporating ever more partners into its framework: the number of partners working through the 3RP approach has risen from 100 in 2012 to 270 in 2018.

The 2018–2019 3RP Regional Strategy Overview emphasizes the importance of focusing in the humanitarian response on "longer term socio-economic impacts of the Syria crisis on neighboring countries," which foregrounds sectors of social policy, including education, as integral to humanitarian work (UNHCR, 2018c, p. 5). The plan operates under the leadership of the national authorities of refugee-hosting countries, thereby reassuring the ownership of national authorities in their role in the delivery of education to refugees, while still granting supranational actors—namely, the United Nations, the lead role in regional coordination and advocacy for both funding and policy change. The 2018–2019 3RP Regional Strategy Overview celebrates the policy shifts that now permit the inclusion of refugees in public schools throughout the region and also highlights a number of other regional priorities as reaching youth, supporting school-to-work strategies, and supporting quality and improving data collection mechanisms.

Other important regional initiatives are being undertaken to facilitate regional coordination. In 2018, UNESCO's regional Beirut office published "Pathways to Empowerment: Recognizing the Competences of Syrian Refugees in Egypt, Iraq, Jordan, Lebanon and Turkey" to encourage national governments to recognize and validate refugees' credentials earned in other countries in the region.

From the perspective of WST, it is striking to note that major reports published by UNHCR and UNICEF stress the extent to which national policies are aligned to global and regional initiatives. For example, a 2018 UNICEF report on the status of Syrians reports that all activities of Jordan's National Response Plan are being implemented "in line with the 'No Lost Generation' initiative" (UNICEF, 2018b, p. 30). Similarly, the 2018–2019 Regional Strategy Overview emphasizes that the educational sector strategy is aligned to the objectives of NLG and also "in line with Sustainable Development Goal Four (SDG4)" (UNHCR, 2018c, p. 34). These documents point to the importance of regional and global discourses in shaping current policies. We now turn to discuss global shifts that have also played a role, including the professionalization of the field and strategic shifts in approaches to funding.

Global: The Professionalization of Education in Emergencies

At the global level, the field of Education in Emergencies (EiE) has grown rapidly in the past two decades (Kagawa, 2005; Lerch, 2017). Once education had been accepted as a universal right for all, regardless of how fragile their nation-state or their citizenship status, then conflict became characterized as a threat to education (Lerch & Buckner, 2018). At the same time, the global commitment to protecting refugee children's rights has been institutionalized and supported by global organizations, initiatives, and resources (Burde et al., 2017). In this section we profile two of these initiatives: the Inter-Agency Network for Education in Emergencies (INEE) and the Supporting Syria and the Region Conference in 2016.

International Network for Education in Emergencies (2000)

The INEE was founded in 2000 at the Dakar Summit to improve communication and coordination in the field of Education in Emergencies. The network has been active, and successful, in elevating education in emergencies to the global humanitarian agenda (Anderson & Hodgkin, 2010). Since its inception in 2000, INEE has spearheaded efforts to advocate for Education in Emergencies, by creating new culture and norms surrounding the field (Bromley & Andina 2010). The network has grown to be the most influential actor in harnessing support for EiE in the area of humanitarian support, by operating as the sole organizational structure through which new ideas regarding emergency in education is mobilized globally (Mendizabal & Hearn, 2011). INEE is a network of more than 14,000 individual members and 130 partner organizations in 190 countries. INEE members are practitioners working for national and international NGOs and UN agencies, ministry of education and other government personnel, donors, students, teachers, and researchers who voluntarily join in the work related to education in emergencies. INEE identifies its core functions as: community building, convening, knowledge management, amplifying and advocating, facilitating and learning, and providing. A key goal of the network is to support the standardization and professionalization of the field. Its most celebrated tool is a document known as the "Minimum Standards for Education: Preparedness, Response, Recovery," or "Minimum Standards" for short. The document was produced through consultation and originally developed in 2004 and subsequently updated in 2010, and designed to address standards of practice in emergency preparedness, response, and recovery and in humanitarian advocacy.

INEE does not pool or provide resources for education; rather, it focuses on providing an intellectual resource, what it calls "global public goods" as its offering to the international community through a global platform. While the INEE network does not focus solely on refugees affected by the Syrian conflict, the sheer numbers and need of Syrian refugees acted as a catalyst for the development of INEE, and the numbers of members in INEE has consistently grown, and governments and civil society organizations working in the region cite the "Minimum Standards" as influencing their work (Buckner et al., 2018; Mendenhall, Russell, &

Buckner, 2017). The continuous growth of INEE sheds light on how the professionalization of the field has shaped the educational response to the Syrian conflict by shaping professional practice. In addition to professionalization, the sheer size of the Syrian conflict has also generated unprecedented global attention, the point to which we now turn.

Supporting Syria and the Region Pledging Conference (2016)

While INEE has supported the professionalization of the field of EiE, the global community has also heavily advocated for increasing donor aid to Syria. The Supporting Syria and the Region Conference, held in London in 2016 with a follow-up pledging conference in Brussels in April 2017, focused on pooling financial resources to support a global humanitarian response to the Syrian conflict.

Various previous efforts had attempted to address the growing financial need of the Syrian refugee crisis. Between 2013 and 2015, successive donor pledging conferences were hosted by Kuwait; however, these annual pledging conferences never fully funded education, and adopted the approach of short-term funding typical of humanitarian sector. By 2016, shifting ideas at the global level strongly argued for better supporting host country governments in long-term planning and funding and the need to address joint needs of education and livelihoods. These same ideas were later endorsed at the World Humanitarian Summit and in the signing of the Refugee Compact in 2016.

In line with these changing ideas, the global community came together in February 2016 to Support Syria, as the 2016 Donor Pledging Conference in London was known (The National Archives, 2018). The Supporting Syria and the Region Conference brought together the major refugee-hosting countries, donors, UN agencies, and civil society organizations to discuss education sector planning, programming, and reporting. The four primary objectives were: raising finances for those affected by the crisis; protection of civilians; supporting political transition in conflict-affected countries, and providing opportunities through economic support and education.

One of the most striking differences between the global response to Syria and past conflicts, including Iraq, is the fact that the most recent donor funding for the Syrian refugee crisis is significantly higher than in past conflicts. In terms of funding, the conference successfully raised US $12 billion in pledges—$6 billion for 2016 and a further $6.1 billion for 2017–2020 (The National Archives, 2018).

There was also an explicit commitment by donors to fund education, based on the idea of education as a human right (Butlar, 2015; Cahill, 2010). The primary outcome of the Supporting Syria and the Region Conference was the consolidation of the education response around three key pillars: access, quality and system strengthening, and the conceptualization of education along a humanitarian-to-development continuum, which supported multi-year and sector-wide planning and funding.

These pledges represent a significant increase in donor assistance to Syria, and point to a recognition of global responsibility for the education of refugees. Nonetheless, we know that such ambitious pledging goals are rarely met. Although UNHCR data shows increasing overall funding dedicated to the Syrian conflict, from $2.98 billion in 2013 to $3.40 billion in 2017, funding appeals have never been fully met. And by the third quarter of 2018, only 52% of the pledges had been received (UNHCR, 2018b). Indeed, the gap between rhetoric and reality is common in education, and seems particularly common when the global community has played a large role in setting policy agendas and has set ambitious educational targets based on rights frameworks. We now turn to discuss this decoupling.

Predictable Unintended Consequences: Aspirational Goals in Politicized Realities

Despite the impressive targets, networks, and funding, the ambitious goals for provision and quality education for refugee education are quite removed from the reality of what is going on, on the ground, where many children remain out of school and where school is not always a safe or engaging place for refugee children. In world society literature, the discrepancy between rhetoric and reality is known as decoupling (Pope & Meyer, 2016). In the case of refugee education, decoupling is widespread: national governments have committed to providing access to public schools, but for issues of both capacity and politics, roughly one in two Syrian refugees remains out of school across the region (UNHCR, 2018c). This decoupling has led to a predictable series of reports that point to donors not actually meeting commitments to funding and national governments not actually meeting commitments to enrolling children (Culbertson & Constant, 2015; Khawaja, 2016).

First, education remains an extremely underfunded sector of humanitarian responses. There is more money than ever before going to EiE in Syria, and yet, still, education remains extremely underfunded, according to Humanitarian Appeals and other monitoring, coordinating, and advocacy documents. For example, of the $873 million called for to meet education goals, only $347 million (40%) had been received by the third quarter of 2018 (UNHCR, 2018b).

Additionally, because regional funding, advocacy, and coordination initiatives have emanated and diffused among global actors based within the international humanitarian and development sectors, they are often more ambitious than what seems realistic at the level of the school and classroom. Indeed, despite significant progress, roughly one in two

Syrian refugees remains out of school. According to the 2018–2019 3RP, Regional Strategic Overview, which is the guiding document for regional coordination, 57% of Syrians aged 5–17 are in school in the five neighboring host countries, while 43% remain out of school (UNHCR, 2018c, p. 34)

The literature points to the ways in which stated policies guaranteeing refugees' access to quality education are far removed from the reality of limited-access, low-quality schooling that may actually harm rather than protect refugees (Aydin & Kaya, 2017; Mendenhall et al., 2017; Buckner et al., 2018). Syrian refugees still face many barriers in accessing quality education (Khawaja, 2016; UNICEF, 2018b). For refugees who are struggling to provide basic needs for their families, it can prove difficult to prioritize education for their children, especially if school and other fees are expected for enrollment and retention. Children may also need to work to support their families. Depending on where they live, and where they can enroll in school, refugees often travel long distances to school, and a lack of safe transportation can be an impediment (UNICEF, 2018a). In some cases, schoolbuses are available for refugee children, but families must pay a certain amount each month; even small fees may pose a barrier for refugee families. Long distances to school also raise concerns over safety and security, as many families are hesitant to allow their children to travel unaccompanied to school due to fear of physical, sexual, and gender-based violence.

In addition, other barriers limit refugees' access to public schools. These include a lack of legal status and documentation needed to officially enroll in schools, such as birth certificates or diplomas needed to access a level. McCarthy (2018) and Buckner et al. (2018) both report that despite official policies permitting access to schooling in Turkey and Lebanon, respectively, school administrators are often unwilling to admit Syrian students into their schools due to pressure from some in their communities.

Even when they can enroll in schools, a variety of factors may impede retention and learning. In both Turkey and Lebanon, the official language of instruction in public schools is not Arabic. In Lebanon, the language of instruction is officially either English or French, with Arabic taught as a subject. In Turkey, early policy decisions by government actors focused on providing refugees in camps access to schooling in Arabic, with no intention of teaching refugees the Turkish language; McCarthy (2018) argues that this decision was made in part to prevent permanent integration into Turkish society. As a result, the language of instruction can be a barrier. Overcrowding in refugee schools can become an impediment to quality, and teachers cannot possibly attend to the needs of all of their students. Many refugee students also encounter forms of discrimination and xenophobia, which can take the form of stereotyping and bullying from teachers, peers, and the community. Additionally, many refugee children will have experienced trauma, and may need additional assistance. National teachers in public schools may not be equipped to support their refugee learners as they struggle to adapt to a new curriculum, language of instruction, and classroom expectations.

At a more basic level, conflict is fundamentally political, which means that despite the rights-based orientation and the rapid professionalization of the field of EiE, schooling for refugees is still provided in fundamentally localized and politicized settings. This results in significant decoupling between the aspirational discourses spreading at the global, regional, and national levels from the local and politicized environments of educational programming in conflict-affected regions. Humanitarian programming, and the inclusion of education into humanitarian responses, is founded on an apolitical mandate of providing life-saving programs to people in need, regardless of who or where. And yet, the Syrian conflict—like all conflicts—is ongoing due to unresolved disputes, interests, and ideologies that have positioned the Assad regime, armed opposition, and other nation-states in opposition. On the ground, contested ideologies affect possibilities for schooling. In both Turkey and Lebanon, informal schools are operating outside state control, and there are political battles over the curriculum in Kurdish-controlled northeast Syria. Moreover, the reality is that the significant aid provided by donors is never fully explained by normative commitments. European donors are concerned with stemming the flow of refugees into Europe, where many governments are increasingly espousing xenophobic policies. These political and geopolitical realities are well known among professionals working in EiE and affect their ability to provide education to refugees.

Conclusion

The dramatic differences between the global responses to three successive refugee policies in the region Palestine, Iraq, and Syria point to the power that the institutionalization of education as a human right has had in how the global development community has responded to the Syrian conflict. By profiling initiatives and policy shifts at the national, regional, and global levels, this study examines both "why" and "how" the global community has institutionalized education as a key domain of the global response to the Syrian conflict. Drawing on the world society tradition in comparative education, we argue that the institutionalization of education as a human right, the intensification of supra-national policy actors, and the professionalization of the field of Education in Emergencies have all resulted in fundamental shifts at the national, regional, and global level.

On one hand, there is reason to think that the response to the Syrian conflict, like the Iraqi crisis before it, has attracted disproportionate attention, as many other ongoing refugee crises, including those in

Afghanistan (2.6 million), South Sudan (2.4 million), and Myanmar (1.2 million) are not as well funded or covered (World Vision, 2018). Nonetheless, Syria also points to the development of a new model of refugee response: a firmly rights-based approach that integrates humanitarian and development frameworks for collective and long-term educational outcomes, and the creation of regional coordination platforms and funding mechanisms. This new model sets a precedent to be taken up in other contexts. It seems as though this model is being modified in other contexts as well: the 2018 "Global Education Monitoring Report" examines the case of Bangladesh, where education was incorporated into the earliest response to displaced Rohingya refugees from Myanmar (UNESCO, 2018a). This is one of the world's newest refugee crises, having begun after the Syrian refugee crisis (2017–2018), and although refugees are not currently allowed in Bangladesh public schools, ongoing advocacy is actively seeking to change this, drawing on strong normative claims. While we do not know what the future holds, the policy shifts in Turkey and Lebanon suggest positive policy change is possible, particularly as global actors and donors increasingly advocate, support, and fund national governments in inclusive educational policies.

Note

1. Turkey signed the 1951 convention on refugees but reserves applicability only to those fleeing Europe.

References

Anderson, A., & Hodgkin, M. (2010). *The creation and development of the global IASC Education Cluster*. Paper commissioned for the EFA Global Monitoring Report 2011, The hidden crisis: Armed conflict and education. Retrieved from https://toolkit.ineesite.org/resources/ineecms/uploads/1116/CreationEd_Cluster.pdf

Aydin, H., & Kaya, Y. (2017). The educational needs of and barriers faced by Syrian refugee students in Turkey: A qualitative case study. *Intercultural Education*, 28(5), 456–473.

Bocco, R. (2009). UNRWA and the Palestinian refugees: A history within history. *Refugee Survey Quarterly*, 28(2–3), 229–252.

British Broadcasting Company (BBC). (2018). *Syria profile: Timeline*. Retrieved April 24, 2018 from www.bbc.com/news/world-middle-east-14703995

Bromley, P. (2010). The rationalization of educational development: Scientific activity among international nongovernmental organizations. *Comparative Education Review*, 54(4), 577–601.

Bromley, P., & Andina, M. (2010). Standardizing chaos: A neo-institutional analysis of the INEE Minimum Standards for Education in Emergencies, chronic crises and early reconstruction. *Compare*, 40(5), 575–588.

Buckner, E., Spencer, D., & Cha, J. (2018). Between policy and practice: The education of Syrian refugees in Lebanon. *Journal of Refugee Studies*, 31(4), 444–465.

Burde, D., Kapit, A., Wahl, R. L., Guven, O., & Skarpeteig, M. I. (2017). Education in emergencies: A review of theory and research. *Review of Educational Research*, 87(3), 619–658.
Butlar, M. (2015). Education emergencies: A plan for success. *Journal for Nurses in Professional Development*, 31(5), 292.
Cahill, K. M. (2010). *Even in chaos: Education in times of emergency* (1st ed.). New York, NY: Fordham University Press.
Chabbott, C. (2003). *Constructing education for development: International organizations and education for all*. New York, NY: Routledge Falmer.
Culbertson, S., & Constant, L. (2015). *Education of Syrian refugee children: Managing the crisis in Turkey, Lebanon, and Jordan*. Washington, DC: RAND Corporation.
Dorman, S. (2014). Educational needs assessment for urban Syrian refugees in Turkey. *YUVA Association Report*, 5.
Double Shift. (2019). Retrieved from: "Double Shift" https://www.double-shift.org/double-shift/double-shift
Fiddian-Qasmiyeh, E., Loescher, G., Long, K., & Sigona, N. (2014). *The Oxford handbook of refugee and forced migration studies*. Oxford, UK: Oxford University Press.
Ministry of Planning and International Cooperation (MPIC). (2018). Jordan Response Plan for the Syrian Crisis 2018–2020. Amman, Jordan.
Kagawa, F. (2005). Emergency education: A critical review of the field. *Comparative Education*, 41(4), 487–503.
Khawaja, B. (2016). *Growing up without an education: Barriers to education for Syrian refugee children in Lebanon*. New York: Human Rights Watch.
Knudsen, A. (2009). Widening the protection gap: The "politics of citizenship" for Palestinian refugees in Lebanon, 1948–2008. *Journal of Refugee Studies*, 22(1), 51–73.
Krafft, C., Sieverding, M., Salemi, C., & Keo, C. (2018, April). *Syrian refugees in Jordan: Demographics, livelihoods, education, and health*. In Economic Research Forum Working Paper Series (No. 1184).
Lenner, K. (2016). *The politics of pledging: Reflections on the London donors conference for Syria*. Policy Brief 2016/03. Florence, Italy: European University Institute.
Lerch, J. C. (2017). *Beyond survival the rise of education in emergencies as global field and profession*. (Dissertation). Stanford University, Stanford, CA.
Lerch, J. C., & Buckner, E. (2018). From education for peace to education in conflict: Changes in UNESCO discourse, 1945–2015. *Globalisation, Societies and Education*, 16(1), 27–48.
McCarthy, A. (2018). Politics of refugee education: Educational administration of the Syrian refugee crisis in turkey. *Journal of Educational Administration and History*, 50(3), 223–238.
Mendenhall, M., Russell, G., & Buckner, E. (2017). *Urban refugee education: Strengthening policies and practices for access, quality and inclusion*. New York, NY: Teachers College, Columbia University. Retrieved from www.tc.columbia.edu/refugeeeducation/urban-refugee-education/project-deliverables
Mendizabal, E., & Hearn, S. (2011). *Inter-agency network for education in emergencies: A community of practice, a catalyst for change*. Paris, France: UNESCO IIEP.
Meyer, J. W., Boli, J., Thomas, G. M., & Ramirez, F. O. (1997). World society and the nation-state. *American Journal of Sociology*, 103(1), 144–181.

Ministry of Education and Higher Education (MEHE). (2014). *Reaching all children with education*. Retrieved from www.mehe.gov.lb/uploads/file/2015/Feb2015/Projects/RACEfinalEnglish2.pdf

Mundy, K. (2006). Education for all and the new development compact. In *Education and social justice* (pp. 13–38). Dordrecht, Netherlands: Springer.

Mundy, K., & Murphy, L. (2001). Transnational advocacy, global civil society: Emerging evidence from the field of education. *Comparative Education Review*, 45(1), 85–126.

The National Archives. (2018). Supporting Syria and the region 2016. *Archived Website*. Retrieved from https://webarchive.nationalarchives.gov.uk/20180313172041/www.supportingsyria2016.com/

No Lost Generation. (2018). *Our vision*. Retrieved from https://nolostgeneration.org/

Pope, S., & Meyer, J. W. (2016). Local variation in world society: Six characteristics of global diffusion. *European Journal of Cultural and Political Sociology*, 3(2–3), 280–305.

Ramirez, F. O., Meyer, J. W., & Lerch, J. (2016). World society and the globalization of educational policy. In K. Mundy, A. Green, R. Lingard, & A. Verger (Eds.), *The handbook of global education policy*. Malden, MA: Wiley-Blackwell.

Seeley, N. (2010). The politics of aid to Iraqi refugees in Jordan. *Middle East Report*, 256, 37–42.

UNESCO. (2018a). *Migration, displacement and education: Building bridges, not walls*. Global Education Monitoring Report. Paris, France: UNESCO.

UNHCR. (2018a). *UNHCR operational data portal*. Retrieved December 9, 2018 from https://data2.unhcr.org/en/situations/syria

UNHCR. (2018b). Financial summary: Q3 2018. *Regional Refugee and Resilience Plan*. Retrieved from https://data2.unhcr.org/en/documents/download/67233

UNHCR. (2018c). Regional refugee & resilience plan (3RP) 2018–2019. *Regional Strategic Overview*. Retrieved from https://data2.unhcr.org/en/documents/download/62229

UNHCR. (2018d). External Statistical Report on UNHCR Registered Syrians as of 15 December 2018. Retrieved from: https://data2.unhcr.org/en/documents/details/67333

UNICEF. (2018a). *Syria crisis October 2018 humanitarian situation report*. Retrieved from www.unicef.org/appeals/files/UNICEF_Syria_Crisis_Humanitarian_Situation_Report_____October_2018.pdf

UNICEF. (2018b). *Assessment of Syrian refugee children in host communities in Jordan*. New York, NY: UNICEF. Retrieved from www.unicef.org/jordan/Assessment_Syrians_in_Jordan_host_communities2018_online.pdf

World Vision. (2018). *Forced to flee: Top countries refugees are coming from*. Retrieved from www.worldvision.org/refugees-news-stories/forced-to-flee-top-countries-refugees-coming-from

3 Teacher Preparation, Classroom Pedagogy, and the Refugee Crisis in National Education Systems

Alexander W. Wiseman and Ericka Galegher

The United Nations High Commissioner for Refugees (UNHCR) reported that 65.3 million people worldwide were forcibly displaced by the end of 2015 (UNHCR, 2016a). At the time of reporting, this was a record for the highest number of refugees and asylum-seekers since the UNHCR began tracking forcible displacement. In 2015, more than half of the refugees and asylum-seekers worldwide were under the age of 18 years old, many of whom were unaccompanied minors (UNHCR, 2016a). The UNHCR also reports that refugee and asylum-seeking youth are out of school at a rate five times the average. In other words, primary education is available to only 50% of refugee and asylum-seeking children, only 22% of them attend secondary school, and only 1% attend university (UNHCR, 2016b). Yet, formal education has historically been a strategic tool in the development of refugee and asylum-seeking youth worldwide (Buckland, 2005).

Evidence suggests that refugee and asylum-seeking youth are innovative and adaptable to different forms of education, and that these traits persist into the labor market (Shakya et al., 2010). In spite of these positive reports, refugee and asylum-seeking youth bring significant social, emotional, and educational challenges to schools in receiving countries. Educational systems need significant resources to address and resolve the unique needs of refugee and asylum-seeking youth. For example, refugee and asylum-seeking youth are often trauma victims, both physically and psychologically (Haffejee, 2015). Evidence shows they need dedicated school-based support as they adjust to unfamiliar contexts, communities, and cultures (McBrien, 2005; Segal & Mayadas, 2005).

Traditional classroom teachers are often unprepared to meet the needs of refugee and asylum-seeking youth who settle in their communities and attend mainstream schools. While teacher training programs for classrooms and schools in conflict and immediate post-conflict zones (e.g., refugee camps) both exist and are deployed by national governments and international organizations worldwide (Shepler & Routh, 2012), pre-service teacher training and in-service professional development in stable, developed nations are rare. In fact, the majority of schools and classrooms in countries receiving refugee and asylum-seeking youth are filled with teachers who are native to the receiving country and have little or no training in teaching or addressing the unique needs of refugee and asylum-seeking youth (MacNevin, 2012; Naidoo, 2013). For example, teachers in mainstream schools in Germany who have Syrian refugees in their classrooms are more likely to be native Germans and less likely to have training related to language, identity, or trauma needs of refugee and asylum-seeking youth.

Given the relevance and importance of formal education to the transition and resettlement of refugee and asylum-seeking youth (Abu El-Haj, 2010; Alba, Sloan, & Sperling, 2011; Hek, 2005), there is a remarkably thin research base on teacher preparation and pedagogy with refugee and asylum-seeking students in stable, developed countries (Pinson & Arnot, 2007). This research investigates teacher preparation to work with refugee and asylum-seeking youth using international education data on teachers, on refugee and asylum-seeking youth, and on the characteristics of formal education, teaching, and learning in destination countries that are member states in the Organization for Economic Cooperation and Development (OECD). The question this research asks is: How does teacher training and professional development in OECD countries' national education systems prepare them to meet both the academic and non-academic needs of refugee and asylum-seeking youth?

Refugee Education and Teacher Preparation

There is little empirical research examining the preparation of mainstream classroom teachers or their role in educating refugees in formal education systems worldwide. The exception is research on teacher training programs specifically for refugee teachers and on training programs for teachers working in conflict zones or refugee resettlement camps. There is also much research on immigrant education, teaching, and learning both within and across national education systems worldwide. There is, however, a growing body of research on the status of refugee and asylum-seeking youth in OECD countries.

Status of Refugees and Asylum-Seekers

There is a subtle-yet-important difference between refugee and asylum-seeking youth. According to the United Nations High Commissioner on Refugees (UNHCR, n.d.),

> A refugee is someone who has been forced to flee his or her country because of persecution, war, or violence. A refugee has a well-founded fear of persecution for reasons of race, religion, nationality,

political opinion or membership in a particular social group. Most likely, they cannot return home or are afraid to do so. War and ethnic, tribal and religious violence are leading causes of refugees fleeing their countries.

The UNHCR (2016a, p. 37) also designates an asylum-seeker as "an individual seeking international protection and whose refugee status is yet to be determined." Germany received more asylum-seekers than any other country in 2015, and most of those were from Syria (UNHCR, 2016a, p. 28). Elsewhere, the United States and Sweden were the second and third largest hosts of asylum-seekers in 2015, with 172,700 and 156,400 new applications respectively (UNHCR, 2016a, p. 38).

The data suggest that although there is much variation in the political and economic contexts of receiving countries, proximity to refugees' home countries plays a major role in determining the number of refugees or asylum-seekers in the destination or host country. Yet, OECD countries in Western Europe, like Germany, were some of the largest receiving countries for refugees and asylum-seekers since 2010.

Immigrant and Refugee Education

Education-related research on refugee and asylum-seeking youth exists, but is largely confounded with research on immigrant youth and focused on (1) academic achievement, (2) the impact of language on student learning and performance, and (3) the gap between student and teacher identities related to educational expectations. While immigrant youth share many characteristics and concerns with refugee and asylum-seeking youth, the conditions under which they immigrate and their experiences (family, community, and school) differ significantly from those experienced by refugee and asylum-seeking youth. Most of the literature reviewed here specifically focuses on immigrant youth, and does not distinguish refugee and asylum-seeking youth, although efforts were made to synthesize the research literature that most closely approximated the conditions of refugees in post-conflict situations and, more specifically, in OECD member states.

Overall, large-scale international assessment results suggest that immigrant students underperform academically compared to native or nonimmigrant students (Meunier, 2011; OECD, 2015). Interestingly, immigrant students' average scores on Program for International Student Assessment (PISA) 2012 were more representative of average scores of students in their home countries than in their host countries (Rubinstein-Avila, 2016), and higher concentrations of immigrant students in schools tends to lead to lower academic performance among native students (Brunello & Rocco, 2013). Although immigrant students underperform on PISA compared to native students in some countries, the performance gap has closed or narrowed in some developed countries (Jakubowski, 2011). This may be because the educational achievement of immigrant youth is influenced by socioeconomic differences between immigrant and native communities as well as relative community size (Levels, Dronkers, & Kraaykamp, 2008). Other factors also play a significant role in immigrant student learning and performance, including access to quality schools, language barriers, and educational policies that disadvantage immigrant and underperforming students like tracking and grade repetition. Yet, in spite of these disadvantages for immigrant youth, their educational expectations and aspirations are significantly higher than their native school peers (Entorf & Minoiu, 2004; OECD, 2015).

High expectations and aspirations, however, cannot overcome language obstacles for immigrant and refugee youth. In fact, language proficiency is the key challenge for immigrant youth regarding both educational attainment and achievement (OECD, 2012). Some research has shown that the language of the receiving countries can make a difference in immigrant students' educational achievement. For example, Schnepf (2007) showed that immigrant students achieve higher in English-speaking countries than in others, but language skills are consistently associated with lower achievement among immigrant students (Entorf & Minoiu, 2004). Also, students who migrate at older ages and who do not speak the language of their host country achieve below natives and students who migrated at younger ages (Azzolini, Schnell, & Palmer, 2012; Cobb-Clark, Sinning, & Stillman, 2012). Research shows that one of the main obstacles to effective teaching of refugee and asylum-seeking students may be a lack of preparation of mainstream classroom teachers to teach new language learners (Lucas & Villegas, 2010). Other research suggests that teachers of refugee and asylum-seeking youth say they need professional development to help them learn how to teach basic reading and address the needs of students who experienced trauma (MacNevin, 2012).

Language differences between immigrant and refugee youth and native populations can also be indicative of identity crises among these youth. Immigrant youth, including refugees and asylum-seekers, often feel like they do not "belong" in their host countries, and may experience isolation or identity crises in their new homes (Abu El-Haj, 2007). These youth often do not have access to the same school experiences that native youth have, and are instead relegated "to the margins of school life" (Gibson & Carrasco, 2009, p. 249). These identity challenges are exacerbated by significantly different expectations of immigrant, refugee, and asylum-seeking youth and their new teachers. For example, the experiences of refugees in school in Western liberal democracies can be characterized as (1) more focused on the freedoms from oppression, want, and other disadvantages rather than the rights and responsibilities of free individuals, and (2) refugees have been "medicalized" as victims of trauma, which marginalizes them rather than celebrating their resiliency (Taylor &

Sidhu, 2012, p. 52). More specifically, evidence shows schools that balance the needs of refugee and asylum-seeking youth without "othering" them have the following characteristics: (1) commitment to social justice, (2) specific policy and support systems, (3) strong principal leadership coupled with a whole-school approach, and (4) inclusive education (Taylor & Sidhu, 2012; Arnot & Pinson, 2005; Dryden-Peterson, 2011).

The research literature suggests that although immigrant youth outperform their native peers in social welfare states (Shapira, 2012), there are many more situations and conditions that lead to underperformance among immigrant and refugee youth (Teltemann & Schunck, 2017). These include language disadvantages compared to native peers, biased political and educational systems in receiving countries, disadvantageous policies for refugees and asylum-seekers, identity issues and educational expectations, and the degree to which educational systems and teachers "other" immigrant, refugee, and asylum-seeking youth. Given these factors, the role of teachers working directly with refugee and asylum-seeking youth is significant. Yet, little research examines the preparation of mainstream teachers to work directly with refugees, particularly on the role of teachers in OECD countries who have recently experienced an influx of refugee and asylum-seeking students coming directly from conflict or post-conflict situations into their classrooms.

Training for Teachers of Refugees and Asylum-Seekers

While research increasingly recognizes that the ethical care of refugee students is a responsibility of mainstream classroom teachers (Hos, 2016), mainstream teachers are not being prepared to work with refugees or asylum-seekers in their classrooms. There is significant research on teacher preparation and pre-service programs related to diversity and multiculturalism, but this does not adequately address the needs of refugee youth and their teachers. For example, research shows that security concerns impact the education of refugee and asylum-seeking students, and can impact teachers' attitudes as well as students' identity development (Collet & Bang, 2016). This is the type of concern that is unique to refugee youth, and that is largely unaddressed by existing teacher preparation or professional development programs. Training in trauma-informed teaching is relatively rare among mainstream teachers, in spite of being a frequently discussed need (Phifer & Hull, 2016; Thomas, 2016). In addition, teachers' concepts of compassion related to refugee and asylum-seeking youth are often unsupported or challenged by national immigration policies (Arnot, Pinson, & Candappa, 2009).

Although research analyzing the educational impact and pedagogy of teachers of refugee and asylum-seeking students is rare, evidence does demonstrate that more direct and tailored instruction positively impacts refugee and asylum-seeking student learning, especially given that these students often have been in overcrowded classrooms, if they were in school at all, prior to arriving in the receiving country (Tobin, Boulmier, Zhu, Hancock, & Meunnig, 2015). And, there are isolated examples of teacher preparation programs that emphasize the unique needs of refugee and asylum-seeking youth in OECD countries. For example, a pre-service teacher preparation program in Australia uses a reciprocal learning approach where pre-service teachers develop refugee students' academic skills and socio-cultural understanding while the refugee students provide the pre-service teachers with an appreciation of the dynamics between teachers and diverse students (Ferfolja, 2009).

In summary, the research that does exist focuses primarily on the needs of immigrant students related to language learning and the impact of youth trauma on classroom experiences. For this reason, there is a stream of research examining the importance of teacher compassion and ethical pedagogy with refugees, but little research on the impact that teacher preparation programs have on mainstream teachers' capacity to teach refugee and asylum-seeking youth in their classrooms. And, there is less evidence related to the unique situation of teachers in OECD countries receiving refugee and asylum-seeking students from conflict situations into their classrooms, and the unique needs of these students compared to those in school in active conflict zones or refugee camps. Most importantly, there is no existing research examining the ways that mainstream pre-service teacher training and in-service professional development in OECD countries prepares teachers to meet both the academic and non-academic needs of refugee and asylum-seeking youth.

Data

The 2015 Programme for International Student Assessment (PISA) provides nationally representative data on 15-year-old students and teachers in 72 national education systems, which includes all 35 OECD countries and 37 partner countries' national education systems (OECD, 2016b). PISA is administered on a 3-year cycle, and data is made publicly available through the OECD. While PISA 2015 provided academic assessment data in science, reading, and mathematics, most of the data for the analysis reported here came from the student and teacher background questionnaires. Background questionnaires provided information about participants' demographics, approaches to learning, and learning environments (OECD, 2016a, p. 10). The teacher background questionnaires were optional, and not all participating countries administered them (OECD, 2016a). Approximately 540,000 students were sampled from a population of about 29 million 15-year-olds in the 72 participating national education systems.

PISA 2015 used a two-stage stratified sampling procedure (OECD, 2016a). The first stage randomly sampled individual schools within each participating national educational system that would likely have 15-year-old students enrolled. A minimum of 150 schools were selected in each national education system. Any school choosing not to participate in PISA 2015 was removed and replaced with replacement schools identified during the initial sampling. The second stage selected 42 students per school with equal probability from a list of each sampled schools' 15-year-old students. No fewer than 20 students per school could be included in the sample. More information on sampling is available in the "PISA 2015 Technical Report" (OECD, 2017). The student-level file used in this analysis includes only those students who are first generation immigrants in order to focus on the community within the student sample that is most likely to include refugee or asylum-seeking students. Approximately 6% of the total student sample were first generation immigrants across all participating countries. In the analyses reported here, 519,334 students and as many as 88,000 teachers are represented by the data for OECD countries only.

The following sections describe the dependent and independent variables included in the analyses below, as shown in Table 3.1, which includes descriptive statistics for all participating students and teachers across all participating OECD countries.

Table 3.1 Descriptive statistics for all students and teachers across all participating OECD countries (PISA 2015)

Variables	N	Min	Max	Mean	Std Dev
Student Outcomes					
Math Achievement Score (PV1MATH)	519334	0	870.51	463.08	103.25
Science Achievement Score (PV1SCIE)	519334	25.10	888.36	469.49	102.37
Reading Achievement Score (PV1READ)	519334	0	882.12	465.65	106.07
Motivation Index (MOTIVAT)	430962	–3.09	1.85	0.09	0.99
Belonging Index (BELONG)	487677	–3.15	2.66	–0.02	0.99
Student Background					
Female (SFEMALE)	519334	0	1	0.50	0.50
Same Language (SAMELANG)	498267	0	1	0.87	0.34
SES(SES)	505728	–9.48	5.99	–0.34	1.21
Teacher Background					
Female (TFEMALE)	88217	0	1	0.6	0.49
Years Teaching (YRSTCH)	86592	0	50	16.63	10.06
Education Level (EDUCATN)	88349	1	5	3.33	0.68
Formally qualified Teacher (TCHREDPR)	88299	0	1	0.91	0.28
Teacher Training					
Teaching in Multicultural and Multilingual Settings (MULTTRAIN)	58881	0	1	0.33	0.47

(*Continued*)

Table 3.1 (Continued)

Variables	N	Min	Max	Mean	Std Dev
Teaching Special Needs Students (SPECEDTRAIN)	58881	0	1	0.41	0.49
Approaches to Individualized Learning (INDVTRAIN)	58881	0	1	0.56	0.50
Cross-curricular Skills (CROSSTRN)	58881	0	1	0.55	0.50
Teacher Professional Development					
Teaching in Multicultural and Multilingual Settings (MULTIPD)	58881	0	1	0.23	0.42
Teaching Special Needs Students (SPECEDPD)	58881	0	1	0.35	0.48
Approaches to Individualized Learning (INDVPD)	58881	0	1	0.38	0.49
Cross-curricular Skills (CROSSPD)	58881	0	1	0.39	0.49
Teacher Professional Interactions and Behaviors					
Professional Development Network of Teachers (PDNETWRK)	78924	0	1	0.6	0.49
Formal Mentoring and Coaching (MENTORING)	77606	0	1	0.63	0.48
Reading Professional Literature (READLIT)	79177	0	1	0.73	0.45
Informal Dialog with Colleagues (INFDIALG)	84840	0	1	0.95	0.21

Student-Level Dependent Variables

At the student level, two types of outcomes are measured: academic and non-academic. The academic outcomes are student achievement scores in mathematics (*PV1MATH*), reading (*PV1READ*), and science (*PV1SCIE*).[1] The non-academic outcomes are students' sense of belonging (*BELONG*) and their motivation to learn (*MOTIVAT*). PV1MATH (N=519334, Mean=463.08, SD=103.25) is the first plausible value mathematics achievement score. PV1READ (N=519334, Mean=465.65, SD=106.07) is the first plausible value reading achievement score. PV1SCIE (N=519334, Mean=469.49, SD=102.37) is the first plausible value science achievement score. BELONG (N=487677, Mean=–0.02, SD=0.99) is an index of students' subjective well-being and sense of belonging at their school. MOTIVAT (N=430962, Mean=0.09, SD=0.99) is an index of students' attitudes, preferences, and self-related beliefs and motivations to achieve.

Student-Level Independent Variables

Student-level independent variables measure key background characteristics like student gender (*SFEMALE*), language (*SAMELANG*), and socioeconomic status (*SES*), as well as likely refugee or asylum-seeking status (*LES2GEN1*). *SFEMALE* (N=519334, Mean=0.50, SD=0.50) is a dichotomous, self-reported variable indicating whether a student is female (1) or male (0). *SAMELANG* (N=498267, Mean=0.87, SD=0.34) is a dichotomous variable indicating that the language spoken at home is the same as the language of testing (1=yes; 0=no). *SES* (N=505728, Mean=−0.34, SD=1.21) is an index of home possessions (Min=−3.09; Max=5.99).

The student-level indicator, which serves as a proxy measure for the likelihood of an individual student having refugee or asylum-seeking status (*LES2GEN1*), was established in two ways. First, students must report that they are first generation immigrants to be included in the pool of potential refugee or asylum-seeking students. Second, they must have been in the country of testing for two years or less at the time of testing in order to increase the likelihood that first generation immigrant students were part of the cohort of refugees historically documented to be immigrating to OECD countries from 2013 to 2015 (Hatton, 2017). We calculated the time each student was in the country by the difference between the age each student reported arriving in the country of testing and their current age at the time of testing. This indicates if a student has been in the country of testing for two years or less at the time the PISA 2015 background questionnaire was administered.

Teacher-Level Independent Variables

Teacher-level variables were categorized three ways to identify the key factors associated with teachers and their preparation or professional development that potentially affects refugee and asylum-seeking student outcomes. These are (1) background indicators, (2) pre-service and in-service training indicators, and (3) professional interactions and behaviors. The following variables were background indicators. *TFEMALE* (N=88217, Mean=0.60, SD=0.49) is a dichotomous indicator of whether the teacher is female (1=female; 0=male). *YRSTCH* (N=86592, Mean=16.63, SD=10.06) indicates the number of years teachers report working as teacher. *EDUCATN* (N=88349, Mean=3.33, SD=0.68) is the highest level of formal education a teacher reports attaining (Min=1; Max-5). *TCHREDPR* (N=88299, Mean=0.91, SD=0.28) is a dichotomous indicator of whether a teacher completed a teacher qualifications program.

Next, we examined the pre-service and in-service training indicators. "Pre-service" indicators provide data about the training that teachers received before becoming classroom teachers, usually during a formal university teacher preparation program or a teacher training institute. "In-service" professional development occurs while the teachers are working as teachers. The following dichotomous variables represent pre-service training and in-service professional development. *MULTTRAIN* (N=58881, Mean=0.33, SD=0.47) indicates whether a teacher received pre-service training in teaching in multicultural or multilingual settings. *MULTPD* (N=58881, Mean=0.23, SD=0.42) indicates whether a teacher received in-service professional development in teaching in multicultural or multilingual settings. *SPECEDTRAIN* (N=58881, Mean=0.41, SD=0.49) indicates whether a teacher received pre-service training in teaching special needs students. *SPECEDPD* (N=58881, Mean=0.35, SD=0.48) indicates whether a teacher received in-service professional development in teaching special needs students. *INDVTRAIN* (N=58881, Mean=0.56, SD=0.50) indicates whether a teacher received pre-service training in approaches to individualized learning. *INDVPD* (N=58881, Mean=0.38, SD=0.49) indicates whether a teacher received in-service professional development in approaches to individual learning. *CROSSTRN* (N=58881, Mean=0.55, SD=0.50) indicates whether a teacher received pre-service training in cross-curricular skills (e.g., problem solving & learning to learn). *CROSSPD* (N=58881, Mean=0.39, SD=0.49) indicates whether a teacher received in-service professional development in cross-curricular skills (e.g., problem-solving and learning to learn).

Finally, variables at the teacher level reflect professional interactions and behaviors that would likely influence refugee and asylum-seeking student learning, outcomes, and socialization. The following dichotomous variables measure these teacher interactions and behaviors. *PDNETWRK* (N=78924, Mean=0.60, SD=0.49) indicates whether a teacher participated in a network of teachers formed specifically for professional development. *MENTORNG* (N=77606, Mean=0.63, SD=0.48) indicates whether a teacher participated in mentoring or peer observation and coaching as part of a formal school arrangement. *READLIT* (N=79177, Mean=0.73, SD=0.45) indicates whether a teacher reads professional literature (e.g., journals, evidence-based papers, thesis papers). *INFDIALG* (N=84840, Mean=0.95, SD=0.21) indicates whether a teacher engages in informal dialog with colleagues on how to improve teaching.

Analyses and Results

The analyses examining the ways that mainstream teacher training and professional development in OECD countries prepares teachers to meet both the academic and non-academic needs of youth likely to be refugees and asylum-seekers were developed in three phases: descriptive, linear, and hierarchical.

Descriptive Analyses

Descriptive analyses address the distribution of refugee and asylum-seeking youth across OECD member states' educational systems, and describe the most common pre-service teacher training and in-service professional development in those systems.

Identifying which students are refugees or asylum-seekers versus those who are simply first generation immigrants is the first task. The PISA 2015 student background questionnaires do not ask students to identify themselves as refugees or asylum-seekers, but they do provide immigrant status (native, first generation, or second generation), age of arrival in country of testing (for immigrant youth), length of time in country since arrival (by proxy), and country of birth. Using these indicators, it is possible to narrow the student file to those students who meet these criteria and self-identify in ways that are consistent with refugee or asylum-seeking status. Refugee and asylum-seeking students, for example, are first generation immigrants, who in 2015 would be in the country of testing for two years or less, and be originally from a country that is or recently was in conflict or unstable. Table 3.2 shows the number and percentage of students in each of the 35 OECD countries that meet each and all of these criteria.

As Table 3.2 shows, the percentage of first generation immigrants arriving in the country of testing two years ago or less is on average 12% across the OECD. Of those students who meet these status criteria, all of them reported that their country of origin was "Other Country," but they did not indicate which country specifically. This means that it is not possible to determine whether these students were forcibly displaced or come from a country experiencing conflict or instability. Yet, since the largest percentage of immigrants worldwide during the period between 2013 and 2015 is refugees and asylum-seekers (UNHCR, 2016a), this is a reasonable proxy indicator of the percentage of students in mainstream schools in OECD countries who are refugees and asylum-seekers. Across all OECD countries in PISA 2015, there are 13,590 first generation immigrants and 1,361 first generation immigrants who arrived two years ago or less. This student sample size is adequate to conduct tests of statistical significance with this data.

Linear Analyses

Table 3.3 shows the results of a linear regression of the school-level aggregate file, which regressed both student academic and non-academic outcomes among first generation and new arrival students on teacher characteristics. These teacher characteristics included background, pre-service training, professional development, and professional interactions and behaviors indicators.

Teacher background has a statistically significant and positive effect on students' academic and non-academic outcomes in primarily two ways. If the teacher is female, and if the teacher has a higher level of formal education, then effects on math, reading, and science scores, as well as

Table 3.2 Number of students in OECD member countries by immigrant and arrival status (PISA 2015)

OECD Member Country	First Generation Immigrants[1]	Arrived 2 years ago or less[2]	% of First Generation Immigrants Arriving 2 Years Ago or Less
Slovak Republic	35	12	34%
Latvia	43	13	30%
Turkey	16	4	25%
Hungary	57	13	23%
Estonia	37	8	22%
Chile	100	19	19%
Slovenia	223	42	19%
Czech Republic	109	16	15%
Poland	7	1	14%
France	252	32	13%
Ireland	581	73	13%
Austria	477	57	12%
Australia	1423	169	12%
New Zealand	677	78	12%
Canada	2139	237	11%
United Kingdom	1086	113	10%
Luxembourg	1093	108	10%
Israel	267	26	10%
Switzerland	614	58	9%
Sweden	395	35	9%
Finland	126	11	9%
Denmark	368	31	8%
United States	382	29	8%
Norway	320	24	8%
Japan	14	1	7%
Greece	170	12	7%
Germany	215	13	6%
Belgium	773	46	6%
Italy	526	31	6%
Portugal	236	13	6%
Spain	556	27	5%
Netherlands	114	5	4%
Mexico	60	2	3%
Iceland	95	2	2%
Korea	4	0	0%
	OECD Average =		12%

[1] OECD N = 13,590
[2] OECD N = 1,361; All first generation immigrants arriving two years ago or less in the country of testing indicated their country of origin as "Other Country." No further specification was indicated in all cases.

Table 3.3 Linear regression of teacher characteristics on student's academic and non-academic outcomes among first generation and new arrival immigrant students across all OECD countries (PISA 2015)

Teacher Indicators	First Generation and New Arrival Immigrant Student Outcomes					
	Academic Outcomes			Non-Academic Outcomes	
	Mathematics Achievement Score	Science Achievement Score	Reading Achievement Score	Motivation Index	Belonging Index
Teacher Background					
Female (TFEMALE)	47.993**	56.429***	79.847***	0.522***	0.194
Years Teaching (YRSTCH)|	0.766	0.228	0.76	-0.008	0.003
Education Level (EDUCATN)	63.789***	45.1***	52.85***	0.19+	0.142+
Formally Qualified Teacher (TCHREDPR)	-33.104	-27.959	-19.888	0.034	-0.149
Teacher Training					
Teaching in Multicultural & Multilingual Settings (MULTTRAIN)	-44.503+	-23.955	-17.049	0.186	-0.383*
Teaching Special Needs Students (SPECEDTRAIN)	48.888*	73.349**	75.197**	0.137	0.293
Approaches to Individualized Learning (INDVTRAIN)	-39.537+	-37.078+	-52.431*	0.161	0.104
Cross-curricular Skills (CROSSTRN)	45.194*	26.35	23.441	-0.132	0.174
Teacher Professional Development					
Teaching in Multicultural & Multilingual Settings (MULTIPD)	-4.628	7.245	-2.384	-0.31	-0.205
Teaching Special Needs Students (SPECEDPD)	57.926*	66.405**	66.062**	0.181	0.17

(Continued)

Table 3.3 (Continued)

| Teacher Indicators | First Generation and New Arrival Immigrant Student Outcomes ||||||
| | Academic Outcomes ||| Non-Academic Outcomes ||
	Mathematics Achievement Score	Science Achievement Score	Reading Achievement Score	Motivation Index	Belonging Index
Approaches to Individualized Learning (INDVPD)	-41.749	-28.067	-14.751	0.433+	0.116
Cross-curricular Skills (CROSSPD)	-19.168	-31.521	-37.739+	-0.19	-0.173
Teacher Professional Interactions & Behaviors					
Professional Development Network of Teachers (PDNETWRK)	-60.799**	-51.703**	-40.022+	0.484*	0.104
Formal Mentoring & Coaching (MENTORING)	69.44***	67.609***	51.291**	0.432*	0.182
Reading Professional Literature (READLIT)	39.027+	31.412	0.073	0.085	-0.016
Informal Dialog with Colleagues (INFDIALG)	128.881*	56.99	78.127	0.189	0.173
(Constant)	41.483	147.265*	94.401	-1.642**	-1.358**
R²	0.166	0.131	0.133	0.092	0.031

+p<.010
*p<0.05
**p<0.01
***p<.001

on motivation and belonging indices, were generally strong, positive, and statistically significant. The exception is that female teachers did not impact students' sense of belonging any differently than male teachers. Years of working as a teacher and completing a teacher qualifications program had no effect on student outcomes. Those completing a qualifications program, however, had large, statistically non-significant, negative effects on student outcomes.

Teachers' pre-service training was a significant indicator of student academic outcomes when they were trained in teaching special needs students. There was also a strong statistically significant effect of teachers' training in cross-curricular skills on students' math scores. Approaches to individualized learning also had a statistically significant negative impact on reading outcomes and marginally significant negative effect on students' math and science achievement scores. There were no statistically significant effects of teacher training on either student motivation or belonging. Surprisingly, teachers who received pre-service training in teaching in multicultural or multilingual settings had one of the few statistically significant negative impacts on student outcomes, specifically on students' sense of belonging. And, multicultural training had a marginally significant ($p<0.10$) negative effect on students' mathematics achievement scores. Otherwise, multicultural and multilingual training were not significant predictors of student academic outcomes.

Overall, teachers' professional development was not a significant predictor of student outcomes. Except for the large, positive, significant effect of approaches to teaching special needs on students' academic outcomes, there was no significant effect on students' academic outcomes. Similarly, there was little effect of teacher professional development on students' non-academic outcomes.

Finally, teachers' professional interactions and behaviors had mixed effects on student outcomes. Teachers who participated in a network of teachers specifically for professional development had a consistently significant negative effect on students' academic outcomes, but a positive and significant impact on students' motivation and no effect on students' sense of belonging. Teachers who engaged in mentoring or peer observation and coaching as part of a formal school arrangement had large, positive, and significant impacts on all students' academic outcomes as well as student motivation, but no impact on students' sense of belonging. Teachers who read professional literature had little to no effect either on students' academic or non-academic outcomes, and teachers engaging in informal dialog with colleagues on how to improve teaching only impacted students' math achievement scores, but nothing else.

Overall, the linear regression shows more impact of both pre-service and professional development teacher activity on likely refugee and asylum-seeking students' academic achievement than their non-academic outcomes. Perhaps the most important results show that multicultural and multilingual training as well as professional networks are either not significant predictors or are strong negative predictors of students' academic or non-academic outcomes, even though teachers' professional networks had a statistically significant, positive impact on motivation. Even more importantly, teachers' training and professional development in individualized learning had significantly negative effects on students' academic outcomes. This is important because these are strategies often used to prepare for immigrant student populations that are marginalized or challenged in mainstream communities (Correa-Velez, Gifford, McMichael, & Sampson, 2017; Gilhooly & Lee, 2017).

Hierarchical Analyses

To investigate the nested relationship between teacher backgrounds, training, professional development, and interactions with student-level characteristics and outcomes, we used hierarchical linear modeling (HLM). For this analysis, we were interested in one OECD member country in particular, Germany. In the year that PISA 2015 was administered, Germany received more refugees and asylum-seekers than any other country, with most of them coming from Syria (UNHCR, 2016a, p. 28). Given the unique experiences of Germany as an OECD destination country for refugees and asylum-seekers during 2015, and the relatively large percentage of those who were children, we conducted the HLM analysis with Germany's PISA 2015 data exclusively. The German PISA 2015 data includes 5,231 students and 240 schools.

The teacher characteristics which potentially influence refugee and asylum-seeking youth are significant predictors of mainstream students' academic and non-academic outcomes. Therefore, to isolate the impact that teacher characteristics and experiences have on student outcomes, we included teacher characteristics as cross-level interaction variables with the student proxy indicator for likely refugee and asylum-seeking status (i.e., first generation immigrant in country less than two years). A cross-level interaction is an interaction where one of the predictors is restricted in its variability to units at level 2. By including these teacher characteristic variables as interaction effects with students' likely refugee or asylum-seeking status, we were able to estimate the effect that teacher-level indicators have on refugee and asylum-seeking students' academic and non-academic outcomes within the larger mainstream student population in Germany.

To simplify the estimation of effects related to teacher training and professional development, we combined training and professional development indicators into single indicators for both training and professional development related to teaching in multicultural and multilingual settings (MULTI), teaching special needs students (SPECED), approaches to individual learning (INDV), and cross-curricular skills such as problem-solving and learning to learn (CROSS). All other teacher variables remained the same. The HLM model is described below for each of the two levels. The first level (1) estimates the amount of variance in individual student-level academic or non-academic outcomes that is explained by student characteristics.

$$Y_{ij} = \beta_{0j} + \beta_{1j}\text{FEMALE}_{ij} + \beta_{2j}\text{SAMELANG}_{ij} + \beta_{3j}\text{SES}_{ij} + \beta_{4j}\text{LES2GEN1}_{ij} + r_{ij} \qquad (1)$$

where Y_{ij} is the estimated average student academic or non-academic outcome for the *ith* student in the *jth* school, and r_{ij} is a student-level residual. Note that all of the regression coefficients in the student-level equation (the βs) are indexed by *j*, indicating that within the multilevel model a student-level regression coefficient is estimated for every *jth* school in the sample. The term β_{0j} is an estimate of an adjusted dependent variable for the *jth* school in Germany. The coefficient β_{4j} represents the indicator of a students' possible refugee status at level 1.

The relative association of teacher characteristics on student academic and non-academic outcomes is shown by comparing the percentage of total variance in the level 2 average student outcome dependent variable associated with either teacher background, training, professional development, or professional interactions aggregated to the school level. The second level estimates the amount of variance in student outcome that is associated with the school-level aggregate of teacher characteristics when variance is accounted for as well as the association of each teacher characteristic variable on the average school-level aggregate student outcome. At the second level (2) of this multilevel model, we include the factors as follows:

$$\begin{aligned}
\beta_{0j} &= \gamma_{00} + u_{0j} \\
\beta_{1j} &= \gamma_{10} \\
\beta_{2j} &= \gamma_{20} \\
\beta_{3j} &= \gamma_{30} \\
\beta_{4j} &= \gamma_{40} + \gamma_{41}\text{TEACHERCHARACTERISTICS}_j
\end{aligned} \qquad (2)$$

where γ_{00} is the school-level aggregated mean of the student outcome variable, and u_{0j} is the residual difference between the school-level mean and the national average. The coefficient γ_{41} represents the cross-level interaction effects of each set of teacher characteristics such as background (TFEMALE, YRSTCH, EDUCATN, TCHREDPR), training and professional development (MULTI, SPECED, INDV, CROSS), and professional interactions (PDNETWRK, MENTORING, READLIT, INFDIALG) with students' possible refugee status and the relationship of that interaction with student academic and non-academic outcomes.

The hierarchical model with cross-level interaction may also be expressed as a mixed model as follows:

$$Y_{ij} = \gamma_{00} + \gamma_{10}\text{HOMEPOS}_{ij} + \gamma_{20}\text{SAMELANG}_{ij} + \gamma_{30}\text{FEMALE}_{ij} + \gamma_{40}\text{LES2GEN1}_{ij} + \gamma_{41}(\text{TEACHERCHARACTERISTICS}_{j} * \text{LES2GEN1}_{ij}) + u_{0j} + r_{ij}$$

The teacher characteristics in level 2 of the model were entered in three separate steps following a baseline model that did not include any level 2 indicators. The first batch included the teacher background variables at level 2 only. The second batch included teacher training and professional development variables at level 2 only. And, the third batch included teacher professional interactions and behaviors at level 2 only. All models and batches were run for each of the five academic and non-academic student outcomes. Table 3.4 represents a composite of the HLM regression results for each of the student academic and non-academic outcomes. The student-level indicators shown in Table 3.4 are for the baseline model only, and the teacher characteristic coefficients show the cross-level interaction effects with student refugee status for each of the student outcomes.

In each of the models run, the student-level background indicators (female, same language, and SES) were all strong, significant predictors of student outcomes. Students' gender estimated students' academic outcomes (math, reading, and science achievement scores) in the expected ways and in alignment with the research on gender and student performance (Else-Quest, Hyde, & Linn, 2010). Students speaking the same language of the test at home also predicted student academic outcomes positively and significantly. The same is true for students' SES. Overall, student background characteristics predicted students' non-academic outcomes (i.e., motivation and sense of belonging) in the ways that existing research suggests, with the exception of the impact of students' speaking the same language of the test at home. Same language had a strong, significant, negative effect on student motivation and a weak, non-significant effect on students' sense of belonging.

Refugee and Asylum-Seeking Status

In the baseline model, for each student academic outcome, likely refugee and asylum-seeking (*LES2GEN1*) status had a strong, significant, negative effect. This suggests that being a refugee or asylum-seeker tends to lower students' achievement in math, reading, and science. Refugee status in the baseline model, however, had a strong, significant, and positive effect on students' motivation and no significant effect on belonging. For the most part, these results remained consistent as the teacher characteristics cross-level interaction effects were added.[2]

Table 3.4 Hierarchical linear model results for the cross-level interaction between teacher characteristics and first generation and new arrival immigrant student status in Germany (PISA 2015)

Independent Variables	Student Academic Outcomes			Student Non-Academic Outcomes	
	Mathematics Achievement Score	Science Achievement Score	Reading Achievement Score	Motivation Index	Belonging Index
Level 1 Student Indicators					
Female (SFEMALE)	−27.71***	−21.88***	7.59***	−0.11***	−0.12***
	(1.98)[1]	(2.04)	(2.07)	(.03)	(.03)
Same Language (SAMELANG)	31.68***	42.20***	31.79***	−0.26***	0.02
	(3.08)	(3.44)	(4.21)	(.05)	(.06)
SES (SES)	15.33***	18.63***	15.79***	0.16***	0.09***
	(1.29)	(1.41)	(1.52)	(.02)	(.02)
First Generation and New Arrival Immigrant Status (LES2GEN1)	−51.13**	−87.97***	−108.15***	0.68*	−0.38
	(19.64)	(22.49)	(20.31)	(.27)	(.34)
Level 2 Teacher Indicators					
Teacher Background					
Female (TFEMALE)	258.70*	403.34***	314.98+	2.78	−3.72
	(126.980)	(95.27)	(180.37)	(3.25)	(4.48)
Years Teaching (YRSTCH)	5.15*	5.87*	7.03+	−0.08	−0.11
	(3.11)	(2.81)	(3.99)	(.08)	(.12)
Education Level (EDUCATN)	−372.46**	−555.13**	−461.12***	7.11+	−6.12
	(123.59)	(214.87)	(142.62)	(3.71)	(7.63)
Formally Qualified Teacher (TCHRE)	−1414.86*	−650.61	−755.07	18.03	−3.25
	(561.95)	(589.08)	(691.05)	(12.82)	(21.85)
Training & Professional Development					
Teaching in Multicultural & Multilingual Settings (MULTI)	237.42**	389.76***	118.96	0.48	−1.09
	(87.16)	(111.21)	(151.74)	(1.)	(1.81)
Teaching Special Needs Students (SPECED)	−159.71	−262.11*	88.59	2.31	2.81
	(116.06)	(115.93)	(161.67)	(1.61)	(2.22)

(Continued)

Table 3.4 (Continued)

Independent Variables	Student Academic Outcomes			Student Non-Academic Outcomes	
	Mathematics Achievement Score	Science Achievement Score	Reading Achievement Score	Motivation Index	Belonging Index
Approaches to Individualized Learning (INDV)	-60.98 (66.06)	-127.34* (57.24)	-3.39 (97.57)	-3.49*** (.74)	-1.15 (1.92)
Cross-curricular Skills (CROSS)	248.91* (100.57)	381.85*** (124.11)	95.91 (158.96)	2.71* (1.07)	2.72 (1.76)
Professional Interactions & Behaviors					
Professional Development Network of Teachers (PDNETWRK)	119.48 (91.84)	64.92 (166.56)	-156.39 (176.1)	0.87 (2.32)	-0.48 (2.07)
Formal Mentoring & Coaching (MENTORING)	178.71** (65.15)	221.04** (106.6)	149.26 (105.46)	-0.94 (1.14)	-0.40 (1.58)
Reading Professional Literature (READLIT)	-10.35 (167.99)	-241.58 (255.66)	-54.63 (218.04)	-0.08 (2.23)	-10.42* (4.3)
Informal Dialog with Colleagues (INFDIALG)	707.67* (299.04)	314.84 (482.65)	837.82 (512.45)	2.74 (6.04)	-3.25 (6.88)
Intercept	495.40*** (4.6)	487.07 (4.98)	484.20*** (5.52)	-0.13* (.05)	0.33*** (.06)
Variance Components					
Level 2 (μ₀)	2558.06	3097.53	3101.82	0.01	0.02
Level 1 (r)	4155.83	4971.09	5021.13	0.78	1.10

[1]Standard errors in parentheses
†p<.10,
*p<.05,
**p<.01,
***p<.001

Teacher Background

When teacher background was added as a cross-level interaction with students' likely refugee and asylum-seeking status, there were mixed effects. Female teachers and more experienced teachers tend to have a strong, positive, and significant effect on likely refugee and asylum-seeking students' academic outcomes. However, teachers with higher education levels tend to have a strong, negative, and significant effect on refugee students' academic outcomes, and teachers with formal qualifications tend to have a negative effect on academic outcomes. Teacher background indicators largely have no significant effect on likely refugee and asylum-seeking students' non-academic outcomes with the only exception being a strong, positive, and marginally significant effect of teachers' education level on students' motivation.

Training and Professional Development

Teachers who have been trained or had professional development in teaching in multicultural and multilingual settings had a strong, positive, and significant impact on likely refugee and asylum-seeking students' math and science achievement, but no significant impact on reading achievement or either of the non-academic student outcomes. Those teachers who are prepared to teach special needs students had no significant effect on student outcomes, except for a negative and significant impact on science achievement. Overall, teachers prepared to support or develop individualized learning had negative influences on student outcomes, especially to science achievement and motivation. Finally, teachers prepared with cross-curricular skills have a strong, positive, and significant effect on students' math and science achievement as well as motivation.

Professional Interactions and Behaviors

Teachers who have developed a network of other teachers related to professional development had no significant effect on any likely refugee or asylum-seeking student outcomes. The most impactful teacher professional interaction was formal mentoring and coaching, but it only strongly and positively impacted students' math and science achievement. Reading professional literature had no effect on any student outcome except for a significant, negative impact on sense of belonging. And, information dialog with colleagues was only associated with a significant, positive increase in students' math achievement. No other student outcomes were influenced by teachers' professional interactions and behaviors.

Discussion

The research presented here set out to answer how teacher training and professional development in OECD countries' national education systems prepare them to meet both the academic and non-academic needs of refugee and asylum-seeking youth. The focus on OECD countries came about because a significant proportion of early 21st century refugee and asylum-seeking families with school-aged children and unaccompanied minors are received by countries in the OECD, namely, Germany. Although there has been small sample and case study research on refugee and asylum-seeking youth and their education in receiving countries, there is little large-scale research examining the effects of teacher training and professional development on refugee and asylum-seeking student outcomes. Part of the gap in this research has to do with the lack of identifying data on refugee and asylum-seeking student status in education.

Using the PISA 2015 data, we created a proxy indicator for likely refugee or asylum-seeking students that combines their status as first generation immigrants with their time since arrival in the country of testing. While this indicator of immigrant status is not limited to students who are refugees or asylum-seekers, it includes those students when they do exist in participating OECD countries. Then, we regressed teacher background, training, professional development, and professional interaction indicators on student outcomes in academic and non-academic areas for the sample of students who fall under the immigrant and arrival status markers necessary to be a refugee or asylum-seeker in all of the participating OECD countries.

The results of this analysis suggest that across all OECD countries, female teachers with higher levels of formal education have the most positive effect on likely refugee and asylum-seeking students' academic and non-academic outcomes. Those teachers who received training or professional development in teaching special needs students also had a strong positive impact on likely refugee and asylum-seeking students' academic outcomes. Teachers trained in cross-curricular skills had a significant, positive effect on math achievement across all OECD countries, and a strong, positive effect on math, science, and motivation outcomes in Germany. From the analysis of the interaction between teachers' professional interactions and behaviors and likely refugee and asylum-seeking student outcomes, the teachers who engaged in mentoring or peer observation and coaching had strong and positive impacts on student academic outcomes and motivation. It appears, however, that likely refugee and asylum-seeking students' sense of belonging is not influenced to a large degree by any teacher background, training, professional development, or professional interactions or behavior.

Finally, we estimated the cross-level interaction effects of teacher characteristics on students' status as first generation and new arrival immigrants (i.e., likely refugee and asylum-seeking students) on academic and non-academic student outcomes. We limited the sample for this final analysis to Germany, which is an OECD country with one of the highest levels of refugee and asylum-seeking immigration within the two years prior to the administration of PISA 2015. The results of our hierarchical linear models suggest that a student's status as first generation and new arrival immigrant had an expected negative impact on their academic outcomes, which existing research predicted. But, we also found that this possible refugee student status was positively related to student motivation, which existing research on aspirations and expectations suggests (Entorf & Minoiu, 2004; OECD, 2015). This suggests that although refugee students may not be academically prepared for schooling in OECD countries, like Germany, they are significantly motivated to learn and succeed.

Teacher characteristics in the HLM analysis in Germany posted slightly different effects than in the linear regression across all OECD countries. Teacher background, for example, had the expected positive impact on likely refugee and asylum-seeking students' academic outcomes, and no significant impact on non-academic outcomes. But, the effect of teachers' education level flipped to become a negative interaction effect for likely refugee and asylum-seeking students within an otherwise mainstream student sample. Formal qualifications for teachers also posted a negative effect on most student outcomes. More experienced teachers, however, tend to have a strong, positive impact on the relationship between students' likely refugee and asylum-seeking status and academic outcomes.

In terms of teacher training and professional development, the key significant and positive interaction effects with a students' likely refugee and asylum-seeking status were in teaching in multicultural and multilingual settings and using cross-curricular skills. But, even these effects were limited to math and science achievement primarily. Teachers prepared in individual learning and to work with special needs students had either a negative or no significant effect on student outcomes when cross-interacted with likely refugee and asylum-seeking student status. Teachers' formal mentoring and informal dialog with colleagues posted the only positive and significant interaction effects with likely refugee and asylum-seeking student status, but again only on students' math and science achievement and not on reading achievement or either of the non-academic student outcomes.

Conclusion

Based on these analyses, receiving countries in the OECD would be wise to work with refugee and asylum-seeking students using primarily female, experienced, and highly educated teachers who have training in teaching special needs as well as in the use of cross-curricular skills. The evidence also suggests that these teachers should engage in formal mentoring and coaching, and keep up a healthy informal dialog with their colleagues about how to improve their teaching. One of the key problems that persists, however, is how to prepare teachers to handle and improve refugee and asylum-seeking students' non-academic outcomes such as their motivation to learn and their sense of belonging in new schools and communities. This non-academic side is perhaps best accomplished in collaboration with social, psychological, and community organizations outside of the formal education system.

The problem of training teachers to teach in multicultural and multilingual settings also is substantiated by the evidence reported here. Although training and professional development related to teaching in multicultural and multilingual settings was either negatively or only marginally significant for math and significantly negative for belonging across all OECD countries, but significant, positive, and strong for math and science achievement in the German case, it is not possible to suggest that training teachers to teach in multicultural and multilingual settings has an impact with refugee and asylum-seeking students, in general. The evidence suggests that training teachers to teach in multicultural and multilingual settings has mixed results, and although it can have a significant and positive effect on academic outcomes in some countries (e.g., Germany), there is no evidence to suggest that this should be broadly implemented across national educational systems and schools. On the other hand, individualized learning had a negative effect both across the OECD countries and in the German case, in particular. Therefore, individualized learning does not significantly interact with students' likely refugee and asylum-seeking status and student outcomes regardless of the context.

While the evidence from existing research shows that refugee and asylum-seeking students bring many challenges with them to schools and their mainstream classrooms—such as high levels of trauma—the evidence presented here suggests that mainstream teachers' effects on likely refugee and asylum-seeking students predominantly impacts students' academic outcomes and at best does not interfere with the motivation to learn that they bring with them. Future research could investigate the ways that interactions with students and peers impact their non-academic outcomes, too.

Notes

1. First plausible value achievement scores are used in the analyses reported here, but similar results were found running all five plausible values for each achievement score as well as an average score across the plausible values.
2. It is important to note that when cross-level teacher background effects were added to the model, students' likely refugee and asylum-seeking status effects increased several times their original strength. For example, refugee status in the baseline model estimating student math achievement scores was -51.13 ($p<.05$), but increased in strength and direction to 2568.79 ($p<.01$) when teacher background characteristics were added as cross-level interactions.

References

Abu El-Haj, T. (2007). "I was born here but my home isn't here": Educating for democratic citizenship in an era of transnational migration and global conflict. *Harvard Educational Review, 77*(3), 285–316.

Abu El-Haj, T. (2010). The beauty of America: Nationalism, education, and the war on terror. *Harvard Educational Review, 80*(2), 242–275.

Alba, R., Sloan, J., & Sperling, J. (2011). The integration imperative: The children of low-status immigrants in the schools of wealthy societies. *Annual Review of Sociology, 37*, 19.1–19.21.

Arnot, M., & Pinson, H. (2005). *The education of Asylum-seeker and refugee children: A study of LEA and school values, policies and practices.* Cambridge: Faculty of Education, University of Cambridge.

Arnot, M., Pinson, H., & Candappa, M. (2009). Compassion, caring and justice: Teachers' strategies to maintain moral integrity in the face of national hostility to the "non-citizen." *Educational Review, 61*(3), 249–264.

Azzolini, D., Schnell, P., & Palmer, J. R. B. (2012). Educational achievement gaps between immigrant and native students in two "new" immigration countries: Italy and Spain in comparison. *The Annals of the American Academy of Political and Social Science, 643*, 46–77.

Brunello, G., & Rocco, L. (2013). The effect of immigration on the school performance of natives: Cross country evidence using PISA test scores. *Economics of Education Review, 32*, 234–246.

Buckland, P. (2005). *Reshaping the future: Education and postconflict reconstruction.* Washington, DC: World Bank Publications.

Cobb-Clark, D. A., Sinning, M., & Stillman, S. (2012). Migrant youth's educational achievement: The role of institutions. *The Annals of the American Academy of Political and Social Science, 643*, 18–45.

Collet, B. A., & Bang, H. (2016). The securitisation of refugee flows and the schooling of refugees: Examining the cases of North Koreans in South Korea and Iraqis in Jordan. *Compare: A Journal of Comparative and International Education, 46*(2), 272–292.

Correa-Velez, I., Gifford, S. M., McMichael, C., & Sampson, R. (2017). Predictors of secondary school completion among refugee youth 8 to 9 years after resettlement in Melbourne, Australia. *Journal of International Migration and Integration, 18*(3), 791–805.

Dryden-Peterson, S. (2011). *Refugee education: A global review.* Geneva: United Nations High Commission for Refugees.

Else-Quest, N. M., Hyde, J. S., & Linn, M. C. (2010). Cross-national patterns of gender differences in mathematics: A meta-analysis. *Psychological Bulletin, 136*(1), 103.

Entorf, H., & Minoiu, N. (2004). *PISA results: What a difference immigration law makes.* IZA Discussion Paper No. 1021. Bonn, Germany: IZA.

Ferfolja, T. (2009). The refugee action support program: Developing understandings of diversity. *Teaching Education, 20*(4), 395–407.

Gibson, M. A., & Carrasco, S. (2009). The education of immigrant youth: Some lessons from the U.S. and Spain. *Theory into Practice, 48*, 249–257.

Gilhooly, D., & Lee, E. (2017). The Karen resettlement story: A participatory action research project on refugee educational experiences in the United States. *Action Research, 15*(2), 132–160.

Haffejee, B. (2015). African refugee youths' stories of surviving trauma and transition in U.S. public schools. *Journal of Muslim Mental Health*, 9(1), 3–23.

Hatton, T. J. (2017). Refugees and asylum seekers, the crisis in Europe and the future of policy. *Economic Policy*, 32(91), 447–496.

Hek, R. (2005). The role of education in the settlement of young refugees in the UK: The experiences of young refugees. *Practice*, 17, 157–171.

Hos, R. (2016). Caring is not enough: Teachers' enactment of ethical care for adolescent Students with Limited or Interrupted Formal Education (SLIFE) in a newcomer classroom. *Education and Urban Society*, 48(5), 479–503.

Jakubowski, M. (2011, December 11). *PISA in focus*. Paris: OECD.

Levels, M., Dronkers, J., & Kraaykamp, G. (2008, October). Immigrant children's educational achievement in Western countries: Origin, destination, and community effects on mathematical performance. *American Sociological Review*, 73, 835–853.

Lucas, T., & Villegas, A. M. (2010). The missing piece in teacher education: The preparation of linguistically responsive teachers. *Yearbook of the National Society for the Study of Education*, 109(2), 297–318.

MacNevin, J. (2012). Learning the way: Teaching and learning with and for youth from refugee backgrounds on prince Edward Island. *Canadian Journal of Education*, 35(3), 48–63.

McBrien, J. L. (2005). Educational needs and barriers for refugee students in the United States: A review of the literature. *Review of Educational Research*, 75(3), 329–364.

Meunier, M. (2011). Immigration and student achievement: Evidence from Switzerland. *Economics of Education Review*, 30, 16–38.

Naidoo, L. (2013). Refugee action support: An interventionist pedagogy for supporting refugee students' learning in greater Western Sydney secondary schools. *International Journal of Inclusive Education*, 17(5), 449–461.

OECD. (2012). *Untapped skills: Realising the potential of immigrant students*. Paris: Author.

OECD. (2015). *Immigrant students at school: Easing the journey towards integration*. Paris: Author.

OECD. (2016a). *PISA 2015 assessment and analytical framework: Science, reading, mathematic and financial literacy*. Paris: Author.

OECD. (2016b). *PISA 2015 results (volume I): Excellence and equity in education*. Paris: Author.

OECD. (2017). *PISA 2015 technical report*. Paris: Author.

Phifer, L. W., & Hull, R. (2016). Helping students heal: Observations of trauma-informed practices in the schools. *School Mental Health*, 8(1), 201–205.

Pinson, H., & Arnot, M. (2007). Sociology of education and the Wasteland of refugee education research. *British Journal of Sociology of Education*, 28(3), 399–407.

Rubinstein-Avila, E. (2016). Immigrant and refugee students across "receiving" nations: To what extent can educators rely on PISA for answers? *The Clearing House*, 89(3), 79–84.

Schnepf, S. V. (2007). Immigrants' educational disadvantage: An examination across ten countries and three surveys. *Journal of Population Economics*, 20(3), 527–545.

Segal, U. A., & Mayadas, N. S. (2005). Assessment of issues facing immigrant and refugee families. *Child Welfare, 84*, 563–583.

Shakya, Y. B., Guruge, S., Hynie, M., Akbari, A., Malik, M., Htoo, S., et al. (2010). Aspirations for higher education among newcomer refugee youth in Toronto: Expectations, challenges, and strategies. *Refugee, 27*(2), 65–78.

Shapira, M. (2012). An exploration of differences in mathematics attainment among immigrant pupils in 18 OECD countries. *European Educational Research Journal, 11*(1), 68–95.

Shepler, S., & Routh, S. (2012). Effects in post-conflict West Africa of teacher training for refugee women. *Gender and Education, 24*(4), 429–441.

Taylor, S., & Sidhu, R. K. (2012). Supporting refugee students in schools: What constitutes inclusive education? *International Journal of Inclusive Education, 16*(1), 39–56.

Teltemann, J., & Schunck, R. (2017). Education systems, school segregation, and second-generation immigrants' educational success: Evidence from a country-fixed effects approach using three waves of PISA. *International Journal of Comparative Sociology*, 1–24.

Thomas, R. L. (2016). The right to quality education for refugee children through social inclusion. *Journal of Human Rights and Social Work, 1*(4), 193–201.

Tobin, T., Boulmier, P., Zhu, W., Hancock, P., & Meunnig, P. (2015). Improving outcomes for refugee children: A case study on the impact of Montessori education along the Thai-Burma border. *International Education Journal: Comparative Perspectives, 14*(3), 138–149.

UNHCR. (2016a). *Global trends: Forced displacement in 2015*. Geneva: United Nations Human Rights Commission.

UNHCR. (2016b). *Missing out: Refugee education in crisis*. Geneva: United Nations Human Rights Commission.

UNHCR. (n.d.). *What is a refugee?* Retrieved February 17, 2017 from www.unrefugees.org/what-is-a-refugee/

4 Creating a Refugee Space in the Canadian School Context
The Approach of an Inclusive Society

Ratna Ghosh, Domenique Sherab, Maihemuti Dilimulati and Narjes Hashemi

> To those fleeing persecution, terror & war, Canadians will welcome you, regardless of your faith. Diversity is our strength #WelcomeToCanada.
> (Justin Trudeau, 28.01.2017, twitter.com)

These words by Canadian Prime Minister Justin Trudeau were made the day following an executive order in the United States that barred entry from seven Muslim-majority countries including Syria, and indefinitely banned Syrian refugees from resettling in the United States (Paling, 2017). This decision was upheld by the Supreme Court although the dissenting justice warned this was "eroding the foundational principles of religious tolerance" (Burke, 2018).

Canada has long been portrayed as a country of welcome to refugees. Indeed, the country has a long history of refugee protection stretching back to the first "refugees" of the American Revolution, African American former slaves, and diverse populations during the twentieth century (Government of Canada, 2018a; Canadian Council for Refugees, 2009; Hynie, 2018; Epp, 2017; McCallum, 2018). Since the Second World War, Canada has admitted over 1.2 million refugees (El-Assal, 2015) and has consistently changed its refugee intake to respond to urgent crises (Lenard, 2016). In recognition of their welcome of refugees, the Canadian people were awarded the Nansen Prize by UNHCR in 1986. The welcome of 45,000 Syrian refugees since 2015 is suggested as a continuation of this history.

It is important to indicate that this history should be understood alongside a history of exclusion of certain refugee groups during its past. In the words of the prime minister:

> We need to acknowledge that our history includes darker moments: the Chinese head tax, the internment of Ukrainian, Japanese, and Italian Canadians during the First and Second World Wars, our turning away boats of Jewish or Punjabi refugees, our own history of slavery. Canadians look back on these transgressions with regret and shame—as we should.

But our history was also filled with many positive moments. The Underground Railroad. The Charter of Rights and Freedoms. The Multiculturalism Act. The Official Languages Act. The welcoming of Ismaili Muslims. The freedom for Jews and Sikhs, Hindus and Evangelicals to practice their religion as they choose.

These positive changes can never right historical wrongs. But they can serve to remind us that, in the phrase so beloved of Martin Luther King Jr., "The arc of the moral universe is long, but it bends towards justice."

(Trudeau, 2015)

Canadian policy toward refugees, as in other countries, is influenced by a composite of humanitarian, political, economic, and demographic as well as strategic concerns (Gibney, 2004; Hampshire, 2013; Salehyan & Rosenblum, 2008). Indeed, Canada did not formally sign on to the 1951 Refugee Convention until 18 years after it came into existence because it could impede their ability to deport people thought to be security risks (Canadian Council of Refugees, CCR, 2009). This history inevitably impacted the ability of the education systems in Canada to respond to refugee students as refugee students arrived with few systems in place to support them. However, lessons learned from earlier arrivals of refugees are feeding into the educational response now.

This chapter begins with a discussion of the foundations of an inclusive society in Canada through its legislations, which act as a moral force and guide to its people and social institutions. It then provides a brief description of refugee law in Canada. Following this, the structure of the education system is briefly explained so that we can then give some examples of best practices in the education of refugees in Canada.

For a country that was exclusionary, the evolution of dynamic social change in the attitudes and policy in previously monocultural groups (British/Anglophone in English Canada, or French/ Francophone in Quebec) can be explained by developments in social science and cultural theories. Post-modern and post-colonial theories lend themselves to concepts such as alterity, ethnicity, and identity focusing on social and political power relations along with a move towards mutual respect and multiple voices (especially those that were previously silenced). Once multiculturalism and anti-racism are accepted as necessary, especially in education, policies, and practices must move beyond to acknowledge and address the compounding effects of intersecting factors such as race and ethnicity along with gender, religion, class, language, and so on.

Legislation: The Foundations of an Inclusive Society

Canada was the first country in the world to adopt multiculturalism as an official policy in 1971. The country declared bilingualism (English and French as the official languages) in recognition of the significant

French-speaking population concentrated in Quebec, and multiculturalism in acknowledgment of the contributions of many cultures and ethnic groups who developed the nation. Although the French and British were settler societies which colonized a country that already had many aboriginal groups called First Nations and Inuit people, it became an immigrant society. At first, its immigration policies were exclusionary and kept nonwhite people out. However, with the need for immigrants in the 1960s, a dramatic change in the selection of immigrants attracted many groups from Asia, Africa, and Latin America (Ghosh & Galcznyski, 2014; Ghosh, 2018). Currently, South Asians and Chinese form the largest immigrant groups (Ghosh, 2017).

Multiculturalism policy stated that the government of Canada would recognize and respect its diverse society, including its many cultures, languages, customs, religions, and so on. Historically, Canadian society and education had been monocultural and assimilationist, and multiculturalism represented a paradigm shift in Canada's identity and certainly in education. Prime Minister Pierre Elliot Trudeau, who had declared the Multiculturalism Policy in 1971, enshrined multiculturalism in the constitution in 1982. Section 27 of the Charter of Rights and Freedoms of the Constitution officially recognized multiculturalism as a national value. Section 27 reads: "This Charter shall be interpreted in a manner consistent with the preservation and enhancement of the multicultural heritage of Canadians" (Government of Canada, 2006). With the Multiculturalism Act in 1988, Prime Minister Brian Mulroney (Conservative Party) provided a legislative framework for multiculturalism. The focus of the act was equality before the law and for pursuing opportunities at all levels and in the field to "ensure that all individuals receive equal treatment and equal protection under the law, while respecting and valuing their diversity" (Government of Canada, n.d.). With the right to pursue one's interest regardless of race or ethnicity, several pieces of Canadian legislation reflect rights guaranteed to all men and women in the Canadian Charter of Rights and Freedoms which is part of the Canadian Constitution.

The architect of multiculturalism policy in Canada, Prime Minister Pierre Elliot Trudeau had as his campaign theme: Canada—A Just Society. His son, Justin Trudeau, now prime minister has as his theme: Diversity is Our Strength: "Our commitment to diversity and inclusion isn't about Canadians being nice and polite—though of course we are. In fact, this commitment is a powerful and ambitious approach to making Canada, and the world, a better, and safer, place" (Trudeau, 2015).

Himself a teacher and a feminist, when he was elected with an overwhelming majority in 2015 Justin Trudeau appointed a cabinet with an equal number of men and women, two aboriginal members of parliament, three Sikh politicians, and a Somalian immigrant as the minister of Immigration, Refugees, and Citizenship. In fact, now 43 years of age, the minister of Immigration, Ahmed Hussen, arrived in Canada as a refugee from Somalia at the age of 16 with just a change of clothes in his bag. He does not speak about himself, but in a rare interview to the *New York Times* (2017) he said: "my experience is not unique. . . . When you go through the refugee experience, it is not a free ride." But he registered for high school in the Toronto area, put himself through his first degree at university, and then went to law school to become a lawyer while also working.

Canada's concept of diversity extends beyond race and ethnicity and spans a broad range of markers of difference from the majority English and French populations, such as culture, language, gender, religious affiliations, sexual orientation, dis/abilities, and economic status (Ghosh & Abdi, 2013). Canadians, especially young Canadians, are comfortable with diversity, although some people hold dissenting views on diversity, immigration, and refugee intakes (Bagley, 2017). Notwithstanding strong legislation against discrimination, incidences of racism and discrimination are experienced by several groups in society and in educational institutions. Unfortunately, attitudes of people cannot be legislated. However, in comparison to other countries globally, Canada continues to stand out for the public's positive attitudes toward newcomers and in the happiness that immigrants themselves report (Perreaux, 2018). Canada took the second spot on global social-progress ranking and second place (after Iceland) in social inclusiveness in the 2016 Social Progress Index. In the 2018 index, only 1.64 points separates it from Norway, which ranks first (Social Progress Index, 2018).

Recently, Canada's commitment to accept Syrian refugees was widely applauded, and they are the largest group to come to resettle in this country since 1980 (Wilkinson & Garcea, 2017). Canada has a history of large refugee resettlement commitments starting with the 37,000 Hungarian refugees fleeing communism in 1956; from Southeast Asia, 60,000 Vietnamese, Cambodian, and Laotian people after the Vietnam war in 1979/80; from Eastern Europe in 1992 and 1994, 11,000 Bosnian, Serbian, and Croatians; and in 1999, 6,000 Kosovars were airlifted and brought to Canada (Wilkinson & Garcea, 2017). More recently, the Middle Eastern crisis has brought 20,000 Iraqi refugees with Syrians following soon after (CIC, 2015; Wilkinson & Garcea, 2017).

The refugees from the European countries were not familiar with English, although some of the East Asian refugees knew some French. So, knowledge of the language of the school is one of the persistent challenges facing refugee students in schools. Depending on how old they are when they go to school, the level of difficulty varies. In the earlier years, efforts were put into language learning for refugee students as they were for immigrant children. Most of the refugee groups were from European countries and largely Christian, although there were some Muslims from Eastern Europe. But with Middle Eastern refugees who were culturally very different and displayed symbols of their religion, attention to refugees became more apparent. In 2016 alone, over 33,000 refugees from Syria and nearly 13,000 refugees from Eritrea, Iraq, Congo, and Afghanistan (Puzic, 2017) came to Canada and were sent all over the country. Schools are facing large numbers of refugee students not only in the metropolitan cities but in the small towns across Canada. Reports indicate that in the small towns which have never even had immigrants, refugees are made to feel welcome by all levels of school staff. #WelcomeRefugees is full of stories of schoolchildren, among others, welcoming refugee children to Canada.

The development of multicultural and anti-racist education, and the need to provide all students with opportunities in education had been seen as enough for refugee children. Immigrant and refugee students were not treated differently (Shakya et al., 2010). It was not until the 1990s that the special needs for victims of trauma, interrupted education, or simply a refugee status (Pillay & Asadi, 2012) have been taken into account leading to the provision of more services as well as policy development. The next section looks briefly at policy development at the federal level, which guides provincial and local school board policies, and practices in schools.

Legislation: Refugee Law

With multiculturalism as one of the identifying features of Canada, immigration policies were changed to encourage people from countries of the geographical South. Even before the formal change to multiculturalism, the Canadian government legislated refugee law in the 1970s following pressure from progressive groups to not only enable resettlement but to ensure increased numbers of resettlement places, both through private and public sponsorship. This has been more recently pronounced with the change from a Conservative to a Liberal government at the federal level and consequent policy resulting in the fast tracking of 45,000 Syrian refugees and upsurge in arrivals of asylum-seekers at the border with the United States.

The first attempt to formally integrate refugee law into Canadian law was made in the Immigration Act of 1976. The act differentiated between different immigrant groups including refugees, families assisted by relatives, and independent immigrants. Due to pressure from churches and voluntary groups, the government legislated the ability for private individuals to sponsor refugees. Although originally envisioned as a small complement to the government assisted program for immigrants as well as refugees, private sponsorship expanded rapidly with the response to the Indo-Chinese crisis (Labman & Pearlman, 2018; Macklin et al., 2018) and has remained a consistent part of Canada's resettlement approach up to the most recent arrival of Syrians (Macklin et al., 2018).

In 2002, the Immigration and Refugee Protection Act (IRPA) changed the eligibility requirements for resettlement to Canada. The shift can be summed up as an increased focus on protection concerns over integration (Hyndman, 2014; Pressé & Thomson, 2007). This shift did not completely do away with concerns about the latter, however, with refugees required to demonstrate "an ability to establish" in Canada (Hyndman, 2014).

In December 2012, a gamut of laws relating to immigration were amended with the introduction of the Protecting Canada's Immigration System Act (Ahmad, 2016). This act (2012) gave the authorities greater ability to incarcerate asylum-seekers for long periods of time (Dawson, 2014), deny the right of appeal, introduce shorter timelines for the refugee claims process, and introduce the idea of safe countries of origin (OCASI). This was widely viewed as an effort to restrict the progressive nature of the law relating to refugees and was condemned by progressive Canadian organizations (Amnesty International, 2012; CCR, 2012; Human Rights Watch, 2012). It is important to note that it is this law which remains in force to this day, impacting refugees already settled in Canada retroactively (Yiu, 2016).

In addition to government assisted refugees (GAR) and privately sponsored refugees (PSR), in 2013, the government introduced another category, namely the Blended Visa Office-Referred (BVOR) process (Hyndman & Hynie, 2016) in an apparent attempt to limit Private Sponsored Refugees (PSR) being used solely for family reunification. This constitutes a private-public partnership over the sponsorship of a refugee (Labman & Pearlman, 2018). The first six months are covered by the government and the second six months covered by a sponsor. This visa class received criticism by various groups because of its suggested dilution of the additionality principle that was a characteristic of private sponsorship (CCR, 2016). To be sure, the BVOR has been used sparingly thus far, largely, it seems, because of lack of understanding of how it works (Labman & Pearlman, 2018).

Regardless of which visa category, resettlement is administered by Citizenship and Immigration Canada (CIC, 2015) (Ahmad, 2016) and refugees arrive as permanent residents. The federal government's centralization of the process of resettlement ends there, with integration services conducted provincially (Jeram & Nicolaides, 2018; McGrath & McGrath, 2013). Jeram and Nicolaides (2018) indicate that integration in Canada is the most decentralized reception regime of the advanced liberal democracies. Importantly, these provincial differences are also complicated by the fact that PSR and BVOR, for a certain time, do not receive support from the provincial or federal government, as they are receiving support from their sponsors, while GAR receive assistance from the federal government for a whole year. After the first year, refugees on each visa group stop receiving assistance from either the federal government and their sponsors but in many cases transition to receive provincial support (Government of Canada, 2017).

Canada's refugee system also accommodates asylum-seekers who, after entering Canada, can make an application for asylum if there is fear or danger when one returns to one's home country. It is important to note that the Canadian authorities must determine the claim of the individual in relation to the Refugee Convention after they have arrived in the country. With the election of Donald Trump and changes to US policy, increasing numbers of asylum-seekers have been arriving in Canada (Shugerman, 2018), which has caused significant debate (Markusoff, 2018; Zilio, 2018) with regard to the federal government's approach to asylum-seekers and refugees.

Research suggests that PSR are more likely to socially integrate than those refugees who arrive as GAR (Drolet & Moorthi, 2018). However, this is not uniformly the case with various distinctive challenges arising as a consequence of the contractual and financial commitments that have been made (Kyriakides, Bajjali, McLuhan, & Anderson, 2018). Indeed as Reza Nakhaie (2018) has indicated, PSR had more service needs related to community services and work, which suggest that they do not receive adequate support on these issues through their sponsors. The way individuals arrive, and their status, may also have bearing on the ability of children to learn. This has certainly been the case for those children who are undocumented, with parents fearful of immigration authorities identifying them through their children (Hanley, Hachey, & Tetrault, 2017; Meloni, Rousseau, Ricard-Guay, & Hanley, 2016). This has been changing in recent years with some school boards across Canada implementing a Don't Ask, Don't Tell policy (Villegas, 2016) and provinces legislating access regardless of status, most recently in Quebec with Project de Loi 144 (amending the Education Act by extending free educational services to preschool children and nonresidents). In contrast, asylum-seekers and refugees formally have access to education for their children. In the following sections of this chapter, we will outline how Canadian educational systems have attempted to respond to the inclusion of refugee students and meet their distinct needs. This has developed since the first major introduction of refugee students in the 1970s and advanced more rapidly in the last decade with major resources developed at the school, school board, and provincial levels.

Education

Educational policy on refugee youth needs to be sensitive to the varied experiences of youth and avoid essentializing a group which is already marginalized. Most importantly, refugee students should not be seen merely as victims but rather seen from the point of view of their strengths and resilience. Brewer (2016) points out the importance of having an "asset perspective" rather than a "deficit perspective" in order to avoid further marginalizing refugee students. This is particularly important for teacher education and classroom practice (p. 136).

Schools, as social institutions, are a reflection of society. As with a generally inclusive culture, there is a strong tradition of supporting refugee youth to integrate into Canadian schools and this is often pointed to as an example of best practice. While multicultural and equality legislation are at the federal level, education at all levels is exclusively a provincial responsibility in Canada, and there is no ministry or department of education at the federal level. The ministers of education of each of the 10 provinces and three territories are responsible through their ministries or departments of education for all aspects of education. While the 13 jurisdictions have many similarities and consult each other in the Council of Ministers of Education of Canada (CMEC), Canada is the second largest country in the world, with great variations in geography and population needs; these are all taken into account in an effort to make education as accessible as possible for all.

Despite education being organized by the provinces and territories, there is a "common commitment to an equal chance in school with fairness and equal access" (Cheng & Yan, 2018, p. 139). This common commitment is what sets the foundation of Canadian education. Following the federal policies and legislation that encourage an inclusive environment, provincial education policies foster a culture of inclusive education, which seeks to support diverse learners, whether it be disabled students or students from a refugee background (Cheng & Yan, 2018). Within this decentralized approach are a number of models being developed to address specific immigrant and refugee students (Ruban, 2017; Stewart & Martin, 2018). Gagné, Schmidt, and Markus (2017) have suggested more recently that the arrival and interest in Syrian refugees has encouraged the strategic development of a progressive education agenda that can support all refugee learners. The following section of the chapter will outline the current state of the art approaches to refugee youth education in Canada, paying particular attention to differences across provinces.

Refugee Education

Different Approaches by Provinces/Regions

Between January 2015 and December 2017, over 94,000 refugees were resettled to Canada (Government of Canada, 2018b). The refugee population included 43% school-age (17 years old and under) youth, arriving to all schools across Canada. While the federal government determines if refugees can enter the country, it is a provincial responsibility to manage educational policies in developing curriculum and resources that respond to the needs of refugees (Brewer, 2016, p. 134).

Although the education of children from all parts of the world at all levels is not new to Canada, the education of the increasing number of refugee children and youth becomes more complex due to the variations in their experiences, which range from violence, fear, and stress to loss of or separation from parents and close family members, and sudden contact with environments that are very different. Moreover, their educational backgrounds may differ, often because of war in their home countries which disrupted their education; those who have grown up without access to schools find it difficult to have to go to school in Canada where schooling is compulsory until age 16. Trauma is often a huge problem, and studies on the mental health of refugees indicate a 30% rate of post-traumatic stress disorder (Stewart, 2017). Uncertainty and vulnerability are compounded with problems of parental employment and barriers of an unfamiliar host culture and language along with possible experiences of discrimination which impact the schooling of refugee children. Even suitable housing is a problem when, as in the case of Syrian refugees, Canadian housing units are for small families whereas Syrian families typically tend to have seven or eight members or more (Friesen, 2017).

Existing literature from Canada highlights that the challenge for refugee youth and young adults to access and succeed in education is far greater than that for children who experience disrupted education and pressure to work (Boyd, 2002; Gunderson, 2002; Hou & Bonikowska, 2016; Kanu, 2008; MacKay & Tavares, 2005; MacNevin, 2012; Wilkinson, 2001). After potentially years outside the formal schooling system, refugee youth and young adults face the daunting prospect of being in school for long periods to get a high school diploma to continue to higher education or vocational training. While education is widely accepted as an important basis for successful integration, entering school at an advanced age can create a sense of anxiety and hopelessness (MacKay & Tavares, 2005).

The need to recognize the role of identities is especially important for refugee youth, not only because childhood and youth are important development phases but also because they are "lost in the spaces between various identities" (Gunderson, 2002, p. 702) due to their often traumatic experiences. They need the opportunities to explore their identities, which are in flux (Brewer, 2016; MacNevin, 2012). Adding to the displacement experience and its administrative challenges, financial pressure, language barriers, overt and covert forms of racism and differences in approaches to teaching and learning contribute to refugee students feeling overwhelmed and unsupported, and dropping out (Baffoe, 2006; Blanchet-Cohen, Denov, Fraser, & Bilotta, 2017). In addition to language and other academic barriers that refugee youth face, they are particularly susceptible to bullying and marginalization, and teachers and administrators need to be supportive and aware so that they are not pushed into oppositional activities such as gangs and violent extremism. A study currently under way is investigating the support services in place in Quebec to ensure youth and young adult refugee students in adult education continue and thrive.

Although Canadian schools deal with diversity in the classroom and in the playground, the different provinces have experienced dissimilar rates of diversity, and their programs have consequently been more or less inclusive. Diversity and inclusion policies and practices not only vary among the provinces but also within the provinces as the administration of schools is done by school boards which have elected officials on their boards. Provinces and cities, which attract a large number of immigrant populations have developed multicultural and anti-racist educational programs, policies, and environments. So, they are more prepared to deal with refugee students.

Studies by Wilkinson, Garcea, Bhattacharyya, Abdul-Karim, and Riziki (2017), Stewart (2017) and Nourpanah (2014), looked at language learning and other experiences and the services availed by Syrian refugees who were sent to the Prairie provinces of Alberta, Saskatchewan, and Manitoba. The results indicated that language learning was their main preoccupation given that over 90% of them spoke only Arabic. They were also concerned about the recognition of their foreign credentials. In Alberta, the province has Inclusive Education as a policy and Manitoba has specific policies for refugees as described below. Further west, in the province of British Columbia, which has had a surge of asylum-seekers, the Ministry of Education published a document entitled "Students from Refugee Backgrounds: A Guide for Teachers and Schools" in 2009, which has been updated in 2011 and 2015. Along with the Teacher's Federation of British Columbia, which has an up-to-date website, the Ministry of Education offers resources to teachers to help in the integration and success of refugee children. Aside from British Columbia, immigrants and refugees have traditionally gone to the metropolitan cities in Ontario as described below, and to Quebec. The province of Quebec has not only taken a large number of refugee children in its cities and also in smaller towns, but it has opened up the Olympic Stadium in Montréal to accommodate the surge of Haitian asylum-seekers in 2018, fleeing the United States, where they had been given refuge after the devastating earthquake in 2016 (McKenna, 2017). More than 9,000 refugee claimants crossed into Canada through unofficial routes along the US border within the first five months of 2018, and 90% of them came to Quebec (Wright, 2018). Although asylum-seekers get health-care benefits first and eligibility questions later (Young, 2017), one of their problems is that they cannot enroll children in school until the families have fixed addresses. However, Quebec has been providing educational activities for children in temporary shelters. Farther east, in the maritime provinces, despite their small populations, all schools have geared up to receive increasing numbers of refugee children in Prince Edward Island, Nova Scotia and New Brunswick.

Language Learning

Bourdieu and Passeron (1990) have convincingly asserted that knowledge of the language of instruction is essential both for student learning and school achievement and for engaging students in their learning. Teachers have a very difficult time teaching content when language skills are inadequate. Teachers find that they are struggling to teach basic language skills when doing more advanced material in secondary schools. MacNevin's study (2012) conducted in Prince Edward Island in the extreme east of Canada indicated that one of the important barriers to learning English is the lack of skills in their first language due to interrupted schooling. Linguistic ability to communicate not only impacts the social well-being of refugees and society as a whole but is imperative for success in schools (Dryden-Peterson, 2011). The Syrian Refugee Integration Initiative was launched by Languages Canada to help refugees arriving in Canada have access to courses provided by the federal and provincial governments to develop language skills, which are crucial to their effective integration in their new country. This initiative is partnering with Canadians citizens who donate their time and resources to offer free tuition for English and French language programs.

Provincial policies are implemented by school boards which administer a group of schools based on a regional, religious, or linguistic basis. Most school boards focus on language learning as a basic need to be able to cope with schoolwork. In all provinces except Quebec, the language of instruction is English, and there are special English classes for the newcomers, although French is taught as a second language because Canada is bilingual. However, bilingual schools and immersion programs (teaching both English and French) are increasing rapidly throughout the country. In the province of Quebec, schooling in French is mandatory and English is taught as a second language. In Quebec, school boards are divided along linguistic lines rather than on a confessional basis (Protestant or Catholic) as stipulated by the constitution in 1867. Quebec's largest school boards are French, and language learning is an important part of the program to have refugee adults and children adapt quickly to the culture in Quebec so that they can function in society. For those who know neither English nor French, learning the language is most important but since many refugee children do not have foundational knowledge of their own languages, learning another language is not easy (Paradis, Genesee, & Crago, 2011).

Teacher Education

Much attention is focused on the need for teachers to be trained to provide special attention to the needs of refugee children (Lopour & Thompson, 2016; Stewart, 2011). Teacher education programs are determined by the ministries of education and taught in universities but certified by the provinces. Research has identified gaps in teacher preparation to deal with refugee children and diagnosing or understanding the impact of trauma on children, especially those from conflict-affected countries (Stewart, 2011). Those who teach refugee children face tremendous challenges not only because of the limited literacy skills of the refugee students but perhaps more because of their role in making those students feel safe and welcome and able to achieve their educational aspirations. Teacher education programs are increasingly becoming sensitive to the special needs of refugee students and the barriers they face. Studies by Richardson MacEwen and Naylor (2018) and Kanu (2008) and a few others show that teachers are eager to help, to know the students' experiences so that they can engage them in the class and help them through the confusing process of identity construction as they grow up.

Exemplary Practices

The education offered to refugee children and youth in Canada varies to a great extent, especially with regard to the individual attention needed to respond to students' experiences of trauma, and in the very important area of the training of teachers. Nevertheless, there are several examples of successful programs in the educational system at all levels in the provinces. We provide here (1) the example of a middle school, (2) an idea of the efforts made at the policy and administrative level in one province, and (3) a brief description of the work of organizations with refugee youth at the tertiary level of education.

The Example of a Middle School

A few studies have investigated best practices for building welcoming communities for newcomer and refugee children in individual provinces (Stewart and Martin, 2018; Wilkinson et al., 2017). In a study on refugee integration in Alberta, Manitoba, and Newfoundland, Stewart and Martin, (2018) found that some schools have successfully implemented programs that encourage social inclusion and intercultural understanding, while others have not. The following is an example of a program in one school in Manitoba which is outstanding in its practices for supporting refugees and creating an inclusive school culture described by Stewart (2017).

We begin with the educational policies that support the kind of inclusion in the school described below. The Manitoba Ministry of Education's website indicates several relevant documents with regard to refugee education. It uses narratives of refugee youth to highlight the unique needs and strengths of refugee students. It also provides insights on best practices for teaching refugee youth (Manitoba Education and Advanced Learning, 2015). The document "Building Hope: Refugee Learner Narratives"

(2015) states that after conducting research with youth of immigrant backgrounds, there was a recognized need to focus on refugees specifically because of their unique characteristics. Another government publication, "Life After War: Education as a Healing Process for Refugee and War-Affected Children" (2012), is a valuable resource that describes some shared experiences of students from war-affected backgrounds, and it provides appropriate pedagogical strategies and programs to facilitate dialog between family members, schools, and other service providers to meet the needs of refugee students (Government of Manitoba, 2012). There are other similar documents such as "Building Hope and War Affected Children: A Comprehensive Bibliography" (Gagné et al., 2017, p. 440). These resources are discussed, analyzed, and studied by teacher candidates in Manitoba so as to prepare pre-service teachers for their diverse future students and their specific needs.

In addition, the Ministry of Education in Manitoba has a variety of other resources available on its website. Some examples are: documents like "The Impact and Effects of War on Children" and sample student narratives which in-service teachers can read to learn about refugee students from different countries such as Burundi, Democratic Republic of Congo, Somalia, Rwanda, Sudan, Afghanistan (Manitoba Education and Advanced Learning, 2015). This is very helpful, since the documents also give a brief summary of the culture and history of conflict in each country. The large numbers of Syrian refugees who have arrived since the publication of these documents must soon have their stories included because of the extreme suffering they have endured.

With these resources from the Ministry of Education in Manitoba, and spurred by the need to make education available to refugee students, a middle school in Winnipeg, the capital of the province of Manitoba in central Canada, has created a culture where all students feel connected and safe (Stewart, 2017). The success of this school in dealing with its refugee children is partly due to the leadership of the school. The principal is himself a former refugee from Vietnam who arrived in Winnipeg as a child in 1979. Together with his staff and students they have created four teams: Humility, Wisdom, Courage, and Truth. In order to enable teachers to have more meaningful relations with the students and understand their challenges, the principal has organized teachers to teach the same students for their three years in middle school—grades seven through nine. With the belief that learning cannot take place when one is threatened, they strive for compassion and care in their daily interactions. Learning takes place when students feel respected and honored, and this is true of all students. With refugee students, this is even more important. As the school principal says, "We know the trauma is there, we recognize that students have had horrific experiences and it is our job to create a space where they can be safe, feel cared for, and be open to learning" (Stewart, 2017).

Based on reflections on the activities, support programs, and teaching strategies offered in the above mentioned school and combining these with the literature on supporting refugee students, Stewart (2017) identifies unique approaches and best practices that are necessary for creating safe, trauma-sensitive schools that relate to learning and teaching in schools. Many of the methods have to do with knowing who teachers are dealing with: (1) know the students, (2) know the community, (3) know the signs of trauma, (4) know who can help (e.g., professionals), and most importantly, (5) know yourself, the teacher.

1. Knowing the story of students is crucial because despite the trauma, there is the story of a survivor. Many refugee students show great resilience, and are capable of success. Teachers need to see their students as having assets rather than deficits. Knowledge of students' background can be crucial to developing relationships but will also give teachers the ability to see mental health issues which may need professional attention; this is especially critical for refugee students whose pre-migratory experiences of war, violence, loss of loved ones, fear, and stress are overwhelming. Such experiences, compounded by the stress of starting a new life, lack of language in the new society, new ways of doing things, and parents' pressures of finding jobs and establishing themselves can lead to anger and emotional behavior, which are not conducive to learning. Students' ability to learn English or French as an additional language (E/FAL) is fundamental to their success as students.
2. To know the community is to collaborate so that all stakeholders are involved in discussions and planning for future activities. Cooperation among teachers, parents and students goes a long way in preventing violence, bullying and other oppositional activities.
3. In Canada, it was estimated that in 2012 about 17% of the 15 and over age group needed mental health interventions (Sunderland & Findlay, 2013). Refugees undoubtedly need help to deal with their trauma and displacement. Attention to this aspect of refugee education is imperative for a peaceful and healthy society, as well as to promote their successful inclusion. Knowing the signs of trauma is essential so that teachers can get professional help, and then they need to know what kind of professional help is needed in each case.
4. Teachers need to be able to identify the specific type of help needed. In a country where medical help is available to each and every person, refugees who come and become permanent residents (later citizens) are eligible for medical health coverage from the moment they arrive. For refugee students, a sense of security, ability to share their stories, knowing that people will listen to them, and a feeling of trust are steps towards healing and mental well-being which will help in learning. School counselors and specialized medical help are available to

all children and youth, and schools can arrange help if the culture of the school is one of empathy and care.
5. Most importantly, teachers must be aware of their own attitudes, their prejudices, their unconscious biases, and their willingness to be patient and understand some of the trauma and behaviors that may be stressful but unavoidable.

It is ultimately what Nel Noddings (1984) has called the ethics of care, caring about others, which is the basis of relationships. It is this, a caring and compassionate relationship among students, teachers, and community that the middle school in Manitoba has succeeded in developing. Concepts of diversity, understanding, and respect for them as students who have different skills help integrate refugees in the classroom.

Efforts Made at the Policy and Administrative Levels

The Province of Ontario

While several provincial ministries of education have implementation documents for creating inclusive classrooms, Ontario is given here as an example of a province which has been at the forefront of equity in education for all students and has been recognized for its success in reducing the impact of socioeconomic background on student achievement. These documents encourage school boards in the province which receive the largest number of immigrant as well as refugee children and youth on creating learning environments that validate all students with a multicultural and anti-racist approach; this extends beyond the prevention of overt discrimination to include the awareness of practices that are discriminatory in their impact. What is significant is that many school boards have expanded the inclusive equity policies to recognize the intersectionality of several discriminatory factors such as ethnicity, gender, class, religion, sexual orientation, and so forth, which compound the impact of negative experiences for many students (Ontario Ministry of Education, 2014a). In a renewed vision for education in Ontario, the goal of the document "Achieving Excellence" (Ontario Ministry of Education, 2014b) focuses on equity and promoting student well-being as measures of success. Supporting well-being is a holistic approach to cognitive, social, emotional, and physical development as well as a sense of identity in order to create positive relationships, be connected, and feel a sense of belonging. With the belief that student learning can best take place when students feel safe, physically and emotionally, and are engaged in their learning that they develop into healthy citizens who have a positive identity. Collaborative learning with the community and other stakeholders is given importance. The Ontario Knowledge Network for Student Well-being has joined with existing communities which work to promote student mental health and prevent bullying among other areas.

These documents and action plans are for all students, and in recognition of the special needs of refugee students, the province of Ontario's Ministry of Education has consulted and planned for the recent wave of 10,000 Syrian refugees. The ministry sent out memos describing the consultations with school boards so that they would be able to show that they are a welcoming and inclusive society. The Population Profile of Syrian Refugees prepared by the federal government provides demographic as well as health and cultural information (Citizenship and Immigration Canada, 2015). Given that refugees were coming under the government plan, they would be given permanent resident status and therefore would be eligible for free public education. Professional development for initial literacy and numeracy assessments and programs such as STEP—steps to English proficiency—was linked to resources for teachers and staff. This was done not only in at the K–12 level but also in the adult education sectors of school boards.

Most importantly, mental health needs were anticipated and schools were put in touch with a Refugee Resource Group to assist in developing new resources and accessing existing ones. These equity and student well-being documents, in addition to resources on bullying and mental health issues are important for refugee children who come from very different cultures, as well as religions that are under attack in North America. Teacher education and professional development is of utmost importance in this area.

A document titled "Capacity Building" was developed in 2016. This document focuses on K–12 education, and states that many refugees coming from all over the world—Afghanistan, Nigeria, Sri Lanka, Colombia, Haiti, and most recently, the newcomers from Syria—all model perseverance and resilience because of what they have been through as a result of conflict and war; so many show gratitude and a strong desire for education (Capacity Building K-12, 2016). As such, in the document, it is recognized and emphasized that refugee newcomers should get the necessary support to feel accepted and valued in schools. Classroom educators need to become "trauma informed," as they should be aware of the three transitional periods that impact refugee student's learning, such as "pre-migration: their life experience in their place of birth, trans-migration: their life experience in the time between leaving their home community and their immigration to Canada, and finally, post-migration: their life experience as they adjust and integrate into their new school and community" (Capacity Building K-12, 2016, p. 2).

In addition, a framework for responsive practice for Ontario educators was developed in 2016. It includes a detailed description of six responsive practices, some of which suggest focus on language learning, supporting students with limited prior schooling, assisting the learning process by using the refugee student's "story," using their prior knowledge to introduce new academic concepts, involving parents, and providing a "same language" buddy that will help the student (if possible).

Further, the "Capacity Building" document notes the importance for developing opportunities for teachers and other education stakeholders (such as government agencies and educational institutions) to collaborate on socio-psychological challenges of refugees for better settlement programs. As such, another short document entitled "Capacity Building K–12: Supporting Students with Refugee Backgrounds, Special Edition # 45," was released in July 2016, after the Syrian refugee resettlement had taken place (Capacity Building K-12, 2016). This document is produced by the Ontario Ministry of Education and targeted at teachers; it contains specific instructional strategies and information for education professionals to keep in mind when working with refugee students. The document also contains references to current research about refugee students for further reading (Capacity Building K-12, 2016). Developing tangent solutions to problems that refugees face can ensure there is enough support for better education outcomes and well-being for refugee children and youth (Capacity Building K-12, 2016).

Moreover, in Ontario, many teacher training programs have to go through a guide which was set out by Ontario Regulation 347/02 "Accreditation of Teacher Education Programs" (Ontario College Teachers, 2014). For example, the University of Toronto's two-year teacher education program (after an undergraduate degree) to become certified teachers in Ontario elementary and secondary schools uses this guide as a part of their program (Gagné et al., 2017). This guide has two sections—Supporting ELLs (English Language Learners) and Mental Health, Addictions, and Well-Being; the first section provides suggestions on how to support students and the second section addresses the "need for teachers to acquire specific knowledge and skills to meet the needs of refugee children who may need to learn English as an Additional Language (EAL) and may be suffering from trauma" (Gagné et al., 2017, p. 432).

In 2008, the Ontario Ministry of Education released a practical guide for in-service Ontario educators about ways to support English language learners with limited prior schooling, which are almost always refugees (Gagné et al., 2017). Since 2014, there is a new course requirement—Supporting ELLs—for the master of teaching program in the Ontario Institute for Studies in Education (OISE). It is noted by the authors of this chapter that, while this is a good course to be added, there is a need for more courses on physical health and educational psychology with a specific focus on refugees' mental health (Gagné et al., 2017). Other resources that are made available to the teacher candidates at the masters in teaching program in Toronto include video and multimedia resources that are a part of the curriculum so that the pre-service teachers can have a first-hand look and make meaningful connections that are relevant to immigrant and refugee students (Gagné et al., 2017, p. 432).

There are professional workshops for teachers in different elementary and secondary schools in Ontario where an ESL/ELD program co-coordinator works collaboratively with school administrators and classroom teachers. The aim is to help teachers become more attuned to how refugees experience school and learning so that they can better accommodate the students' needs, especially those who have underdeveloped home language and/or literacy skills (Gagné et al., 2017). Further, the Settlement Workers in Schools (SWIS) Program is an initiative funded by Immigration, Refugees and Citizenship Canada (IRCC). The SWIS program places settlement workers from community agencies in elementary and secondary schools that have high numbers of newcomer students (SWIS, 2018). In Ontario, approximately 200 settlement workers from 20 different settlement agencies are based in schools in over 20 school boards across the province (SWIS, 2018).

Higher Education

According to WES (World Education Services, 2018), only 1% of the entire eligible refugees currently have access to higher education. With this dismal background, Canada has been working hard to help refugees access higher education through various ways. For example, since 1978, World University Service of Canada, (WUSC) through its Student Refugee Program (SRP) has placed refugee students from various locations around the world into Canadian universities (Loo, Streitwieser, & Jeong, 2018). With its long-standing agreement with Immigration, Refugees and Citizenship Canada, SRP has been actively supporting the refugee youth in resettling and preparing for admissions to higher education in various universities, colleges, and community colleges across Canada. Currently, SRP is the only program that has been focusing on both refugee resettlement and refugee access to higher education in Canada. Since its launch, this program has supported over 1,800 young refugees in over 80 higher educational institutions across Canada (Loo et al., 2018). Facing the recent Syrian refugee crisis, WUSC has reached out to more than 200 postsecondary academic institutions across the country and effectively contributed to the enrollment of many Syrian refugees into Canadian postsecondary educational institutions since 2015.[1]

Moreover, York University's Borderless Higher Education for Refugees (BHER) program has been providing training to untrained refugee teachers already working in the field through funding provided by the Canadian government (Lopour & Thompson, 2016). More specifically, this program has provided gender equitable teacher training programs to working, untrained teachers who can then contribute to the community;

this addresses the additional barriers females face in pursuing an education. Equally important, BHER has been offering a mentorship program for local women, pairing them with international scholars and students who can help them challenge and overcome gender-related discrimination or obstacles in accessing education and the job market. At the same time, it has been offering both onsite and online high-quality courses for the refugees in the Global South actively coordinating with the local partners. For example, currently under this program, York University, Kenyatta University, the University of British Columbia, and Moi University are working together to offer refugee youth the opportunity to earn internationally recognized certificates, diplomas, and degrees in the refugee camps in Dadaab, Kenya.[2]

Loo et al. (2018) look at the higher education systems of four Western countries (Canada, the United States, France, and Sweden) and find that Canada, as a whole, has been faring particularly well in terms of integrating refugees. While many Canadian higher educational institutions have not been directly involved in helping refugees access tertiary education, they have been assisting refugee families to resettle in Canada through partnerships with various community organizations as well as fundraising. In the same vein, according to a review conducted by Streitwieser, Loo, Ohorodnic, and Jeong (2018), along with Germany, Canada has been "most notable" in terms of supporting refugees in accessing higher education (p. 20). This is a very positive sign, because higher education plays a key role in the successful integration of refugees into their host society, as such a process can have "wide ramifications for individual refugees, the refugee community, and the general common good" (MacLaren, 2010, p. 109), through leading to improved skills, increased empowerment, heightened confidence, and more cohesiveness among various communities (Crea, 2016).

Assessment of Credentials

A huge barrier for many refugees is the recognition of their qualifications in order to gain admission to educational institutions for further studies (CICIC, 2017, p. 8). Some key barriers that many refugees face in relation to assessment of their education qualification are: "incomplete or interrupted education, missing diplomas and other forms of documentation, an inability to verify documentation with the issuing institution; and the impact of war and disasters on quality of their accreditation (CICIC, 2017, p. 8)." Several new programs have been initiated by the government of Canada on foreign credential evaluation of refugees and new educational policies to support refugees while attending to their unique circumstances. In 2016, the Canadian Information Centre for International Credentials (CICIC) held a two-day national workshop on assessing the qualifications of refugees in Canada. Included among the

93 participants were members of the Alliance of Credential Evaluation Services of Canada (ACESC), professional regulatory bodies, postsecondary educational institutions, academic credential assessors, government departments and agencies, and recognition experts. The objective of this workshop was to assist refugees to enter the labor market and access further education by building knowledge on alternative ways of credential assessment. The workshop focused on the legal frameworks for assessing refugees' credentials, the risks faced by organizations assessing these qualifications, and issues faced by refugees who are going through this process.

In addition, the unique circumstances of individual countries were detailed (CICIC, 2017). For instance, refugees from Iraq, Syria, and Afghanistan each face similar but unique challenges based on their situation and country of origin. In the end, this workshop resulted in suggestions and approaches for best practices that are neither exhaustive nor mutually exclusive. It also highlighted the need for organizations to adopt a case-by-case approach for each of their clients. The guidelines are listed below:

1. Governance: assessment services should have procedures for alternative assessment processes when refugees can't provide documentation.
2. Building awareness: organizations should provide appropriate training to their staff to build understanding and their cultural competence to develop and carry out appropriate procedures specific to refugees' needs.
3. Eligibility: all applicants who don't have access to verifiable documentations of their qualifications for reasons beyond their control should have access to an alternative assessment of their qualification. Organizations should document their rationale for using an alternative approach in each case.
4. Minimum documentation required: many refugees may have access to some sort of documentation, such as student-issued copies of transcripts, or degrees etc.
5. Translation requirement: if and where organizations have the capacity to accept and review a document in its original language, requirements for official or certified translations may be waived.
6. Sworn affidavits: these should include the information needed to conduct an assessment, such as name, age, location, place of birth, attempts made to obtain documents, name of institution, titles, grades, etc.
7. Use of competency-based assessments: where applicable, eligible applicants should be given the opportunity to be assessed by an expert in the field when there is no documentation.
8. Use of prior learning assessment: recognition bodies should assess the applicant based on their competencies.

9. Sharing documents: with consent of the applicant this could assist with work and study opportunities.
10. Contacting institutions: sometimes if the refugee person is unable to contact the institutions, the Canadian agency may be able to contact them on the applicant's behalf.
11. Transparency and public communication: recognition bodies, where resources permit, are recommended to meet with prospective applicants by phone or person, to explain the process and determine the documentation.
12. Transparency in the assessment report: assessment services should provide a report for other recognition bodies about the basis of their assessment.
13. Fees: where possible, application fees should be waived or reduced for a refugee likely to have financial barriers. (CICIC, 2017).

Conclusion

Refugees who come to Canada can be categorized into three types: government-sponsored (GAR), privately sponsored (PSR), and Blended Visa Office Referred (BVOR). In addition, there are undocumented refugees who enter through the border between Canada and United States, as well as asylum-seekers. A refugee's status determines the amount of assistance and services he or she receives. For the first three categories who are given immigrant status, their health and education are free. Refugees generally come from countries with very different climates and cultures than Canada. They also have faced traumatic and life-threatening experiences, and their children and youth who must go to school face many barriers, including interrupted education in the pre-migratory phase. In school, they encounter a language of instruction which most often they do not know, and they face challenges due to their unpreparedness for the level of education for their age. This study attempts to identify policies and practices in the Canadian educational systems that increase refugee students' sense of belonging and contribute to their success in school.

One of the many challenges faced by refugees is encountering the involvement of several levels of administration. First, there is the federal government, which admits refugees into the country and assigns the government-sponsored refugees to different regions. After that, the refugees deal with the provincial governments. A further complication is that education is not a federal subject and provincial governments are responsible for educational policies as well as curriculum development and resources in the publicly funded schools. Policies at the highest level filter down through the provinces to the school boards and then to schools to influence students' learning as well as teacher education, their attitudes, and methods of practice.

The three examples showcased above clearly indicate that Canada's policies and social justice practices go a long way in setting the stage for an inclusive society. The national policy of multiculturalism, refugee law, and several legislated social policies impact Canadian society and its values. While federal policies serve as a guide, education is a provincial responsibility, and the various provinces have had different experiences with immigrants and refugee students; their policies vary in the extent to which they are attentive to the special needs of refugee children. However, most provinces are conscious of the need to develop in refugee children a feeling of belonging so that they can contribute to, as well as enjoy the rewards that Canada can provide. The recent group of Syrian refugees has brought attention to refugee education while also increasing awareness of their resilience and eagerness to get a good education. Provincial and school board policies as well as school practices are increasingly mindful that refugee students are capable of performing well in school despite their often traumatic past experience, and that they can be an asset to the community. Teachers, in particular, face severe challenges in helping refugee students adapt to the school environment; support from teachers and other adults, in addition to peer support, is of the utmost importance. The example of the school in Manitoba shows that compassion and care by the school administration, the teachers, and staff and the opportunity given to refugee students to share their experiences create an inclusive environment in the classroom and school. On the other hand, without such support, refugee children and youth and their families struggle to adapt to Canadian society and the school system.

While national and provincial policies guide practice at the school level, there are major constraints. Provincial and school board budgets, particularly in the smaller provinces, are not sufficient to develop the resources that are needed in the classrooms and schools for refugee children such as mental health professionals and assessments, dealing with trauma, and improved language learning. Most importantly, much more attention needs to be paid to improve teacher education so that teachers are able to understand trauma, identity confusion, help in language development, and prevent the marginalization of students—one of the main causes of dropping out and getting involved in oppositional activities. Professional development for in-service teachers is of crucial importance in order to meet these needs.

The majority of Canadians continue to support refugees who have left their home countries mainly due to war, persecution, and various forms of violence. On the whole, Canadian schools strive to give children and youth a safe place to live and learn and help them overcome the challenges they face as they adjust to a new language, unfamiliar schools, and a different culture. Many other countries are accepting large numbers of refugee students. Those who have had the experience of diverse societies and classrooms usually have developed some policies for inclusion. National policy guidance is crucial because it shows political will and acts as a moral force. All the stakeholders at all levels in the educational system must recognize the special needs of refugees and work with compassion and care toward their success in schools. Schools are social institutions and must have the support of the larger society to work together toward a peaceful and harmonious world.

Notes

1. For more information please see Finding Hope in Higher Education, https://srp.wusc.ca/about/
2. For more information please see http://bher.apps01.yorku.ca/about-bher/, www.bher.org/about-bher/dadaab-camps/ and Living, Learning and Teaching in Dadaab, http://lltd.educ.ubc.ca/media/dadaab-camps/

References

Ahmad, T. (2016). Refugee law and policy: Canada. *The Law Library of Congress*. Retrieved from www.loc.gov/law/help/refugee-law/canada.php

Amnesty International. (2012). *Unbalanced reforms: Recommendations for bill C-31*. Retrieved from www.amnesty.ca/get-involved/lead-in-your-community/unbalanced-reforms-recommendations-bill-c-31

Baffoe, M. (2006). *Navigating two worlds: Culture and cultural adaptation of immigrant and refugee youth in Quebec (Canadian) educational context* (PHD). School of Social Work and Department of Integrated Studies in Education. Retrieved from http://digitool.library.mcgill.ca/webclient/StreamGatefolder_id=0&dvs=151965921946,1~220.

Bagley, S. (2017). Is Canada a model for compassionate migration policy? In S. W. Bender & W. F. Arrocha (Eds.), *Compassionate migration and regional policy in the Americas* (pp. 193–216). London: Palgrave Macmillan.

Blanchet-Cohen, N., Denov, M., Fraser, S., & Bilotta, N. (2017). The nexus of war, resettlement and education: War-affected youth's perspectives and responses to the Quebec education system. *International Journal of Intercultural Relations*, 60, 160–168.

Bourdieu, P., & Passeron, J. (1990). *Reproduction in education, society and culture* (2nd ed.). London, England: Sage.

Boyd. M. (2002). Educational attainments of immigrant offspring: Success or segmented assimilation? *International Migration Review*, 36(4), 1037–1060.

Brewer, A. (2016). An outline for including refugees in Canadian educational policy. *Canadian Journal for New Scholars in Education*, 7(1), 133–141.

Burke, D. (2018, June 28). Does the Supreme Court have a double standard on religion? *CNN*. Retrieved from www.cnn.com/2018/06/26/politics/does-the-supreme-court-have-a-double-standard-on-religion/index.html

Canadian Council for Refugees. (2009). *A Brief history of Canada's responses to refugees*. Retrieved from http://ccrweb.ca/en/brief-history-canadas-responses-refugees

Canadian Information Centre for International Credentials (CICIC). (2017). *Assessing qualification of refugees: Best practices and guidelines*. Council of Ministers of Education, Canada. Retrieved from www.cmec.ca/Publications/Lists/Publications/Attachments/376/Best_Practices_and_Guielines.pdf

Capacity Building K-12. (2016, July). Supporting students with refugee backgrounds: A framework for responsive practice. *Ontario Ministry of Education*. Retrieved from www.edu.gov.on.ca/eng/literacynumeracy/inspire/research/cbs_refugees.pdf

CCR. (2012). *Concerns about changes to the refugee determination system*. Retrieved from http://ccrweb.ca/en/concerns-changes-refugee-determination-system

CCR. (2016). *Statement on blended visa officer referred refugees*. Retrieved from http://ccrweb.ca/en/BVOR-statement

Cheng, L., & Yan, W. (2018). Immigrant student achievement and educational policy in Canada. In L. Volante, D. Klinger, & O. Bilgili (Eds.), *Immigrant student achievement and education policy* (pp. 137–153). The Netherlands: Springer, Cham.

Citizenship and Immigration Canada. (2015, November). *Population profile: Syrian refugees*. Retrieved from http://lifelinesyria.ca/wp-content/uploads/2015/11/EN-Syrian-Population-Profile.pdf

Crea, T. (2016). Refugee higher education: Contextual challenges and implications for program design, delivery, and accompaniment. *International Journal of Educational Development, 46*, 12–22.

Drolet, J., & Moorthi, G. (2018). The settlement experiences of Syrian newcomers in Alberta: Social connections and interactions. *Canadian Ethnic Studies, 50*(2), 101–122.

Dawson, C. (2014). Refugee hotels: The discourse of hospitality and the rise of immigration detention in Canada, *University of Toronto Quarterly, 83*(4), 826–846.

Dryden-Peterson, S. (2011). Refugee education: A global review. *UNHCR, the UN Refugee Agency*. Retrieved from www.unhcr.org/hu/wp-content/uploads/sites/21/2016/12/Dryden_Refugee_Education_Global-Rvw.pdf

El-Assal, K. (2015, January 21). Why does Canada accept refugees? *The Conference Board of Canada*. Retrieved from www.conferenceboard.ca/commentaries/immigration/default/hot-topics-in-

Epp, M. (2017). Refugees in Canada: A brief history. *The Canadian Historical Association Immigration and Ethnicity in Canada Series, No.5*. Retrieved from www.cha-shc.ca/download.php?id=2488

Friesen, J. (2017, November 12). Syrian exodus to Canada: One year later, as look at who the refugees are and where they went. *The Globe and Mail*. Retrieved from www.theglobeandmail.com/news/national/syrian-refugees-in-canada-by-the-numbers/article33120934/

Gagné, A., Schmidt, C., & Markus, P. (2017). Teaching about refugees: Developing culturally responsive educators in contexts of politicised transnationalism. *Intercultural Education, 28*(5), 429–446.

Ghosh, R., & Galcznyski, M. (2014). *Redefining multicultural education: Inclusion and the right to be different* (3rd ed.). Toronto, Ontario: Canadian Scholars' Press.

Ghosh, R. (2017). *South Asian immigration to Canada in our immigration Saga: Canada @150: Canadian issues*. Spring Issue. Montreal: Association for Canadian Studies.

Ghosh, R. (2018). Multiculturalism in a comparative perspective: Australia, Canada and India. *Canadian Ethnic Studies Journal, 50*(1).

Ghosh, R., & Abdi, A. (2013). *Education and the politics of difference: Select Canadian perspectives* (2nd ed.). Toronto: Canadian Scholars' Press.

Gibney, M. J. (2004). *The ethics and politics of asylum: Liberal democracy and the response to refugees.* Cambridge: Cambridge University Press.

Government of Canada. (n.d.). Canadian multiculturalism: An inclusive citizenship. *Government of Canada.* Retrieved from https://web.archive.org/web/20140312210113/http:/www.cic.gc.ca/english/multiculturalism/citizenship.asp

Government of Canada. (2006). Guide to the Canadian Charter of Rights and Freedoms. *Human Rights Program, Canadian Heritage.* Archived from the original on 19 July 2006. https://web.archive.org/web/20060719192337/http:/www.pch.gc.ca/progs/pdp-hrp/canada/guide/general_e.cfm

Government of Canada. (2017, April 20). *Syrian refugee integration: One year after arrival.* Retrieved from www.canada.ca/en/immigration-refugees-citizenship/services/refugees/welcome-syrian-refugees/integration.html

Government of Canada. (2018a). *Canada: A history of refuge.* Retrieved from Government of Canada www.canada.ca/en/immigration-refugees-citizenship/services/refugees/canada-role/timeline.html

Government of Canada. (2018b). *2018 annual report to parliament on immigration.* Retrieved from www.canada.ca/en/immigration-refugees-citizenship/corporate/publications-manuals/annual-report-parliament-immigration-2018/report.html

Government of Manitoba. (2012). Life after war: Education as a Healing Process for refugee and war-affected children. *Manitoba Education School Programs Division.* Retrieved from www.edu.gov.mb.ca/k12/docs/support/law/full_doc.pdf

Gunderson, L. (2002). Voices of the teenage diasporas. *Journal of Adolescent & Adult Literacy, 43*(8), 692–706.

Hampshire, J. (2013). *The politics of immigration: Contradictions of the liberal state.* Cambridge: Polity Press.

Hanley, J., Hachey, A., & Tetrault, A. (2017, September 18). *Le droit international a l'education: un droit toujours brime pour les enfants sans statut au Quebec.* Le Reseau EdCan. Retrieved from www.edcan.ca/articles/le-droit-international-leducation/?lang=fr&fbclid=IwAR2nFtbyinYMUiyRJQarZyEEiW467eX_R5i0uzw8HDD4wC_ZmQls498AQhw

Hou, F., & Bonikowska, A. (2016). *Educational and labour market outcomes of childhood immigrants by admission class.* Retrieved from www.statcan.gc.ca/pub/11f0019m/11f0019m2016377-eng.htm

Human Rights Watch. (2012, March 16). *Letter to Canadian MP's on C-31 Law.* Retrieved from www.hrw.org/news/2012/03/16/letter-canadian-mps-c-31-law

Hyndman, J. (2014). *Refugee research synthesis 2009–2013.* Retrieved from http://ceris.ca/wp-content/uploads/2015/05/CERIS-Research-Synthesis-on-Refugees-19-May-2015.pdf

Hyndman, J., & Hynie, M. (2016). *From newcomer to Canadian: Making refugee integration work: The public forum for the public good.* Retrieved from http://policyoptions.irpp.org/magazines/may-2016/from-newcomer-to-canadian-making-refugee-integration-work/

Hynie, M. (2018). Canada's Syrian refugee program, intergroup relationships and identities. *Canadian Ethnic Studies*, *50*(2), 1–14.

Jeram, S., & Nicolaides, E. (2018). Intergovernmental relations on immigrant integration in Canada: Insights from Quebec, Manitoba, and Ontario. *Regional & Federal Studies*, 1–21. doi:10.1080/13597566.2018.1491841

Kanu, Y. (2008). Educational needs and barriers for African refugee students in Manitoba. *Canadian Journal of Education*, *31*(4), 915.

Kyriakides, C., Bajjali, L., McLuhan, A., & Anderson, K. (2018). Beyond refuge: Contested orientalism and persons of self-rescue. *Canadian Ethnic Studies*, *50*(2), 59–78.

Labman, S., & Pearlman, M. (2018). Blending, bargaining, and burden-sharing: Canada's resettlement programs. *Journal of International Migration and Integration*, *19*(12), 439–449.

Lenard, P. T. (2016). Resettling refugees: Is private sponsorship a just way forward? *Journal of Global Ethics*, *12*(3), 300–310.

Loo, B., Streitwieser, B., & Jeong, J. (2018, February 6). Higher education's role in national refugee integration: Four cases. *World Education News + Reviews*. Retrieved from https://wenr.wes.org/2018/02/higher-educations-role-national-refugee-integration-four-cases

Lopour, J., & Thompson, A. S. (2016, September 20). This is Canada's opportunity to improve education for refugees. *Huffington Post*. Retrieved from www.huffingtonpost.ca/jacqueline-lopour/canada-refugee-education_b_12085938.html

MacKay, T., & Tavares, T. (2005). *Building hope: Appropriate programming for adolescent and young adult newcomers of war-affected backgrounds and Manitoba schools: A preliminary report for consultation and discussion*. Retrieved from www.edu.gov.mb.ca/k12/cur/ diver-sity/eal/building_hope.pdf

Macklin, A., Barber, K., Goldring, L., Hyndman, J., Kortewag, A., Labman, S., & Zyfi, J. (2018). A preliminary investigation into private refugee sponsors. *Canadian Ethnic Studies*, *50*(2), 35–57.

MacLaren, D. (2010). Tertiary education for refugees: A case study from the Thai-Burma border. *Refuge*, *27*(2), 103–110.

MacNevin, J. (2012). Learning the way: Teaching and learning with and for youth from refugee backgrounds on Prince Edward Island. *Canadian Journal of Education*, *35*(3), 48–63.

Manitoba Education and Advanced Learning. (2015). Building hope: Refugee learner narratives. *Minister of Education and Advanced Learning, Government of Manitoba*. Retrieved from www.edu.gov.mb.ca/k12/docs/support/building_hope/building_hope_interactive.pdf

Markusoff, J. (2018, August 3). Why the explosive debate over asylum seekers could define the next federal election. *Macleans*. Retrieved from www.macleans.ca/news/canada/why-the-explosive-debate-over-asylum-seekers-could-define-the-next-federal-election/

McCallum, J. (2018). *Canada has a proud history of doing the right thing for refugees*. Retrieved from www.theglobeandmail.com/opinion/canada-has-a-proud-history-of-doing-the-right-thing-for-refugees/article27475500/

McGrath, S., & McGrath, I. (2013). Funding matters: The maze of settlement funding in Canada and the impact on refugee services. *Canadian Journal of Urban Research*, *22*(1), 1–20.

McKenna, K. (2017 August 2). Montreal's Olympic Stadium used to house surge in asylum seekers crossing from U.S. *CBC News*. Retrieved from www.cbc.ca/news/canada/montreal/olympic-stadium-houses-asylum-seekers-1.4231808

Meloni, F., Rousseau, C., Ricard-Guay, A., & Hanley, J. (2016). Invisible students: Institutional invisibility and access to education for undocumented children. *International Journal of Migration, Health and Social Care*, *13*(1), 15–25.

Nakhaie, M. R. (2018). Service needs of immigrants and refugees. *International Migration and Integration*, *19*(1), 143–160.

Noddings, N. (1984). *Caring, a feminine approach to ethics & moral education*. Berkeley: University of California Press.

Nourpanah, S. (2014). A study of the experiences of integration and settlement of Afghan government-assisted refugees in Halifax, Canada. *Refuge: Canada's Journal on Refugees*, *30*(1), 57–66.

OCASI, Bill C-32 Must Be Withdrawn. (n.d.). Retrieved from www.ocasi.org/bill-c-31-must-be-withdrawn

Ontario College Teachers. (2014, February 7). *College formalizes certification requirements related to Ontario's enhanced teacher education plans*. Retrieved from www.oct.ca/public/media/announcements/enhanced-ed

Ontario Ministry of Education. (2014a). *Equity and inclusive education in Ontario schools: Guidelines for policy development and implementation*. Toronto: Queen's Printer for Ontario.

Ontario Ministry of Education. (2014b). *Achieving excellence: A renewed vision for education in Ontario*. Toronto: Queen's Printer for Ontario.

Paling, E. (2017, January 29). Trudeau tells refugees: "Canadians will welcome you." *Huffington Post Canada*. Retrieved from www.huffingtonpost.ca/2017/01/28/trudeau-refugees_n_14461906.html

Paradis, J., Genesee, F., & Crago, M. B. (2011). *Dual language development and disorders: A handbook on bilingualism and second language learning* (2nd ed.). Baltimore, MD: Paul H. Brookes Publishing.

Perreaux, L. (2018, March 22). Canadian attitudes towards immigrants, refugees remain positive: Study. *The Globe and Mail*. Retrieved from www.theglobeandmail.com/canada/article-canadian-attitudes-toward-immigrants-refugees-remain-positive-study/

Pillay, T., & Asadi, N. (2012). *Participatory action research and educational liberation for refugee youth in Canada*. Paper presented at the Canadian Society for Studies in Education Annual Conference, Waterloo, ON.

Pressé, D., & Thomson, J. (2007). The resettlement challenge: Integration of refugees from protracted refugee situations. *Refuge: Canada's Journal on Refugees*, *24*(2), 48–53.

Puzic, A. (2017). *Record number of refugees admitted to Canada in 2016, highest since 1980*. Retrieved from www.ctvnews.ca/canada/record-number-of-refugees-admitted-to-canada-in-2016-highest-since-1980-1.3382444

Richardson, E., MacEwen, L., & Naylor, R. (2018). *Teachers of refugees: A review of the literature*. Highbridge House, Berkshire: UK: Education Development Trust.

Ruban, F. (2017). Welcoming refugee children to the Alberta classroom. *Alberta Teachers' Association*, *12*(1), 1–22. Retrieved from www.teachers.ab.ca/SiteCollectionDocuments/ATA/Publications/Human-Rights-Issues/Just-In-Time/Just%20in%20Time%2012–1%20(April%202017).pdf

Salehyan, I., & Rosenblum, M. R. (2008). International relations, domestic politics, and asylum admissions in the United States. *Political Research Quarterly*, *61*(1), 104–121.
Settlement Workers in Schools. (2018, March 26). Settlement at work. *WIKI*. Retrieved from http://wiki.settlementatwork.org/index.php/Settlement_Workers_in_Schools_%28SWIS%29
Shakya, Y. B., Guruge, S., Hynie, M., Akbari, A., Malik, M., Htoo, S., . . . Alley, S. (2010). Aspirations for higher education among newcomer refugee youth in Toronto: Expectations, challenges, and strategies. *Refuge*, *27*(2), 65–78.
Shugerman, E. (2018, June 26). Supreme Court upholds Trump travel ban from several Muslim-majority countries. *Independent*. Retrieved from www.independent.co.uk/news/world/americas/us-politics/supreme-court-travel-ban-trump-upholds-countries-muslim-ruling-latest-a8417781.html
Social Progress Index. (2018). *Social progress imperative*. Retrieved from www.socialprogress.org/
Stewart, J. (2011). *Supporting refugee children: Strategies for educators*. Toronto: University of Toronto Press.
Stewart, J. (2017). *A culture of care and compassion for refugee students: Creating a state of nhân dao*. Education Canada Network. Retrieved from http://www.cea-ace.ca/educationcanada/article/culture-care-and-compassion-refugee-students
Stewart, J., & Martin, L. (2018). *Bridging two worlds: Supporting newcomer and refugee youth A guide to Curriculum implementation and integration*. Toronto: CERIC Foundation House.
Stewart, M., Anderson, J., Beiser, M., Mwakarimba, E., Neufeld, A., Simich, L., & Spitzer, D. (2008). Multicultural meanings of social support among immigrants and refugees. *International Migration*, *46*(3), 123–159.
Stewart, M., Dennis, C. L., Kariwo, K. E., Kushner, N., Letourneau, K., Makwarimba, E., & Shizha, E. (2015). Challenges faced by refugee new parents from Africa in Canada. *Journal of Immigrant and Minority Health*, *17*(4), 1146–1156.
Streitwieser, B., Loo, B., Ohorodnic, M., & Jeong, J. (2018). *Access to higher education for refugees: A review of interventions in North America and Europe*. Graduate School of Education & Human Development, George Washington University. Retrieved from https://gsehd.gwu.edu/sites/default/files/documents/working_paper_2_bernhard_streitwieser_final_3.25.18_3.pdf
Sunderland, A., & Findlay, L. C. (2013). *Perceived need for mental health care in Canada: Results from the 2012 Canadian community health survey: Mental health*. Statistics Canada. Retrieved from www.mooddisorders.ca/sites/mooddisorders.ca/files/downloads/mentalhealth_statcan11863-eng.pdf
Trudeau, J. (2015, November 26). *Diversity is our strength, address by the Right Honourable Justin Trudeau, Prime Minister of Canada*. Retrieved from https://pm.gc.ca/eng/news/2015/11/26/diversity-canadas-strength
Villegas, F. J. (2016). "Access without fear"! Reconceptualizing "access" to schooling for undocumented students in Toronto. *Critical Sociology*, *43*(7–8), 1179–1195.
WES (World Education Services). (2018). *Refugee access to higher education*. Retrieved from https://wenr.wes.org/wp-content/uploads/2018/02/Feb18_LSJ1.png
Wilkinson, L. A. (2001). *The integration of refugee youth in Canada*. Retrieved from www.collectionscanada.gc.ca/obj/s4/f2/dsk3/ftp04/NQ60357.pdf

Wilkinson, L. A., & Garcea, J. (2017). *The economic integration of refugees in Canada: A mixed record*. Washington, DC: Migration Policy Institute.

Wilkinson, L. A., Garcea, J., Bhattacharyya, P., Abdul-Karim, A., & Riziki, A. (2017, June 27). *Resettling in the Canadian prairies: A survey of Syrian refugees in Canada's prairies: A final report submitted by immigration refugees and citizenship Canada-integration branch, prairies & Northern territories.* Edmonton, Alberta: Alberta Association of Immigrant Serving Agencies. Retrieved from https://umanitoba.ca/faculties/arts/research/media/Syrian_refugee_report.pdf

Wright, T. (2018, June 4). Ottawa to give $50 million to Quebec, Ontario and Manitoba for asylum-seeker costs. *The Canadian Press*. Retrieved from https://globalnews.ca/news/4248111/ottawa-to-give-50m-to-quebec-ontario-and-manitoba-for-asylum-seeker-costs-2/

Yiu, G. (2016, March 28). Conservatives' bills continue to haunt immigrants and refugees. *Huffington Post*. Retrieved from www.huffingtonpost.ca/gabriel-yiu/bill-c-31_b_9555414.html

Young, L. (2017, August 23). Asylum seekers get health-care benefits first, and eligibility questions later. *Global News*. Retrieved from https://globalnews.ca/news/3690481/asylum-seekers-benefits-eligibility/

Zilio, M. (2018, August 14). Illegal border crossings from U.S increase by nearly 23 per cent from June to July. *The Globe and Mail*. Retrieved from www.theglobeandmail.com/politics/article-illegal-border-crossings-from-us-increase-by-nearly-23-per-cent-from/

5 A Comparative Policy Analysis of the Comprehensive Refugee Response Framework in Uganda and Kenya

Tshegofatso D. Thulare, Christin Spoolstra, Eileen Dombrowski, Rachel Jordan, and Rehemah Nabacwa

A Comparative Policy Analysis of the Comprehensive Refugee Response Framework in Uganda and Kenya

There are an estimated 16.1 million refugees around the world as calculated by the United Nations High Commission for Refugees (UNHCR), and fewer than 1% are submitted for resettlement. Instead, the vast majority of the world's refugees—86%—are hosted in developing regions, with more than a quarter in the world's least developed countries (UNHCR, 2015). Running counter to the narrative that the West is bearing the burden of resettlement, 80% of refugees are hosted in countries next to their country of origin, and just 10 countries are hosting 60% of the world's refugees (Dempsey, 2018; UNHCR, 2018d). As stated in a report commissioned by the UNHCR, "access to education is a basic human right and is linked to poverty reduction, holding promises of stability, economic growth, and better lives for children, families, and communities" (Dryden-Peterson, 2011, p. 8). However, education in many refugee camps remains inconsistent and unstable, and there remains a disconnect between the proclamation of "education for all" and the experience of children living in refugee camps. With 52% of refugees worldwide under the age of 18, this crisis will be generationally compounded, and many in the field are concerned not just with this lost generation but also with future peace and stabilization efforts in the refugees' countries of origin (Türk, 2016; Martinez, 2018). Of the 7.4 million school-aged children under the UNHCR's mandate, over half are out of school (UNHCR, 2018e). As president of the World Bank Jim Yong Kim warns, "the consequences of inaction will haunt us for generations" (Martinez, 2018, para 17).

Current efforts at providing safety, refuge, and basic sanitation for displaced people are failing, and the ability to provide consistent and quality education opportunities even more so. A radical change in how countries respond to the ever-growing crisis is needed. The Comprehensive Refugee Response Framework (CRRF) is currently being piloted by the UNHCR as that paradigm shift. The CRRF is the mechanism for implementing the ideals of the 2016 New York Declaration for Refugees and Migrants (NY Declaration). The role of education in this push, particularly expanding the enrollment of refugees in primary through tertiary institutions will be crucial to realizing the end goal of "enhanced self-reliance" for displaced people, also allowing them to meaningfully contribute to their host communities (UNHCR, 2018c). Questions remain about whether this envisaged all-encompassing framework is that radical response the world has been waiting for. For those in the field of Education in Emergencies, it remains to be seen whether this declaration will lead to the political will needed to enact its goals within the countries it targets.

Given this uncertainty in a fast-changing policy landscape with multiple actors and messages emanating from different parts of the international arena, this study looks to answer the question: What do the perspectives of implementers tell us about the ability of host countries to incorporate the objectives of the CRRF into national policy? Understanding what the CRRF is asking of education will be a mammoth task with serious implications for host nations' education plans and their ability to provide adequately and equitably. Within this context, we seek to synthesize the grand ideals of the CRRF through the perspectives of multiple implementers, policymakers, and education experts from two piloting countries in the horn of Africa, Uganda and Kenya. This synthesis guides an initial reflection of the implications of adopting the CRRF's values through a thoughtful discussion on the current anxieties implementers and policymakers share as pilot rollout occurs in Uganda and Kenya.

Key Informant Interviews (KIIs) with individuals who work on the ground were conducted in both these countries. Informants identified work directly in implementation of local public education and education for displaced people or are in positions that give strategic guidance to such provision. The research presented is intended to inform both local and international actors while contributing a sober reflection for policymakers and implementers about the very real considerations those on the ground face.

Methodology and Structure

The study is structured into three sections. Section I is a textual analysis of the CRRF and the UN policies related to the creation and adoption of the Framework. Identifying and presenting these key documents, the section brings together discrete foundational documents that outline the main tenets of the Framework while situating the events that led to the development of the CRRF as it stands. Documents consulted span from the time the NY Declaration was signed in September 2016 and include official and draft versions of the pending Global Compact on Refugees as they have built upon each other. Drafts and final versions published on key UN websites and portals were treated as official international policy intentions and were tracked to highlight where and when intentions changed. The analysis also kept in mind that some of these documents were works-in-progress and will continue to change over the next few years; thus the limitations to the comprehensiveness of this synthesis should be noted. Given the multitude of policies and international conventions that govern the status of refugee and displaced people in the global arena, key priority was given to recent UN policies that made mention of the Global Compact on Refugees and the CRRF. The section concludes by highlighting the guiding core objectives of the CRRF: (1) reduce strain on host countries; (2) increase self-reliance among refugees; (3) increase opportunities for third country solutions; and (4) strengthen conditions for repatriation to countries of origin (UN, 2016, p. 20).

Section II takes a closer look at Uganda and Kenya to answer our guiding question: What do the perspectives of on-the-ground implementers and policymakers tell us about the ability of host countries to incorporate the objectives of the CRRF into national policy? The informant discussions are organized under the Framework's core objectives as a way to give structure to their reflections. The countries are chosen because both have played major roles in providing sanctuary for neighboring countries and are both one of the 13 countries to pilot the CRRF. Both countries have a history of providing education for citizens alongside established refugee settlements where education programming has been a feature, but they differ vastly in how they have provided this education. The national policy framework and initiatives of both countries make for a particularly rich comparison given the differences in starting points and institutional mechanisms that can be leveraged during their pilot participation. Thus, the analysis uses the four core objectives of the Framework to describe the experience of each country's CRRF participation against current national education efforts. It concludes with a discussion that compares these experiences while also commenting on the grand ideals of the Framework.

Officials interviewed included representatives from national education ministries, key international donor organizations, and members of UN agencies. For the purposes of anonymity, names, official designations, and institutional affiliations are not cited in this study, but a coded list with general descriptions of their designations and key takeaways from their interviews is provided in Appendix 1. Quotations have been paraphrased by the interviewers and member-checked by the informant in question. As policy and program implementers are deeply aware of the needs of displaced people as well as the balancing of state development priorities, their expertise was sought to help reflect on the CRRF's grand task of countries long-embroiled in their own economic woes. Given how early it is in implementation of the CRRF across both countries, some of the perspectives shared may be speculative. However, they are an important addition to the conversation, due to the implementers' varied experience within the contexts and history of being witness to the multiple reform efforts and response plans before this Framework. Prioritizing the voices of those embedded in such deep knowledge while reflecting on the possible outcomes of a policy is necessary to informing dialog on the current crisis. But, before the CRRF policy is outlined, it is important to situate the call for education in the drive to provide basic human rights for displaced people.

Overview of the Problem: The Drive to Provide

Since the adoption of the Universal Declaration of Human Rights, the enshrinement of education in Article 26 as a basic human right for all has been well accepted and arguably forms the backbone to the strong calls to educate forcibly displaced persons (UNHCR & Global Education Monitoring Report, 2016). Multiple theoretical positions have helped place the education of refugees at the center of the crisis. Some have focused on the human development imperative for successful integration and psychological well-being (Anderson, Hamilton, Moore, Loewen & Frater-Mathieson, 2004). Known as the mental health perspective, this view places significance on the recovery of children that have gone through loss and trauma and the healing role that education can play. Through regularity and community-based healing, the perspective holds that a sense of balance can and must be restored to children in crisis (Sinclair, 2001). The second perspective has focused on the need to acclimatize and support refugees during displacement and resettlement (Anderson et al., 2004). Placing significance on the role education can have in dealing with language and cultural barriers faced during their transition and early settlement lives, the emphasis here is on education as a tool for refugees. Closely associated is the perspective that rationalizes the need to expand education to allow refugees access to job opportunities and economic readiness for their integration into new communities.

The perspectives above are underpinned by a human rights based framework that fully accepts the Universal Declaration and commits to ensuring its realization. The United Nations, through the UNHCR and other agencies, has been a pivotal actor in facilitating the relief efforts of displaced people. Education is critical to the UNHCR's approach to ending the intergenerational impact of refugee status, as education provides normalcy and leads to healing from trauma (UNHCR, 2018e). A senior member of the UNHCR touts education as vital to international security and as key to a durable solution to the conflicts producing the refugee crisis:

> Educated refugees provide leadership in displacement situations and in rebuilding communities recovering from conflict. Through education, refugees can become agents of social transformation. The future

security of individuals and of our societies is inextricably connected to the transferable skills, knowledge, and capacities that are developed through quality education.

(Türk, 2016, p. 10)

However, despite such claims and the fact that access to education is often listed as a primary need by refugees themselves, it is rarely prioritized in relief efforts, and less than 2% of funding for refugee support is spent on the education sector (Education Cannot Wait, n.d.).

Section I

The Comprehensive Refugee Response Framework: A Policy Synopsis

Currently, the UN is leading a formalized paradigm shift in the management of the global refugee crisis. Moving away from encampment and a traditional relief lens, the UN is now promoting a more holistic development approach that integrates refugees with host populations and promotes more sustainable solutions for both refugee and host populations (Uganda, The World Bank, & UNHCR, 2016b; UNHCR Uganda, 2017). In September 2016, all 193 members of the United Nations signed the NY Declaration during a General Assembly to "strengthen the international response to the global refugee crisis and grow support to meet the needs of refugee and host communities" (Action for Refugee Education, 2018, p. 1).

A critical component to achieving this goal is for the international community to commit to "a more equitable sharing of the burden and responsibility for hosting and supporting the world's refugees" (UN, 2016, p. 13). Included in an annex to the NY Declaration was the CRRF. Taken together, these agreements commit to protecting the rights of refugees and to supporting their host countries (UNHCR, n.d.a). In extending beyond the relief model to reflect a "whole of society approach" (UNHCR Uganda, 2017, p. 5), the UNHCR is attempting to address the mismatch between the sustainability of refugee care and the development concerns of the host population (Patton, 2016b). The intention is to have the CRRF guide the country-specific response plans, including response plans for refugee education.

Since host countries are often vulnerable populations tasked with the care of incoming refugee communities, this UN agreement seeks durable solutions that take into consideration host population needs and realities (Uganda, The World Bank, & UNHCR, 2016b, 2013). The CRRF outlines four primary objectives: (1) reduce strain on host countries; (2) increase self-reliance among refugees; (3) increase opportunities for third country solutions; and (4) strengthen conditions for repatriation to countries of origin (UN, 2016, p. 20). It serves as a guide for nations, public and private stakeholders, as well as refugees themselves to coordinate together, removing the traditional parallel systems of humanitarian and development aid to achieve durable solutions under common principles (UNHCR Uganda, 2017; UNHCR, 2018c). An example of what a multi-stakeholder approach might look like, one that is truly integrated into national state structures, is Ethiopia. Similar to the Department of Refugees in the Office of the Prime Minister in Uganda, a government ministry in Ethiopia has been set up specifically for the purposes of handling the refugee crisis. The Administration for Refugee and Returnees Affairs (ARRA) leads the coordination effort with the international aid community, acting as the authority and voice of the government. Working through an inter-agency task force led in conjunction with the UNHCR Ethiopia, the ARRA participates on the following task forces that enforce the UNHCR's Regional Response Strategy; health, nutrition, protection, security, shelter/infrastructure, water sanitation and hygiene known as the WASH program, and education (UNHCR, 2016c). A partner implementation model is used where various local and international donor organizations and NGOs participate in the task forces, and each is responsible for specific programs for the camps they work in. Thus, education for refugees in Ethiopia is largely driven by these partners with recent efforts by the ARRA to collaborate with the Federal Ministry of Education to establish an Education Management Information System (EMIS) to integrate refugee data with the national education system (UNHCR, 2016c). Focusing on refugees' development as opposed to the traditional emergency relief model is intended to contribute to refugees' self-reliance and skill development, allowing for more solutions in their countries of origin upon voluntary repatriation (UNHCR, 2018c).

The United Nations intends to follow the NY Declaration with a Global Compact on Refugees (GCR), specifying commitments and approaches to ensure the success of the vision put forth by the NY Declaration. This GCR, which is expected to be signed in December 2018, contains two major components: (1) the already-published CRRF and (2) the advice gleaned from the Framework's implementation in pilot countries on how to operationalize and contextualize the CRRF and the ideals of the NY Declaration (UNHCR, n.d.b). Guided by the Sustainable Development Goals' pledge to "leave no one behind" (UNHCR, n.d.a, p. 2), the GCR seeks to "operationalize the principles of burden- and responsibility-sharing" to protect the rights of the refugees while also supporting host communities (UNHCR, 2018c, p. 2).

The CRRF and subsequent GCR echo the commitments made in the NY Declaration to provide quality education from primary through secondary. This would include ensuring that refugee children are enrolled within a few months of their initial displacement as well as providing for early childhood education and tertiary and vocational opportunities

(UN, 2016). While education is specifically addressed only three times within the text of the CRRF, it is a critical component of the UNHCR's new strategic self-reliance approach and a key strategy for advancing the social cohesion between refugees and host populations. Thus, education is critical to the success of the CRRF's principle of an integrated development approach (Türk, 2017).

In 2017, 13 countries agreed to apply the CRRF, with Uganda being among the first to commit (International Review of the Red Cross, 2017). In fact, many of the principles enshrined in the NY Declaration and operationalized in the CRRF have been embedded in Uganda's approach to refugee management for decades. The CRRF is even being tested in regional responses to crises such as the Somalia situation, to which Djibouti, Ethiopia, Uganda, and the United Republic of Tanzania have agreed to work together in addressing the crises by following the principles of the CRRF (UNHCR, n.d.a). However, Tanzania has since dropped out of the commitment, citing severe underfunding as a barrier to their continuation (Tanzania Withdraws from UNHCR Comprehensive Refugee Response Framework, 2018). These initial applications of the CRRF will guide the formation of the Global Compact on Refugees and advise future applications of the CRRF (UNHCR, 2018b).

From the above, it is seen that the CRRF is pushing more than any other proposed initiative, as its promulgators claim to challenge countries, specifically host countries, to modify their own policies and development programs to include displaced people and thereby merge the emergency relief world with that of the political, economic, and social development structures in their countries. To understand what this means for these countries, we turn our attention toward the case studies.

Section II

The CRRF and Refugee Education: Policy Assessment in Uganda and Kenya

Ugandan Refugee Context

Uganda has, relative to its gross domestic product (GDP), the highest refugee population in Africa (UNHCR Uganda, 2017) with refugees in some regions accounting for one-third of the total population (Uganda, The World Bank, & UNHCR, 2016b). Since 1961, Uganda has hosted an annual average of 168,000 refugees (Uganda, The World Bank, & UNHCR, 2016b), but as of July 2017 there were over 1.3 million refugees within Uganda (UNHCR Uganda, 2017), having fled from South Sudan, the DRC, Burundi, Somalia, Rwanda, and other countries (UNHCR, 2017). Refugees in Uganda are granted rights often denied in other neighbor-hosts: the right to documentation, to work, to movement, and to education (UNHCR, 2016b; Patton, 2016a). As a key informant from a local government agency observes, this attitude is rooted in a history of fluid movement across borders (KII 5, 2018). However, poverty among refugees in settlement districts impacts the economy of the surrounding communities, which are typically already less developed than other parts of the country (Uganda, The World Bank, & UN Uganda, 2017b). When refugees were supported while neighboring Ugandans went without, the disparity was viewed by many to be "morally repugnant" (Uganda, The World Bank, & UNHCR, 2016a, p. 20). To rectify that imbalance and promote social cohesion between the two populations, Uganda created a 70–30 rule in which at least 30% of refugee-aid must be allotted for host communities (Patton, 2016a). A 2016 assessment of Uganda's refugee management revealed 81% of Ugandans believe their country is doing well with refugee management, and 89% believe that Uganda is setting a positive example for the rest of the world (International Rescue Committee [IRC], 2018).

Uganda is known for its self-reliance and resilience approach to refugee management (Patton, 2016b). The CRRF in many ways reflects Uganda's Refugee and Host Population Empowerment (ReHoPE) framework, which began implementation in 2016, as well as long-applied refugee management approaches of self-reliance and sustainability (Gouby, 2017). Education services for refugees are integrated into Uganda's public education systems (Patton, 2016a), and refugees, along with Ugandans, legally have universal access to primary and secondary schooling.

Despite a well-praised policy, refugee education in Uganda still faces significant barriers, primarily access, education workforce, and school infrastructure, all of which will be examined below through the lens of CRRF Uganda (UNHCR, 2013). At the most basic level, too few funds have meant too few schools are available. Primary schools serving refugees on average have a child-classroom ratio of 150:1. Funding limitations also result in shortages in teaching and learning resources, including textbooks (Uganda, UN, & UNHCR, 2017). Ultimately, "inadequate and insufficient infrastructure drives down enrollment, retention and achievement rates" (UNHCR, 2013, p. 13). As such, 57% of school-aged refugees are not in school (Uganda, 2018).

CRRF Uganda: Case Study Discussion

Uganda officially launched the CRRF in March 2017 (UNHCR Uganda, 2017), becoming the first country to commit to applying their contextualized CRRF (International Review of the Red Cross, 2017). In fact, Uganda's strategic approach to refugee self-reliance predates the NY Declaration by two decades and partly inspired the development of the CRRF (Gouby, 2017). For Uganda, the CRRF means a continuation of their strategic approach and building on existing programs to "harness a whole-of-society approach" (Uganda, 2018, p. 7). Uganda's application of the CRRF to refugee education can be examined through two primary programs: The ReHoPE Strategic Framework and the Education Response Plan (ERP). ReHoPE is designed as a "self-reliance and resilience strategic framework" for engaging both communities more actively as agents in their own development (UNHCR, 2016b, p. 16; Patton, 2016b). Basic services for refugees are merged with those for the local populations, such as handing over the UNHCR-run schools to the district education offices (Patton, 2016b). Building upon ReHoPE's work to integrate refugees into the local education systems, the education-specific component of the CRRF in Uganda is their newly released Education Response Plan for 2018–2021. The ERP responds to current obstacles and planned responses to ensure that both refugee and Ugandan children have access to quality education at all levels, including early childhood and tertiary education, in order to respond to past access barriers stemming from lack of infrastructure and human resources (UNHCR, 2018a). CRRF Uganda is now analyzed by its contextualized approach to achieving the CRRF's four objectives.

CRRF OBJECTIVE 1: REDUCE STRAIN ON HOST COUNTRIES

With limited international support, the continued influx of refugees entering Uganda stretches already limited resources and threatens the self-reliance strategy so central to Uganda's policies (UNHCR Uganda, 2017). A rapidly increasing refugee population is pushing Uganda back into the relief paradigm of aid to focus almost solely on "urgent, life-saving needs" such as food, shelter, water and sanitation, and sexual- and gender-based violence prevention and response (UNHCR, 2016b, p. 69, 2016c). Livelihood and stabilization programs critical to a self-reliance approach are among those from which funds have been re-appropriated (UNHCR, 2016b). In addition to overcrowded classrooms, a growing refugee population also means an inability to keep up with the demand for school infrastructure and teacher certification, resulting in poor learning outcomes. The ERP estimates an additional 3,000 classrooms and 1,750 teachers are needed to reach the government standards for appropriate student-to-classroom and student-to-teacher ratios within the current ERP target areas (Uganda, 2018). The ERP intends to address many of the shortcomings in the current education system, focusing on many of the challenges that arose from formalizing education integration under ReHoPE. Key informants, though, doubt whether there is enough local buy-in to implement integrated education as well as if there is enough communication among aid agencies and government institutions to work on a singular plan toward unified outcomes objectives (KII 3, 2018; KII 6, 2018).

Key informant interviews also reveal several concerns with the ERP's ability to address these issues sustainably. Already Uganda is behind schedule for school construction, and beyond that, there is uncertainty as to which agency should build infrastructure in an integrated model: Should it be external agencies or should the government itself be taking on this responsibility? (KII 3, 2018). Merging both agency- and government-run development systems largely meant for Ugandans with humanitarian systems for refugees creates a tension between the former parallel systems, which is a common theme in the KIIs. The integrated approach, which is so critical to the CRRF, relies upon the provision of schooling through existing Ugandan systems. However, some programs, such as accelerated learning and early childhood education programs, are still operating parallel to government schools and run by relief agencies and NGOs (KII 4, 2018). While access has been extended to Ugandan students, both programs are viewed as being primarily an advantage for refugee students, so, as discussed in the ERP, they have created a point of contention for parliamentarians and other government actors (Uganda, 2018; KII 2, 2018; KII 3, 2018). In addressing access concerns in these parallel systems, key informants doubt the government's willingness to raise the cap on teacher positions as an increasing number of teachers means higher annual expenditures for the Ugandan government. Instead, Uganda has been relying upon aid organizations to provide classroom assistants, particularly to address the multilingual classrooms which arise in this integrated approach (KII 6, 2018).

The CRRF is meant to reduce the resource burden on host countries, but Uganda's first Solidarity Summit on Refugees resulted in only $350 million in pledges, contrasted with the goal of $2 billion (Alfred, 2017). This underwhelming response supports the belief of 91% of Ugandans that their country has "taken on a larger share of the responsibility and cost of hosting refugees compared to other countries" (IRC, 2018, p. 13). Unless the ERP is sufficiently supported to address foundational concerns of access such as classroom and teacher shortages, learning outcomes for students from refugee and host populations are threatened (Uganda, 2018). Many of the recommendations within the ERP and Uganda's CRRF rely upon making improvements that will create long-term costs of care and upkeep on behalf of the Ugandan government. As international funding support is scarce, as evidenced by the low financial commitments made at the recent Solidarity Summit, Uganda has been hesitant about making such improvements and addressing barriers to refugee education.

CRRF OBJECTIVE 2: INCREASE SELF-RELIANCE AMONG REFUGEES

Educational achievement is a critical component of the CRRF's self-reliance approach to durable solutions. Not only is it a positive tool for the mental health of refugee children, which helps address the long-term consequences of the conflict (Lutheran World Federation, 2015), but within Uganda secondary education and beyond has been shown to correlate with an increase in employment status (Uganda, The World Bank, & UNHCR, 2016a). Traditionally, educational opportunities for refugees were prioritized at the primary level; however, the NY Declaration calls for increased attention to early childhood education as well as tertiary education, including vocational training, because higher education "acts as a catalyst for the recovery and rebuilding of post-conflict countries" (UN, 2016, p. 15). While the Education Response Plan does call for increased support for pre-primary education, it also includes cuts from adolescent and psychosocial response programming (KII 6, 2018), both of which are key to the mental health perspective of refugee education. Despite calls for increased secondary school access, primary school access is still the main focus of implementers. However, a 2016 assessment revealed that a primary-level education only had limited impact on a refugee's employment status and earning capacity (Uganda, The World Bank, & UNHCR, 2016a), so a prioritized inclusion of secondary and vocational education is needed to achieve the CRRF's second objective of increased self-reliance among refugees.

To transition away from the temporary humanitarian relief lens to a self-reliance lens (Uganda, The World Bank, & UN Uganda, 2017a), ReHoPE builds upon the 70–30 rule by replacing the parallel systems of development and humanitarian relief with integrated ones (Uganda, The World Bank, & UNHCR, 2016a). As part of a self-reliance model intended to improve conditions in refugee communities, relieve some of the burden on the host communities, and equip refugees with skills needed for eventual repatriation (Refugee and Host Population Empowerment [ReHoPE], n.d.), refugees will begin to pay for some of these integrated services, including education (Patton, 2016b). Given 61% of refugees in Uganda are under 18 years of age (UNHCR Uganda, 2017), this self-reliance approach raises unique concerns. Many children who have dropped out of school cite feeling overworked as they have more duties at home for agriculture production (another key component of the self-reliance strategy) (Bouscaren, 2016). Furthermore, 85% of children not enrolled in school explained that they could not afford the school fees and related expenses (Uganda, The World Bank, & UNHCR, 2016a). Another criticism of this self-reliance narrative is that the policy is in danger of viewing self-reliance as the inverse of dependency. Previously, a self-reliance policy shift in a Ugandan settlement district was fraught with challenges, as refugees were fearful to be seen as independent and risk losing support from both the UNHCR and the government of Uganda (Easton-Calabria & Omata, 2018).

CRRF OBJECTIVE 3: INCREASE OPPORTUNITIES FOR THIRD COUNTRY SOLUTIONS

For 2017 and 2018 combined, UNHCR estimated that 104,200 refugees in Uganda were in need of resettlement as part of the CRRF's key pillar of durable solutions (UNHCR Uganda, 2017). With Uganda as a CRRF pilot country, the UNHCR is presenting resettlement based on protection needs and the nature of displacement as a priority durable solution: "resettlement is a tangible demonstration of solidarity between Uganda and the international community" (UNHCR Uganda, 2017, p. 24). However, resettlement relies upon the international community, and resettlement opportunities have proven so limited for refugees from Uganda that many refugees chose to seek refuge instead in Egypt or European countries, which have been able to attract more resettlement offers (Hovil, 2018).

CRRF OBJECTIVE 4: STRENGTHEN CONDITIONS FOR REPATRIATION TO COUNTRIES OF ORIGIN

The ultimate aim of the NY Declaration, CRRF, and Global Compact is to achieve durable solutions for the refugee crisis, including "voluntary repatriation, local solutions and resettlement and complementary pathways for admission" (UN, 2016, p. 19). Of those, the primary end goal is the safe and dignified repatriation to countries of origin (UN, 2016). For Uganda, repatriation is one of the sole goals as there are no citizenship pathways for refugees (Uganda, The World Bank, & UNHCR, 2016a). To support this envisioned future of repatriation and reconstruction, the CRRF calls on host countries to contribute to growing self-reliance among refugees by "pledging to expand opportunities for refugees to access, as appropriate, education, health care and services, livelihood opportunities and labour markets" (UN, 2016, p. 20). Educational achievement is a critical component of this self-reliance approach to durable solutions; however, key informant interviews revealed how this provision of education can counter the goal of repatriation as refugee groups prefer to stay in Uganda where there is better access to and quality of education (KII 6, 2018). While a primary goal of ReHoPE and the Uganda CRRF is to build refugees' skills and capacities for an eventual return to their country of origin (Uganda, The World Bank, & UNHCR, 2016a), Uganda hopes that this skill building will also contribute in the short term to improving the communities where refugees are hosted, relieving some of the community's burden for supporting refugees (ReHoPE, n.d.). Though Uganda's response plan to transforming the educational goals of the CRRF into reality is relatively new, we see that its history is a long one with regards to incorporating many of the values the Framework espouses.

Kenyan Refugee Context

When we turn to Kenya, we see it has one of the largest refugee populations in the world and, as of 2014, hosted 607,223 registered refugees and asylum-seekers, mainly from Somalia, South Sudan, Ethiopia, Democratic Republic of the Congo (DRC), Eritrea, Burundi, and Uganda

(Mendenhall et al., 2015). The Kakuma refugee camp, which is about 125 kilometers from the South Sudanese border, was established in 1992, primarily to accommodate 16,000 children and youth fleeing the conflict in Sudan (Lutheran World Federation, 2015). The Kakuma refugee camp covers a total area of approximately 25 square kilometers and is one of the largest single-site and multi-ethnic refugee camps in the world. Over 55% of the camp's population is under the age of 17, with disproportionate numbers of children arriving every day—65% of current new arrivals. Of these new arrivals, 25% are unaccompanied minors, which increases the challenges of care (Lutheran World Federation, 2015). Kenya's other refugee camp, Dadaab, was established in 1991 to address refugees fleeing Somalia. Partially due to a drought occurring in southern Somalia in 2011, the population of Dadaab increased from 135,000 in 1991 to 369,294 in 2016 (Sugow & Ndegwa, 2017).

Unlike the integration approach in Uganda, the Kenyan government decreed in 2013, after violence by Al-Shabab, that all refugees in urban centers must return to a refugee camp in Dadaab or Kakuma. This was mainly addressed toward Somali refugees and coincided with threats to close the Dadaab camp (Mendenhall et al., 2015). The main actor in the refugee camp arena, the UNHCR, runs both the Kakuma and Dadaab camps. It continues to pursue legal challenges to ensure that both camps remain open, as well as to confront harassment, bribery, assault, arbitrary arrests, and deportation faced by refugees (Mendenhall et al., 2015).

CRRF Kenya: Case Study Discussion

Despite agreeing to be a pilot country, Kenya has not yet implemented the CRRF. However, in March 2018, the Refugee Affairs Secretariat shared a draft of its national plan to implement a CRRF Road Map. This plan includes implementation of the Nairobi Declaration on Durable Solutions, which was signed by the Inter-Governmental Authority on Development's (IGAD) member states in 2017 and commits to supporting Somali refugees (Global CRRF Portal, 2018). In addition, the Road Map includes plans to assist refugees who have legitimate claims to citizenship or residency to obtain legal status and improve the self-reliance and inclusion of refugees in Kenya (Okoth, 2018).

This builds on Kenya's previous commitment to supporting refugees, starting with their commitment at the Leaders' Summit on Refugees in 2016, where they pledged to develop the Kalobeyei Integrated Settlement. This was a settlement to benefit refugees and residents of Turkana County, due to its proximity to Kakuma Camp and that camp's issues with overpopulation. They pledged to implement the "Guidelines on Admission of Non-Citizens to Institutions of Basic Education and Training in Kenya," a guide which facilitates enrollment of refugees within Kenyan schools (Leaders' Summit on Refugees, 2016). In 2017, Kenya also passed a bill that provides 500,000 refugees with the right to work and to farm (Wesangula, 2017).

CRRF OBJECTIVE 1: REDUCE STRAIN ON HOST COUNTRIES

Prior to the early 1990s, when the refugee population in Kenya expanded rapidly and national security became a concern, the strain on Kenya's resources was considered manageable (Burns, 2010). However, when the situations in Sudan and Somalia became increasingly unstable in the 1990s and refugees began to flee to Kenya in great numbers, the strain on Kenya increased rapidly. Rising numbers of refugees from Somalia also intensified national security concerns, as the number of bombings by al-Shabaab increased in the early 2000s (Burns, 2010). In addition to security concerns, Kenya is still in the process of improving its own education system for Kenyan children, aside from the strain of supporting the education of refugees within the country.

One KII reported that an agreement was enacted between the UNHCR and Kenya, wherein local schools near Kalobeyei Integrated Settlement received support from the UNHCR. This went a long way toward reducing the strain on the local community, as well as reducing tensions related to misconceptions that refugees were benefiting while Kenyan children were not (KII KE 1, 2018). Another KII had the perspective that the UNHCR was, since its initial involvement, more involved in managing the refugee response than in many other countries, such as Ethiopia, and that the Kenyan decree that refugees should leave resulted in greater amounts of UNHCR funding. However, the KII felt that while funding should come from UNHCR and other donors, Kenya should have greater control over managing the education of refugees than it currently does, but through the Ministry of Refugee Affairs and with increased technical support and capacity building from partner organizations (KII KE 2, 2018).

CRRF OBJECTIVE 2: INCREASE SELF-RELIANCE AMONG REFUGEES

Due to the 2013 decree that all refugees must leave urban areas and live in either Kakuma or Dadaab refugee camps, self-reliance among refugees in Kenya is fairly limited. Though some refugees do still live in Nairobi and other areas, they do so illegally and without the right to work (Burns, 2010). However, this may change following the passage of the 2017 Refugees Bill, which provides refugees with the right to work. Several KIIs spoke of small steps that have already been taken in some camps, including administering of the Kenya National Exam in several camps, the opening of secondary and technical schools, and the opening of a Primary Teachers' College within one camp to train refugees to be teachers (KII KE 1, 2018). This increases the self-efficacy of refugees within the camp by giving both access to continuing education as well as a venue (teaching) to then apply these gained skills. In addition, for those refugees who choose to become teachers, this gives them access to work experiences that they could apply outside of the camp as well as within it.

Another KII reported that about 50% of refugee teachers received some training as primary teachers under the Kenyan curriculum within Dadaab camp (KII KE 2, 2018). However, another KII was clear to note that many of these increases in the self-reliance of refugees should only happen within a refugee camp, and with the sole purpose of having the refugee return to his or her country of origin (KII KE 3, 2018). This reflected the broader perspective of the KIIs interviewed, in that integration is supported only to a certain point and within very clearly defined parameters. Most KIIs interviewed were in strong support of refugees attaining educational training, certificates, and exam scores for their value and transferability in either a third country or their country of origin but were uncomfortable with the idea of refugees accessing Kenyan services outside of a refugee camp, as well as establishing long-term residency within Kenya itself. Due to these perspectives, further expansion of refugee programs and increasing opportunities for self-reliance could lead to tensions between Kenyans and the refugee population.

CRRF OBJECTIVE 3: INCREASE OPPORTUNITIES FOR THIRD COUNTRY SOLUTIONS

Between 1992 and 2006, 84,420 refugees were resettled from Kenya to a third country; between 2001 and 2005, this constituted 20.4% of refugee resettlement cases worldwide (Jansen, 2008). This pattern remains fairly steady to the present day, where the UNHCR projected that 6,537 refugees, primarily from Somalia and the DRC, would be proposed for resettlement in 2017 (UNHCR Kenya, 2018). However, with the sharp cuts to the US refugee resettlement program following the election of Donald Trump, it is uncertain if similar third country resettlement rates will continue to be possible in the future (Refugee Council of Australia, 2017). UNHCR had been negotiating with the United States for 15,000 refugees to be resettled there if Kenya follows through on decrees to close Dadaab refugee camp. They made it clear during the 2017 Annual Tripartite Consultations on Resettlement (ATCR) that, given the United States' reduction in the number of refugees it is willing to accept, other international partners would be needed to assist (Refugee Council of Australia, 2017). One KII expressed the need for a greater international commitment for third country resettlement and highlighted all of the skills that refugees gain in Kenya that could be meaningfully applied to a third country. The interviewee shared that they had seen Sudanese, Rwandan, and Somali refugees coming into Kenya with no education and leaving with income-generating skills, which showed what an asset education can be (KII KE 1, 2018).

CRRF OBJECTIVE 4: STRENGTHEN CONDITIONS FOR REPATRIATION TO COUNTRIES OF ORIGIN

Kenya's current CRRF road map includes implementation of the Nairobi Declaration on Durable Solutions, a large part of which focuses on the reintegration of Somali refugees back into Somalia. As Somalia begins to stabilize, the UNHCR also anticipates large numbers of Somalis to voluntarily repatriate back to Somalia—in 2017, they estimated that 79,500 Somalis would return (UNHCR Kenya, 2018). However, many KIIs were skeptical of the feasibility of these Somali refugees being able to safely return and willingly stay in Somalia. One KII shared that despite the current focus on voluntary repatriation, if there were issues in their country of origin, the refugees would often return to Kenya (KII KE 1, 2018). Another KII had similar experiences with Somali refugees, due to the security issues still at play within the country. He reported that as soon as refugees were sent back to Somalia, many ended up coming back to Kenya due to the danger they were still experiencing in Somalia. As a result, the refugees in Dadaab preferred third country resettlement to going back to Somalia (KII KE 1, 2018). This has broader implications, as many refugees within Kenyan refugee camps are being educated in a language not their own and on a skill set that may not necessarily apply to their country of origin. As a result, refugees become tied to the customs and future of Kenya rather than of their home country, which may lead to their unwillingness to stay once repatriated.

Although Kenya is making progress toward fulfilling the goals of the CRRF, particularly with the new Refugees Bill including the right to work, it is difficult to see full achievement as long as refugees are restricted to refugee camps. Additionally, without consistent stability in countries of origin and access to third country repatriation, options for refugees in Kenya remain limited.

Section III

Discussion

Looking at these two country case studies in their experience with implementing the CRRF, a question posed by KIIs is how the aims of the CRRF are to be reached through on-the-ground policies, particularly given the, at times, unclear political will and divergence between implementers and policymakers. Both Uganda and Kenya are implementing contextualized versions of the CRRF, having made distinct commitments to begin moving toward the vision of the NY Declaration. However, both countries,

Uganda in particular, face implementation concerns as one of the key policy documents for the CRRF Uganda, the Education Response Plan, was designed at such a high national level that local implementers are not invested in realizing the plan.

For example, where provision of schooling has expanded to include refugee communities in public institutions, relief has been felt in one corner while strain has been felt in another. In integrating traditional relief programs, such as schools solely for refugee children, into the host country's public schools, relief agencies have more resources available in their efforts. However, in increasing enrollment in public schools, there is a rising financial pressure felt in the public education system, which is already evident in both Kenya and Uganda. While Uganda and Kenya have different approaches and challenges in regard to refugee education, one need certainly echoes across their responses: underfunding. While "education remains a key prerequisite for self-reliance and effective integration," (Uganda, The World Bank, & UNHCR, 2016a, p. 33), enrollment numbers are high and quality levels remain low due to an absence of international burden sharing. Though reducing strain on host countries is the CRRF's first objective, this chronic underfunding along with the rapid entry of new refugees limits host countries' ability to address the long-term nature of this crisis and could ultimately hinder development in this region for generations to come (UNHCR, 2016a). Critics of the CRRF and the Global Compact also point to the voluntary nature of any commitments made under the GCR, claiming that without any enforcement mechanisms, sufficient support will not materialize (Lieberman, 2018). This concern has already become apparent with Tanzania dropping out of the CRRF due to underfunding as well as Uganda's appeal in its first-ever Solidarity Summit reaching less than 2% of their pledges' goal (Alfred, 2017).

The large gains made by both countries toward the CRRF's second objective of increased self-reliance seems at first encouraging. This includes the employment opportunities created as a direct result of expanding educational opportunities such as the teacher training colleges in some camps of Kenya and the continuation of Uganda's right to work policy. However, the informants identify key tensions to the potentially uneasy reluctance by both countries to wholly support this pillar. The first is the direct impact that funding these activities has on taking away from other services, whether within the aid funding stream or within the national bureaucratic stream. The second tension lies in determining what it means to have a self-reliant refugee citizenry eager (if not desperate) to participate in the economy and earn an income. For instance, in working toward longer-term solutions, the Ugandan Education Response Plan struggles to rectify the immediate demands for teachers and school structures through government systems with the attitude among government actors that even enabling the certification of teachers from refugee communities would have implications on the wage bill and, in turn, Uganda's limited education budget (KII 3, 2018). And, though not explicitly mentioned, this would in turn increase the job competition market.

Finally, as to how education is positioned to increase third country resettlement, the CRRF's third objective, this is still largely unanswered. While the opportunity for its role is demonstrated in the anecdotal reflection by one key informant working in Kenya (KII KE 1, 2018), without durable commitment backed by intentional policies financed by resettlement countries, third country resettlement will not be a durable nor feasible solution shifting even larger responsibility and financial pressure on to current host countries. At the signing of the NY Declaration, while pledges to resettle refugees doubled from previous commitments, the secretary-general of Amnesty International cautioned that the 360,000 places offered globally must be considered within the worldwide context of more than 20 million refugees. While a previous version of the Declaration committed to achieving a global 10% rate of refugee resettlement each year, that provision was removed in order to reach a final agreement (Dowd & McAdam, 2017). Even as the number of refugees rises, countries are increasingly unwilling to open their borders (Yarnell, 2017). In each country, key informants doubt the effectiveness of the CRRF's fourth objective of voluntary repatriation. The second objective of increasing self-reliance is believed to link with this fourth objective of strengthening conditions for repatriation to countries of origin, but the practical mechanisms of achieving these objectives, such as stronger access to public education, creates a pull for refugees to stay within the host country where they perceive stronger opportunity as noted by key informants in both Kenya and Uganda. Though Uganda is demonstrating to the world that the CRRF has vast potential, it will ultimately fail unless other nations fulfill their obligation and provide for equitable burden sharing (Rosenberg, 2018).

In conclusion, the CRRF is putting forth ideals that are being used to justify the expansion of public education provision in countries such as Kenya and Uganda that have for years struggled to extend quality education to their own youth. For countries that are already embattled with providing adequately and equitably, it would seem that the recent CRRF push to integrate refugees into national societal structures runs the risk of creating more parallel systems that are unsustainable than expanding durable solutions. What emerges from this synthesis is not a uniform, one-size-fits-all experience, echoing what comparativists have well understood when initiating international policy: context matters both at a global scale but also in thinking through implementation at the national and local levels to understand how this context will shape and interplay even with the sincerest of grand values. What the perspectives of on-the-ground implementers and policymakers tell us about the extent that host countries will be able to incorporate the objectives of the CRRF into national policy is that, though different in structure, both countries have been involved in looking to reduce strain and subsequent fallout regardless of the push to adopt the CRRF country-wide. The primary motivator for the creation of the CRRF is to integrate refugee support within national development goals in order to address the harsh dichotomy faced by many host countries. However, the depth of resources needed to implement the reforms suggested within the CRRF have been so resource-heavy that host countries increasingly feel strain from the policy reforms intended to lighten their load. The perspectives of the informants highlight this consistently. What they also highlight is that without actual financial commitment from the rest of the international community, these gains cannot be sustained.

References

Action for Refugee Education. (2018). *Charter for action*. Retrieved from www.actionforrefugeeeducation.net/charter-for-action/

Alfred, C. (2017, December 28). Year in review: The refugee crisis in 2017. *News Deeply*. Retrieved from www.newsdeeply.com/refugees/articles/2017/12/28/year-in-review-the-refugee-crisis-in-2017

Anderson, A., Hamilton, R., Moore, D., Loewen, S., & Frater-Mathieson, K. (2004). Education of refugee children: Theoretical perspectives and best practice. In R. J. Hamilton & D. Moore (Eds.), *Educational interventions for refugee children: Theoretical perspectives and implementing best practice*. London: Routledge Falmer.

Bouscaren, D. (2016, October 23). As South Sudan fights, refugees flow into Uganda. *National Public Radio (NPR)*. Retrieved from www.npr.org/sections/parallels/2016/10/23/498398234/as-south-sudan-fights-refugees-flow-into-uganda

Burns, A. (2010). Feeling the pinch: Kenya, Al-Shabaab, and East Africa's refugee crisis. *Refuge: Canada's Journal on Refugees*, 27(1).

CRRF Global Digital Portal. (2018). [Web Page]. Retrieved from http://www.globalcrrf.org/crrf_document/nairobi-declaration-on-durable-solutions-for-somali-refugees-and-reintegration-of-returnees-in-somalia-23-march-2017/

Dempsey, M. (2018, June). Western leaders ignore new peak in global displacement at their peril [Open Editorial]. *News Deeply*. Retrieved from www.newsdeeply.com/refugees/community/2018/06/28/western-leaders-ignore-new-peak-in-global-displacement-at-their-peril

Dowd, R., & McAdam, D. J. (2017). International cooperation and responsibility-sharing to protect refugees: What, why, and how? *International and Comparative Law Quarterly*, 66, 863–892.

Dryden-Peterson, S. (2011). *Refugee education: A global review*. Geneva: United Nations High Commission for Refugees.

Easton-Calabria, E., & Omata, N. (2018). Panacea for the refugee crisis? Rethinking the promotion of "self-reliance" for refugees. *Third World Quarterly*, 39(8), 145-1474 doi:10.1080/01436597.2018.1458301

Education Cannot Wait [ECW]. (n.d.). *The situation*. Retrieved from www.educationcannotwait.org/the-situation/

Gouby, M. (2017, November 22). What Uganda's struggling policy means for future of refugee response. *News Deeply*. Retrieved from www.newsdeeply.

com/refugees/articles/2017/11/22/what-ugandas-struggling-policy-means-for-future-of-refugee-response

Hovil, L. (2018). *Uganda's refugee policies: The history, the politics, the way forward* [Special Series Working Paper]. Retrieved from https://reliefweb.int/sites/reliefweb.int/files/resources/IRRI-Uganda-policy-paper-October-2018-Paper.pdf

International Review of the Red Cross. (2017). Interview with Filippo Grandi. *International Review of the Red Cross, 99*(904), 17–29.

International Rescue Committee [IRC]. (2018, June). *Uganda: Citizens' perceptions on refugees*. Retrieved from www.rescue.org

Jansen, B. J. (2008). Between vulnerability and assertiveness: Negotiating resettlement in Kakuma refugee camp, Kenya. *African Affairs, 107*(429), 569–587.

Key Informant Interview 1 [KII1]. (2018, Sep 21). Personal interview.

Key Informant Interview 2 [KII2]. (2018, Sep 27). Personal Interview.

Key Informant Interview 3 [KII3]. (2018, Sep 28). Personal Interview.

Key Informant Interview 4 [KII4]. (2018, Oct 9). Personal Interview.

Key Informant Interview 5 [KII5]. (2018, Oct 11). Personal Interview.

Key Informant Interview 6 [KII6]. (2018, Oct 10). Personal Interview.

Key Informant Interview Kenya 1 [KII KE 1]. (2018, Nov 14). Telephone Interview.

Key Informant Interview Kenya 2 [KII KE 2]. (2018, Nov 19). Telephone Interview.

Key Informant Interview Kenya 3 [KII KE 3]. (2018, Nov 19). Telephone Interview.

Leaders' Summit on Refugees. (2016). *Summary overview document leaders' summit on refugees*. Retrieved from https://refugeesmigrants.un.org/sites/default/files/public_summary_document_refugee_summit_final_11-11-2016.pdf

Lieberman, A. (2018, August 2). Global Compact for Refugees moves forward, but without clear path for implementation. *Devex*. Retrieved from www.devex.com/news/global-compact-for-refugees-moves-forward-but-without-clear-path-for-implementation-93179

Lutheran World Federation. (2015). *Rapid assessment of barriers to education in Kakuma Refugee Camp* (Report). Retrieved from https://kenyadjibouti.lutheranworld.org/sites/default/files/documents/Barriers%20to%20Education%20in%20Kakuma%20Refugee%20Camp%20Assessment_0.pdf

Martinez, M. (2018, September 24). World leaders voice strong support for new refugee deal at UN General Assembly. *UNHCR News*. Retrieved from www.unhcr.org/news/latest/2018/9/5ba9270d4/world-leaders-express-resounding-support-new-deal-refugees-un-general-assembly

Mendenhall, M., Dryden-Peterson, S., Bartlett, L., Ndirangu, C., Imonje, R., Gakunga, D., . . . Tangelder, M. (2015). Quality education for refugees in Kenya: Pedagogy in urban Nairobi and Kakuma refugee camp settings. *Journal on Education in Emergencies, 1*(1), 92–130.

Okoth, F. (2018). *The comprehensive refugee response framework: A perspective from Kenya*. Retrieved from https://za.boell.org/2018/10/09/comprehensive-refugee-response-framework-perspective-kenya

Patton, A. (2016a, August 20). Is Uganda the best place to be a refugee? *The Guardian*. Retrieved from www.theguardian.com/global-development-professionals network/2016/aug/20/is-uganda-the-best-place-to-be-a-refugee

Patton, A. (2016b, September 21). In Uganda, a new approach for refugees: And for Ugandans. *Devex*. Retrieved from www.devex.com/news/in-uganda-a-new-approach-for-refugees-and-for-ugandans-88774

Refugee and Host Population Empowerment (ReHoPE). (n.d.). *Bridging the gap between humanitarian and development programming: ReHoPE strategic framework*. Retrieved from https://d10k7k7mywg42z.cloudfront.net/assets/ 5667425fd4c96170fe082173/REHOPE_2_Page_Brief_141015.pdf

Refugee Council of Australia. (2017). *UNHCR appeals for support to address refugee resettlement needs in Africa*. Retrieved from https://reliefweb.int/sites/reliefweb.int/files/resources/ATCR_2017-Final-Report.pdf

Rosenberg, T. (2018, August 21). A new deal for refugees [Op Ed]. *The New York Times*. Retrieved from www.nytimes.com/2018/08/21/opinion/refugee-camps-integration.html

Sinclair, M. (2001). Education in emergencies. In J. Crisp, C. Talbot, & D. Cipallone (Eds.), *Learning for a future: Refugee education in developing countries*. Geneva: United Nations High Commission for Refugees.

Sugow, M. I., & Ndegwa, P. (2017). Food voucher choice and refugees' livelihoods in Dadaab refugee camp, Kenya. *International Academic Journal of Human Resource and Business Administration*, 2(4), 108–127.

Tanzania Withdraws from UNHCR Comprehensive Refugee Response Framework. (2018, February 13). *News Deeply*. Retrieved from www.newsdeeply.com/refugees/executive-summaries/2018/02/13

Türk, V. (2016). Statement by Volker Türk. *International Journal of Refugee Law*, 28(4).

Türk, V. (2017). 68th session of the executive committee of the High Commissioner's Programme: Statement by Volker Türk. *International Journal of Refugee Law*, 29(4), 696–710. https://doi.org/10.1093/ijrl/eex043

Uganda. (2018). *Education response plan for refugees and host communities in Uganda*. The Ministry of Education and Sports, the Republic of Uganda. Retrieved from www.globalcrrf.org/crrf_document/education-response-plan-for-refugees-and-host-communities-in-uganda_final/

Uganda, UN, & UNHCR. (2017). *Translating New York Declaration commitments into action: Requirements for a comprehensive refugee response in Uganda*. Proceedings from the Uganda Solidarity Summit on Refugees, June 22–23, Kampala. Retrieved from http://solidaritysummit.gou.go.ug/sites/default/files/UgandaComprehensiveRefugeeResponse1_20_June_2017.pdf

Uganda, The World Bank, & UNHCR. (2016a). *An assessment of Uganda's progressive approach to refugee management*. Retrieved from http://documents.worldbank.org/curated/en/259711469593058429/An-assessment-of-Ugandas-progressive-approach-to-refugee-management

Uganda, The World Bank, & UNHCR. (2016b, September 15). *Refugee and host population empowerment: ReHoPE strategic framework*. Retrieved from https://d10k7k7mywg42z.cloudfront.net/assets/5667425fd4c96170fe082173/REHOPE_2_Page_Brief_141015.pdf

Uganda, The World Bank, & UN Uganda. (2017a, June). *ReHoPE: Refugee and host population empowerment: Strategic framework: Uganda*. Retrieved from https://reliefweb.int/report/uganda/rehope-refugee-and-host-population-empowerment-strategic-framework-uganda-june-2018-0

Uganda, The World Bank, & UN Uganda. (2017b, June). *ReHoPE: Refugee and host population empowerment: Strategic framework: Uganda* [brochure]. Retrieved from https://reliefweb.int/report/uganda/rehope-refugee-and-host-population-empowerment-strategic-framework-uganda-june-2018-0

UNHCR. (n.d.a). *Comprehensive refugee response framework*. Retrieved from www.unhcr.org/comprehensive-refugee-response-framework-crrf.html

UNHCR. (n.d.b). *Towards a global compact on refugees*. Retrieved October 15, 2018 from www.unhcr.org/towards-a-global-compact-on-refugees.html

UNHCR. (2013). *The UNHCR Uganda strategy for refugee education: 2013–2016*. Retrieved from http://fenu.or.ug/wp-content/uploads/2013/02/The-UNHCR-Uganda-Strategy-forRefugee-Education.pdf

UNHCR. (2015). *Global trends: Forced displacement in 2015* [Report]. Retrieved from https://www.unhcr.org/statistics/unhcrstats/576408cd7/unhcr-global-trends-2015.html

UNHCR. (2016a, July). *South Sudan fighting sees more refugees fleeing into Uganda than in the first 6 months of 2016*. Retrieved from www.unhcr.org/en-us/news/briefing/2016/7/579724704/south-sudan-fighting-sees-refugees-fleeing-uganda-first-6-months-2016.html

UNHCR. (2016b, August). *Revised South Sudan regional refugee response plan: January–December 2016*. Retrieved from www.unhcr.org/578f2da07.pdf

UNHCR. (2016c, September). Ethiopia education fact sheet. *UNHCR: The UN Refugee Agency*. Retrieved at data.unhcr.org/horn-of-africa/download.php?id=2026

UNHCR. (2017). *Uganda: UNHCR refugees and asylum-seekers*. Retrieved from http://data.unhcr.org/SouthSudan/documents.php?page=1&view=grid&Country%5B%5D=229

UNHCR. (2018a). *Applying comprehensive responses (CRRF) in Africa*. Retrieved from www.unhcr.org/publications/operations/5a8fcfff4/applying-comprehensive-responses-crrf-africa.html

UNHCR. (2018b). *Bringing the New York declaration to life: Applying the Comprehensive Refugee Response Framework (CRRF)*. Retrieved from www.unhcr.org/593e5ce27

UNHCR. (2018c, July). *The global compact on refugees: Final draft*. Retrieved from www.unhcr.org/5b3295167.pdf

UNHCR. (2018d). *The global compact on refugees: UNHCR quick guide*. Retrieved from www.unhcr.org/events/conferences/5b6d574a7/global-compact-refugees-unhcr-quick-guide.html

UNHCR. (2018e). *Turn the tide: Refugee education in crisis*. Retrieved from www.unhcr.org/5b852f8e4.pdf

UNHCR and Global Education Monitoring Report. (2016, May). *No more excuses: Provide education to all forcibly displaced people: Policy paper number 26*. Retrieved from http://unesdoc.unesco.org/images/0024/002448/244847E.pdf

UNHCR Kenya. (2018). *Figures at a glance*. Retrieved from www.unhcr.org/ke/figures-at-a-glance

UNHCR Uganda. (2017). *Comprehensive refugee response framework Uganda: The way forward*. Retrieved from https://data2.unhcr.org/en/documents/details/63266

United Nations [UN]. (2016). Resolution adopted by the General Assembly on 19 September 2016 (A/RES/71/1). New York.

Wesangula, D. (2017). Kenya to give work and hope to refugees after decades in limbo. *The Guardian*. Retrieved from www.reuters.com/article/us-kenya-refugees/kenya-to-give-work-and-hope-to-refugees-after-decades-in-limbo-idUSKBN19B269

Yarnell, M. (2017, December 29). *The global compact on refugees: Reasons for hope* [blog post]. Retrieved from www.refugeesinternational.org/blog/2017/12/29/the-global-compact-on-refugees-reasons-for-hope

Appendix 1
Key Informant Interview Key

KII Code	Country of Work	Organization Type	Date of Interview	Format of Interview	Length of Interview	Key Takeaways
KII 1	Uganda (Kampala)	Government	21 Sept 2018	In person	45 minutes	Government is committed to refugee education as a long-term solution. Some tensions between priorities of NGO partners and government policy (ex. ECD).
KII 2	Uganda (Kampala/West Nile)	Donor Agency	27 Sept 2018	in person	50 minutes	ReHoPE has been a best practice, if difficult to specifically identify budget split. Challenges around parallel systems, harmonizing guidelines for accelerated learning.
KII 3	Uganda (Kampala)	Donor Agency	28 Sept 2018	in person	75 minutes	CRRF as guiding document to drive consensus. Fears to commit to permanent structures, higher ed on assumption refugees will return to country of origin. More needs to be done to break down barriers for refugees; treat refugee and host communities as one group.
KII 4	Uganda (Kampala/West Nile)	Implementing NGO	9 Oct 2018	in person	60 minutes	Key challenge to integration is around remote and sparsely distributed host communities—how to ensure these are reached/heard. High demand for more child protective services—refugee populations very vulnerable.
KII 5	Uganda (West Nile)	Government	11 Oct 2018	in person	35 minutes	Best practices have been in integrating work plans. Government is critical to coordination, inspection while partners bringing in technical expertise. High levels of collaboration and capacity building means local government can carry programs forward. Need to be realistic about spending.

(*Continued*)

(Continued)

KII Code	Country of Work	Organization Type	Date of Interview	Format of Interview	Length of Interview	Key Takeaways
KII 6	Uganda (Kampala/West Nile)	Donor Agency	10 Nov 2018	in person	70 minutes	ERP in itself is an achievement, but needs aggressive coordination and integration to ensure it is operationalized. Some tension around purpose of ERP document as an advocacy tool or government guideline.
KII KE 1	Kenya (Nairobi)	Implementing NGO	14 Nov 2018	phone	35 minutes	Integration of refugees and host communities varies by camp, but now host communities can access many of the same resources—this has helped to bridge gaps and ease tensions. Refugees take national exams, have some access to some higher education (though limited).
KII KE 2	Kenya (Daddab)	Implementing NGO	19 Nov 2018	phone	40 minutes	Since 1991, a lot has been done toward integration of refugees in the education system. Key role of donors is to provide financial support. Major concern now for Kenya refugee situation is security—government very sensitive to this, and forces need more capacity building on refugee rights.
KII KE 3	Kenya (Kakuma)	Implementing NGO	19 Nov 2018	phone	30 minutes	Government has taken lead on education standards, with partners coming in with funding and provision. Focus is on providing refugees with education/certification for third country/home country repatriation, or with livelihoods and income-generating skills within refugee camp.

Part 2

Local Adaptations for Refugees' Educational Transitions

6 Female Refugees' Transitions Into Higher Education
Comparative Perspectives From Germany, Egypt, and Kyrgyzstan

Lisa Damaschke-Deitrick, Ericka Galegher, and Maureen F. Park

Introduction

After years of neglect, access to education has recently emerged as a powerful tool to mitigate the effects of conflict by promoting equality and stability as well as providing a safe haven during times of conflict (Burde et al., 2017; Smith, 2010; UNHCR, 2018). Post-conflict, education can help stabilize and rebuild societies and lives. Education plays a key role in empowering women and girls and is crucial to enabling them to fully participate in post-conflict peace building efforts (Kirk, 2003). Nevertheless, aid agencies, governments, and educational research overlook the importance of continuing refugees' access to educational opportunities into higher education (HE), access which literature suggests has significant positive implications for female refugees.

Globally, women's participation rates in HE have continued to improve; substantial gains in educational attainment mean there are now more women than men enrolled in HE, most notably in Europe and North America (Morley, 2010). Access to HE is an important component of Sustainable Development Goal 4 (SDG), which aims to ensure equal access to postsecondary education, (UNESCO, n.d.). However, despite the specific inclusion of refugees in the SDGs, gender parity does not exist for female refugees in HE. Gender disaggregated enrollment data is scarce; however, one study in Australia indicates that refugee women account for only 40% of tertiary enrollment (Ferede, 2018). This is despite the "almost universal desire to attend university" for refugees who have completed secondary education (Dryden-Peterson & Giles, 2010, p. 4). Even more worrisome are statistics from the UNHCR, which estimates only 1% of refugees have access to higher education (UNHCR, 2016b), although access varies based on host country and country of origin (Ferede, 2018). The gap between supply and demand of university-aged refugees has led to calls of a potential "lost generation" (Barakat & Milton, 2015), the negative side effects of which literature suggests could be great.

In conflict and post-conflict situations, the normalizing influence of education is critical as it "feeds hope and future aspirations, and provides an essential bridge to future livelihoods" and "promote[s] stability in post-conflict societies" (Mundy & Dryden-Peterson, 2011, p. 7). Enabling access to education is crucial in order to provide opportunities for future employment or continued study (Mundy & Dryden-Peterson, 2011), as well as integration into the host country. Very little research has been conducted on the educational experiences of refugees after secondary school, despite the fact that these educational opportunities can have a profound positive impact on female refugees. Many refugees are well educated and academically suited for university studies. Often, refugees have higher skills and levels of education than the general population of their home countries (OECD, 2013). Despite persistent claims of a potential "lost generation" and crisis of HE amid the current unprecedented level of university-qualified displaced persons, the opportunities and gender-specific focus remain scarce. For example, displaced university-qualified Syrian males are three times more likely than females to resume their tertiary studies (Institute of International Education, 2016). And despite their many hardships, the experiences of the refugee women in this study highlight the important window of opportunity that exists as a result of their displacement, which the international community must utilize.

Through a comparative analysis of the integration of refugee women into universities in Kyrgyzstan, Germany, and Egypt, this research explores the ways in which the specific needs of refugee women can be supported through HE. This study explores the perspective of female refugees' experiences in HE through a capabilities approach by asking: How do female refugees perceive their university experiences in their host countries? What role do universities play in facilitating their transitions into these host communities? This analysis compares Germany, a country with state-sponsored support but significant cultural and linguistic differences, with Kyrgyzstan and Egypt, which provide significantly less support for refugees but are more culturally similar to the refugee population studied. This research seeks to fill the dire gap in studying refugees' academic experiences in HE and provide vital information to higher education institutions to better address the diverse and complex needs of female refugee students.

Gender and Higher Education

Research is scarce on girls' education in conflict zones, but does indicate that girls, in particular, are especially vulnerable to the negative effects of conflict in terms of access to education (Kirk, 2003; Chinen, Coombes, De Hoop, Castro-Zarzur, & Elmeski, 2017). Conflict and crisis situations affect women and girls differently than men and boys; safety and security become of increased concern, and rates of early marriage and teen pregnancy tend to increase (Kirk, 2008). However, studies indicate that adequate support and teacher training as well as community involvement can have a positive impact on gender roles and attitudes (Chinen et al., 2017). Further, there is some evidence that conflict situations can create new opportunities for girls to access education (see Kirk, 2008; Manchanda, 2001).

Post-conflict, refugee girls and women face additional challenges and barriers to education. As the number of female refugees and migrants increases (UNHCR, 2018), so has the incidence of gender-based violence against refugee women; this has been called the "hidden" aspect of the refugee crisis (Freedman, 2016; UNHCR, 2018). Female migrants and refugees experience sexual and gender-based violence in their country of origin, while traveling, and even at their resettlement location (UNHCR, 2018). In addition to the past trauma, (Rothkegel et al., 2008; Schick et al., 2018), upon resettlement, girls and women face additional gendered challenges; existing gender disparities and disadvantages are often exacerbated (Liebig, 2018) as they are expected to assume the role of caregiver, translator, and breadwinner (Tuliao, Najjar, & Torraco, 2017).

Despite the challenges and constraints faced by female refugees, access to education, and postsecondary education, in particular, is fundamental to full participation in society (see Allwood & Wadia, 2010; Dryden-Peterson, 2010). Zeus (2011) points to studies highlighting the importance of providing refugees access to skills development during displacement in order for them to draw upon these skills later. In addition to the high rate of return in labor market outcomes, as well as intergenerational benefits (Liebig, 2018), access to tertiary education helps give agency to refugee women. Postsecondary education can "open new spaces that do not currently exist and that can be transformative" (El Jack, 2010).

HE promotes self-reliance, enabling female migrants and refugees to "gain knowledge, voice, and skills which will give them access to better employment opportunities and earnings" (El Jack, 2010, p. 19). Their educational attainment and entry into the workforce are important steps toward independence, empowerment (Tuliao et al., 2017), and equality. Providing migrant and refugee women access to higher education helps shift the gender imbalance and gender relationships within society (El Jack, 2010).

Despite the persistent emphasis on the importance of education for refugees, and specifically, its role in supporting transitions for refugees and host communities, HE for refugees is consistently overlooked by policymakers, aid agencies, and donors (Avery & Said, 2017; Barakat & Milton, 2015; Dryden-Peterson, 2010; Dryden-Peterson & Giles, 2010; Kirk & Sherab, 2016; Magaziner, 2015). Research and funding consistently focus on primary and secondary education despite the right to HE being codified in a number of international legal frameworks (see Ferede, 2018, p. 10). Nevertheless, it is largely overlooked by the global education movement as outlined by Dryden-Peterson (2010), in part due to the perception by donors and aid agencies that investment in HE favors the elite and is therefore contrary to equity goals of the UN and development community.

The deemphasis on HE for refugees has significant consequences considering the prioritization of increasing access to primary and secondary education by aid agencies and the increasing number of university-aged refugees. Dryden-Peterson and Giles (2010) argued that the expansion of the educational continuum or "pipeline" at the primary and secondary levels necessitates the continuation of opportunities into HE. Lack of such opportunities potentially demotivates young refugees to persist through school, resulting in negative impacts on the individual and societies (Dryden-Peterson & Giles, 2010).

This is problematic as current refugee crises, specifically the Syrian refugee crisis, affect university-aged students at levels previously unseen (Streitwieser, Miller-Idriss, & De Wit, 2017). In fact, UNESCO statistics state that in 2011 when the Syrian war started, nearly 26.2% of the school-aged population was enrolled in tertiary education (Stanton, 2016), and in 2016, it was estimated that 100,000 to 200,000 university-aged Syrians sought refuge elsewhere (Streiwieser et al., 2017). As a result, HE institutions have a vital role to play in receiving countries to utilize and cultivate this influx of human capital (Stanton, 2016; Streitwieser et al., 2017). Many universities in the United States and Europe are already equipped with the infrastructure and programs which can be adapted and deployed to assist refugee students (Streitwieser et al., 2017). Examples of these programs are outlined in reports on higher education institutions (HEI) assisting refugees across Europe (see Jungblut & Pietkiewicz, 2017) and interventions available by US institutions (see Stanton, 2016; Streitwieser, Loo, Ohorodnik, & Jeong, 2018; Watenpaugh, 2016). However, there is still not a comprehensive European Union–wide or even member state solution to providing greater access to HE for refugee students. Programs at present are largely individual institution initiatives (Jungblut & Pietkiewicz, 2017; Streitwieser et al., 2018).

Rather than the traditional short-term perspectives of education, researchers increasingly call for a paradigm shift from short-term, immediate relief to long-term, development goals that meet the increasingly protracted refugee situations throughout the world (Dryden-Peterson, 2010). In fact, it is estimated that those displaced young people, nearly 30% university-aged students from Syria, will remain displaced for an average of 17 years (Watenpaugh, 2016). Recognizing this shift is important as literature highlights the long-term importance of HE.

Literature on refugees and HE consistently cites a number of potential long-term benefits for increasing refugees' access to HE. Specifically, refugee access to HE is vital to long-term societal goals of combating radicalization, society building, peace building, and reconstruction and reconciliation in post-conflict situations (Avery & Said, 2017; Barakat & Milton, 2015; Dryden-Peterson & Giles, 2010; Streitwieser et al., 2017; Watenpaugh, 2016). On the individual, short-term level, HE creates a sense of empowerment (Zeus, 2011), supports refugees' ability to make decisions about their own lives (Dryden-Peterson, 2010; Gateley, 2015), helps "shed the stigma of refugee status" (Crea & McFarland, 2015, p. 241), and potentially reduces the psychosocial trauma and emotional pressure many refugees experience (Avery & Said, 2017). Additionally, skills acquired in HEI will undoubtedly support refugee communities (Avery & Said, 2017; Wright & Plasterer, 2010)

Investment in quality HE has implications for receiving countries as well. A government report from Norway cites significant problems for receiving countries when inadequate education is provided to refugees and asylum-seekers in the form of socioeconomic losses and even monetary losses to the state (Jungblut & Pietkiewicz, 2017). This exemplifies the advantages of continuing the education pipeline through HE for both individuals and receiving countries. In fact, HE can also be viewed as a long-term investment in creating future economic and political partnerships once refugee students return to their homelands (Streitwieser et al., 2017). Additionally, hosting refugee students enriches the campuses and student bodies of these institutions (Millner, 2016) as well as promotes many HEI's internationalization objectives (Streitwieser et al., 2017).

Despite these individual and societal level benefits, university-aged refugees face a number of challenges to accessing HE. Research highlights five main challenges refugees face: lack of documentation and credentials; lack of information; language; discrimination; and finances (Avery & Said, 2017; Dryden-Peterson & Giles, 2010; Gateley, 2015; Jungblut & Pietkiewicz, 2017; Watenpaugh, Fricke, & King, 2014). Additionally, in many host countries refugees lack information and legal access to labor markets (Avery & Said, 2017; Watenpaugh, Fricke, & King, 2014). Despite minimal efforts by HEIs, donors, and aid agencies to provide opportunities, currently they do not meet the significant demand from university-aged students who desire to continue or complete their disrupted educational careers. Some of these challenges are being addressed in the EU, for example, through the Council of Europe's credential recognition system (Jungblut & Pietkiewicz, 2017). Nevertheless, research highlights the deeply embedded de-prioritization of HE in refugee crises by policymakers, donors, communities, and aid agencies like the UN as the greatest obstacle to meaningfully mobilizing the resources and beneficial role of HE to support refugee crises and societies (Dryden-Peterson, 2010; Watenpaugh, 2016). Overall, research generally focuses on access to HE rather than the experiences of refugees within these institutions and even more lacking is research on females' access and experiences within HE.

Theoretical Framework

This research draws from the capabilities approach, which is inextricably linked to education as a human right. The right to education of migrants, refugees, and internally displaced people is protected by international law (see UNHCR, 2011). This mandate, however, does not extend to higher education. Zeus (2011) argues that the assumption that refugees are only "temporarily displaced," leads to the denial of many of their rights, among them, access to higher education.

As a means to examine equal access to education, Sen's explanation of the capability approach serves as a useful model to examine access to higher educational opportunities for female refugees. He defines capability as "the opportunity to achieve valuable combinations of human functionings—what a person is able to do or be" (Sen, 2005, p. 153). While the marginalization of female refugees through limited access to higher education can be viewed as a denial of rights, this disenfranchisement is "not only related to whether one receives an education; rather, a capabilities approach allows us to examine how the process and practices of being educated can foster wellbeing" (DeJaeghere & Lee, 2011). HE is necessary for women to expand their opportunities and other capabilities (Nussbaum, 2000, p. 78). Not only does this approach highlight the advantages for individual female refugees but also the potential benefits continued educational opportunities may have for post-conflict societies.

Methodology

Data

Primary data were gathered for this study and Institutional Review Board approval as well as consent by individual participants were obtained. Interviews were conducted in Kyrgyzstan, Germany, and Egypt throughout 2016, 2017, and 2018. Qualitative content analysis of interviews was conducted. The coding system was developed using interrater reliability coding to ensure the reliability of the code system, which was developed deductively, through the theoretical framework and literature, as well as inductively through the interviews.

Participants[1]

The refugee women were all either currently enrolled in universities or had completed their studies. All are current or former refugees, asylum-seekers, or internally displaced persons (see Wiseman et al., 2019). In Kyrgyzstan, the population included five female refugees originally from Afghanistan; they studied in both public and private universities in Kyrgyzstan. Participants were recruited through several organizations working with refugee populations. In Egypt, four individual interviews and one focus group discussion consisting of three participants were conducted with female refugee participants who were enrolled in both private and public universities from Syria and Yemen. Participants were recruited through organizations and programs working with refugees in Egypt. In Germany, the interviewed refugee students were enrolled in a preparatory refugee study program at a public university. The women were from Syria, Iran, and Iraq. Contact was established through an institutional partnership with the university. Five individual interviews were conducted with female refugee students.

The educational and socioeconomic backgrounds of the women interviewed were mixed. In Germany, many of the interviewed women came from educated families, and some had attended well-known universities in Syria before the war, but most of them were unable to finish their degree. In Egypt, three women from Yemen and Syria who attended a private university all had previous bachelor's degrees; one even had a master's degree. None of the women's mothers had a university degree, and only the woman attending a private university from Yemen had a father who obtained a university degree. In Kyrgyzstan, the women interviewed came from less educated families of lower socioeconomic backgrounds; only one had a parent with a master's degree, the majority (especially mothers) had completed less than secondary education. However, two of the women had previously earned bachelor's degrees.

Country Contexts

Germany

The German constitution recognizes the rights of refugees for asylum. After the end of the Cold War, Germany saw an increase of refugees from former Yugoslavia, but also from countries like Ethiopia and Eritrea, as well as from the Republic of Congo and Senegal among others in the early 1990s. As a response to the increase in refugees, Germany tightened its asylum law and restricted anybody who entered from a "safe third country" to claim political asylum. This led to a significant decrease in the numbers of refugees (Bundeszentrale für politische Bildung [BpB] & Institut für Migrationsforschung und Interkulturelle Studien [IMIS], 2017).

This changed with the conflict in Syria and the arrival of hundreds of thousands of refugees in Germany. In 2015, the Federal Office for Migration and Refugees (BAMF) registered about 477,000 refugees, even though the actual number arriving in Germany in 2015 was much higher, around 890,000 (Beauftragte der Bundesregierung für Migration, Flüchtlinge und Integration [BBMFI], 2016). For the authorities, it became increasingly difficult to accommodate the large number of refugees. This situation led to a controversial social debate on the German refugee law. In the course of the "refugee crisis" Germany tightened its legislation on migration and asylum. In addition, the closure of the so-called Balkan route in March 2016 led to a decline in numbers.

Approximately 64% of adult refugees (of whom the majority were Syrian) arriving between 2013 and 2016 had a high school degree; 20% had a degree in higher education or vocational training (Brücker, Rother, & Schupp, 2017). These statistics suggest there is a significant number of current and future university-qualified refugees with the potential for entry or reentry into higher education. Germany recognizes foreign qualifications for employment more than other European countries. Nevertheless, obtaining recognition of a foreign degree is often a long bureaucratic process, and missing qualifications are still an obstacle for many. Refugee women, especially, have greater difficulties integrating into the German labor market (UNESCO, 2018; Liebig, 2018). The "2019 Global Education Monitoring (GEM) Report" notes that refugees in Germany were segregated into less academic school streams. Almost 85% of those over age 16 were placed in special classes separate from mainstream education, creating a barrier for them to start a university career (UNESCO, 2018).

With refugee status, a student is eligible to apply to a German university and receive free admission to study. The student must have a higher education entrance qualification recognized in Germany. Otherwise the student must pass a qualification assessment exam. Students who have been awarded refugee status and/or subsidiary protection are entitled to apply for financial support (Deutscher Akademischer Austauschdienst [DAAD], n.d.a). With federal funding, the German academic exchange service, DAAD, developed the following measures to support easier access to university for refugees:

- Recognizing skills and qualifications
- Ensuring academic qualification: Language and subject-related preparation
- Supporting integration at universities

(DAAD, n.d.a).

As part of this effort, universities have been offering special programs for refugees as preparation for entering a formal study program. These programs mainly concentrate on German language learning and preparatory knowledge for different subjects (DAAD, n.d.a). One exemplary refugee program implemented at a German university is presented in the following section.

Egypt

Due to its geographic position in North Africa, Egypt has historically been a transit point for refugees from the Middle East and sub-Saharan Africa. According to UNHCR (2017a), there are 211,104 registered asylum-seekers or refugees, and over half (123,033) are from Syria, although the estimated number of Syrians living in Egypt is much higher. Refugees in Egypt come from 63 different countries with a majority coming from Syria, Sudan, Ethiopia, Eritrea, South Sudan, Iraq, Somalia, and Yemen. Registration as a refugee or asylum-seeker is only done in Egypt through UNHCR under the legal guidance of the 1954 memorandum of understanding between the Egyptian government and UNHCR. However, registration does not grant residency. After registering with UNHCR, the asylum-seeker or refugee must register with the Ministry of Foreign Affairs. The bureaucratic process and lack of information regarding this process is extremely complex and time-consuming. Despite most refugees initially perceiving their stay in Egypt to be only temporary, seeking final resettlement in third countries or through dangerous sea crossings, most find themselves in largely uncertain and protracted situations in Egypt (Al-Sharmani, 2014).

Despite being one of two "non-Western member[s] of the drafting committee of the 1951 Geneva Convention relating to the Status of Refugees (and its 1967 Protocol)," Egypt has reservations on personal status, rationing, access to public education and relief as well as access to the labor market and social security (Al-Sharmani, 2014, p. 60). Although Egypt has historically provided admissions and temporary permits to refugees, the state does not provide the basic social, economic, and legal support to adequately provide long-term safety and security for refugees. The financial costs and often changing and complex bureaucratic red tape required to renew visas and residency permits are additional challenges refugees face. Additionally, since the Arab Spring, Egypt's political and economic climate has been in great flux, creating even more instability for refugees already in marginalized conditions.

Refugees have different degrees of access to free public education depending on their country of origin. Access to Egypt's higher education system has changed along with the changing administrations. In general, some refugees based on country of origin, such as Syrians, graduating with an Egyptian secondary diploma and depending on their score on the final national examinations, can access the higher education system largely free of charge like Egyptians. However, many university-aged students from Syria arrived with interrupted studies. Only under the Mohammed Morsi administration was the policy opened to allow Syrians without an Egyptian secondary diploma to access higher education institutions in Egypt largely free of charge. However, upon the removal of Morsi, the policy was reversed. Now refugees without an Egyptian secondary school diploma can only access higher education in Egypt as a foreigner, which requires significantly large financial resources or a scholarship.

Kyrgyzstan

Kyrgyzstan is a mountainous, landlocked Central Asian country that gained independence from the Soviet Union in 1991; it remains the only democracy in the region. Although classified as a "lower-middle-income country" (World Bank, 2019), and heavily reliant on development aid and migrant labor remittances, Kyrgyzstan has a long history of welcoming refugees (UNHCR, 2016a), and is a signatory to the 1951 UN convention on the status of refugees; refugee protection is enshrined in its constitution. Since 1998, more than 10,000 refugees from neighboring Afghanistan and Tajikistan have entered the country, fleeing civil wars and prolonged conflict (RFE/RL, 2013). In 2017, there were 341 refugees and 105 asylum-seekers in Kyrgyzstan, 125 of whom were new arrivals. In 2015, there were 9,100 stateless people (UNHCR, 2016a). While most refugees and asylum-seekers come from Afghanistan, smaller numbers come from Syria, Uzbekistan, and Ukraine. Although 80% of the refugees are Afghans, because of the complicated path to citizenship, fewer than 100 Afghan refugees obtained Kyrgyz citizenship between 1996 and 2013 (RFE/RL, 2013).

Post-independence, Kyrgyzstan embarked upon an ambitious process of higher education reform, (Shadymanova & Amsler, 2018). There are now more than 50 public and private higher education institutions in the country (ADB, 2015), including a number with international affiliations (Shadymanova & Amsler, 2018). In a vestige of the Soviet education system, women continue to play a strong leadership role in higher education, and female enrollment is around 55% (ADB, 2015) Because refugee access to HE depends on asylum status, a limited number are able to access the opportunity. In Kyrgyzstan, few programs provide refugee support for HE. However, since 2002, the UNHCR's DAFI (Albert Einstein German Academic Refugee Initiative) has provided university scholarships to more than 40 refugee students (UNHCR, 2017b).

In addition to locally available scholarships like DAFI, current and former Afghan refugees have been able to access HE as recipients of a third-party scholarship funded by a foreign government. These five-year scholarships cover four years of undergraduate work as well as a one-year college preparatory program at a private university.

Case Studies Results

The following individual case studies present the experiences of refugee women in universities in Germany, Egypt, and Kyrgyzstan. Their stories highlight their shared dreams, challenges, and paths to HE. Thus, each case study is unique in its perspectives.

Female Experiences in a German University

Program Description

The following section describes a refugee program at a public university in Southwest Germany. The university is located in the state of Baden-Württemberg, one of the largest territorial states. Like all states in Germany, Baden-Württemberg has been obligated to take in refugees. The state strongly encouraged its universities to help facilitate the transition of refugees by implementing study programs for refugee students.

In fall 2016, the preparatory program Integrating Refugees in Higher Education (Integra) was launched. The objective is to efficiently enable qualified refugees to start a regular university study program (DAAD, n.d.b). The goal is to intensively prepare them (26–30 hours a week) for regular studies within nine months. The free program (as all HE is free of charge in Germany), co-funded by the German academic exchange service, DAAD, consists of courses focused on three components: the development of language skills, facilitating societal and cultural participation, and specialized courses in various academic disciplines (DAAD, n.d.b).

During the academic year, the first semester offers mainly German language courses and courses on German culture, including history and politics, life in Germany, and religion and intercultural training. These classes are predominantly taught in English. The second semester focuses on subject-specific knowledge and terminology as well as German language followed by a possible German language exam. The program offers a buddy program, in which refugee students are matched with German students (buddies) for support; it also offers excursions and other joint cultural activities (DAAD, n.d.b). The refugee program cooperates with the university's psychotherapeutic counseling service to provide access to treatment for post-traumatic stress syndrome for participants and their families; it also provides student counseling, free enrollment as "guests" to access resources and courses (without credit), and an internet platform for information.

Status

Most interviewed women in the refugee program were from Syria and had arrived in Germany in 2015 or 2016. Other students in the program came from Iran, Iraq, and Afghanistan. The interviewed women were between 23 and 27 years old. The women explained that they had difficulties entering the labor market in Germany solely with their qualifications from their home country. As refugees, the women are eligible to study at a German university. However, they first have to demonstrate sufficient language skills and pass a German language exam before they are eligible to apply for a regular study program.

They described bureaucracy and administration within and outside of the university context as complicated. The legal situation and particularly the asylum-seeking laws were also described as challenging. The women talked about their frustration when things had taken a long time and they had not been able to move forward with their plans. For instance, it took about two years since the arrival in Germany for all of the interviewed women to start the preparatory study program for refugees. Before, it took a long time to get out of the refugee homes and complete the bureaucratic processes to get their status recognized. They explained that finally being able to study in the refugee program gave them and their families hope and pride.

Societal Context

The women described Germans as uninformed about Syria in the interviews, specifically regarding religion and culture. Yara said "Germans are not unfriendly but uninformed" toward her background. Sara highlighted that "there are a lot of wrong ideas about my home country, the culture and Islam" in German society. Most women were eager to teach their German acquaintances about their culture and religion.

ADAPTING

Most women said they had been in Germany for more than two years and were adapting mostly well to the German society. However, language challenges were a recurring issue in the interviews. All of the interviewed women were English speakers and described learning German as their biggest challenge. This also presented tremendous social constraints as the language barrier made it difficult to socialize with German students. The women said that they mostly spent time with other Arabic-speaking students. They spoke English with German students at the university because of their lack of German language skills.

Institutional Context

All interviewed women described courses and studies as challenging due to the language barrier. For example, Yara said: "German language is hard and teaching tempo is quick." Some women complained that they did not learn enough about the use of academic language in their preparatory courses. However, most women stated that preparatory subjects like intercultural communication, life in German society, or history and politics were helpful for understanding life in Germany. Different competency levels by the students in the courses were described as another challenge. For example, Haya said that she felt pressured by other students that she was not advanced enough.

IDENTITY AT UNIVERSITY

In the courses that were part of the preparatory refugee program, the students were identified as refugees. They were also allowed to take classes outside their program (noncredit). In these courses, the students usually did not identify themselves as refugees. Thus, professors were not always aware when they had refugees as students in their classes. Sara noted that nonaffiliated professors with the program sometimes did not recognize the skills and knowledge of refugee students due to the language barrier. She stated that she had the experience that a non-affiliated professor believed that she was uneducated and treated her accordingly.

The separation between refugee students and German students was described as problematic in the interviews. Reasons for this separation were not only due to language differences, but also cultural differences as well as different experiences. Nevertheless, all interviewed women highlighted the importance of interaction with German students to break this barrier. Other obstacles were of a practical nature. For instance, some women did not live in town, so they had to figure out how to pay for their transportation.

The "buddy" program was described as significantly helpful for adjusting to everyday life and for making friends with German students. Abeer described the program as "useful for learning to speak and how to live in Germany. Assisting students help with information on how to study German outside the course, in daily life." Yara explained that she was lucky that one of the affiliated female professors supported her also outside of the program by teaching her German. Having support by native Germans, in particular professors and students, seemed to have made the biggest impact for adjusting to life in Germany.

Access

The women stated that they received help from German nongovernmental organizations to get papers and apply for residency and to find accommodation. The women supported themselves financially with the help of state money. In general, the women chose not to talk much about their financial situation in the interviews.

Most women learned about the refugee program through social media like Facebook. Others heard about the program from friends. The women applied and subsequently had face-to-face interviews to test their English and German skills before they were accepted into the program. Due to the many applications, only about half of the applicants were accepted in the program.

Agency

FAMILY

Most of the interviewed women fled without their family from home, and some of them still had parents or siblings in their home country. These family situations presented a tremendous burden for the women. Abeer and Haya described their family obligations in Germany, which included caring for and supporting their own children and family members in addition to their studies. These obligations were time and money constraints for the women who had to balance their commitments at home with tight study plans.

All women described their families as being supportive of their academic career plans. Most women said that their parents, siblings, or friends helped them with the application to the refugee program. They were all highly motivated to have a strong career in the future, such as becoming a pharmacist, doctor, or dentist. Sara called herself an "independent woman." The women felt supported by their friends and family in their career plans.

DEGREES

All of the interviewed women came with previous university experience in their home country. For example, Sara studied four years of pharmacy and Yara four years of computer science. Most of them were unable to finish their studies before they were forced to leave their home. Abeer from Syria already had a bachelor's degree. However, she felt the need to have a German degree to work in her desired career. Most women were hoping to get a permanent residence permit and find a good job in Germany in the near future. The women described the refugee program as a helpful start to prepare them for their study plans afterward.

Finally, despite the difficulties the women faced in the past, they were all highly goal oriented and motivated. For example, they made clear that they wanted to learn German as fast as possible and study very hard to be able to support their families. Some of them wanted to use their degree to go back and contribute to the rebuilding and development of their home country in the future.

Female Experiences in Universities in Egypt

Although access to HE in Egypt is guaranteed to all Egyptians with a secondary school diploma, the system has struggled to keep up with the massive expansion in demand. In 2015, there were 54 universities, 23 of them public, along with 141 private higher institutes with approximately 2,624,705 registered students (EACEA, 2017). The total number of refugee students is unknown as they are largely registered as international students. However, according to UNHCR, more than 4,300 Syrians were attending public HEI in 2016 (2017a).

Status

All of the women described the difficulties they faced with their legal status—not necessarily to acquire refugee status, but to acquire and maintain legal residency to stay in Egypt. Residency is often tied to education as enrollment in schools and universities provides legal justification to maintain residency in Egypt until completion of studies. In general, this residency applies to the family as well. The process of doing government paperwork and residency is long and arduous. Additionally, women often stated they had to reapply every six months, spending significant amounts of time and money in the process.

Finally, Syrian women described the uncertainty of whether or not the Egyptian government would grant them access to higher education largely free of charge similar to Egyptians. This uncertainty is connected to the unstable political climate Egypt faced since the 2011 uprisings. Syrians were allowed to access higher education free of charge like Egyptians during the presidency of Mohamed Morsi. The Syrian women attending the public universities in this study all accessed higher education because of this policy. However, after his departure, this policy remained unclear for some time until finally the policy was reversed. In fact, Nora went back to Syria during the war to finish her bachelor's degree as a result of this policy uncertainty. Currently, only Syrians who graduate with an Egyptian secondary school diploma can access higher education free. This poses serious limitations on those whose university degree was disrupted due to war. Overall, problems related to their status, both as foreigners or as refugees, were most often connected to bureaucratic difficulties in renewing their documents, the transient political climate as well as their legal status, discrimination in public universities, and lack of access to services and financial exemptions due to their refugee and foreign status.

LABOR MARKET

Lack of legal access to Egypt's labor market was described by all women as one of the biggest obstacles and one that causes a great deal of "suffering." Apart from volunteering, work opportunities are largely relegated to the informal job market. All described the time constraints and additional pressure they faced being a university student and working. Many of the women interviewed in public universities had family who depended on the extra income. Most of the women see the importance of education in expanding their job opportunities, but these opportunities for them remain largely outside of Egypt. They also realized their access to these opportunities is also uncertain. There exists a potential inability to transform the acquired educational abilities into valuable opportunities, valuable in the fact that many stated opportunities in their field were not available in Egypt or they were legally constrained in accessing these job markets. As Salma described her volunteer work in an INGO in Egypt:

> A promotion wasn't available for me. Although I worked very hard. I always feel like I am trapped in one place that I can't move from. [...] It's absolutely the work permit. And they stated that many times, we would like to have you for this position, but we can't because of the policies of the place they can't hire a refugee.

Unemployment and underemployment are significant problems many Egyptians face. As a result, Egypt has reservations on formal access to the labor market and other government services under the justification to protect these services for their own citizens.

Access

FINANCES

All of these women cited financial constraints. They were able to overcome financial limitations through accessing government, institutional, and third-party scholarships. Two of the women attending private universities acquired institutional scholarships which covered their tuition, room and board, transportation, and medical insurance. The third woman attending a private university had an institutional scholarship and third-party scholarship which together covered her expenses. One Yemeni woman attending a public university acquired a scholarship from the Yemini government. However, due to the war which continues in Yemen, her funds were very unstable and came only sporadically. She stated that she last received her scholarship money more than six months ago. The lack of steady financial support through the government scholarship, lack of formal access to job opportunities, and time constraints related to family and school obligations were very burdensome.

INFORMATION

Information regarding scholarships, universities, and university registration processes was largely acquired online through self-initiated searches. Many of the women described finding this information through refugee-initiated online platforms often on social media networks like Facebook. Others acquired this information through word of mouth from their friends and other refugee students. Some described trying to get support and information from refugee-related NGOs but often found little help as these organizations often lacked information and support for higher education.

SERVICES

Nearly all women cited the lack of support and services from the UN, NGOs, and the government to assist refugees, and in particular, those trying to access higher education. There was a persistent focus by the women on the need to access services to help improve their academic English abilities, health services, and access to job opportunities. Finally, one Yemeni woman, Farah, stressed the difference between Yemeni and Syrian refugees and the services as well as focus placed on Syrian refugees in comparison. In her perspective, the status of a Syrian refugee included more services, support, and access to financial help than were available to a Yemeni refugee.

> Even there are some things that are free for them. But for us no, even there are some scholarships that are special for them or subsidies, but us no. We are between not refugees and not normal. We are in the middle.

Institutional Context

PUBLIC VERSUS PRIVATE

The most significant differences faced by these women were largely related to the differences between the preexisting institutional services available in the private university in comparison to the public universities. Private universities were already equipped and had services available for all students, which the refugee students could access free of charge. These included access to a writing center, counseling services, and cultural and sports activities. In contrast, public universities had no such services. The women often complained of difficulties in registration, administration officials purposefully making their registration process difficult, discrimination from students, and overall lack of support from the university and university professors. The women only found support from their friends and social networks.

Women in the private university often cited the significant support they got from their professors, classmates, and colleagues at work. The university was flexible and adapted to the needs of the refugee students as they developed. However, these women faced significant challenges in the private university largely related to the high level of academic English required in classes and amount of writing and research which were required. Additionally, they all cited the significantly higher quality education they are receiving in comparison to their universities in Yemen and Syria, which was a welcomed challenge.

Academic challenges among public university students was mixed. Farah stated the university was more modern and higher quality her previous university in Yemen. However, the other three Syrian woman had similar complaints to many Egyptian students—namely, the lack of contact with professors, overcrowded classrooms, and difficulties registering. Overall, private university students had access to both academic and non-academic support. The women were also required to take English language preparation courses before enrolling in their core subject classes. No such courses existed for those enrolled in Egypt's public universities, although only one is taking her courses in English rather than Arabic. All of the students in the public universities are enrolled as regular Egyptian or international students. No specific services or support are available for them, and as a result, they largely rely on each other for support and information.

DISCRIMINATION

The women who attended public universities described the largest degree of discrimination primarily from fellow Egyptian students, mainly other Egyptian women classmates, as well as from members of the university administration and government officials. Although all of the women except one described discrimination or the possibility of exploitation, whether this discrimination was directly related to their status as refugees or as foreigners is unclear. Overall, the women described their desire to hide their refugee status and blend in as much as possible with Egyptians. The women who attended the public universities described the need to hide their refugee status because of an assumed stigma attached with being labeled a refugee both within society and at their university. As Farah stated there are hundreds of Yemeni students studying throughout Egypt, but "I don't say, and they don't say either. Everyone is hiding this. So we don't know each other." Nevertheless, she and others did not describe significant cultural challenges in adapting to their universities. All cited similar difficulties related to time constraints, finances, higher quality, and academic language demands.

Societal Context

ADAPTING

Overall the women all stated they could adapt well in Egyptian society. Most, not all, acquired enough of the Egyptian dialect to blend in over time. Since Egypt was also similar religiously, many women often stated religion or wearing the veil was not an issue as they assumed others faced in Europe. Nevertheless, most did not describe their stay in Egypt as long-term and saw it as something temporary until they could return to their country, particularly if resettlement was not available.

Agency

All of the women were extremely motivated to continue their studies and utilize the skills and knowledge they acquired to better their futures as well as to go back to rebuild their countries. As reflected by the language skills and work experience of the private university students, it is clear that English language abilities provide refugees with a significant advantage accessing scholarships and universities. The women, who otherwise would not have access to Egypt's public universities if not for the Morsi-era policy for university-aged Syrian refugees, were extremely grateful for the opportunity to attend university and felt significantly more empowered as a result. Just the opportunity to learn new skills and move around gave Karima a sense of freedom and normalcy.

GENDER

Throughout the interviews, only the focus group discussion with the Syrian women in public universities cited issues related to gender. The women in the private universities described the support and encouragement they received from their families to pursue their university degrees. The Syrian women in the public universities, in contrast, stated their families and often their brothers did not support their decision to enroll as most "don't want their girls to go and study outside the home." However, over time and seeing the emotional toll that the war had on their children, they described the attitudes of their parents changing as a result. They eventually saw the opportunities and potential futures attending university in Egypt could provide for their daughters, and they became supportive. The women stated that their displacement to Egypt provided them with the opportunity to attend university, which they likely would not have had in Syria.

Female Experiences in Universities in Kyrgyzstan

The following section explores the experiences of five female students from Afghanistan as they navigate HE in Kyrgyzstan. Their path to Kyrgyzstan and HE is varied, although all originally left Afghanistan to escape Taliban rule. Three grew up in Pakistan, one in Iran, and one sought asylum in Kyrgyzstan and is the only one with official mandate refugee status. Each woman's educational experience is unique; some earned degrees before studying in Kyrgyzstan; another received a DAFI scholarship to attend a state university in Kyrgyzstan.

Status

All but one of the women interviewed received a full scholarship and stipend to attend the university. Perhaps because this financial burden was eliminated, with student status guaranteed, few mentioned the legal status issues experienced by the other women in the study. Interestingly, although only one was classified as a mandate refugee in Kyrgyzstan, all respondents referred to themselves as refugees. Although not directly addressed in the interviews, this shared identity was never mentioned as a challenge. Only two women focused on the limitations of their legal status on their ability to legally work.

Because the university enrolled a significant number of Afghans as well as students from neighboring Central Asian countries, some with a history of conflict, the women did not express an initial need to try to blend in or "hide" their refugee status or country of origin while on campus. For them, this shared status and shared past served as a unifier, in a way, and helped them navigate the challenges of adapting to a new country and university. It provided them with a built-in support system. This did not necessarily protect them, however from stigma attached to their country of origin. All spoke of experiencing discrimination and "otherness," based on prevalent local stereotypes of Afghanistan. Malalai described an especially intimidating experience that occurred away from the university where she was accused of being a terrorist. This sort of discriminatory experience, unfortunately, was not isolated; however, it occurred with greater frequency away from the university setting.

Societal Context

Because all the women interviewed fled Afghanistan during their early schooling years, they were exposed to educational and cultural opportunities that would not have otherwise been available to them had they remained in Afghanistan for the duration of their primary and secondary education. Many noted that because of their experiences as refugees in Pakistan and Iran, their families had adopted less conservative views regarding education, girls' access to education, and gender roles.

CULTURAL

Although Kyrgyzstan neighbors Afghanistan and is a Muslim-majority country, the Soviet influence remains strong, and women do not typically wear the hijab or scarves. For many refugees, this was the first obvious cultural difference, and keenly felt.

> I had culture shock when I first came here. Here, they aren't very conservative, like us. . . . [I]t was actually good, but it was difficult for me to adapt. I felt that people were looking at me the first few days.

In addition to the visible cultural differences, the women also noted more subtle differences. Local students often assumed because they were from

Afghanistan, they would prefer to stay within their own social circle; few made any initial advances toward developing friendships.

LANGUAGE

Because of their education in Pakistan and Iran, the majority of the women arrived with a strong command of English. However, outside of the university, very few people spoke English. While English allowed them to succeed academically, it limited their social interaction with Russian-speaking peers, and also restricted movement outside of campus, minimizing their exposure to the Kyrgyz culture. Although none of the students planned on remaining in Kyrgyzstan post-graduation, several cited language as a barrier to developing deeper social networks and future employment opportunities.

GENDER

Many of the women grew up studying in single-sex classrooms; the coeducational environment they experienced at the university was described as both shocking and freeing. Mariam, initially uncomfortable with coeducation, described the university experience as transformative and empowering. "I was seeing that nobody judged you, it doesn't matter what you wear, how you talk. . . . [I]t doesn't matter if you are a man or a woman. People were very open minded, and I liked that."

Nadia explained how her earlier refugee experience in Pakistan had, in fact, prepared her for the university experience.

> I can talk or share my ideas with males easily. This really prepared me for this experience, there was no shock. Any kind of thing, I can handle it. I had it from my childhood. So I was given more access because I was a refugee.

Institutional Context

The critical role of institutional support was highlighted in the interviews. The one-year college preparatory program was frequently mentioned as one of the key factors in facilitating the transition to university life. This program, designed to provide intensive academic support including critical thinking as well as academic writing skills, also helped develop leadership skills. In addition to academic support, the program helped the women develop valuable social connections within their peer groups. Soraya, who did not participate in the orientation program explained the challenges she had integrating:

> It was very difficult because everyone knew each other. All were Afghans and I didn't have any friends at first, even from Afghanistan.

The Kyrgyz and other nationalities, no one would talk to me, they had their own groups. I would be by myself, and sit by myself, because I didn't speak Russian, and they would always speak in their own language.

LANGUAGE

Beyond the social context, issues of linguistically exclusionary practices extended into the classroom. English is the language of instruction at the private university. However, because many of the local students spoke Russian more fluently, classroom discussions, and even instruction frequently devolved into Russian. Mariam expressed her frustrations with this:

> It is totally challenging. I expect my teacher to teach me, and it is not always like that. In my course, they should be teaching in English, but they use Russian, and it makes me sort of angry. And sometimes they [other students and teachers] say, "if it is a big deal, then you should learn our language as well."

This was perceived by many of the students as one of their greatest challenges at the university. While the Afghan students generally possessed a high degree of English language fluency, many of their counterparts did not, and they felt that the faculty often perpetuated this issue by using Russian. As a result, they felt this exclusion both within and outside the classroom.

QUALITY/VALUE OF DEGREES

Overwhelmingly, the respondents spoke of the value of an English language liberal arts degree from a foreign accredited university; they felt this opportunity was invaluable in terms of accessing future jobs or graduate school opportunities. However, some women were disappointed in the limited variety of degrees offered; they felt constricted by their choice of field of study. Despite this, they acknowledged the importance of continuing their studies in order to secure a more stable future.

NON-ACADEMIC

After the orientation program, the school provided little formal support for the students. However, many mentioned the important role academic and non-academic clubs played in their ability to adjust to university life. Several women joined the model UN, and through this had the opportunity to travel and participate in international conferences; for several, this was the highlight of their university experience. In addition, some helped form a women's club. These opportunities to develop and participate in social networks provided the women needed socio-emotional support, mentorship, and leadership skills.

Access

With one exception, all women were awarded four- or five-year scholarships to attend the private university. In addition to tuition support, the women were provided a monthly living stipend, accommodation in a dormitory, and travel to and from Afghanistan. Without this financial support, they all agreed that this opportunity would not have been possible. In fact, at the time of the interview, Malalai, a previous DAFI recipient, was facing tremendous financial challenges and was uncertain if she would be able to continue her studies if she did not receive a scholarship.

A few of the women also explained that they had also received a scholarship to attend the American University in Kabul, but had instead chosen this university, some citing security as a key factor.

> One thing that I love here so much is the security, the freedom that the students have. Sometimes, I get jealous because I have so many friends who don't have this opportunity. Maybe you heard about the huge attack in Afghanistan at the American University?

While some sought refuge and security in this university in Kyrgyzstan, for Zahira, and others, their earlier refugee experience ultimately enabled them to pursue an education.

> We were living in a remote village. If I had not gone to Pakistan, I would have had to walk two hours to get to school, if I could even go. And even if I could get an education, as a girl, I may not be allowed to go to Kabul and study.

Mariam explained that because of the more open gender attitudes toward education in Pakistan, her father changed his mind about the importance of girls' education. Ultimately, this led to her academic success and ability to attend a university with her family's support.

Agency

A recurring theme throughout all the interviews was the prominent role of agency in allowing the women to attend university. While some women had previously earned degrees, they all independently decided on the need for this degree. The path was varied, and for some, extremely challenging. Malalai described how her mother sold her gold wedding dowry to pay for tuition at the state university. Before she was awarded a DAFI scholarship, she could not afford bus fare, and was forced to walk for several hours each day, sometimes in brutally cold weather, to attend class.

Woven throughout the interviews as well was the recurring theme of gender. The women frequently mentioned older sisters, female cousins, or friends who had either identified the scholarship opportunity or motivated them and encouraged them to apply. Malalai, who received support through the UNHCR, described her experience working with a female mentor: "She asked me if I wanted to study, and I said yes, it is my dream to study. And I was flying! I was really happy. She really helped me."

This female support network continued into the university; female mentors and peers encouraged some women to attend a women's conference, and later develop the women's club. They also provided access to other women in the broader expatriate community who helped them navigate the challenges of university life.

Although the women all acknowledged the benefits of studying in a university that afforded them personal freedom as well as safety, they overwhelmingly expressed their desire to return to Afghanistan and contribute to the development of the country. Their choice of degrees, including international relations and psychology, reflected their aspirations to work for international organizations or NGOs to help rebuild the country.

Finally, these women viewed education as both an escape and also path to empowerment.

> If I wasn't in school, my parents would make me get married. Right now, they think I should even be engaged in school. But I am going to continue and hopefully get a master's degree before I consider that. And I have told them that.

Many acknowledged that their situation would be very different had they stayed in Afghanistan. "In Afghanistan, it would be hopeless. I would not have a job, and it would be very difficult to leave the house. Here, I am studying, I will have a job, and I have freedom."

Comparative Analysis and Discussion

Status

In Egypt and Germany, the length of time and bureaucracy were most often criticized. The four-year student status the women in Kyrgyzstan obtained significantly decreased stress and problems related to their status in the country. Similarly, student status in Egypt also grants many refugees residency status. However, in Egypt the universities do not facilitate government paperwork concerning status, and most universities categorize refugees as simply international students, thus creating greater financial burdens and obstacles to accessing higher education. Additionally, the women in Egypt and Kyrgyzstan were significantly restricted in their legal access to formal labor markets. These labor restrictions substantially inhibit these women from reaching their full potential post-graduation, and for some, this obstacle increased feelings of uncertainty.

The women described discrimination occurring mostly in the university setting rather than outside the university. However, women in Egypt and Kyrgyzstan did describe instances of discrimination outside the university context. The lack of discrimination in Germany may be attributed to the sheltered refugee course at the university and the "Refugees Welcome" climate prevalent among the German public at this time. Additionally, the prevalence of discrimination and apathy from professors and students occurring within the university setting was striking and suggests that all universities need to be more proactive in creating intercultural awareness within the university community.

Societal Context

As expected, the language barrier in Germany was the greatest obstacle to connecting with local Germans and society. Language also significantly restricted the connections and exposure the Afghan women made with the local Kyrgyz culture, as well as their ability to forge social networks within the university setting. In Egypt, however, language and remaining in the Middle East were often cited as reasons for seeking refuge in Egypt. Once the women learned enough of the local dialect, it was easy to blend in with local communities. Although they did not highlight it as an obstacle, women did discuss the more liberal culture in both Kyrgyzstan and Egypt. In all countries, the women stated that the local population was largely uninformed about what was occurring in their countries, and there was an overall lack of outreach from the local populations. Overall, local communities in all countries did little to encourage connections and communication between refugee communities and host country communities.

Institutional Context

Academic Services

In both Germany and Kyrgyzstan, the curriculum of the preparatory programs included courses such as intercultural communication, society, and history and politics. These courses facilitated the students' understanding of their new host country. In Kyrgyzstan and Germany, the one-year college preparatory program, designed to prepare students for all aspects of university life, both academic and social, was frequently mentioned as one of the key factors in facilitating the transition to university life in the new country. In Germany, the quick pace of classes and varied academic levels of the students were highlighted as challenges. The universities in Egypt did not provide the same preparatory programs. However, students at the private universities did have access to various high-quality academic and non-academic services including English preparatory classes, a writing center, counseling, and extracurricular activities similar to those available in the preparatory programs. In contrast, students enrolled in Egyptian public universities received far less institutional support; they reported numerous challenges both academically and socially and were often forced to rely on one another for support and information.

Across all three country contexts, the students highlighted the need for intensive, extended academic support in the language of instruction. In addition to the academic challenges language presented, students, especially in Germany and Kyrgyzstan, acknowledged the linguistic exclusion they sometimes experienced within the institution from both peers and professors.

Non-academic Services

The role of institutional support was frequently highlighted. In Germany, women felt that they did not have enough institutional support in practical issues, including access to transportation to the university. Women in the private Egyptian university praised the supportiveness and flexibility of staff and faculty. In Kyrgyzstan, some women felt that the university did not provide a sufficient variety of degrees, and felt constrained, although powerless to make changes. Access to a variety of extracurricular programs supported by the university and advisers helped mitigate this, for some. Although the women in private Egyptian universities did not have a preparatory program, their access to clubs, cultural activities, and sports provided them with similar advantages.

Overall, their university experiences did not facilitate or ease their transition into society or host communities. In fact, the time constraints associated with their academic work and for many, family obligations and work made it nearly impossible to make friends or cultivate a social network within or outside the university. This finding supports recent research that governments need to prioritize access to formal labor markets to further encourage these transitions as well as utilize the skills, knowledge, and motivation of these refugee graduates (Ferede, 2018).

Access

Information regarding the various higher educational opportunities and scholarships was overwhelmingly shared online through various social media networks, including Facebook. In addition, many of the refugees were encouraged to pursue HE by other female friends or relatives who were currently studying, highlighting the important role of gender support (Ferede, 2018). INGOs and other refugee-related organizations were less reliable in terms of providing information related to access to higher education and scholarship opportunities.

The differences in financial access among respondents underscores the challenges in accessing higher education for refugees. While the majority of the women in Kyrgyzstan were studying on full scholarships with stipends, and thus free from the financial burden, the financial situation for women in Egypt was more precarious. Refugee status afforded the women in Germany access to higher education without a significant financial burden. However, women with family obligations often mentioned additional financial constraints in Germany and Egypt.

These women's experiences highlight their motivation and perseverance in the face of significant obstacles to accessing HE. All faced challenges related to finances, obtaining scholarships, access to information, support services, and for some, family obligations and objections to continuing their education at the university level. Additionally, language requirements for many scholarships, specifically English language requirements, significantly reduces access to HE for many refugees and potentially exacerbates previous claims that HE for refugees creates an elite niche. However, as many of the women emphasized, access to English language and academic writing preparatory courses is needed. Such courses could open the door for many more marginalized women to access scholarships and training to overcome the financial and linguistic hurdles associated with accessing HE.

Nevertheless, these women were motivated to continue their studies and eventually were able to access the financial support and navigate the complex bureaucracies in their host countries largely through their own persistence and the support of the refugees around them. In conclusion, the refugees and their refugee networks were the greatest facilitators of access to information, resources, and support.

Agency

The most significant finding of this study was that despite the life-altering experience of becoming a refugee and the devastation, trauma, and disadvantages that are often attached to and described by the women, this displacement was in fact the impetus behind accessing and continuing their education through opportunities unavailable in their home countries. For the women in Kyrgyzstan, their initial displacement to Pakistan and Iran changed their families' views on girls' education, providing many of them with the opportunity to continue and complete their schooling. Most stated that if it were not for their displacement, they probably would not have completed secondary school. Their access to the private university in Kyrgyzstan was an escape from early marriage and their experience encouraged a sense of freedom, security, and empowerment.

Most of the women in Germany had access to universities in Syria. However, Germany gave them the chance in their perception to have a more prestigious career, and the motivation to return and utilize these degrees and knowledge if they return to Syria. Similarly in Egypt, the women who attended the private university stated that they otherwise would never have the opportunity to study in such a high-quality and prestigious university that will, in their opinion, open doors for them occupationally and through the linguistic and academic skills they acquire. The Syrian women in the public universities stated that moving to Egypt and having access to HE without having to pay tuition allowed them to access and finish their university degrees, which they would never have been allowed to do in Syria, largely because of family objections, which for some changed once they moved to Egypt. Rasha did not finish primary school in Syria, but in Egypt, she was able to complete her primary and secondary education through home schooling and continue on to finish her bachelor's degree. Farah highlighted the higher quality of the public university she is now attending in Egypt; however, the lack of support from the government of Yemen's scholarship program, lack of support from the university, and her family obligations still created significant challenges to her current situation and future opportunities. The universities and local community organizations largely overlook the additional burden and pressure many of the women faced as a result of family obligations. Nevertheless, like the women in Kyrgyzstan and Germany, all described feelings of empowerment, freedom, and increased motivation as a result of their HE experience. At least for the time being, HE provided the women with a safety net.

Unexpectedly, the women cited few gender-specific issues. Gender issues were discussed most by the women in Kyrgyzstan and the Syrian women in Egypt's public universities. It is possible this is related to the educational and socioeconomic backgrounds of these women who come from more marginalized backgrounds (see Galegher, 2019). Additionally, this study did not capture those women who were unable to access HE and potentially those who may benefit most from such an opportunity.

As a university student, some of the women had the opportunity to cultivate a new identity. "The identity of 'student' is not heavy with loss but rather hopeful with possibility" (Ferede, 2018, p. 8). For many, it also provided them with relief from past traumas and the potential to start a new path. As university students, the women felt opportunistic, confident, and independent. Nearly all of the women, however, did identify with and feel more comfortable creating relationships and social networks with other international students. Thus, it is important for universities to cultivate and facilitate such support networks.

Finally, supporting research that suggests increased access to HE is necessary for postwar reconstruction, nearly all of the women had aspirations of returning to their home countries to help rebuild. Not only do these women have the motivation and aspirations to be key components to rebuilding their societies, but through their HE experiences, they have now acquired the skills, educational degrees, networks, and knowledge to capably and effectively fulfill such roles.

Conclusion

Overall, HE did not significantly facilitate integration into the host society for these women in Germany, Kyrgyzstan, or Egypt as expected and as research often suggests. Women found support largely through their own refugee communities and felt greater acceptance interacting with other international students. These interactions also cultivated their "student" identities. These findings support the need for a community-wide, holistic approach to supporting refugees in host communities. Although HEIs often have preexisting structures that can be utilized to support refugee women, the academic and non-academic services did not cultivate long-term interest and support from local communities and, in many instances, administrators, professors, and local students. However, the preparation program for refugees in Germany does increase the overall success rate of refugees continuing their studies. Additionally, gender-specific services related to child care and family obligations must be addressed by universities and communities. Discourse consistently focuses on preparing refugees for integration. However, supporting and encouraging refugee transitions must include engagement and awareness not only with refugee communities but equally as important with local communities and individuals.

These women's experiences support both the individual and societal benefits of HE (Ferede, 2018). Although limited in job opportunities in their current host countries, they are all highly motivated to continue to pursue higher education or to return home and contribute to rebuilding efforts. For those receiving scholarships or state support, education for many of the participants was an escape not only from war, but also marriage, home life, and underemployment. Through these educational transitions, many of the women realized their nascent potential. Additionally, they have the potential to become important role models for refugee girls encouraging persistence through secondary schooling when refugee girls tend to drop out (Ferede, 2018). However, the gap still remains between transforming these capabilities into opportunities post-graduation. Universities and governments have an important role to play in facilitating connections to professional networks to utilize these important change-makers.

Note

1. Pseudonyms have been used to protect the confidentiality of the participants.

References

Afghan Refugees Picket UN, Demand Kyrgyz Citizenship. (2013). Retrieved from www.rferl.org/a/kyrgyzstan-afghan-refugees-un/25202525.html

Allwood, G., & Wadia, K. (2010). Refugee women and NGOs. In *Refugee women in Britain and France* (pp. 152–170). Manchester, UK: Manchester University Press. Retrieved from www.jstor.org/stable/j.ctt155jb8c.12

Al-Sharmani, M. (2014). Refugee migration to Egypt: Settlement or transit? In F. Düvell, I. Molodikova, & M. Collyer (Eds.), *Transit migration in Europe* (pp. 55–77). Amsterdam, Netherlands: Amsterdam University Press.

Asian Development Bank (ADB). (2015). *Assessment of higher education: Kyrgyz republic*. Retrieved from www.adb.org/sites/default/files/institutional-document/175940/higher-education-kgz.pdf

Avery, H., & Said, S. (2017). Higher education for refugees: The case of Syria. *Policy & Practice: A Development Education Review*, 104–125.

Barakat, S., & Milton, S. (2015). *Houses of wisdom matter: The responsibility to protect and rebuild higher education in the Arab world*. Doha, Qatar: Brookings Doha Center.

Beauftragte der Bundesregierung für Migration, Flüchtlinge und Integration. (2016, December). *11. Bericht der Beauftragten der Bundesregierung für Migration, Flüchtlinge und Integration. Teilhabe, Chancengleichheit und Rechtsentwicklung in der Einwanderungsgesellschaft Deutschland* [11th report of the commissioner of the federal government for migration, refugees and integration: Participation, equal opportunities and legal developments in the immigration society Germany]. Berlin, Germany. Retrieved from www.bundesregierung.de/breg-de/suche/11-bericht-der-beauftragten-der-bundesregierung-fuer-migration-fluechtlinge-und-integration-teilhabe-chancengleichheit-und-rechtsentwicklung-in-der-einwanderungsgesellschaft-deutschland-729972

Brücker, H., Rother, N., & Schupp, J. (2017). IAB-BAMF-SOEP-Befragung von Geflüchteten 2016: Studiendesign, Feldergebnisse sowie Analysen zu schulischer wie beruflicher Qualifikation, Sprachkenntnissen sowie kognitiven Potenzialen [*2016 IAB-BAMF-SOEP survey of refugees: Study design, field results and analyzes on educational and professional qualifications, language skills and cognitive potentials*]. Retrieved from www.bamf.de/SharedDocs/Anlagen/DE/Publikationen/Forschungsberichte/fb30-iab-bamf-soep-befragung-gefluechtete-2016.html

Bundeszentrale für politische Bildung, & Institut für Migrationsforschung und Interkulturelle Studien. (2017). *Focus migration: Country profile: Germany*. Bonn & Osnabrück, Germany. Retrieved from www.bpb.de/gesellschaft/migration/laenderprofile/58349/germany

Burde, D., Kapit, A., Wahl, R. L., Guven, O., & Skarpeteig, M. I. (2017). Education in emergencies: A review of theory and research. *Review of Educational Research*, 87(3), 619–658.

Chinen, M., Coombes, A., De Hoop, T., Castro-Zarzur, R., & Elmeski, M. (2017). Can teacher-training programs influence gender norms? Mixed methods experimental evidence from northern Uganda. *Journal on Education in Emergencies*, 3(1), 44–78. https://doi.org/10.17609/N81T0D

Crea, T. M., & McFarland, M. (2015). Higher education for refugees: Lessons from a 4-year pilot project. *International Review of Education, 61*, 235–245.

DeJaeghere, J., & Lee, S. K. (2011). What matters for marginalized girls and boys in Bangladesh: A capabilities approach for understanding educational well-being and empowerment. *Research in Comparative and International Education, 6*(1), 27–42. Retrieved from https://journals.sagepub.com/doi/pdf/10.2304/rcie.2011.6.1.27

Deutscher Akademischer Austauschdienst [DAAD]. (n.d.a). *Refugees at universities: How the DAAD is helping*. Retrieved from www.daad.de/der-daad/fluechtlinge/infos/en/43153-refugees-at-universities-how-the-daad-is-helping/

Deutscher Akademischer Austauschdienst [DAAD]. (n.d.b). *Refugee Programm an der Universität Tübingen* [Refugee program at the University of Tübingen]. Retrieved from www.daad.de/der-daad/fluechtlinge/steckbriefe/de/49897-refugee-programm-an-der-universitaet-tuebingen/

Dryden-Peterson, S. (2010). The politics of higher education for refugees in a global movement for primary education. *Refuge: Canada's Journal on Refugees, 27*(2), 10–18.

Dryden-Peterson, S., & Giles, W. (2010). Introduction: Higher education for refugees. *Refuge: Canada's Journal on Refugees, 27*(2), 3–9.

Gateley, D. E. (2015). A policy of vulnerability or agency? Refugee young people's opportunities in accessing further and higher education in the UK. *Compare: A Journal of Comparative and International Education, 45*(1), 26–46.

Education, Audiovisual and Culture Executive Agency [EACEA]. (2017). *Overview of the higher education system: Egypt*. Brussels, Belgium: European Union. Retrieved from https://eacea.ec.europa.eu/sites/eacea-site/files/countryfiches_egypt_2017.pdf

El Jack, A. (2010). "Education is my mother and father": The "invisible" women of Sudan. *Refuge, 27*(2), 19–31.

Ferede, M. (2018). *Higher education for refugees*. Paper commissioned for the 2019 Global Education Monitoring Report Migration, Displacement and Education: Building Bridges, not Walls. Paris, France: UNESCO. Retrieved from https://unesdoc.unesco.org/ark:/48223/pf0000266075/PDF/266075eng.pdf.multi

Freedman, J. (2016). Sexual and gender-based violence against refugee women: A hidden aspect of the refugee "crisis." *Reproductive Health Matters, 24*(47), 18–26. https://doi.org/10.1016/j.rhm.2016.05.003

Galegher, E. (2019). Refugee experiences in higher education: Female perspectives from Egypt. In S. Jornitz & A. Wilmers (Eds.), *Transatlantic perspectives on education research*. Leverkusen, Germany: Barbara Budrich Verlag.

Institute of International Education. (2016). *Jusoor, IIE launch scholarships for Syrian university women*. New York, NY: Institute of International Education. Retrieved from www.iie.org/Why-IIE/Announcements/2016/09/2016-09-14-Jusoor-IIE-Partnership-Brings-18-Syrian-Women-to-US-Canadian-Universities

Jungblut, J., & Pietkiewicz, K. (Eds.). (2017). *Refugees welcome? Recognition of qualifications held by refugees and their access to higher education in Europe*. Brussels, Belgium: European Students' Union.

Kirk, J. (2003). *Women in contexts of crisis: Gender and conflict*. Commissioned Paper for the EFA Monitoring Report. Retrieved from http://unesdoc.unesco.org/images/0014/001467/146794e.pdf

Kirk, J. (2008). Addressing gender disparities in education in contexts of crisis, postcrisis, and state fragility. In M. Tembon & L. Fort (Eds.), *Girls' education* in the 21st century, gender equality, empowerment, and economic growth (pp. 153–180). Washington, DC: World Bank. Retrieved from http://citeseerx.ist.psu.edu/viewdoc/download?doi=10.1.1.158.7031&rep=rep1&type=pdf#page=184

Kirk, K., & Sherab, D. (2016). *Access to higher education for refugees in Jordan*. Amman, Jordan: Arab Renaissance for Democracy and Development (ARDD)-Legal. Retrieved from https://reliefweb.int/sites/reliefweb.int/files/resources/access_to_higher_education_for_refugees_in_jordan.pdf

Liebig, T. (2018). Triple disadvantage? A first overview of the integration of refugee women. OECD Social, Employment and Migration Working Papers, 216. Paris, France: OECD Publishing. http://dx.doi.org/10.1787/3f3a9612-en

Magaziner, J. (2015, December 7). The importance of higher education for Syrian refugees. *World Education News and Reviews*. Retrieved from http://wenr.wes.org/2015/12/the-importance-of-higher-education-for-syrianrefugees/#.VmdQ-49fa1A0.email

Manchanda, R. (2001). Ambivalent gains in South Asian conflicts. In S. Meintjes, A. Pillay, & Turshen (Eds.), *The aftermath: Women in post-conflict transformation* (pp. 99–120). London: Zed Books.

Millner, W. (2016). Displaced students enriching the University of Evansville. In *Supporting displaced and refugee students in higher education: Principles and best practices*. New York, NY: Institute of International Education.

Morley, L. (2010). Gender equity in higher education: Challenges and celebrations. *International Encyclopedia of Education*, 629–635. Retrieved from www.sussex.ac.uk/wphegt/documents/gender_equity_in_higher_education_presentation_-_vaxjo.pdf

Mundy, K., & Dryden-Peterson, S. (Eds.). (2011). *Educating children in conflict zones: Research, policy and practice for systemic change, a tribute to Jackie Kirk*. New York: Teachers College Press.

Nussbaum, M. (2000). Women's capabilities and social justice. *Journal of Human Development*, 1(2), 219–247. Retrieved from http://pdfs.semanticscholar.org/54fe/81caecc14bb20e69242bd7123b6f796c25b4.pdf

OECD. (2013). The fiscal impact of immigration in OECD countries. In *International Migration Outlook 2013*. Paris, France: OECD Publishing.

Rothkegel, S., Poluda, J., Wonani, C., Papy, J., Engelhardt-Wendt, E., Weyermann, B., & Hennig, R. (2008). *Evaluation of UNHCR's efforts to prevent and respond to sexual and gender-based violence in situations of forced displacement*. Geneva: Policy Development and Evaluation Service, UNHCR. Retrieved from www.unhcr.org/48ea31062.pdf

Schick, M., Morina, N., Mistridis, P., Schnyder, U., Bryant, R. A., & Nickerson, A. (2018). Changes in post-migration living difficulties predict treatment outcome in traumatized refugees. *Frontiers in Psychiatry*, 9, 476.

Sen, A. (2005). Human rights and capabilities. *Journal of Human Development*, 6(2), 151–166. Retrieved from www.unicef.org/spanish/socialpolicy/files/Human_Rights_and_Capabilities.pdf

Shadymanova, J., & Amsler, S. (2018). Institutional strategies of higher education reform in Post-Soviet Kyrgyzstan: Differentiating to survive between state and market. In J. Huisman, A. Smolentseva, & I. Froumin (Eds.), *25 years of transformations of higher education systems in Post-Soviet countries* (pp. 229–257). London, UK: Palgrave Macmillan and Cham. https://doi.org/10.1007/978-3-319-52980-6_9

Smith, A. (2010). The influence of education on conflict and peace building. *Paper commissioned for the EFA Global Monitoring Report 2011 the hidden crisis: Armed conflict and education*. Paris, France: UNESCO. Retrieved from https://unesdoc.unesco.org/ark:/48223/pf0000191341

Stanton, A. (2016). Best practices: Making use of existing university resources to welcome and integrate refugee students. In *Supporting displaced and refugee students in higher education: Principles and best practices*. New York, NY: Institute of International Education.

Streitwieser, B., Loo, B., Ohorodnik, M., & Jeong, J. (2018). *Access to higher education for refugees: Interventions in North America and Europe*. Working Paper. Washington, DC: The George Washington University Graduate School of Education and Human Development.

Streitwieser, B., Miller-Idriss, C., & De Wit, H. (2017). Higher education's response to the European refugee crisis. In J. Gacel-Avila, E. Jones, N. Jooste, & H. de Wit (Eds.), *The globalization of internationalization: Emerging voices and perspectives* (pp. 29–39). London, UK: Routledge.

Tuliao, M., Najjar, K., & Torraco, R. (2017). Talent development of refugee women. In F. M. Nafukho, K. Dirani, & B. Irby (Eds.), *Talent development and the global economy: Perspectives from special interest groups* (pp. 41–60). Charlotte, NC: Information Age Publications. Retrieved from http://digitalcommons.unl.edu/cgi/viewcontent.cgi?article=1082&context=cehsedadfacpub

UNESCO. (n.d.). *Higher education and the sustainable development goals*. Retrieved from https://en.unesco.org/themes/higher-education/sdgs

UNESCO. (2018). *Global education monitoring report 2019: Migration, displacement, and education: Building bridges, not walls*. Paris, France: Author. Retrieved from https://en.unesco.org/gem-report/report/2019/migration

UNHCR. (2011). *The 1951 convention relating to the status of refugees and its 1967 protocol*. Retrieved from www.unhcr.org/about-us/background/4ec262df9/1951-convention-relating-status-refugees-its-1967-protocol.html

UNHCR. (2016a). *The Kyrgyz republic: Factsheet*. Retrieved from www.unhcr.org/protection/operations/500016f59/kyrgyz-republic-fact-sheet.html?query=kyrgyz%20republic%20refugees

UNHCR. (2016b). *Aiming higher: The other one percent: UNHCR education report 2016*. Retrieved from www.unhcr.org/aiming-higher.html

UNHCR. (2017a). *Egypt: Factsheet*. Cairo, Egypt: United Nations High Commission for Refugees. Retrieved from http://reporting.unhcr.org/sites/default/files/UNHCR%20Egypt%20Factsheet%20-%20September%202017.pdf

UNHCR. (2017b). *The other one per cent: Refugee students in higher education*. UNHCR. Retrieved from www.unhcr.org/publications/education/5bc4affc4/other-percent-refugee-students-higher-education-dafi-annual-report-2017.html

UNHCR. (2018, February 9). *Refugee women and children face heightened risk of sexual violence amid tensions and overcrowding at reception facilities on Greek islands*. [Press Release]. Retrieved from www.unhcr.org/news/briefing/2018/2/5a7d67c4b/refugee-women-children-face-heightened-risk-sexual-violence-amid-tensions.html

Watenpaugh, K. D. (2016). Principles for the protection and support of refugee university students: A global imperative and the definitive challenge to the human right to education. In *Supporting displaced and refugee students in higher education: Principles and best practices*. New York, NY: Institute of International Education.

Watenpaugh, K. D., Fricke, A. L., & King, J. R. (2014). *The war follows them: Syrian university students and scholars in Lebanon*. Institute of International Education and UC Davis. Retrieved from www.iie.org/Research-and-Publications/Publications-and-Reports/IIE-Bookstore/The-War-Follows-Them-Syrian-University-Students-And-Scholars-In-Lebanon#.V567XEOrJD8

Wiseman, A. W., Damaschke-Deitrick, L., Galegher, E., & Park, M. (2019). The contested expectations of education as a panacea for refugee transitions. In A. W. Wiseman, L. Damaschke-Deitrick, E. Galegher, & M. Park (Eds.), *Comparative perspectives on refugee youth education*. Abingdon, UK: Routledge.

World Bank. (2019). *The World Bank in the Kyrgyz republic*. Retrieved from www.worldbank.org/en/country/kyrgyzrepublic/overview

Wright, L., & Plasterer, R. (2010). Beyond basic education: Exploring opportunities for higher learning in Kenyan refugee camps. *Refuge: Canada's Journal on Refugees*, 27(2), 42–56.

Zeus, B. (2011). Exploring barriers to higher education in protracted refugee situations: The case of Burmese refugees in Thailand. *Journal of Refugee Studies*, 24(2), 256–276.

7 Emergency Education for Rohingya Refugee Children in Bangladesh
An Analysis of the Policies, Practices, and Limitations

Mahbub Alam Prodip and Johanna Garnett

Introduction

More than one million Rohingyas from Myanmar (Burma) have fled to Bangladesh as refugees over the last 40 years. On 25 August 2017, attacks by the Arakan Rohingya Salvation Army (ARSA) on 30 police outposts in Maungdaw, Buthidaung, and Rathedaung townships in northern Rakhine State (formerly Arakan) resulted in Myanmar military counterinsurgency operations, and nearly 700,000 Rohingyas fleeing. They joined previously displaced Rohingya, and one year later, around 800,000 Rohingya are living in two registered refugee camps, new spontaneous settlements, and makeshift settlements and among host communities in Teknaf and Ukhiya *upazilas* (administrative regions) around the barren hills of Cox's Bazar in southern Bangladesh (Joint Rapid Needs Assessments (JRNA), 2017; UN News, 2018b).

This massive refugee emergency has become one of the world's worst humanitarian and human rights catastrophes. The Myanmar military, the Tatmadaw, has been accused of using disproportionate force in Rakhine State with state counselor, Aung San Su Kyi, vilified for her lack of response for defending the Rohingya (UN News, 2018b). According to the United Nations, this humanitarian crisis constitutes "elements of genocide" and has resulted in accusations of "ethnic cleansing" (UN News, 2018b).[1]

A year after the attacks, Myanmar says it is willing to begin the process of repatriating refugees from Bangladesh; however, despite claims that it has built transit centers to receive Rohingya returnees to western Rakhine State, at the time of writing, the situation is at a stalemate and actions on the ground in Rakhine seem counterproductive to repatriation.[2] Very few genuinely believe the right conditions for the return of the Rohingya refugees are present (Uddin, 2018).

Around 415,000 of these Rohingya refugees are children, many orphaned by the violence. The majority of these children do not have access to educational opportunities and there are fears for a "lost generation" (Children on the Edge, 2018; UN News, 2018a). It is argued that, as part of the humanitarian response, children who have newly arrived in Cox's Bazar urgently need educational opportunities and assistance to help them in processing the horrific events they have lived through and provide them with skills for the future (Children on the Edge, 2018; Global Education Cluster, 2018).

A number of international non-governmental organizations (INGOs) and non-governmental organizations (NGOs) in Bangladesh are offering non-formal educational opportunities to refugee children in both registered camps and makeshift settlements. Some of the INGOs and NGOs, such as United Nations International Children's Fund (UNICEF), United Nations High Commissioner for Refugees (UNHCR), Save the Children International (SCI), and OBAT Helpers initiate and manage funds for offering Emergency Education (EE) to Rohingya refugee children in the camps. In order to implement these EE programs, some national and local NGOs such as Bangladesh Rehabilitation Assistance Committee (BRAC), Community Development Center (CODEC), MUKTI, Dhaka Ahsania Mission (DAM), and Young Power in Social Action (YPSA) are directly involved with the execution of emergency related issues in the camps and makeshift settlements (GEC, 2018).

The situation in the camps for Rohingya refugees is precarious due to overcrowding, disease, lack of suitable shelter, and prevailing weather conditions. Women and young girls are particularly vulnerable due to lack of basic facilities, and sexual violence is rife (UN News, 2018a). Facilitating education in these circumstances is particularly challenging. With this backdrop, the objective of this study is to analyze the non-formal and informal education policies and practices in place for Rohingya refugee children in Bangladesh. This study also explores the limitations of EE for Rohingya refugee children during this time of great transition and flux.

This research is based on fieldwork in mid-2018, where one of the authors conducted semi-structured interviews with education providers, teachers, and parents of Rohingya refugee students, while observing, firsthand, some of the processes and practices being applied (almost literally) on the ground. The study begins with a review of the literature on education in emergencies (EiE) and prior research into EiE for refugees in camps. It then presents a brief overview of Rohingya exclusion in Myanmar and the Rohingya refugee situation in Bangladesh before examining local adaptations for educational transitions for this displaced, stateless,[3] and traumatized population.

Education in Emergencies: International Context

Education has officially been recognized as a human right through the adoption of the Universal Declaration of Human Rights (UDHR) in

1948 (UNICEF, 2007). A rights-based approach to development means empowering marginalized groups, challenging oppression and exclusion, and changing power relations (Uvin, 2010, p. 172). Programs should therefore "respect the dignity and individual autonomy of all those whom it claims to help, and create opportunities for their participation" (Uvin, 2010, p. 170).

Education is viewed as integral to development (Buckland, 2004; Dryden-Peterson, 2015a; Pigozzi, 1999; Sen, 2005) and national, if not global, security (Cardarelli, 2018; Deane, 2016). In recent years, a rights-based approach has become the focus in the education sector. The aim of a human rights–based approach to education is simple. It wants to respect and promote a child's dignity and optimum development through offering and assuring a quality education (UNESCO, 2011). UNICEF (2007) has developed a conceptual framework of a rights-based approach for education for all (EFA). The framework emphasizes: the right to access education; the right to quality education, and respect for human rights in education (UNICEF, 2007, p. 27). With a view to ensuring quality education, it is necessary to pay attention to the relevance of the curriculum, the teacher's role, and the code of the learning environment. A rights-based approach requires an obligation to identify and respect the human rights of children such as their identity, agency, and integrity while they are in school (UNICEF, 2007).

Whereas a needs-based approach is on safeguarding extra capital for delivery of services to the particular groups, a rights-based approach aims to distribute existing capitals more equally and to assist marginalized individuals to claim their rights to those capitals. As Sen (2005) notes, a rights-based approach emphasizes "the capacity to lead the kind of life he or she has reason to value," of which education is key. The international community approaches EiE from a rights-based approach and this ideology shapes the provision of education for the Rohingya refugees in Bangladesh. It is their right to have access to quality education.

Education is also a humanitarian concern, viewed as integral to relief programs and as an aspect of relief-development transition due to its role in psychological coping and conflict prevention. It is particularly critical for children and youth affected by conflict, as a part of an emergency response and for lifelong recovery (Burde, Kapit, Wahl, Guven, & Skarpeteig, 2017; Burde, Guven, Kelcey, Lahmann, & Al-Abbadi, 2015; Cardarelli, 2018; Dryden-Peterson, 2017; Mendenhall, 2014; Sinclair, 2007; Stichick Betancourt & Khan, 2008; UNESCO, 2001; Zeus, 2011). Research indicates "higher rates of symptoms and mental disorders in refugees, compared with the general population" (Williams & Berry, 1991, p. 632, cited in Drumm, Pittman, & Perry, 2004). Further, education is often a priority for families despite difficult circumstances (Sinclair, 2007).

Education in emergency situations for refugees can be traced back to the creation of the UNHCR in 1950 during the aftermath of the Second World War. It has expanded over the ensuing decades to incorporate uprooted people in Africa, Asia, and Latin America displaced by conflict (UNHCR, 2018).[4] A new discourse of humanitarian intervention and protection appeared in the international community in the 1990s in response to armed conflicts post the Cold War. The international community has recognized education as a "fourth pillar" of humanitarian assistance in such crisis status quo along with health care, water, food, and shelter (Kagawa, 2005). During the 1990s many UN agencies and INGOs began to prioritize education as an essential component of humanitarian response (Mendenhall, 2014, p. 67) primarily in post-conflict societies.

However, the importance of education systems to meet the needs of traumatized and displaced populations due to human-made and natural disasters was not truly recognized until the 1996 mid-decade meeting on EFA in Amman, and not ratified until the EFA 2000 conference in Dakar (UNESCO, 2001). Education in emergency situations for refugees, and stateless people, is now recognized as a vital aspect of psychosocial recovery for war-affected children (Drumm et. al., 2004; Machel & Salgado, 2001; Sinclair, 2007; UNESCO, 2001; Williams & Berry, 1991; Zeuss, 2011), and programs are facilitated under the umbrella organization of the Inter-Agency Network for Education in Emergencies (INEE).

The notion that education is inevitably a force for good is challenged by some who argue that there are both constructive and destructive impacts of education; it has two faces. These critics argue that "whilst the provision of good quality education can be a stabilizing factor, educational systems can be manipulated to drive a wedge between people, rather than drawing them closer together" (Bush & Saltarelli, 2000, p. v.). Education for refugees in settlements can reproduce systems of inequality (Oh & van der Stouwe, 2008; Preston, 1991). Further, the discourse surrounding EiE, as a "social" or "emergency" imaginary might reiterate prevailing power relations rather than mitigate, or contest, them (Versmesse, Derluyn, Masschelein, & De Haene, 2017).

Despite research highlighting the importance of education provision in emergencies, historically it has been a second-order priority in conflict and post-conflict contexts (Deane, 2016), and research on crisis and post-crisis education is limited (Burde et al., 2015). Existing studies tend to be either observational or focusing on participants' views of programs to assess the strength and quantity of the existing evidence of effective practices and program interventions in countries and regions affected by crises (Zeus, 2011). The bulk of research is conducted by, or on behalf of, organizations and results in calls for further investment, funding, and resources.

Most research has been done on immigrant populations rather than refugees in the emergency phase. Research on education for refugees tends to focus on formal and/or non-formal education in countries of settlement i.e. the United States, Australia, and Lebanon (Dryden-Peterson, 2016, 2015b). Research on EiE in refugee camps is a smaller subset of the EiE literature primarily because of issues regarding access for researchers (Jacobsen & Landau, 2003). Research into EiE for Rohingya is even more limited, primarily conducted by aid agencies and organizations. Prodip (2017) and Letchamanan (2013) are exceptions.

Prodip (2017) studied Rohingya refugee children in Nayapara camp in Bangladesh and concluded that while their educational status was better in the camp than it was in Myanmar, there was clear gender discrimination; girls were able to access education but were treated differently by the teachers. In her study of Rohingya refugees in Malaysia, Letchamanan (2013) argued that they require special consideration because they are stateless and unlikely to be able to return. Oh and van der Stouwe (2008) examined education and inclusion in seven predominantly Karen refugee camps along the Thai-Burmese border and explored the positive and negative impacts on inclusion, diversity, and tolerance in a refugee context. They noted issues regarding the curriculum that tend to affirm the cultural notions of a particular sub-group, and the language of instruction creates educational disadvantages for significant parts of the camp. All three noted that that displacement has both positive and negative effects on refugee children's education, and there is a need for a more structured and stable environment with adequate resources.

As can be seen from the above discussion, there is a global expectation that Rohingya refugee children have access to some form of education during their stay in the various camps within Bangladesh. However, as also noted, there are competing aspects of education, which can result in issues of inclusion and diversity in camps, whereby certain, marginalized groups, such as the disabled or girls, have inequitable access to programs. Before discussing this, the history of the Rohingya and their experiences are discussed.

A Historical Overview of Rohingya Exclusion in Myanmar

The Rohingya are an ethnic minority, originating from the Indian subcontinent, and comprise about 30% of the population in Rakhine State in the west of Myanmar, where they have lived for several centuries. They are predominately Muslim as a result of contact with Islamic traders in the 9th to 14th centuries. There were approximately 1 million Rohingya living in Myanmar in early 2017 (BBC News, 2018; Ibrahim, 2016). Like the Buddhists they live alongside, the majority of Rohingya reside in villages and work as paddy (rice) farmers, fishermen, and small businesspersons/traders.

Despite their long presence in the area, Rohingya are not recognized as one of the official ethnic groups of Myanmar. The word *Rohingya* is banned in the country. They are either referred to as "Bengalis" or "Rakhine Muslims." The Rohingya have been denied citizenship since the implementation of the 1982 Nationality Law.[5] Instead, they are deemed "resident foreigners." As such they have no property rights, are only provided with very basic state primary schooling, cannot hold public office, and their freedom of movement is restricted (Ibrahim, 2016; Lewa, 2009). State pogroms against the Rohingya, military land grabs, and violence, particularly in 1978, 1991–1992, 2001, and 2009 resulted in around 300,000 Rohingya fleeing to Bangladesh (Ibrahim, 2016; Imran & Mian, 2014; Lewa, 2009; Prodip, 2017; Wade, 2017; Zinnat, 2016).[6]

The recent conflicts in northern Rakhine State, and ensuing refugee crisis, can be traced back to riots and communal clashes in early 2012. The government responded to those earlier uprisings by incarcerating up to 140,000 Rohingya in about 30 camps around Thandwe and Sittwe (Ibrahim, 2016). A tenuous peace existed in Rakhine for a few years following these uprisings in 2012. However, there were sporadic and localized clashes until violence escalated rapidly on the night of 25 August 2017, resulting in an influx of refugees into neighboring Bangladesh.

Rohingya Refugees in Bangladesh

The Bangladesh government has regularly unlocked its border to accept Rohingyas as refugees on humanitarian grounds despite having limited opportunities (Imran & Mian, 2014). Bangladesh initially accommodated Rohingyas in 21 camps in the southeastern region in Cox's Bazar during the influxes of 1991–1992 (Zinnat, 2016). With the help of UNHCR, a total of 236,000 Rohingyas were repatriated from 1992 to 2005 through the negotiations between Bangladesh and Myanmar. The communal conflicts between the Buddhist and Muslim communities in 2012 in Rakhine state resulted in 90,000 Rohingyas seeking shelter near the border of Bangladesh (HRW, 2012; O'Sullivan, 2013). The government of Bangladesh, however, denied accommodating Rohingyas for the first time, arguing that they had already provided shelter for more than 400,000 Rohingya people (Imran & Mian, 2014). However, between 2013 and 2016 a consistent, increased flow of Rohingyas entered Bangladesh to escape military oppression (Zinnat, 2016). In October 2016, more than 87,000 Rohingyas came to Bangladesh, as a military operation was under way to suppress rebellious activity along the border of the two countries (Asrar, 2017). Most of the newly arrived Rohingyas were settled in the new Balukhali makeshift settlement in Ukhia Upazila (ACAPS & NPM, 2017). One of the camps, Kutupalong, now shelters more than 620,000 refugees, making it the largest and most densely populated refugee settlement in the world, and the challenges have been immense (Reardon, 2019.

After 2005, until now, Myanmar has not allowed Rohingya repatriation despite agreements, and the status and treatment of Rohingyas in

Bangladesh has become a contentious issue (Zinnat, 2016). Providing resources for the Rohingya refugees is not mandatory for the government of Bangladesh, as it refused to sign the 1951 Refugee Convention or its 1967 Protocol, like other countries in Asia.[7] Bangladesh is also not a party to the 1954 and 1961 Stateless Persons Conventions (Abrar, 2015). As a result, the government of Bangladesh does not adopt or follow any domestic and international regulations that can permit the initiation of an administrative process to address the matter of Rohingya refugees or to secure asylum seekers' rights. Therefore, the government of Bangladesh has the absolute right to refuse to provide shelter and support to the Rohingya refugees (MSF, 2010; Prodip, 2017). It is within this context that policies and practices surrounding EE for the Rohingya refugee children are examined.

Emergency Education for Rohingya Refugee Children

Among the total refugees that live in different locations in Cox's Bazar in Bangladesh, 415,000 are children, almost 55% (Education Sector Dashboard [ESD], 2018; JRNA, 2017). More than 53.6% of Rohingya refugee children are in age group 3–14 at primary level and do not have access to either primary education or temporary learning centers in all locations (ESD, 2018). Only 5% of Rohingyas are living in two registered camps in Cox's Bazar. The registered refugee children of these two camps have access to formal primary education (JRNA, 2017). Around 98.1% in the age group 15–24 at the higher secondary level or above do not have access to EE in all locations (ESD, 2018).

Children out of the learning environment both at the primary and secondary level are more vulnerable to exploitation, child labor such as engaging in income-generating activities, the collection of firewood, and household activities, and particularly girls may experience sexual exploitation through early forced marriage. Thus, formal or non-formal education should be assimilated into child-friendly spaces in the camps (GEC, 2018). In response to this necessity of education for refugee children, the government of Bangladesh has allowed and approved some INGOs and NGOs to use the handbook titled "Minimum Standards for Education in Emergencies," implemented by the INEE, to offer basic education to Rohingya refugee children in the camps and makeshift settlements (Disaster Forum, 2007). Locally developed materials are used in learning centers, which align with the standards of INEE. In 2008, some of the INGOs and NGOs[8] prepared a local guidance note titled "Education Sector Standards for Rohingya Response" to provide education to refugee children (Cox's Bazar Education Sector, 2018).

The main focus of EE for the Rohingya refugee children is to provide basic literacy and numeracy up to ages 5 to 14 along with basic psychosocial and recreational support activities (GEC, 2018). Currently, 14 implementing partners have established around 1,200 safe and protective learning spaces, and it is recorded that approximately 141,000 Rohingya refugee children (around a third) have access to these spaces (Education Sector Dashboard, 2018).

In this backdrop, the aim of this study is to explore the issues surrounding the provision of EE for Rohingya refugee children currently receiving education in Bangladesh. The specific research questions are given below:

1. What are the practices of EE policy in classrooms for Rohingya refugee children in Cox's Bazar in Bangladesh?
2. What kinds of successes has the EE policy brought to the Rohingya refugee children in Cox's Bazar in Bangladesh?
3. What are the limitations that restrict education providers to provide effective EE to Rohingya refugee children in Cox's Bazar in Bangladesh?

Methodology

Primary Data

The researcher reached the respondents nominated by the BRAC NGO. Balukhali Camp 2 in Ukhiya Upazila in Cox's Bazar was chosen as the study area because: (1) more than 30,000 newly arrived Rohingya refugees are living in this makeshift settlement; (2) the government of Bangladesh has allowed and relegated the provisions of EE to a number of INGOs and NGOs to educational facilities for Rohingya refugee children in this makeshift settlement. Among the NGOs, BRAC has 64 learning centers in Balukhali camp 2; and (3) the researcher had easier access to respondents in comparison to other camps and makeshift settlements.

An open-ended questionnaire was developed in order to address the research questions of this study; primary data was collected through semi-structured interviews, key informant interviews, and focus group discussions. The questionnaire mainly focused on the practices of the EE policy for Rohingya refugee children in classrooms in learning centers, the success of the EE policy, and the limitations that both education providers and receivers faced in line with the EE policy. The questionnaire was given to education providers, parents of students, teachers, and the Rohingya language facilitators. In total, 18 respondents have received open-ended questionnaires.

The semi-structured interviews were conducted with four teachers of two learning centers of BRAC; two Bengali and two Burmese teachers were interviewed. The key informant interview included the team leader of the education sector, the program officer, and two technical officers of

BRAC, and four parents of Rohingya refugee children. One focus group discussion was undertaken with six participants. These participants were Rohingya language facilitators appointed by BRAC, who worked in the camp on a daily basis. Data analysis was performed through conversation analysis. Informed consent was obtained from respondents in order to preserve their privacy and anonymity. The total number of participants in semi-structured interviews and key informant interviews were four and eight, respectively. And, the number of participants in one focus group discussion was six.

Results

Practices of EE Policy

As mentioned above, education in emergency provision for Rohingya refugee children in Bangladesh is developed by the local implementing partners such as BRAC following INEE standards. EE for Rohingya refugee children is divided into three types including early learning, basic learning, and life skill learning. Within the curriculum, each module lasts for two hours. Early learning is prepared for children ages 5 to 6 in the camp, whereas basic learning and life skill learning are prepared for the children ages 7 through 10 and 11 through 14, respectively. Each session of three types of education is divided into several sub-sessions. These sub-sessions include different activities such as greetings and physical exercise, rhymes, song and storytelling, life skills, Burmese language such as listening, speaking, pre-reading and pre-writing, creative work such as drawing and crafts, play such as guided play and free play, math and science such as health and hygiene, and closing with a good-bye session (BRAC Education Programme, 2017; INEE, 2012).

Standards of Learning Centers

According to the INEE standards, the ratio of classroom to children is 1:35, and this can be expanded to a maximum of 1:40 per shift in emergency situations. In a day, a maximum of three shifts can be arranged with each shift lasting two to three hours (Cox's Bazar Education Sector, 2018). The findings of this study suggest that education providers are trying to maintain the standard of the INEE. By reviewing the documents of BRAC Learning Centre 82 in the Balukhali makeshift settlement, it was found that the number of pupils in class ranges from 37 to 40. The opinion of a team leader of BRAC education sector is stated below:

> We are always conscious to maintain the standards of INEE. Our learning centers are currently running for three shifts a day, 6 days a week. Each shift is for two hours. We cannot accommodate more

than 40 children in one shift. Children are divided into three to four groups for creating a better friendly atmosphere.
(Participant, Team Leader, BRAC Education Sector)

INEE standards require the establishment of learning centers where at least 40% of spaces should be kept for recreation for refugee children (Cox's Bazar Education Sector, 2018). From interviews with teachers of learning centers, results indicate that learning centers have enough space for the recreation of the refugee children. The students have different activities such as playing, drawing, and physical exercise in learning centers. The importance of having recreational space for the refugee children was reported by all four teachers. The opinion of a Bengali teacher summarizes these results:

Our children do not come here only for reading and writing. Apart from studying, we have different activities for refugee children. We start the educational session with a good morning song. Playing and physical exercise are the main ways to provide EE to the Rohingya refugee children. A number of locally developed materials such as charts, cards, board etc. are used while teachers deliver their session in the learning centers. Through physical exercise children can learn about color, shape, alphabet, and numbers.
(Participant, Bengali Teacher, Learning Center)

Hiring of Teachers and Language Facilitators

INEE determines the minimum standards of hiring head teachers, teaching coaches, teachers (host and Rohingya community teachers), and language facilitators (within the refugee community) (Cox's Bazar Education Sector, 2018). The findings of this study suggest that learning centers do not have head teachers and teaching coaches. There are only two teachers; one is Bengali, and another is Rohingya. Both teachers are female. The researcher has also observed that lack of head teachers and teaching coaches do not have negative consequences for children's education in the classrooms. Recruited female teachers taught Rohingya children by maintaining standards of the locally developed materials (Author's Observation, 2018). The team leader of BRAC education sector explained why they recruited female teachers only:

Currently, we have only female teachers. Usually, females are lovely and have maternal attitudes. In crisis situations, female teachers can interact with refugee children on a very friendly basis and stand beside them with a loving character. This kind of behavior helps children to reduce traumatized behavior.
(Participant, Team Leader, BRAC Education Sector)

BRAC easily recruited six language facilitators to run education programs in 64 learning centers. Language facilitators basically work as a language interpreter inside and outside the classroom while necessary. The distinct languages between the education providers and receivers, particularly the team leaders, program officers, and technical officers, result in communication challenges. In these circumstances, BRAC employees always take language facilitators with them when they visit learning centers. The team leader of BRAC education sector explained why they recruited language facilitators, as noted below:

> Our employees face problems in terms of language. All employees of the education sector (except Bengali teachers) in learning centers speak only in the Bengali language. Thus, they do not understand the language of the Rohingya people. As a result, we recruited six language facilitators, and they make a bridge between employees and Rohingya communities. We consider them (language facilitators) valuable assets.
> (Participant, Team Leader, BRAC Education Sector)

One of the Rohingya language facilitators explained how they work for both education providers and receivers in the camp, as noted below:

> Bengali teachers and education providers face language barriers in communicating with Rohingya teachers, parents, and children in the camp. As a result, we worked as facilitators to solve any issues related to EE. If education providers failed to understand them we helped each other by translating language from Burmese to Bengali or Bengali to Burmese.
> (Participant, Language Facilitator, Learning Center)

The language facilitators receive necessary educational materials and equipment such as a bag, umbrella, and shoes from BRAC. They work as per the requirement of BRAC and receive honorarium per day, not monthly.

Rohingya facilitators receive 800 BDT per day. As they work 6 days a week, their income ranges from 19,000 to 20,000 BDT per month. The amount they receive is higher than the teachers of the learning centers.[9] However, during public holidays, they do not receive any payment from BRAC. Thus, their income is suddenly reduced as noted below:

> We are six language facilitators, working together with BRAC in the learning centers in the camp and receive 800 BDT daily. We cooperate with them when they are in trouble. We basically make our community understand what education providers say.
> (Participant, Language Facilitator, BRAC Education Sector)

Although the language facilitators do not receive any payment during holidays, they are happy with their job. They think that they can work for a long time in the camp and earn money regularly. The experience of one language facilitator is stated below:

> Many INGOs and NGOs work in this camp. They need Rohingya language facilitators to work with the Rohingya community. I worked with UNDP for a few days. Their salary was very lucrative as they pay 3,000 BDT per day. However, their project was only for three months. When I got an offer from BRAC I joined immediately and gave up the job with UNDP. Although this job is also on a daily basis and payment is low, I think this program will be sustained for many years.
> (Participant, Language Facilitator, BRAC Learning Centre)

WASH Facilities

WASH facilities should be combined with every classroom, a standard required by INEE. Standards also suggest that there should be separate toilets for boys and girls in each learning center and the standard of toilets or wash facilities should be 1 toilet per 30 girls and 1 toilet per 60 boys. Toilet facilities need to be built downstream from the water-points and classroom (Cox's Bazar Education Sector, 2018). However, the author observed that learning centers do not have enough WASH facilities. Toilets were built downstream from the water-points and classrooms; there are no separate facilities for boys and girls, and each learning center has only one toilet (Author's Observation, 2018).

Interviews with the program organizer of BRAC education sector specified a few reasons that have resulted in limited washing facilities in the learning centers. These include a scarcity of land as well as resistance from the block head (Majhi)[10] of the Rohingya refugee community in the camp. These lead to poor washing facilities in learning centers:

> We are very open to making a separate latrine for boys and girls. However, we face two main problems. First, we do not have enough space to build two latrines. Second, the block head of the Rohingya community does not agree to build more latrines. The reason behind this is greed; they seek bribes when we want to build learning centers or latrines.
> (Participant, Program Organizer, BRAC Education Sector)

Emergency Learning Packages and Educational Equipment

The basics of English, Burmese, general knowledge, math, and science are needed to be taught to refugee children and those living in the makeshift settlement (See Guidance Note, Cox's Bazar Education Sector, 2018). Education providers tried to maintain the standards of emergency learning packages in the makeshift settlement. The basics of all subjects, developed by the local implementing partners, are taught to refugee children. However, there has been a lack of standardized curriculum and textbooks (Author's Observation, 2018). According to the INEE guidelines, educational equipment in emergency situations should be given free to refugee children (See Cox's Bazar Education Sector, 2018). Results suggest that children receive free materials such as books, a bag, pen, pencil, and writing paper. They also get one pack of nutritious biscuits during class time. Moreover, teaching materials are also accessible and readily available in the learning centers (Author's Observation, 2018).

Summary

Overall, the results suggest that education providers tried to implement the policies and standards of INEE into classrooms in learning centers despite having some problems. They maintained the learning center's standards, educational equipment, and emergency learning packages. However, they could not fulfill the needs of INEE in the case of hiring teachers in learning centers and WASH facilities. Lack of funding limits education providers to recruit head teachers and head coaches, whereas limitations of WASH facilities comes from a scarcity of land and resistance from the Rohingya community heads in the camps.

Successes of Emergency Education

Creating Child-Friendly Spaces

Rohingya refugee children have experienced great trauma and violence as they witnessed brutal atrocities committed by the military in Myanmar. They have witnessed villages burned, infants thrown into rivers, children and mothers shot (Theirworld, 2017). These children are severely traumatized, and safe spaces or safe schools are needed urgently to offer a sense of security and normality to Rohingya refugee children (Theirworld, 2018).

The findings of this study suggest that a lively and safe environment is being offered in the form of learning centers to refugee children aged 5 to 14 years in the makeshift settlements. The team leader for BRAC's EE sector explained how a lively educational environment can reduce trauma for Rohingya refugee children in the camp:

> We tried to create a safe and lively learning center for Rohingya refugee children in the camp. Refugee children like their learning center more than their tiny shelter. Their living place is too small to study. A small living shelter is for five to ten people where children do not

have space to study. The learning center is decorated with various charts and pictures, and children enjoy staying there. Moreover, teachers are very friendly with the refugee children; like a mother. As a result, children prefer to come to the learning center rather than their small makeshift house.
(Participant, Team Leader, BRAC Education Sector)

He also added that learning how to read, write, and calculate numbers is not the only goal of EE for Rohingya refugee children. Apart from learning, children also go to learning centers for enjoyment. It is expected that enjoying their lives in learning centers can be helpful to decrease traumatized attitudes as stated below:

It is difficult to say that we are 100% successful in decreasing trauma in the children. However, the majority of the refugee children who attend learning centers regularly have come out from the brutal atrocities that they have witnessed in Myanmar. They can share their sorrow [sad] stories with the teachers as well as activists of BRAC and donors who came to visit our learning centers. As a result, they are forgetting their violent past gradually day by day.
(Participant, Team Leader, BRAC Education Sector)

Reducing Trauma

Results from interviews with parents of Rohingya children are supported by the findings of Severijnen and Ridwan Steinbock in their report for World Vision, Save the Children and Plan International (2018). The joint report of these organizations found that joyful education in learning centers helps refugee children reduce their mental pressure. Children found learning centers to be places where they can play with their friends while learning to read and write (Severijnen & Ridwan Steinbock, 2018). Consequently, memories of their traumatic past become less frequent. One interview with a parent of refugee children elucidates his experience regarding the success of EE in reducing trauma:

Our children are disremembering the widespread violence by the Myanmar military that they have witnessed in their homeland. When they came to Bangladesh at first, they frequently recalled their days in Myanmar. Now, they barely talk to us about the violent situation of their home country. They go to school regularly and receive a joyful education. As a result, children are emerging from the traumatized status quo.
(Participant, Parent of Rohingya Refugee Children, Balukhali Camp 2)

Another significant finding relates to how EE helps to minimize traumatized behavior of refugee children in Bangladesh. Education providers provide them with different kinds of toys with which they can play and refresh their minds. Refugee children also draw various pictures, which create a lovely scenery and provoke ecstatic moments. Teachers also tell them interesting stories both in Burmese and Bengali (Chittagonian) languages. The view of one teacher is given below:

> When they came to Bangladesh they were mentally shocked and traumatized as they had witnessed violence in their home country. Children are given various toys that they can enjoy and forget their past. We also tell different stories which also help to reduce traumatized behavior. Children also draw various pictures, which in turn help them to be calm (normal).
> (Participant, Rohingya Teacher, Learning Center)

EE has a positive effect on reducing trauma in Rohingya refugee children in Bangladesh. According to the opinion of the education sector Program Organizer of BRAC, their behavior was "strange and aggressive" when they first arrived in Bangladesh. They did not accept the host people cordially and gently. Anxiety was with them all the time. After receiving a safe space for education, it has been noted that there has been a gradual change. Now, the program organizer notes, the children are comparatively calmer than in the past:

> At first, when we went to establish schools, Rohingya children have shown antagonistic behavior toward us, and we were sometimes fearful to talk to them. Now, the situation has been changed as we have provided them with a friendly environment for education in the learning center.
> (Participant, Program Organizer, BRAC Education Sector)

Interviews with the team leader of the BRAC education sector reveal that the majority of the refugee children are now polite and gentle compared to when they first arrived. Teachers have taught refugee children how to communicate with others gently and to be friendly. Refugee children get the opportunity to meet different groups of people such as peers, friends, teachers, education providers, and national and international NGO workers. Children interact with them and observe how they communicate with others and try to act in the same way.

Rohingya refugee children probably did not get the proper environment in Myanmar for being polite and social. Their rough and tough behavior has been changed progressively after receiving education in learning centers. I observed that refugee children are comparatively more modest than previously.

(Participant, Team Leader, BRAC Education Sector)

Independence

The findings of this study suggest that EE has resulted in children achieving a sense of self-dependency. It appears that the children now know how to read, write, and calculate numbers, and this knowledge has assisted them in gaining confidence, as noted below:

> Education is not an individual asset rather it is considered as global equality for anyone. Rohingya refugee children are marginalized in their own country, and most of them did not receive any sort of education. We taught them how to read, write, and count. This kind of education in emergency makes them self-dependent. Nobody knows what they can achieve in the near future. I believe that they can present themselves as a member of the world.
>
> (Participant, Team Leader, BRAC Education Sector)

Overall, the findings of this study revealed that EE has brought positive outcomes for the Rohingya refugee children in the camps. Education providers established child-friendly spaces, which in turn helps reduce the traumatized behavior of the Rohingya children. Moreover, EE assists children to be self-dependent and more confident.

Limitations of Education in Emergencies

Lack of Certification

Refugee children in registered camps receive a certificate of participation or attendance after finishing their studies (Cox's Bazar Education Sector, 2018). However, newly arrived refugee children do not receive any kind of certificate from the learning centers in the makeshift settlements in Balukhali camp 2 in Cox's Bazar:

> Certification is very important for any level of education. We do not have any way to offer them certificates. We, with other implementing partners, are still negotiating with the Bangladesh government to provide certificates to refugee children for EE. It is not logical when we cannot hand over a certificate to the students after offering education for five to six years.
>
> (Team Leader, BRAC Education Sector)

Further, lack of formal certification is resulting in a lack of interest by many parents in sending their children to the learning centers. Rohingya parents think education is meaningless without a certificate. As a result, education providers spend significant amounts of time convincing Rohingya parents to send their children to the learning center:

> As we cannot offer any sort of certificate to Rohingya children, parents of children do not want to send their kids to the learning center. They think education in the camps will not bring any positive results for their children's careers, even when they return to Myanmar. They believe that children cannot do anything without a formal certificate. As a result, we have worked hard to manage Rohingya parents. We arrange monthly meeting and uphold others benefits of education although they will not receive a certificate.
> (Participant, Team Leader, BRAC Education Sector)

Lack of Integrated Curriculum and Textbooks

There is no standardized curriculum in the learning centers to be taught to refugee children (GEC, 2018). Education providers have developed a local teacher's guide and continue activities in the camps, but they have yet to develop an integrated textbook for children. This was discussed by the team leader of BRAC's Education Sector:

> An appropriate curriculum is necessary for any discipline such as math and literature. The biggest challenge of this program is that we are not able to provide an integrated curriculum and textbook in the learning center. We have only developed a teacher guide and workbook. But these are not enough to offer quality education to refugee children. We need a universal textbook. Otherwise, it will be very difficult to carry out this program for long time.
> (Participant, Team Leader, BRAC Education Sector)

Limited Time and Interruptions in Learning

The findings of this study suggest that a two-hour session does not allow enough time for teachers to facilitate sufficient learning for 35 to 40 children. It was observed that no sooner have teachers finished one session the children of the following session would be standing in the corridor waiting for their turn. This issue was noted by the team leader of BRAC's education sector:

> We cannot offer more time to refugee children in the learning center. We run three shifts a day as we lack space in establishing more learning centers. Each shift is two hours only. We witnessed that children of other age groups are roaming around school before finishing the first shift.
> (Participant, Team Leader, BRAC Education Sector)

Children have different kinds of events in the classroom. It was observed that some of them played instead of listening to their teachers. It was also observed that coming to learning centers depends on children's wishes, and some children do not regularly attend scheduled sessions.

Teachers are also busy maintaining formalities when the officials of various INGOs and NGOs come to visit the learning centers. As a result, it was felt that the natural progression of education is hampered because children did not maintain a time schedule and teachers are obliged to respond to the activists and officials of the INGOs and NGOs (Author's Observation, 2018).

Limited Involvement in Education

Despite findings that education is seen as a priority (Sinclair, 2007), there is limited involvement in education for Rohingya refugees. There are three main reasons for this: lack of encouragement from BRAC, need for income-generating activities, and an uncertain future. BRAC does not offer ample food to encourage children to attend school regularly. As a result, sometimes refugee children would prefer to attend the learning centers, which provide more food than the BRAC learning centers.

A Turkish INGO, Small Kindness Bangladesh, provides rice, beef, and vegetables in every day as a lunch. Thus, refugee children run after good food, which hampers children's education in the learning centers. Two program organizers explained how lack of motivation of BRAC promotes children to prefer to attend other learning centers as stated below:

> Some of the students have left our learning centers as they get better food in another school run by the Turkish government. They get rice, fish, and beef in that school. As a result, we found education is not an important issue for them.
> (Participant, Program Organizer, BRAC Education Sector)

> Their first intention is to take food. Food is the first and foremost priority, followed by shelter and latrine. These three things are very important to them rather than any other work in the camp.
> (Participant, Program Organizer, BRAC Education Sector)

Consequently, some children engage in income-generating activities rather going to the learning centers. Additionally, challenges for regular attendance in the learning center are as follows:

> Parents of Rohingya refugee children do not have any interest in sending their children to the learning centers in the camp. They ask

their children to collect relief, firewood, and take care of babies of their family. Thus, they do not come to learning centers regularly.
(Participant, Program Organizer, BRAC Education Sector)

Rohingya refugee children are more curious to earn money than the education that we provide in the camp. They collect vegetables, fish and meat to sell in the market. When they get money by selling goods they forget about education.
(Participant, Bengali Teacher, Learning Centre)

We receive rations fortnightly. We send our children to receive the rations. However, these rations are not good quality. Thus, we need to earn extra money to buy quality food. In this circumstance, we allow our children to be involved in income generating activities.
(Participant, Parent of Rohingya Refugee Children, Balukhali Camp 2)

Lack of parents' interest is also another reason for lower attendance rates of refugee children in the learning centers. Even though parents are well counseled once a month about the importance of education, they are reluctant to force their children to come to learning centers regularly. Some of the parents of refugee children think that education is good for nothing as their future is uncertain, as they are unsure if they can return to their own homeland. Consequently, parents do not take education as a serious matter. A Bengali teacher in the learning center in Block C in Balukhali makeshift settlement shared her experience:

Every month we call a parents' meeting in each block. We discuss the importance of education in crisis. We advise them if they can return to their homeland, education would be a great asset in the near future. However, parents are not serious about their children's education as their future is uncertain. They think that they have to survive in this situation for a long time and depend on the service of the Bangladesh government, national and international NGOs, and donor agencies. Parents also believe that children will take responsibility of their family in the future. As a result, work is better than education.
(Participant, Bengali Teacher, Learning Center)

Limitations of Language Facilitators

As stated earlier, the language of education providers and receivers varies. Thus, BRAC has recruited six language facilitators in the learning centers. However, the number of languages facilitators that they appointed are not enough to cover 64 learning centers in the camp. In some cases, language facilitators cannot provide better and timely services to education providers and education receivers, if problems arise. The team leader of BRAC education center explained why they appointed only six language facilitators and the problems they face in the camp:

> We need more language facilitators. We found more Rohingya people who are sufficiently educated and capable to work with us. They can speak both in Rohingya and English languages. A few of them can also communicate well in the Bengali language. However, we cannot appoint more facilitators as we do not have enough funds. As a result we face problems while we need them in learning centers. As they are only six, we cannot get their services properly; sometimes we need to visit many centers at a time.
> (Participant, Team Leader, BRAC Education Center)

Religious Studies and Their Impact on Girls' Education

Rohingya parents consider Islamic education/madrasahs a significant and useful alternative way of formal education in Myanmar (REACH, 2015). Likely, a few madrasahs, apart from temporary learning centers, are established by Islamic organizations in Bangladesh to provide Islamic education in the makeshift settlements.[11] A significant portion of Rohingya children prefer madrasahs to learning centers. Rohingya parents also want their children to attend for religious studies. Both parents and children are significantly influenced by the religious leaders (*mullah*) in the camp.

> They are fond of Islamic study. Religious leaders (mullah) influence them by asking; "Do you want eternal life or a temporary life on this earth? If you want eternal life you should come to madrasah to study Islamic education. If you like to stay on this temporary earth you can go to learning centers." This kind of statement influences both parents and children for not receiving EE. They [parents and children] think that we are almost dead. They think that they do not have any hope to rise, struggle, and go back to Myanmar again. Thus, life on a temporary earth is meaningless to them, and Islamic education gets more priority than the EE.
> (Participant, Program Organizer, BRAC Education Sector)

Islamic education in madrasahs has more negative impact on adolescent girls compared to boys. Most of the parents always follow the advice from religious leaders when making decisions about their adolescent girls. When girls turn 9 or te10 years old, they usually do not want to allow girls to go to learning centers. The findings from interviews from both teachers and parents are supported by the study of REACH (2015). Most of the Rohingya parents do not want to send their girls to school after they reach sexual maturity, so they can abstain from mixing with men (REACH, 2015). Adolescent Rohingya girls are prohibited from education due to strong patriarchal norms justified through extreme, arguably incorrect interpretations of religion mentioned by one Rohingya teacher:

> Islamic/madrasah education is the first priority of the Rohingya refugee children; especially of the adolescent girls. Parents think that general education is prohibited for adolescent Muslim girls, as suggested by the mullah. Girls' main responsibility is to take care of family members. If girls do not know Islamic education, they will not be loyal to the family members of their husband's house. Because, Islamic education teaches how to be gentle and loyal to their husbands and family members, which is absent in general education. Thus, parents do not want their adolescent girls to study in the learning centers in the camp.
> (Participant, Bengali teacher, Learning Center)

> Girls who are 10 years old are not allowed to go outside of their home according to the norms of the Rohingya community. Rohingya people strictly believe that Islam does not allow female education especially for adolescent girls. Thus, Rohingya girls face problems of freedom of mobility in receiving education.
> (Participant, Rohingya teacher, Learning Center)

An interview with program organizers of BRAC revealed that they have to take extra initiatives to help parents understand the importance of sending their adolescent girls to learning centers. One program organizer shared his experience as given below:

> We frequently talk to the parents about sending their adolescent girls to the learning centers. Every month we arrange a meeting with parents, and our teachers and language facilitators tried to make them understand the importance of sending their adolescent girls to schools. Our counseling works a little as some of the adolescent girls come to learning centers.
> (Participant, Program Organizer, BRAC Education Sector)

The author's observation suggested that the attendance of adolescent girls is very low in learning centers. Some of the adolescent girls came to learning centers by wearing the veil (Author's Observation, 2018).

Heavy Landslides

Rohingyas are living in hilly areas in Ukiah in Cox's Bazar in Chittagong. Comparatively low land is mostly used for makeshift shelter for Rohingya refugees. In this circumstance, several makeshift learning centers are established in hilly areas. Hilly areas are not the ideal place for making schools or learning centers, especially during the rainy season. Rain causes heavy landslides and destroys makeshift learning centers that were made in hilly places.

> The best places are used for shelters, latrines, mosques, and madrasahs in the camp. Learning centers come last. Thus, we need to establish learning centers mostly in hilly areas. When rain comes, learning centers collapse quickly. We need to repair learning centers again and again. As a result, the natural atmosphere of education is frequently distorted.
> (Participant, Program Organizer, BRAC Education Sector)

Roads are very narrow and not made of brick and cement. During the rainy season roads become very slippery and unfeasible for the refugee community. Sometimes, rain causes permanent damage to kutcha roads. As kutcha roads are made of sand and mud, it is very easy for them to be destroyed during the rainy season. Slippery and damaged roads are dangerous for children to use. For children's safety, parents do not allow their children to go to learning centers during the rainy season, and attendance rates during this time are very low.

> Due to heavy rain, the road is very slippery. My son was going to the learning center during the rainy period. However, he fell down and became injured. As a result, I never send my other children to the learning centers if rain comes, even if it is only a little rain.
> (Participant, Parent of Rohingya Refugee Children, Balukhali Camp 2)

Unhealthy Environment

During the rainy season, the environment of the camps deteriorates. The open sewers and sub-standard toilets tend to overflow in the heavy rain and the smell becomes intolerable, resulting in loss of interest from both teachers and students to interact with each other during the rainy season. Moreover, classes were disturbed by loud and persistent noise from nearby construction and road building hampering teachers' ability to conduct classes and distracting the children (Author's Observation, 2018).

Conflict Between Bengali and Rohingya Teachers

As previously noted, in each learning center two teachers are recruited to provide educational services to the Rohingya refugee children in the camp. One Bengali teacher teaches mathematics and English, and another Rohingya teacher teaches Burmese, mathematics, and English. In a few learning centers, interviews with language facilitators suggest a "cold conflict" exists between Bengali and Rohingya teachers with Bengali teachers trying to dominate Rohingya teachers. The monthly honorarium of Bengali teachers is higher than the Rohingya teachers, and this unequal salary structure results in conflict. The locally developed guidance note determines the salary structure of the teachers of learning centers.

> Unequal salary structure creates conflict between Bengali and Rohingya Teachers. Bengali teachers receive 12,000 BDT per month, whereas Rohingya teachers obtain only 7,500 BDT per month. Bengali teachers try to show their supremacy over Rohingya teachers as they get almost double the salary. Sometimes Rohingya teachers lose their motivation to teach children for a low salary.
> (Participant, Language Facilitator, BRAC Education Sector)

Sometimes Bengali teachers used slang language and treated Rohingya teachers very badly. Bengali teachers tried to control Rohingya teachers by labeling them asylum-seekers receiving the best support they can get from Bangladesh, and as a result Rohingya teachers should follow the instructions of Bengali teachers. One of the Rohingya language facilitators shared his experience in the following way:

> I found several cases where Bengali teachers treated Rohingya teachers very badly. Bengali teachers think that they provide shelter, food, and other services to Rohingya refugee community in the camp. Thus, Rohingya teachers should listen to them. In this circumstance, Rohingya teachers lose their interest to teach children spontaneously in learning centers.
> (Participant, Language Facilitator, BRAC Education Sector)

Overall, the findings of this study suggest that both education providers and receivers faced some significant challenges toward implementing EEs due to human-made and natural factors.

Conclusion

Based on a human rights approach, education, as an aspect of humanitarian relief should permit individuals to acquire their socioeconomic purposes and to achieve the skills, values, knowledge, and attitude that bring about responsible and active citizenship (UNESCO, 2011. This research set out to answer the following questions: What are the practices of EE policy in classrooms for Rohingya refugee children in Bangladesh? What kind of successes has the EE policy brought to the Rohingya refugee children in Bangladesh? What limitations restrict education providers in providing effective EE to Rohingya refugee children in Bangladesh?

Findings are that education providers are practicing the EE policy in learning centers in the camps in Bangladesh. The programs being offered by INGOs and NGOs for Rohingya children in the camps in Bangladesh are assisting in psychosocial issues for the Rohingya refugee children in the camps. Further, INGOs and NGOs are trying to facilitate EE, but it is not going far enough for a few issues such as lack of hiring head teachers and head coaches as well as limited WASH facilities in the makeshift settlements. To ensure quality education, it is necessary to develop a standardized curriculum and an integrated textbook, the teacher's role, and a code of the learning environment.

Overall, policies of INEE are well practiced in classrooms in learning centers despite failures due to lack of funds and local resistance from the Rohingya community. However, both education providers and receivers faced a few significant problems in offering/receiving EE in the camps. Despite challenges and limitations, children can benefit more if education providers can work on getting more children into schools.

As noted in the introduction to the study, it is unlikely that the Rohingya refugees currently residing in Bangladesh will be repatriated in the near future, and they are experiencing a protracted crisis. Therefore, EE for Rohingya refugee children in Bangladesh will be long-term, ongoing process. At this stage, education is being viewed as a relief activity rather than development activity by the education providers. Consequently, some policy recommendations are given below in order to improve the quality of EE for Rohingya refugee children in Bangladesh.

1. Education providers should consult with the Ministry of Education in Bangladesh to prepare a common learning framework that can anticipate an integrated curriculum and textbook as well as provide certificates recognized by the government of Bangladesh.
2. As over 66% of Rohingya refugee children do not have access to any sort of education, more learning centers must be established in the camps.
3. Education providers can hire more employees in managerial positions from the Chittagong region in order to decrease the language barriers.
4. Training can be offered to the parents of Rohingya children as well as religious leaders to enhance girls' education in the camps.
5. Training can also be offered to Rohingya parents to help them understand the importance of education in an emergency situation. It is expected that this kind of training can change the mind-set of parents and can reduce children's engagement in income-generating activities during school time.
6. Salary discrimination between Bengali and Rohingya teachers should be reduced.

Finally, further research is required in order to understand the effectiveness of EE of Rohingya refugee children in Bangladesh. Future research can examine the following issues: Why do education providers fail to offer EE to the majority of the refugee children in the makeshift settlements in Bangladesh? How does the impact of formal education on Rohingya children in registered camps differ from the non-formal education in the makeshift settlements in Bangladesh? What is the future of Rohingya children without education in the makeshift settlements?

Notes

1. In August 2018, the United Nations Human Rights Council (UNHRC) released the "Independent International Fact-Finding Mission on Myanmar Report." The findings of this report implicating the Tatmadaw and recommending prosecution by the International Criminal Court (ICC) (OHCHR, 2018).
2. There is evidence that the military is operating a scorched earth policy (www.amnesty.org.au/myanmar-military-land-grab-as-security-forces-build-bases-on-torched-rohingya-villages/). In November 2018 Bangladesh and Myanmar attempted to repatriate thousands of refugees but were forced to postpone plans due to international pressure and fear of further violence by the refugees themselves (Uddin, 2018).
3. A "stateless person" is someone who is not recognized as a national by any state (Goris, Harrington, & Kohn 2009, p. 4).
4. There are 68.5 million displaced peoples in 2018, comprising 25.4 million refugees (UNHCR, 2018).
5. "Full citizenship is primarily based on membership of the "national races" who are considered by the state to have settled in Myanmar prior to 1824. Despite generations of residence in Myanmar, the Rohingya are not officially recognized and are therefore excluded from full citizenship" (http://burmacampaign.org.uk/media/Myanmar%E2%80%99s-1982-Citizenship-Law-and-Rohingya.pdf).
6. Rohingya have also fled in large numbers to Thailand (Oh & van der Stouwe, 2008; Zeus, 2011) and Malaysia (Letchamanan, 2013).
7. Article 22 of Refugee Convention 1951 requires contracting government to refugees the same treatment as is accorded to nationals with respect to elementary education.
8. All partners participating in working groups for standards are BRAC, CODEC, ISDE, MUKTI, OBAT Helpers, PLAN, SCI, UNHCR, and UNICEF.
9. Salary of Rohingya and Bengali Teacher is 7,500 and 11,000 BDT, respectively.
10. Each camp is divided into many blocks and each block has one leader, known as *majhi*.
11. Madrasah is a Muslim religious learning space where the Qur'an and associated Islamic texts are taught, set up and run by communities and operating independently of the government curriculum.

References

Abrar, C. R. (2015). Opening doors to Rohingyas: Duty, not charity. Foreign Affairs Insights and Reviews. Retrieved from https://fairbd.net/opening-doors-to-rohingyas-duty-not-charity/

ACAPS, & NPM. (2017). *Review: Rohingya influx since 1978*. Thematic Report, 11 December. Retrieved from www.acaps.org/special-report/review-rohingya-influx-1978

Asrar, S. (2017, October). Rohingya crisis explained in maps. *Aljazeera*. Retrieved from https://www.aljazeera.com/indepth/interactive/2017/09/rohingya-crisis-explained-maps-170910140906580.html

BBC News. (2018, April 24). *Myanmar Rohingya: What you need to know about the crisis* (online). Retrieved from www.bbc.com/news/world-asia-41566561

BRAC Education Program. (2017). *Teachers guide for early learning, non-formal basic education and life skills*. Dhaka, Bangladesh.

Buckland, P. (2004) *Reshaping the future: education and post-conflict reconstruction*. Washington, DC: World Bank.

Burde, D., Guven, O., Kelcey, J., Lahmann, H., & Al-Abbadi, K. (2015). What works to promote children's educational access, quality of learning, and well-being in crisis-affected contexts. In *Education rigorous literature review*. London, UK: Department for International Development (UK).

Burde, D., Kapit, A., Wahl, R. L., Guven, O., & Skarpeteig, M. I. (2017). Education in emergencies: A review of theory and research. *Review of Educational Research*, 87(3).

Bush, K. D., & Saltarelli, D. (2000). *The two faces of education in ethnic conflict: Towards a peacebuilding education for children*. Florence, Italy: UNICEF. https://www.unicef-irc.org/publications/pdf/insight4.pdf

Cardarelli, R. (2018). Solving the education crisis of displaced children: A most important goal for education diplomacy. *Childhood Education*, 94(3), 61–66.

Children on the Edge. (2018). *Education for Rohingya refugee children*. Retrieved from www.childrenontheedge.org/bangladesh-education-for-rohingya-refugee-children.html

Cox's Bazar Education Sector. (2018, June). *Joint education needs assessment: Rohingya refugee in Cox's bazar*. Report. Retrieved from https://reliefweb.int/sites/reliefweb.int/files/resources/cxb_jena_assessment_report-180607.pdf

Deane, S. (2016). Syria's lost generation: Refugee education provision and societal security in an ongoing conflict emergency. *IDS Bulletin: Transforming Development Knowledge*. Institute of Development Studies (UK), 47(3), 35–52.

Disaster Forum. (2007). *The minimum standard for education in chronic crisis and early reconstruction* (Bengali Version). London, UK: DS Print. Redesign.

Drumm, R. D., Pittman, S. W., & Perry, S. (2004). Social work interventions in refugee camps. *Journal of Social Service Research*, 30(2), 67–92.

Dryden-Peterson, S. (2015a). *Refugee education: A global review*. New York, NY: United Nations High Commissioner for Refugees.

Dryden-Peterson, S. (2015b). *The educational experiences of refugee children in countries of first asylum*. Washington, DC: Migration Policy Institute.

Dryden-Peterson, S. (2016). Three principles for global support to refugee education. *Brookings Education* (online). Retrieved from www.brookings.edu/blog/education-plus-development/2016/09/21/three-principles-for-global-support-to-refugee-education/

Dryden-Peterson, S. (2017). Refugee education: Education for an unknowable future. *Curriculum Inquiry*, 47(1), 14–24.

Education Sector Dashboard. (2018). *Education sector 4W analysis*. Retrieved from https://www.humanitarianresponse.info/en/operations/bangladesh/document/education-sector-4w-analysis

Gallano, H. R. (2018). *Education capacity self-assessment. Transforming the education humanitarian response of the Rohingya refugee crisis, Cox's Bazar, Bangladesh, working document*. Retrieved from https://reliefweb.int/sites/reliefweb.int/files/resources/education_capacity_self-assessment_cxb_education_1803.pdf

Global Education Cluster. (2018). *Education cluster Secondary Data Review (SRD): Rohingya crisis*. Retrieved from https://reliefweb.int/report/bangladesh/education-cluster-secondary-data-review-sdr-rohingya-crisis

Goris, I., Harrington, J., & Kohn, S. (2009). Statelessness: What it is and why it matters. *Forced Migration Review*. Refugee Studies Center, University of Oxford, UK.

Human Rights Watch (HRW). (2012, August 22). *Bangladesh: Assist, protect Rohingya refugees*. Retrieved from www.hrw.org/news/2012/08/22/bangladesh-assist-protect-rohingya-refugees

Ibrahim, A. (2016). *The Rohingyas: Inside Myanmar's hidden genocide*. London: Hurst & Company.

Imran, H. F. A., & Mian, M. N. (2014). The Rohingya refugees in Bangladesh: A vulnerable group in law and policy. *Journal of Studies in Social Sciences*, 8(2), 226–253.

INEE. (2012). *Minimum standards for education: Preparedness, response and recovery*. New York, NY: UNICEF Education.

Jacobsen, K., & Landau, L. B. (2003). The dual imperative in refugee research: Some methodological and ethical considerations in social science research on forced migration. *Disasters*, 27(3), 185–206.

Joint Rapid Needs Assessment (JRNA). (2017). *Education in protection and emergencies*. Retrieved from https://www.humanitarianresponse.info/sites/www.humanitarianresponse.info/files/documents/files/eie-cpie-jrna_report_rohingya_refugee_response_18_coxs.pdf

Kagawa, F. (2005). EE: A critical review of the field. *Comparative Education*, 41(4), 487–503.

Letchamanan, H. (2013). Myanmar's Rohingya refugees in Malaysia: Education and the way forward. *Journal of International and Comparative Education*, 2(2), 86–97.

Lewa, C. (2009). North Arakan: An open prison for the Rohingya in Burma. In *Forced migration review*. Oxford, UK: Refugee Studies Center, University of Oxford.

Machel, G., & Salgado, S. (2001). *The impact of war on children*. London: Hurst Publishers.

Médecins Sans Frontières (MSF). (2010). *Bangladesh: Violent crackdown fuels humanitarian crisis for unrecognized Rohingya refugees*. Retrieved from www.doctorswithoutborders.org/news-stories/special-report/bangladesh-violent-crackdown-fuels-humanitarian-crisis-unrecognized

Mendenhall, M. A. (2014). Education sustainability in the relief-development transition: Challenges for international organizations working in countries affected by conflict. *International Journal of Educational Development*, 35, 67–77.

Oh, S., & van der Stouwe, M. (2008). Education, diversity and inclusion in Burmese refugee camps in Thailand. *Comparative Education Review*, 52(4), 589–617.

O'Sullivan, K. (2013, June 22). The plight of refugee: The uncertain future of Rohingya refugees. *The Fair Observer*. Retrieved from www.fairobserver.com/article/uncertain-future-rohingya-refugees

Pigozzi, M. J. (1999). *Education in emergencies and for reconstruction: A developmental approach*. New York, NY. United Nations Children's Fund Working Paper Series Education Section Programme Division.

Preston, R. (1991). The provision of education to refugees in places of temporary asylum: Some implications for development. *Comparative Education*, 27(1), 61–81.

Prodip, M. A. (2017). Health and educational status of Rohingya refugee children in Bangladesh. *Journal of Population and Social Studies*, 25(2), 135–146.

REACH. (2015, November). *Joint education sector needs assessment, North Rakhine state, Myanmar*. Assessment Report. Retrieved from https://reliefweb.int/sites/reliefweb.int/files/resources/reach_report_rakhine_joint_education_needs_assessment_november_2015.pdf

Reardon, C. (2019, February). Angelina Jolie urges end to injustice that have driven nearly one million Rohingya into exile in Bangladesh. UNHCR. Retrieved from https://www.unhcr.org/news/latest/2019/2/5c5c0be54/angelina-jolie-urges-end-injustices-driven-nearly-million-rohingya-exile.html

Sen, A. (2005). Human rights and capabilities. *Journal of Human Development*, 6(2), 151–166.

Severijnen, E., & Ridwan Steinbock, L. (2018). *Childhood interrupted: Children's voice from the Rohingya refugee crisis*. Report for Save the Children, World Vision & Plan International. Retrieved from https://reliefweb.int/sites/reliefweb.int/files/resources/Childhood%20Interrupted%20Non-embargoed%20low%20res.pdf

Sinclair, M. (2007). *Education in emergencies*. Commonwealth Education Partnerships. Retrieved from http://citeseerx.ist.psu.edu/viewdoc/download?doi=10.1.1.465.9965&rep=rep1&type=pdf

Stichick Betancourt, T., & Khan, K. T. (2008). The mental health of children affected by armed conflict: Protective processes and pathways to resilience. *International Review of Psychiatry*, 20(3), 317–328.

Theirworld. (2017). *Rohingya refugee children need urgent help to reduce trauma*. Retrieved from https://theirworld.org/news/traumatised-rohingya-refugee-children-need-urgent-help

Theirworld. (2018). *Safe spaces help Rohingya refugee children recover trauma*. Retrieved from https://theirworld.org/news/safe-spaces-young-rohingya-refugee-children-recover-from-trauma

Uddin, N. (2018, November 23). Ongoing Rohingya repatriation efforts are doomed to failure. *Al Jazeera*. Retrieved from www.aljazeera.com/indepth/opinion/ongoing-rohingya-repatriation-efforts-doomed-failure-181122124753014.html

UNICEF. (2007). A human rights-based approach to education for all. Retrieved from https://www.unicef.org/publications/files/A_Human_Rights_Based_Approach_to_Education_for_All.pdf

United Nations Educational, Scientific and Cultural Organisation (UNESCO). (2001). *Thematic study: Education in situations of emergency and crisis:*

Challenges for the new century. Retrieved from http://unesdoc.unesco.org/images/0012/001234/123484e.pdf

United Nations Educational, Scientific and Cultural Organisation (UNESCO). (2011). *UNESCO and education: Everyone has the right to education*. Retrieved from http://unesdoc.unesco.org/images/0021/002127/212715e.pdf

United Nations High Commission for Refugees (UNHCR). (2018). *History of UNHCR*. Retrieved from www.unhcr.org/en-au/history-of-unhcr.html

United Nations Human Rights Council (UNHRC). (2018, August 24). *Report of the independent fact-finding mission on Myanmar*. Retrieved from www.ohchr.org/EN/HRBodies/HRC/MyanmarFFM/Pages/ReportoftheMyanmarFFM.aspx

UN News. (2018a). *UNICEF warns of "lost generation" of Rohingya youth, one year after Myanmar exodus*. Retrieved from https://news.un.org/en/story/2018/08/1017632

UN News. (2018b). *No other conclusion, ethnic cleansing of Rohingyas in Myanmar continues: Senior UN rights official*. Retrieved from https://news.un.org/en/story/2018/03/1004232

Uvin, P. (2010). From the right to development to the rights-based approach: How "human rights" entered development. In A. Cornwell & D. Eade (Eds.), *Deconstructing development discourse; Buzzwords and Fuzzwords* (pp. 163–174). Warwickshire, UK: Practical Action Publishing.

Versmesse, I., Derluyn, I., Masschelein, J., & De Haene, L. (2017). After conflict comes education? Reflections on the representations of emergencies in "education in emergencies." *Journal of Comparative Education*, 53(4), 538–557.

Wade, F. (2017). *Myanmar's enemy within: Buddhist violence and the making of a Muslim "other."* London: Zed Books.

Williams, C. L., & Berry, J. W. (1991). Primary prevention of acculturative stress among refugees: Application of psychological theory and practice. *American Psychologist*, 46(6), 632–641.

Zeus, B. (2011). Exploring barriers to higher education in protracted refugee situations: The case of Burmese refugees in Thailand. *Journal of Refugee Studies*, 24(2), 256–276.

Zinnat, M. A. (2016, June 18). 3 lakh Rohingyas staying illegally. *The Daily Star*. Retrieved from www.thedailystar.net/frontpage/three-lakh-illegal-rohingyas-1241512

8 Immigrant Latina Youth and Their Education Experiences in the United States

Gabrielle Oliveira and Mariana Lima Becker

The immigration experiences of immigrant Latinx[1] populations are quite diverse and deserve exploration. Immigrant Latino/a youth often find themselves caught between two worlds, neither fully American nor fully part of their parents' country. Many also arrive without having experienced formal education in their countries of origin nor literacy in their native language (Boehm, 2012; Noguera, 2006). In this study, we argue that immigrant Latinx youth's narrative of centering education and formal schooling in their lives appears as a way to connect to the expectations their migrant mothers create. These immigrant Latinx youth are a particularly vulnerable population as they bear the gender ideology of patriarchal societies (Dreby, 2010; Hirsch, 2003; Hondagneu-Sotelo, 2007; Oliveira, 2018). There is growing evidence that immigrant youth are susceptible to a variety of hardships and pressures that many adults, including their parents, do not fully understand (Bellino, 2017; Gonzales, 2016). In this study, we show through the story of Stella, an undocumented immigrant Latinx youth from Mexico who arrived in the United States in her teens, how she and other Latinx immigrant youth navigate the newfound school system and how their mothers' expectations shape their experiences. Her story represents trends that are present in the educational experiences of other immigrant Latinx youth in this research. We show through their stories that they arrive to the United States with high hopes for their schooling experience; however, they face a number of obstacles as they enter US formal education.

Stella left Mexico to reunify with her mother in New York City. She was smuggled through the border and endured brutal conditions during her crossing. Her town in Mexico had recently been the target of a series of retaliation attacks by different drug cartels, and her mother in New York City grew increasingly worried. Stella did not apply for asylum. Family members and friends advised her against it. According to the Department of Homeland Security (DHS), 667 Mexican nationals who submitted an affirmative US asylum application were granted asylee status in 2015. That number is higher than the norm. For example, only 202 affirmative Mexican asylum cases were approved in 2013. In the case of Mexican nationals that are already in the United States and are in removal proceedings, the probability of gaining asylum is ever more grim. Only 203 out of nearly 9,000 applications in 2015 were eventually approved by immigration judges. That is a grant rate of only 2.3% Mexican asylum claims, compared with a 48% approval rate for all countries overall in the immigration courts (DHS, 2015).

Stella's story is one filled with multi-layered trauma that includes maternal separation, the insecurities of living in her town in Mexico, the difficulties of border crossing, and the hardships of living in the United States with no legal protections whatsoever. While immigrant and refugee youth's experiences differ greatly based on myriad factors, including whether they are undocumented or have had exposure to long-term persecution or war, many face common obstacles such as language barriers, discrimination in their new communities, and difficulty adjusting to new educational and social settings. More often than not refugees, asylum-seekers, and undocumented migrants are described as having similar experiences of prearrival and post-arrival in the United States. While it is important to provide context as to how youth arrived into the United States, it is also crucial to understand the parallels that exist between young people who are labeled refugees and undocumented immigrants. In this study we use the story of Stella, not a refugee, but an undocumented immigrant Latinx youth to show how both immigrant and refugee young people share similar struggles. Perhaps readers and policymakers will take note of how experiences are different and the same in many instances and find ways to make changes relevant to these populations.

Data for this research is deeply ethnographic as this study was conducted with immigrant youth in the United States and Mexico. In this study, we first describe the context of gender and Latin American migration in the United States, and the conceptual framework that contributes to our understanding of female youth's views of education in the United States. Next, we outline the methods used to collect data. We then present the story of Stella. Stella's story is more than an anecdote; her story represents much of the struggle lived by other undocumented immigrant Latinx adolescents who ultimately use education as a way *in*: a way into their new lives in the United States, a way into what their immigrant mothers' had *sacrificed* for. On the one side, undocumented Latinx immigrant youth are a vulnerable population in the United States; on the other hand, they are expected to succeed and do well. This study ultimately argues that education and schooling are at the top of undocumented Latina immigrant youth's goals. However, the hardships that come with the experiences of schooling were not expected by youth nor by their parents.

The Education of Immigrants and Refugees in the United States

In this section of the chapter we aim at providing a short overview of the similar hurdles placed by society for immigrants and refugees alike. These categories of immigrants and refugees can be quite problematic as circulating assumptions of their past and present permeate societal expectations and collective consciousness. We use the literature below to show where and when intersectionality appears between the groups and call attention to practices done in school that may exclude minoritized groups whether classified as refugees or immigrants. Trauma filled narratives exist in the lives of both immigrant populations and refugees. From a political standpoint, refugees face war persecutions and may live in several different nations and camps before arriving to the United States. The assumption behind immigrant populations is that they are "volunteers" and they make conscious choices to *leave*. This assumption is problematic and removes the complexity of the interplay between agency, structure, and the historical contexts between nations.

The rising global mobility, where over 3% of the world's population is living outside of their country of origin, involves migrants who left their homes for a multitude of reasons as well as a growing 65 million individuals classified as refugees, internally displaced persons, or asylum-seekers (Bajaj & Bartlett, 2017; Murray & Marx, 2013). While the public discourse and attitudes toward migrants in the United States have been highly politicized and often times dominated by the "authorized vs. unauthorized" immigration debate, Murray and Marx (2013) emphasize the importance of acknowledging the heterogeneity among migrant groups and differentiating the perceptions and orientations toward each specific group. In order to understand circulating opinions about and attitudes toward unauthorized immigrants, authorized immigrants, and refugees, Murray and Marx (2013) found significant distinctions in attitudes toward and beliefs about different immigrant groups. Overall, the participants perceived unauthorized immigrants as a greater realistic threat and the source of greater intergroup anxiety than authorized immigrants. The former group was also targeted for greater prejudicial attitudes. In contrast, the participants reported positive attitudes toward refugees and resettlement programs in the United States. However, despite Murray and Marx's findings, the current political landscape in the United States has proven hostile to migrant groups, considering the recent reduction[2] in the number of refugees eligible for resettlement and the restriction of immigrants from specific predominantly Muslim countries imposed by the Trump administration (Mendenhall & Bartlett, 2018).

Despite the notably varied and highly contentious opinions about and attitudes toward different migrant groups, refugees and undocumented immigrants in the United States differ in terms of the central role played by legality in their lived experiences. More precisely, while obtaining and living by the legal status of refugee shape this group's experiences in the new country, the lack of legal status regulates the experiences of undocumented immigrants. In this milieu, these groups' construction of a new life with the added layer/complexity of legal status (or lack thereof) has spurred investigations regarding the potential role of education in affording these populations with opportunities for success.

The education of immigrant and refugee youth in the United States has been emphasized in the literature as a potential site for the promotion of health and achievement of newly arrived adolescents (McNeely et al., 2017), the integration of immigrant youth, and the development of skills needed in the labor market (Rubinstein-Avila, 2016), and often their "sole point of engagement with the host country" (Bajaj & Bartlett, 2017, p. 26). However, despite the importance and potential of schooling, studies have also shown that immigrant and refugee youth face significant challenges upon entrance in the US public school system. For example, the case study conducted by Roxas and Roy (2012), which originally was intended to chart the success of one Somali Bantu male high school student over the course of one year, became a study of how this student faced considerable obstacles in school. The authors identified key, intersecting factors that affect the schooling experiences of Somali Bantu young men, including the resettlement of refugee families in urban areas with high poverty rates, difficulties faced by family members to find jobs that pay beyond minimum wage, and the enrollment of refugee students in poorly funded schools with discipline and attendance issues, poor academic performance, and poorly prepared teachers to work with English learners and address these students' needs. Interestingly, drawing from interviews with teachers, Roxas and Roy (2012) report that the focal student's refugee status and strategies to tentatively succeed in his classes were invisible to his educators who "maintained a meritocracy ideology about schooling" (p. 484).

Another study that illustrates the often covert obstacles for migrant youth rooted in US schools can be found in Solano-Campos (2017) who investigated the experiences of bilingual and multilingual immigrant and refugee children from a fourth-grade classroom in a state-funded International Baccalaureate school in a large refugee resettlement area. The author found that despite the international school's explicit commitment to language diversity and inclusiveness of all students, "proficiency in dominant, colonial languages by English proficient speakers was valued over refugee students' mother tongue bilingualism" (p. 46). Solano-Campos identified processes that ultimately neglected minoritized students' linguistic repertoires, namely linguistic tokenism, linguist subordination, and linguistic compartmentalization.

Despite institutional and societal challenges encountered by immigrant and refugee students in the United States, the role of school leaders and educators in challenging negative views about these students and supporting them in the acquisition of academic English while learning subject-area content cannot be understated. In a study that investigated the school experiences of resettled refugees in two international high schools, Mendenhall and Bartlett (2018) documented school-wide engagement and promising pedagogical practices to address these students' needs and strengthen learning experiences for all students. These practices involved all teachers' commitment to teach both content and language, use students' native languages in their lessons, draw upon technology and encourage peer language support, avoid student tracking in favor of heterogeneous groups in content classes, assessments through portfolio projects, and the implementation of culturally responsive curriculum and pedagogy. Mendenhall and Bartlett also emphasized the importance of extracurricular support through school-based activities or clubs and tutoring to ultimately bolster these students' self-confidence, as well as interpersonal and leadership skills. Moreover, Bajaj and Bartlett (2017) argued that traditional curricula grounded in middle-class, European-descent values and experiences also marginalizes migrant students. Showing the significant high school graduation rates from the schools that participated in the study, Bajaj and Bartlett proposed the adoption of what they call "critical transnational curriculum," an approach that incorporates students' interests, needs, and transnational understandings of their own past and present experiences, as well as future aspirations into the classroom. This pedagogical approach and curricula "can offer newcomer students important preparation for life, post-secondary transitions, and the development of a critical understanding of social inequalities and civic participation" (p. 33).

Furthermore, since parental involvement is often related to students' positive schooling experiences and academic achievement, it is crucial to understand the involvement of immigrant and refugee parents in their children's school. In their long-term study involving two elementary schools, Koyama and Bakuza (2017) showed that immigrant parental engagement was affected by teachers' and administrators' deficit perceptions of parents' linguistic abilities. In addition, migrant parents perceived the lack of language support (e.g., translators) as obstacles to their involvement in schools. Despite this, it is valid to highlight that a considerable number of parents in the study were either trying to understand and navigate the expectations related to parental engagement in US schools or were already involved in their children's school. This process was facilitated at times by a few teachers who deliberately included refugee parents in their classes or invited them to be classroom and/or after-school volunteers. The study presents promising examples of refugee parents who developed new identities associated with some authority in school settings, were able to negotiate positions, advocated for their children and at times even challenged school practices (e.g., infrequent parent-teacher meetings), and actively participated in a parents' advisory council.

In sum, the research literature above sheds light on some of the great hurdles that refugee and immigrant youth encounter as they participate in the US school system, findings that challenge discourses that place schools as prime places for achievement and integration (McNeely et al., 2017; Rubinstein-Avila, 2016). Some of the studies revisited here also share promising practices that can be enacted to improve these students' schooling experiences, such as culturally responsive pedagogies and increased parental involvement in school affairs. While these studies contribute to a more nuanced understanding of the education provided to refugee and immigrant populations in the United States, there is still a need for investigations centered on undocumented youth's experiences in K–12 educational settings, particularly taking into account the dynamics of gender that affect these youth's experiences. Acknowledging the centrality of legal status and trauma that shape the lived experiences of both refugees and undocumented immigrants, this study provides insight into the latter group's relationship with schooling. Through the narratives of one undocumented Latinx adolescent, Stella, we examine the intersection between transnational migration, schooling experiences, and gendered roles and expectations.

The Education of Latinx Youth in the United States

Despite the nationwide demographic change and growing number of first- and second-generation Latinx children and youth in K–12 public schools in the United States, many in the field of education have not fully accounted for the complexity of Latinx immigration (Sánchez & Machado-Casas, 2009). Bondy (2015) identifies the need in research on education and immigration to go beyond assimilationist or cultural differences perspectives that ultimately frame youths' experiences and identities in terms of binaries (e.g., origin/destination, push/pull, immigrant/citizen). Instead, the author argues that the field of education would greatly benefit from studies that account for the complex transnational processes that shape youth identity and belonging. Basch, Glick-Schiller, and Szanton-Blanc defined transnationalism as,

> The processes by which immigrants forge and sustain multi-stranded social relations that link together their societies of origin and settlement. We call this process transnationalism to emphasize that many immigrants today build social fields that cross geographic, cultural and political borders.
>
> (1994, p. 7)

Thus, the idea of transnationalism emerges "as an important lens with which to 'see' immigrant students in general" (Sánchez & Machado-Casas, 2009, p. 5). Furthermore, since contemporary discussions and research on Latinx education are often characterized by an emphasis on quantitative indicators of educational performance, there is also a need for qualitative work and pedagogical interventions that encompass students' voices, views, and narratives (DeNicolo, González, Morales, & Romaní, 2015; Fernández, 2002).

Several authors that investigate Latinx immigrant and second-generation schooling experiences report that these students are likely to experience marginalization and have their language resources underused and misunderstood in US school settings (Fernández, 2002; Gitlin, Buendía, Crosland, & Doumbia, 2003; Palmer & Martínez, 2013; Rodríguez, 2009), as they are often perceived as "lacking" social and cultural capital valued in US society (Enriquez, 2011). In addition, the belief systems of the predominantly white teaching staff emerge as a key factor in understanding these students' schooling experiences, especially in the midst of reports of white teachers' negative views about Latinx culture(s) and families fed by myths and stereotypes (Marx, 2008), color blindness, and assimilationist discourse (Herrera & Rodrigues Morales, 2009).

Studies illustrate the complex interplay of factors that impact the educational experiences of Latinx students in US public schools. Katz (1999) showed that a group of immigrant students from Central America and Mexico attributed their growing alienation from school to teacher discrimination against Latinos. On the other hand, the teachers in the study pointed to the pressure to comply with institutional factors (such as tracking, English-only curriculum, high teacher turnover) as significant obstacles in building positive relationships with their Latino students. Fernández (2002) identified that being an immigrant, a native speaker of Spanish, and a Latino student in classrooms led by predominantly white teachers were key elements in a male youth's narratives about his relationship with schooling. More precisely, in response to the low expectations held by their schoolteachers and the vocation-oriented curricula, this student and his peers adopted alternative practices over attending school. These activities involved family or work obligations, as well as parties and socializing, which ultimately allowed these youth to build a sense of identity and community.

While public schools are "one of the most important institutions in the lives of immigrant children" (Gonzales, 2010, p. 471) due to their power to reproduce or transform social inequalities, undocumented immigrants constitute a particularly vulnerable student population and face legal and financial hurdles that ultimately affect their high school completion and transition to postsecondary education. Comparing the high school experiences of high- and lesser-achieving undocumented Latino youth, Gonzales (2010) explored the relationship between school stratification, access to resources and networks needed for postsecondary matriculation, and educational success. The author conducted 78 life history interviews and ethnographic research to document the high school experiences of 1.5 generation, undocumented, Mexican-origin youth in

Southern California. He found that the negatively tracked students and the students in general track classes reported feeling disconnected from their school, being negatively labeled, neglected by teachers and counselors, and isolated from important services. On the other hand, the positively tracked students (or college-goers) experienced small, supportive learning environments and had access to networks that exposed them to colleges, teachers, and information. In fact, such networks have proved to be crucial for undocumented students, since many rely on them when applying to college and looking for non-governmental financial aid. Additionally, positively tracked students in the study also reported enjoying school and the freedom that it provides, describing it as a place to escape from worries and problems at home. Thus, Gonzales argued that "educational advancement is shaped, at least in part, by students' position within the school hierarchy—that is, their curriculum tracks" (p. 482). These findings highlight the need for school officials to incorporate all students into the school culture and provide them with information about the different pathways to postsecondary education. Smaller class sizes and ongoing college counseling are also recommended to foster greater proximity to teachers and school officials.

Other studies have also shed light on the challenges faced by undocumented youth as they transition into adulthood, a process that occurs concurrently with a transition into illegality (Gonzales, 2011). More precisely, while children have the legal right to K–12 education and their student records are out of reach from immigration authorities, the experience of young adults is shaped by their unauthorized residency status, since they "cannot legally work, vote, receive financial aid, or drive" (p. 605). Díaz-Strong, Gómez, Luna-Duarte, and Meiners (2010) gathered more than 40 oral histories of undocumented students in the Chicago metropolitan area and suggested that this population are under severe psychological stress. Similarly to Gonzales (2011), the authors also emphasized the high school years as the period when undocumented youth become "all too aware of the grim futures awaiting for them in the United States: physically demanding low-wage work, no opportunities for economic advancement, and sometimes even deportation" (p. 29). To improve these youths' ability to attend community colleges and universities, Díaz-Strong and colleagues encouraged widespread support for bills that allow in-state tuition for undocumented students, comprehensive immigration reform that includes all immigrants, and greater awareness among university faculty, staff, and high school personnel concerning institutional policies and available resources that can help these students.

To better understand the experiences of undocumented Latinx students who make it to college in California, Perez Huber and Malagon (2007) exposed multiple levels of oppression including race, class, gender, language, and immigration status. While there are factors that affect the paths of all Latina/o community college and four-year university students, such as the positive effects of strong family ties and the negative effects of racial discrimination on campus, the authors documented the unique challenges often faced by Latina/o undocumented students as they navigate through higher education institutions. More precisely, through the narratives of six undocumented Latinas/os, Perez Huber and Malagon identified the need for social support (e.g., peer, family member, student organization) "to offer guidance and share resources specific to undocumented college students" (p. 850). However, it is valid to highlight that the motivation and ability to look for such social support networks were often at odds with some of these students' need to work part-time or full-time while attending school. Other aspects that are unique to the experiences of these students are the ineligibility for federal and state financial aid programs, which places an extraordinary financial burden on their families, and "feelings of fear, criminality, and invisibility" (p. 855) that stemmed from negative campus climate.

Building on studies that explore the intersections between ethnicity, immigration status, and youths' perceptions and attitudes toward schooling, our study incorporates the lens of gender to understand the schooling experiences of one undocumented Latina high schooler, Stella, in the United States. More precisely, our analysis attempts to account for the gendered expectations that framed Stella's schooling experiences and attitudes toward education in Mexico and in the United States. Before turning to our analysis of participants' narratives and the discussion of the data, the next section explores important studies and perspectives on Latinas' gendered schooling experiences that inform our study.

Latina: Gender and Education

Within the Mexican migration context, Oliveira (2018) reported that boys in Mexico who were separated from their mothers experienced challenges associated with schooling, as they cut classes and asked their caregivers if they could stay home rather than go to school many mornings. On the other hand, girls in Mexico demonstrated superior academic performance[3] and engagement, as well as better grades and school behavior. The author argued that maternal expectations and gender role expectations participated in the different construction of school experiences for boys and girls. Interestingly, the narratives of the girls in the study related success in school to the desire to be reunified with their mothers, live up to their mothers' expectations, receive material gifts, and the idea of school as a place to be free. Oliveira (2018) explains that gendered ideologies within Latin America contribute to the formulation of some of these narratives, but they don't address the full picture.

Focusing on a high school setting in the United States, Cammarota (2004) argued that views of schooling among Latina/o youth are often developed in relation to resisting oppressive circumstances that intersect with racialized and gendered experiences. The author pointed out that the differential treatment given to Latinas and Latinos in society and at school leads to different responses and resistances toward education. While the male youth in the study responded to the frequent criminal treatment at school by resisting and cutting class, Latinas' resistance entailed graduating and receiving a high school diploma, actions that may ultimately engender a "status change for them among men and women in the home, community, and society at large" (p. 54).

Other authors document Latina youth academic success as a way to counter stereotypes that mark them and their communities as criminals or cultural/racial/sexual threats (Bondy, 2015; Chang, 2011). Moreover, Latinas' success in school has also been related in the literature to the affordance of local opportunities and positive identities. In a case study by Bartlett (2007), a Latinx adolescent in a US bilingual high school defied negative labels and expectations of school failure by drawing on the local, school-based model of success and ultimately was able to position herself as a "good student." As the young woman in the study increasingly mastered bilingual literacy practices valued at school, she projected an image of herself that aligned with the local model of school success, which in turn provided her with key opportunities to develop her English skills.

Despite several examples of Latinas' reported desire and efforts to succeed academically and "prove them wrong" (Yosso, 2002, p. 56), these youth may face what Lapayese (2013) called "the miseducation of Latinas" in schools in the United States, a cycle of oppression rooted in gender, race, language, and socioeconomic status. In other words, beyond the subtractive language policies enacted in many schools across the country and the frequent cultural and racial mismatch between these students and the school personnel, other school-based issues participate in the systematic marginalization of these youths. Some examples include "gender and cultural bias in the curricula, educational issues raised by sexual harassment and high teen pregnancy, gendered student-teacher interactions, [. . .] an insufficient amount of teachers who are prepared to work with Latina students and segregation in lower financed schools" (p. 489).

In interviews with Latina educators who work in middle and high school settings in the Los Angeles area, Lapayese (2013) reported that Latina students (and the teachers in the study) were often affected by perceptions of them as hypersexual and unintelligent. These teachers also reported that the Latina students in their schools were often placed in non-college preparatory general education classes under the assumption that they would eventually drop out. Such assumptions, perceptions, and "miseducation" practices may shed light on why Latina students have one of the highest dropout rates in the United States, are under-enrolled in gifted and talented education courses, and are notably absent in university undergraduate and graduate programs (Lapayese, 2013; Sy & Romero, 2008; Zambrana & Zoppi, 2002).

Besides identifying school-based and societal factors that participate in the construction of these students' gendered experiences in US schools, studies on Latinx immigration and education have also provided glimpses into Latinas' transnational schooling experiences by investigating young women's narratives about navigating different school systems. For example, Rodríguez (2009) shed light into the transnational schooling experiences of three second-generation Dominican young women in both the Dominican Republic and the United States. One of the participants in the study viewed her experiences in Dominican schools as crucial in the development of her school identity and thinking, and she also related this positive assessment to the teachers' demonstration of care for their students. In contrast, this young woman's account of her US schooling revealed her awareness of being tracked into remedial classes, having inexperienced teachers, and attending a poorly funded school. Throughout the narratives of the Latina youth in the study, there is a pervasive sense of not being valued in US schools or feeling marginalized due to their nationality, linguistic practices, and skin color.

The trend in Latinas' accounts of facing marginalization, as well as the mismatch between their previous (schooling) experiences and what they now face in the United States, is also reported in studies that explore the experiences of older, first generation migrant women in the United States, especially in the workplace. In her case study of four adult, educated, working Latinas living in North Carolina, Thorstensson Dávila (2008) shed light on the impact of schooling, particularly English as a Second Language (ESL) instruction, on these women's lives and professional aspirations. In addition to the frustration over native English speakers' unwillingness to mitigate their linguistic challenges, all participants mentioned their gender as a barrier to learning English and attaining professional mobility. In this context, the English classroom, which represented the possibility to improve their English language skills, offered the potential to reverse their negative experiences as women in the workplace.

Turning to Latinx presence in higher education, Sy and Romero (2008) drew on US census data to point out that Latinas who make it through high school are not likely to enroll in or graduate from four-year university programs. However, concerning the Latinas who do pursue higher education, there are few studies that explore these young women's experiences as they transition to college. Sy and Romero (2008) conducted interviews with first- and second-generation Latina college students[4] to understand their different types of family responsibilities and how these responsibilities affected their college experiences. More precisely, considering Latinx cultural values that stress "family needs and the self-sacrificing role of women" (Sy & Romero, 2008, p. 216), the authors investigated the potential effects of conflicting pressures and demands on these Latinas' academic performance. Sy and Romero found that for the participants in the study, going to college entailed increased levels of independence while also maintaining a clear focus on the family needs and increased responsibility to support the family by "giving back."

Despite the several accounts of gendered and racialized experiences in US schools by Latina youth, it is important to highlight that studies have also shown the transformative power of educational spaces for Latinx students that build on culturally sensitive practices of storytelling and narration of lived experiences (DeNicolo et al., 2015; López-Robertson, 2012). The potential of education as a space for liberation (Bartlett, 2003) and the complexity of Latinx transnational lives and schooling experiences carry implications for curricula, language teaching, and professional development. While identifying as Latinx may provide youth with prestige among peers (Rodríguez, 2009), there is a growing need for culturally responsive policies, practices, and curricula that validate the cultural heritage of ethnic groups (Gay, 2010).

This brief review of the literature reveals the complexities involved in Latina youth's experiences in US schools; an entanglement of conflicting factors that is also present in Stella's account, as shall be seen in the remaining sections of this study. More precisely, Stella's lived experiences align with the studies revisited here in that, for example, she also saw education as a place to succeed (Cammarota, 2004) and overcome the challenges in her personal life (Oliveira, 2018). However, the in-depth examination of Stella's transnational experiences sheds a new light on the gendered expectations related to success in school, as well as the hurdles involved in navigating US schooling and forging a new student identity (as an eleventh grader) in the United States.

Methods

Data for this research come from a multi-sited ethnographic study that sought to "follow the people" and their stories (Marcus, 1995, p. 106). Thus, this study presents findings, insights, and reflections of Gabrielle Oliveira's engagement with members of what the author refers to as "transnational care constellations" that include mothers in New York City, their children in New York City and Mexico, and their children's caregivers in Mexico. Gabrielle Oliveira traveled frequently between different states in Mexico and New York over a 32-month period in order to capture the dynamism of transnational caregiving and communities that are both here and there. Research was conducted in the Mexican states of Puebla, Hidalgo, Veracruz, Mexico, Morelos, and Tlaxcala, but time was spent mostly in Puebla. In the United States, research focused on the New York City neighborhoods of East Harlem (Manhattan), Sunset Park (Brooklyn), Jackson Heights (Queens), and the South Bronx. During three years Oliveira conducted interviews and observations with several mothers and their children in the United States and then went to Mexico to meet their children and caregivers. Through these many interactions, the author collected structured, semi-structured, and group interviews conducted in Spanish with 68 youth (31 in the United States.); in-depth interviews with 31 caregivers (30 grandmothers and one aunt) and 55 mothers; informal interviews with 36 family members, 21 teachers, and 9 fathers; and participant observation documented through field notes with 12 transnational constellations. Ethnographic observation took place in their homes, schools, places of work, church, parks, friends' homes, restaurants, street fairs, and playgrounds. Interviews and observations were carried out in Spanish and English depending on the preference of the participants. For the purposes of this study only the English translations are available. Following a well-established tradition in anthropology, the author changed all the names of interviewees to protect their privacy.

Sacrifice and the (Mis)Match in Education Expectations

Stella was 16 years old and had been in the United States for two months at the time of our first interview. Her mother, Camila, had finally succeeded in bringing Stella across the border from the state of Veracruz in Mexico to the United States. But that did not come easy. Stella's mother, Camila, lived with her partner, Esteban, in Sunset Park, Brooklyn. Esteban was from Guatemala. They owned a grocery store in the neighborhood and lived in a two-bedroom house with their three US born children, all Stella's half-siblings. Stella had two other sisters, Ana (age 18) and Lilly (age 16), in Mexico who were not brought over.

Camila had a tough life. Her first husband, 20 years her senior, left her with the three girls in Mexico and came to the United States. A few years later he sent enough money for her to cross into the United States. He promised her they would go back in a year to be with their three daughters. However, when she arrived in New York City, he already had a new partner and asked Camila if the three of them could live together. Camila said she felt ashamed and terrible about the situation. She went to a friend's house and asked her if she could stay there until she had enough money to go back to Mexico. It was not the first time her husband had been disloyal. He had an affair with Camila's mother when they lived in the same house in Mexico. Camila told me she had forgiven them both. What she worried about was the shame of returning home "with nothing." Camila explained to me, "I could not take the shame of not being able to send money back home . . . after leaving my children with my mother. . . . [C]an you imagine coming back with nothing: no husband, no money?"

Camila worked as a cleaning lady and at a laundry services shop; she also became part of a cooperative at the Assistance and Education Center in Sunset Park. Through a friend Camila met her husband, Esteban, and together they had three children, Antonio (age 10), Natalia (age 7), and

Nina (age 5). The three children attended school, and Antonio was in the process of applying for a private school because of his strong grades. Camila, like other mothers in Sunset Park, was able to secure private tutoring for her children and she was an active participant in school-related activities. Antonio told me his mom was always watching him and he thought that if he did not do well in school, he would get in trouble. Natalia told me that she wanted to be like her big brother and earn good grades. Antonio was promised a new video game if he got into the private school he was applying to. Even though Antonio did well in school, Camila did not feel she helped him with homework or even to be a better student. The three children spoke English to each other in the home. Camila constantly interrupted them and said, "no te entiendo" (I don't understand you) when they spoke in English to her. Like in other households, children spoke to each other in English and mothers felt excluded from conversations.

The academic achievement of her daughters in Mexico, including Stella, was very important to Camila. Camila told me multiple times how she always thought her daughters in Mexico were very smart and capable of so much. "The problem," she told me, "is that I can't be there to enforce and discipline them." Camila blamed herself for everything that went wrong in her daughters' lives back in Veracruz. Her 18-year-old daughter Ana had two children already and from different fathers. Ana was a great student but since she had her first baby, she was no longer attending school. Her other daughter, Lilly, was pregnant but had a scholarship for high school at a private school in Jalapa, the main city in Veracruz. Camila worried about Lilly dropping out of school, but above all, she worried that her daughters in Mexico did not love her anymore. She told me:

> I have love reserved for my daughters in Mexico. I feel guilty to give all my love to the children here, so I save some for the kids there. I know deep down that my children there don't love me as much . . . yo no puedo reclamar, es mi culpa, yo fui quien las deje . . . no es culpa de ellas (I can't complain, it's my fault, I was the one that left them, it's not their fault). Camila continued, They say to me, you left us, abandoned us, and then I stop them and I explain to them that I am helping them and they say "I want to be like you" mamá, someone that works hard.

Camila had dreams about reuniting with her daughters. She said that in her dreams she cries and hugs each one of them and they talk for hours. It was almost a last piece of hope she hung on to. One day Camila told me she was going to try to bring her daughter Stella to the United States. Camila worried that Stella, like her sisters, would also find a boyfriend and become pregnant. She told me she needed to act fast. A few months later Camila sent me a text message telling me that Stella was indeed en route to New York City. She hired a "coyote" that a friend of hers knew well and paid him half of the total price, US$2,500 at the beginning of Stella's journey. It took Stella three weeks to cross into the United States, not counting her arrests, and another week to arrive in New York City. Stella took a bus from her town in Veracruz to the border of Tamaulipas and Texas and attempted to cross several times. She was caught by border patrol twice, but because she was a minor she was not charged with any criminal activity. It was what the Obama administration called "catch and release." Stella was put into a temporary government foster home on the US side the first time and then one on the Mexican side the second time until her grandmother signed authorizations for release. Her experiences of multiple arrests at age 15 and 16, interactions with Immigration and Customs Enforcement (ICE) at the border, smugglers who were often men who intimidated her caused Stella to develop multiple health issues such as anxiety and depression as diagnosed by a social worker in New York City. She was in these foster homes for 7 to 10 days each time and even though there were children being held there for longer, her time in these institutions were enough to have her fearing the dark and being alone. Stella described what she was leaving behind in Veracruz. "If you don't obey and follow what the *men* (as in the drug cartel workers) say, then you can put yourself in danger. . . . [W]e just never knew when things would be asked from us."

Camila was on the edge of her seat for these weeks as Stella tried to cross. She worried that she had put her daughter in potential danger and she told me, "If anything happens to her, I will never be able to live with myself." However, Camila was worried about the state of her town in Mexico and how Stella would fare there. Stella eventually succeeded in crossing and Camila paid the rest of the money to the coyote once she made it to New York City. Stella was put in a van in Texas that brought her to New York City. This was another long journey where Stella went from front seat to backseat to the trunk depending on which way they were taking. The hardships of border crossing stayed with Stella.

"When I saw her, I cried and cried and hugged her and thanked the Lord for her safety. I was so happy to see my baby girl." Stella told me that day, "I was happy to see my mamá, but I'm so tired and it was so tough." The day they were reunited Oliveira attended a small party at Camila's house. Stella stood in the corner and asked her mother several times if she could just go to sleep. Camila was disappointed from the start and was upset that Stella was not into the party she had arranged. Antonio, Natalia, and Nina were fascinated by Stella and wanted to talk to her, play with her, and show her things. Stella struggled with English, but her siblings made an effort to speak in Spanish.

Camila told Stella at the party, "this is your chance, *mi hija*, this is your chance to make this worth it." By "this" Camila meant her own migration. Stella stood in front of her mother, somewhat paralyzed for a few seconds. Moments later she ran to her room. She locked herself in there and did not come out for a few hours. She later said, "I did not ask to be here." Even though Stella was looking forward to coming to the United States, she was not expecting to go through all the hardships she did during the border crossing. Her feelings about her journey were still raw, but her mother's education expectations were there. This (mis)match in terms of high expectations of accomplishing the schooling and education dreams of a parent were in direct contrast with Stella's lived experience.

In the following months, Stella's situation became more precarious. Since Stella arrived in New York, her mother's husband was having privacy issues and had essentially moved out. By privacy issues, Camila explained that her husband did not feel comfortable living in his two-bedroom home with a *new* teenage girl. Camila said that he liked walking around in shorts with no shirt on and watching television and did not feel he could do that with Stella at home. Camila felt pretty strongly about her children coming first. "If he tells me it's my daughter or him, I will take my daughter, no question." I asked if he had given her that choice. She responded, "No, but I am ready. I can sense in his actions that's what he means. She [Stella] feels really bad and she cries. But I tell her not to cry, it's not her fault."

Stella was working at the grocery store Camila opened and was dating one of the boys who worked there. Esteban was not pleased with the fact that Stella was dating another employee. She also did not speak any English yet and could barely communicate with her siblings. Stella told me she felt really anxious and she got headaches and intense chest pains that prevented her from breathing from time to time. She wanted to go back to Mexico. Stella said that because she felt good in the home where she grew up, she didn't really focus on why her mother left. Her sisters, on the other hand, "siempre quejábanse porque la mama no esta" (always complained about their mother's absence). Camila interrupted her and said, "I have given more financially to them in Mexico than to the kids here! I always gave them money for birthdays, school, *dia de los niños*; there are many women that come here and don't send money to their children. I wasn't one of them."

When school started in September, Camila did not enroll Stella, she said, because of a vaccine requirement. After speaking to Camila again it became clear she didn't have the patience to help Stella find the paperwork to help register for school and felt that school would not be good for her, since she was undocumented. Camila told me:

> You know that saying we make plans and God laughs? I think that's what is happening. . . . I got Stella out of Mexico so she could be someone and have opportunities, then she gets here doesn't go to

school. . . . [S]he told me she can't find her papers from school in Mexico, so I can't enroll her . . . and she has a boyfriend; she put an earring on her eyebrow. Maybe she was better off in Mexico! This is very confusing to me. I try to talk to her about taking care of herself sexually, I want to be her friend.

Stella said she felt intimidated by school and worried about not having papers. She liked school in Mexico, she said:

I was a good student there, I was doing well and I was going to do *prepa* (high school) at the best school in Jalapa. Since I got here my stepfather is always leaving because of me, my mamá cries a lot, my siblings speak English among themselves, and I feel like I have no future because I don't have papers. I really like my boyfriend. I was promised a better school, a better life, better education here. I decided to come because they told me my degree in Mexico was not as good as a degree in the United States.

Stella, at 16, did not think she would be able to attend school in New York City. In many ways, she also spoke about the guilt and sacrifice of migration and the shameful feelings of having "nothing to show" for her own mobility. The fear of not matching her mother's education expectations weighed on this teen, and she struggled to find support in navigating the brand new school system she had to engage with.

Stella's experience was similar to a number of other youth interviewed and observed in this research. During the time she was separated from her mother, schooling and education were topics constantly discussed on the phone. Thus, the idea that once Stella arrived in the United States, schooling and education would "fall into place" did not materialize for either mother or daughter. Like other youth though, Stella tried to figure out how to be part of school and as she said, "go back to class."

One day still in September there was a tutor helping one of Stella's half-siblings in her house. Stella had just gotten back from working at the small grocery store and entered the house to find her brother doing homework. The tutor, Ms. Vega, said hello in Spanish and told Stella she was from Peru. Stella nodded and walked to the bathroom. A few minutes later Stella came out of the bathroom:

STELLA: Do you think I should ask for help with school?
GABRIELLE: That sounds like a good idea.
STELLA: Can you also talk to her and maybe you come too?
GABRIELLE: Sure.
STELLA: I think it's time I go back to the class.

Stella asked Ms. Vega questions about paperwork for enrollment in school and showed her what she had brought from Mexico. The different papers indicated grades for middle school and high school. All the words were in Spanish. Ms. Vega had some questions:

MS. VEGA: Why are you not in school?
STELLA: Because they said I am missing the vaccine.
MS. VEGA: Then take the vaccine.
STELLA: But they said I need identification.
MS. VEGA: Any identification works.
STELLA: What if they know I don't have papers here?
MS. VEGA: That doesn't happen. School is different from the police; get the vaccine and bring your birth certificate or anything you have.
STELLA: Did you hear, mamá? (Stella directed the question to her mother)
MS. VEGA: Camila, she can go to school! Have her go to school! Do you want to go to school Stella?
STELLA: I *need* [emphasis added] to go to school.

Several days later Stella registered for school and enrolled in eleventh grade. She was in the ESL classroom, and her first few days of school proved difficult. Stella, like the other youth interviewed in this research, experienced struggles with membership in a group or multiple groups in school; feelings of insecurity about herself; and with the rupture of how she was once in her own school in Mexico and how she was now in her current school. Stella explained to me:

> I did not understand what it meant to be put in another classroom. I know many things, but I think they don't know that I know . . . and it's probably because I don't know how to say it. Made me feel different and without value. I felt like I needed to apologize for not knowing English.

Stella described how even though she had been a good student in Mexico, her past did not change how she was perceived by others in the present. She *needed* to go to school. She said it herself. That need was informed both by her own goals and by the narrative of sacrifice her mother had constructed about migration. Potentially matching her mother's education expectations had Stella dedicate herself to making education a priority. When I interviewed her English teacher, a 28-year-old Puerto Rican woman called Inez, she voiced a concern:

> A lot of kids get here to our school knowing nothing about American education. They are at a disadvantage. We may help them with language, but language is only the tip of the iceberg; we don't know

about what they have been through . . . and I'll tell you . . . worst we don't know about their papers and that's a problem.

Inez, like other school administrators, was at times frustrated with her own perceived inability to assist youth who had recently arrived to the United States and for the most part were undocumented. The principal at Stella's school echoed the concerns:

> There is only so much we can do . . . at least it feels that way. Most of these families have a social worker breathing down their necks and now there is the added pressure of not being legal. That's a problem! That causes anxiety. You don't have to be an expert to know that. What we are able to do here [at the school] is minimal, and we need to know more about all the other sides of the struggle.

Stella was, in fact, doing well in school. Her grades in English and math were higher than in social studies, history, and biology. Her stepfather was back living in her house, and her mother, Camila, had a sense of pride when describing Stella's accomplishments:

> Maybe, maybe it was worth it; but now will she be able to go to university? She has asked me many times, and I don't know if I can promise her that. Imagine she fights hard and works hard, does well, but her dreams of becoming a doctor or a lawyer are not real because I brought her here without papers. And there are no ways to get papers now. We spent a lot of money with lawyers, I don't know. . . . [T]he other day when I met her teacher . . . you know the one who speaks Spanish . . . she asked me how I was planning on supporting Stella with her college dreams!

Stella began to stay in school until much after 2:40 p.m., when classes finished. She participated in clubs, she did homework along other young women, and used that space to ultimately exist outside of her home. Stella, like other girls in this research, argued that education by way of schooling gave her a space and place where she had the potential to be valued for her own merits. It was not so much about her high grades or the report card, but the *promise* that formal schooling had for those years. Stella reflected on her future, on her undocumented status and on being a Latina immigrant girl:

> I guess I am what I am. I am living here and now I like it. . . . [A]fter all the pain of years of separation, the border, the crossing, being caught . . . I now finally go to school. I like to do something that I can be good at, because you know us girls sometimes can't do nothing. Always being ordered around like I am someone's worker. But I get

to have a space now and my mamá doesn't understand much of it, which makes the space even more only mine.

Discussion

Stella's story is part of a larger set of patterns identified in this research: a (mis)match of a promise of an education in the United States and the reality of her situated self. As a young woman, Stella, along with other youth interviewed, showed a clear commitment to the promise of education after migration. Stella explained her commitment to the path of education as a space where she had the opportunity to be valued by own merits of achievement. Stella saw school as an equalizer of opportunities, where one's lack of formal documentation, in theory, could not stop one's own achievement. Stella alluded to different gender constructs: "us girls sometimes can't do nothing," she contended. "Always being ordered around" was another way of explaining her role in the household, for example. Stella described her school and her education as a liberating space where hope for a better future existed.

Previous studies have discussed the links between gender and schooling. Skinner and Holland (1996) stated that getting an education has "gendered dimensions." Bartlett's work with literacy (2003) discussed the narrative that exists in young women's minds regarding education as a space for liberation. Similarly, Murphy-Graham (2012) argued that the participation of women in a secondary education program in Honduras increased women's gender consciousness, which in turn heightened their desire for change in the domestic sphere. She found that in many instances women were able to negotiate a new sharing of responsibilities with their spouses. Based on ethnographic research in a secondary school in Amman, Adely (2012) posited that young women in Jordan saw education as making them more marriageable, thus enhancing their future prospects. Stella's interplay with ideas of schooling and education is no different. She builds on the space that education represents as her desire to *exist* someplace else strengthens.

Stella expressed similar feelings when she expressed that she *needed* her education in order to be valued by her own merits. Her mother had made several decisions that had deeply impacted Stella's life: first when Camila migrated herself to the United States and left Stella and then when she brought Stella to the United States. These moments of rupture and reassemble of relationships left Stella in a liminal legal space (Menjívar & Abrego, 2009), where she was constantly trying to find her path and in this case through education. A significant proportion of undocumented students have navigated US K–12 schools successfully despite the challenges of migration and discrimination—in addition to the typical difficulties faced by all adolescents. Many have the academic preparation to pursue a postsecondary education, but their economic and social mobility is severely restricted by their undocumented status (Gonzalez, 2009). This was the case presented in this study. The wondering doubts about one's future that ultimately cast a shadow over educational experiences were present in Stella's life. Stella's story shows both the difficulties as well as the victories undocumented immigrant youth face upon arrival.

Conclusion

The expectations mothers in New York City develop about their children in Mexico are related to their migration. They rationalize migration as a way to provide for their children and to give them better lives. That logic is turned upside down when reunifications take place. In the case presented above, reunification and the promise of an education don't come without obstacles. Even though it was ultimately the mother who was able to bring her daughter to the United States, she was not able to assist her regarding enrollment and school tasks. The struggles with language, legal status, work schedule, and an overwhelming feeling of being impotent when facing a teacher at a New York City public school influenced much of the interactions with school.

It was the goal of this study to position the story of one Latinx undocumented immigrant adolescent into the literature of education as panacea for refugee and immigrant youth. Measuring the academic performance of immigrant and refugee girls and boys around the world has been the mission of different international agencies as well as local and federal governments. Much of education policy comes from the type of "big data" produced by elaborate regressions, large samples, and longitudinal studies. In this study, our aim was to discuss what these reports do not assess: the particularities of these young women and their families have implications not only for girls' schooling experiences, but also for their roles in society. The choice of having a youth-centered approach and focusing on the narratives that girls used to describe their education experiences was not by chance. Educational attainment helps young women develop their sense of belonging in their new homes, but not without hurdles.

Youth like Stella worry about not being able to return to their homelands and about the fear of living in the shadows. Her story is the narrative of a young immigrant's journey: departure, crossing, arrival, schooling, and attempts at claiming the promise of education. Will Stella become a DREAMER? Will she be able to do justice to the promise of education she holds so close to her heart? We have attempted to show how through the narrative of one story, like the one of Stella, practitioners and scholars alike would understand these microcontexts and how larger policies impact everyday life.

Notes

1. We use the term Latinx, like other scholars, to move beyond gender binaries and to be inclusive of the intersecting identities of Latin American descendants. Latinx includes people who are trans, queer, agender, non-binary, gender non-conforming, or gender fluid. We use the terms Latino or Latina when cited authors do so in their own work or to intentionally foreground the unique gendered experiences of women and girls (i.e. Latina/s).
2. Mendenhall and Bartlett (2018), drawing on Thornton (2017), reported that the Trump administration is reducing the number of refugees eligible for resettlement from 85,000 in 2016 to 50,000.
3. Oliveira (2018) defines academic achievement in her study as "a combination of academic performance indicated by grades, homework completion, in-class behavior, and the overall educational experience that feeds aspirations for the future" (p. 162).
4. The participants in this study were either currently attending a four-year college program, had attended some college, or had completed a four-year college degree (Sy & Romero, 2008).

References

Adely, F. (2012). *Gendered paradoxes: Educating Jordanian women in nation, faith, and progress.* Chicago: University of Chicago Press.

Bajaj, M., & Bartlett, L. (2017). Critical transnational curriculum for immigrant and refugee students. *Curriculum Inquiry, 47*(1), 25–35. doi:10.1080/03626784.2016.1254499

Bartlett, L. (2003). World culture or transnational project? In K. M. Anderson-Levitt (Ed.), *Local meanings, global schooling* (pp. 183–200). New York: Palgrave Macmillan.

Bartlett, L. (2007). Bilingual literacies, social identification, and educational trajectories. *Linguistics and Education, 18*(3), 215–231. doi:10.1016/j.linged.2007.07.005

Basch, L., Schiller, N. G., & Blanc, C. S. (1994). *Nations unbound: Transnational projects: Postcolonial predicaments, and deterritorialized nation-states.* Amsterdam: Gordon and Breach.

Bellino, M. J. (2017). *Youth in postwar Guatemala: Education and civic identity in transition* (Childhood Studies Series). Rutgers, NJ: Rutgers University Press.

Boehm, D. A. (2012). *Intimate migrations: Gender, family, and illegality among transnational Mexicans.* New York: State University of New York Press.

Bondy, J. M. (2015). Hybrid citizenship: Latina youth and the politics of belonging. *The High School Journal, 98*(4), 353–373. doi:10.1353/hsj.2015.0012

Cammarota, J. (2004). The gendered and racialized pathways of latina and latino youth: Different struggles, different resistances in the urban context. *Anthropology & Education Quarterly, 35*(1), 53–74. doi:10.1525/aeq.2004.35.1.53

Chang, A. (2011). Undocumented to hyperdocumented: A jornada of protection, papers, and PhD status. *Harvard Educational Review, 81*(3), 508–521. doi:10.17763/haer.81.3.d84532vu27772424

DeNicolo, C. P., González, M., Morales, S., & Romaní, L. (2015). Teaching through testimonio: Accessing community cultural wealth in school. *Journal of Latinos and Education, 14*(4), 228. doi:10.1080/15348431.2014.1000541

Díaz-Strong, D., Gómez, C., Luna-Duarte, M. E., & Meiners, E. R. (2010). Dreams deferred and dreams denied. *Academe*, 96(3), 28–31.

Dreby, J. (2010). *Divided by borders: Mexican migrants and their children*. Berkeley: University of California Press.

Enriquez, L. (2011). "Because we feel the pressure and we also feel the support": Examining the educational success of undocumented immigrant Latina/o students. *Harvard Educational Review*, 81(3), 476–500. doi:10.17763/haer.81.3.w7k703q050143762

Fernández, L. (2002). Telling stories about school: Using critical race and latino critical theories to document latina/latino education and resistance. *Qualitative Inquiry*, 8(1), 45–65. doi:10.1177/107780040200800104

Gay, G. (2010). *Culturally responsive teaching* (2nd ed.). New York [u.a.]: Teachers College Press.

Gitlin, A., Buendía, E., Crosland, K., & Doumbia, F. (2003). The production of margin and center: Welcoming-unwelcoming of immigrant students. *American Educational Research Journal*, 40(1), 91–122. doi:10.3102/00028312040001091

Gonzales, R. G. (2010). On the wrong side of the tracks: Understanding the effects of school structure and social capital in the educational pursuits of undocumented immigrant students. *Peabody Journal of Education*, 85(4), 469–485.

Gonzales, R. G. (2011). Learning to be illegal: Undocumented youth and shifting legal contexts in the transition to adulthood. *American Sociological Review*, 76(4), 602–619.

Gonzales, R. G. (2016). *Lives in Limbo: Undocumented and coming of age in America*. Berkeley: University of California Press.

Gonzalez, E. R. (2009). Battered immigrant youth take the beat: Special immigrant Juveniles permitted to age-out of status. *Seattle Journal for Social Justice*, 8(1), 409–444.

Herrera, S., & Rodrigues Morales, A. (2009). Colorblind nonaccomodative denial: Implications for teachers' meaning perspectives toward their mexican-american english learners. In R. Kubota & A. Lin (Eds.), *Race, culture, and identities in second language education: Exploring critically engaged perspectives* (pp. 197–214). New York: Routledge.

Hirsch, J. (2003). *A courtship after marriage: Sexuality and love in Mexican transnational families*. California: University of California Press.

Hondagneu-Sotelo, P. (2007). *Doméstica: Immigrant workers cleaning and caring in the shadows of affluence, with a new preface*. Berkeley: University of California Press.

Katz, S. R. (1999). Teaching in tensions: Latino immigrant youth, their teachers, and the structures of schooling. *Teachers College Record*, 100(4), 809–840. doi:10.1111/0161-4681.00017

Koyama, J., & Bakuza, F. (2017). A timely opportunity for change: Increasing refugee parental involvement in U.S. schools. *Journal of Educational Change*, 18(3), 311–335. doi:10.1007/s10833-017-9299-7

Lapayese, Y. V. (2013). Morena pedagogy: Latina educators and latina youth in urban schools. *Gender and Education*, 25(4), 486. Retrieved from https://search.proquest.com/docview/1372352400

López-Robertson, J. (2012). "Esta página me recordó": Young latinas using personal life stories as tools for meaning-making. *Bilingual Research Journal*, 35(2), 217–233. doi:10.1080/15235882.2012.703634

Marcus, G. E. (1995). Ethnography in/of the world system: The emergence of multi-sited ethnography. *Annual Review of Anthropology, 24*(1), 95–117.

Marx, S. (2008). Popular white teachers of latina/o kids. *Urban Education, 43*(1), 29–67. doi:10.1177/0042085907306959

McNeely, C. A., Morland, L., Doty, S. B., Meschke, L. L., Awad, S., Husain, A., & Nashwan, A. (2017). How schools can promote healthy development for newly arrived immigrant and refugee adolescents: Research priorities. *Journal of School Health, 87*(2), 121–132. doi:10.1111/josh.12477

Mendenhall, M., & Bartlett, L. (2018). Academic and extracurricular support for refugee students in the US: Lessons learned. *Theory into Practice, 57*(2), 109–118. doi:10.1080/00405841.2018.1469910

Menjívar, C., & Abrego, L. (2009). Parents and children across borders: Legal instability and intergenerational relations in Guatemalan and Salvadoran families. In N. Foner (Ed.), *Across generations: Immigrant families in America*. New York: New York University Press.

Murphy-Graham, E. (2012). *Opening minds, improving lives: Education and women's empowerment in Honduras*. Nashville: Vanderbilt University Press. Retrieved from http://muse.jhu.edu/books/9780826518309

Murray, K. E., & Marx, D. M. (2013). Attitudes toward unauthorized immigrants, authorized immigrants, and refugees. *Cultural Diversity & Ethnic Minority Psychology, 19*(3), 332–341. doi:10.1037/a0030812

Noguera, P. A. (2006). Latino youth: Immigration, education, and the future. *Latino Studies, 4*(3), 313–320.

Oliveira, G. (2018). *Motherhood across borders: Immigrants and their children in Mexico and New York*. New York: New York University Press.

Palmer, D., & Martínez, R. A. (2013). Teacher agency in bilingual spaces: A fresh look at preparing teachers to educate latina/o bilingual children. *Review of Research in Education, 37*(1), 269–297. doi:10.3102/0091732X12463556

Perez Huber, L., & Malagon, M. C. (2007). Silenced struggles: The experiences of latina and latino undocumented college students in California. *Nevada Law Journal, 7*, 841–1012.

Rodríguez, T. (2009). Dominicanas entre la gran manzana y quisqueya: Family, schooling, and language learning in a transnational context. *The High School Journal, 92*(4), 16–33. doi:10.1353/hsj.0.0029

Roxas, K., & Roy, L. (2012). "That's how we roll": A case study of a recently arrived refugee student in an urban high school. *The Urban Review, 44*(4), 468–486. doi:10.1007/s11256-012-0203-8

Rubinstein-Avila, E. (2016). Immigrant and refugee students across "receiving" nations: To what extent can educators rely on PISA for answers? *The Clearing House: A Journal of Educational Strategies, Issues and Ideas, 89*(3), 79. doi:10.1080/00098655.2016.1168350

Sánchez, P., & Machado-Casas, M. (2009). At the intersection of transnationalism, latina/o immigrants, and education. *The High School Journal, 92*(4), 3–15. doi:10.1353/hsj.0.0027

Skinner, D., & Holland, D. (1996). Schools and the cultural production of the educated person in a Nepalese hill community. *The Cultural Production of the Educated Person: Critical Ethnographies of Schooling and Local Practice*, 273–299.

Solano-Campos, A. (2017). Language ideologies in a U.S. state-funded international school: The invisible linguistic repertoires of bilingual refugee students. *Journal* of *Research in International Education, 16*(1), 36–54. doi:10.1177/1475240 917692759

Sy, S. R., & Romero, J. (2008). Family responsibilities among latina college students from immigrant families. *Journal of Hispanic Higher Education, 7*(3), 212–227. doi:10.1177/1538192708316208

Thornton, L. (30 January 2017). What legal obligation does the US have to accept refugees? *The Independent*. Retrieved from http://www.indepen dent.co.uk/news/world/politics/what-legal-obligation-does-the-us-have-to-accept-refugees-a7552621.html

Thorstensson Dávila, L. (2008). Language and opportunity in the "Land of opportunity." *Journal of Hispanic Higher Education, 7*(4), 356–370. oi:10.1177/1538192708321652

U.S. Department of Homeland Security. (2015). *Yearbook of immigration statistics 2015*. Retrieved from www.dhs.gov/immigration-statistics/yearbook/2015

Yosso, T. J. (2002). Critical race media literacy: Challenging deficit discourse about chicanas/os. *Journal of Popular Film and Television, 30*(1), 52–62. doi:10.1080/01956050209605559

Zambrana, R. E., & Zoppi, I. M. (2002). Latina students. *Journal of Ethnic and Cultural Diversity in Social Work, 11*(1–2), 33–53. doi:10.1300/J051v11n01_02

9 Teacher Professional Development in Crisis Contexts
Teachers' Reflections and Stories of Change in Kakuma Refugee Camp

Mary Mendenhall, Arianna Pacifico and Shenshen Hu

Introduction

Teachers are essential to the learning process and are considered the "single most important school variable influencing student achievement" (Schwille, Dembélé, & Schubert, 2007); yet, there remains a paucity of quality professional development opportunities for teachers working in crisis contexts (Sesnan, Ndugga, & Said, 2013; Mendenhall et al., 2015). Amid the immense challenges inherent to crisis contexts that entail refugees or internally displaced persons, teachers are expected to: facilitate the transition back to school for students with delayed or disrupted education; help students learn a new language of instruction (in some cases); provide psychosocial support and tend to students' social-emotional needs given the effects of war and conflict on their development; ensure that students are achieving learning outcomes (Mendenhall, Gomez, & Varni, 2018); and help prepare students for an "unknowable future" that might entail returning home, remaining in their host country or community, resettling to a third country, or some other unpredictable outcome not yet identified (Dryden-Peterson, 2017). Despite the high expectations and responsibilities placed on teachers in these settings, they are rarely consulted about their experiences and perspectives, inevitably leading international, national, and local actors to miss out on the wisdom teachers can bring to any decisions about improving educational policies and practices for both teachers and learners (Burns & Lawrie, 2015). As these actors collectively wrestle with the challenges of upholding the right to education for all children and aim to achieve quality education in the process (UN General Assembly, 2015), it is incumbent on national governments and the Education in Emergencies community to focus on the critical role of the teacher. In these efforts, these actors also need to find ways to expand opportunities for teachers to participate in the development and refinement of the policies and practices that directly impact them and their efforts to achieve these goals.

The case study presented on the Teachers for Teachers initiative designed and implemented in Kakuma Refugee Camp in Kenya captures teachers' reflections and "stories of change" (Baú, 2016) about the type of support they need and find effective in their own efforts to become better teachers. We prioritize teachers' reflections in an effort to expand the discussion about what is needed to better support teachers working in crisis contexts and how teachers can have a stronger presence in collaborative efforts to provide quality education for children and youth whose lives have been uprooted by conflict and disaster.

Supporting Teachers in Crisis Contexts

According to the 2019 Global Education Report, there is no global data available on teachers working in refugee education contexts (UNESCO, 2018). Nevertheless, there are "mass shortages, especially of qualified teachers [. . .] across displacement settings, both at the onset of crises and in cases of protracted displacement" (UNESCO, 2018, p. 69). Qualified teachers may have fled, they may have been directly targeted amid the violence, or there were already very few teachers available (Burde, Guven, Kelcey, Lahmann, & Al-Abbadi, 2015; UNESCO IIEP, 2010). In these settings, individuals from the community, with at most a high school diploma and only their own educational experiences to draw on, may be recruited to become what Kirk and Winthrop (2007) call "spontaneous" and "tentative" teachers—*spontaneous* in their sudden and unforeseen role as teachers and *tentative* in either their desire to remain teachers or in their confidence to perform the ascribed duties. Nevertheless, these individuals may have other valuable traits to contribute to the educational opportunities being provided. Kirk and Winthrop (2013) recognize these individuals as "alternatively qualified" teachers to "highlight the context-specific qualities and abilities that inexperienced and unqualified teachers in crisis and post-crisis contexts do have" (p. 126). Recognizing and building on these assets, these teachers still require additional training and support in order to provide quality educational opportunities to their students. Unfortunately, the professional development that is available for these teachers is "episodic, its quality variable, its duration limited and support or follow-up for teachers almost non-existent" (Burns & Lawrie, 2015, p. 7). Nevertheless, the focus on quality education in the Sustainable Development Goals (United Nations, 2015) demands a move away from short-term interventions that have been prevalent, and instead requires more robust efforts to support the number one predictor of student learning—the teacher (Schwille et al., 2007).

Quality Teacher Professional Development: What Is Needed?

There are numerous studies and frameworks about what quality teacher professional development entails (see Hill, Beisiegel, & Jacob, 2013;

Timperley, 2008). The majority of these resources stem from non-crisis-affected contexts. Recently, Linda Darling-Hammond, a prominent scholar on teacher education, and her colleagues reviewed 35 studies that "demonstrated a positive link between teacher professional development, teaching practices, and student outcomes" (Darling-Hammond, Hyler, & Gardner, 2017, p. v). They defined effective professional development as "structured professional learning that results in changes in teacher practices and improvements in student learning outcomes" (p. v). Across the 35 studies, they found seven features of effective professional development. These features and their definitions state that professional development:

1. **Is content-focused:** Professional development (PD) that focuses on teaching strategies associated with specific curriculum content and supports teacher learning within teachers' classroom contexts.
2. **Incorporates active learning:** Active learning engages teachers directly in designing and trying out teaching strategies, providing them an opportunity to engage in the same style of learning they are designing for their students.
3. **Supports collaboration:** High-quality PD creates space for teachers to share ideas and collaborate in their learning, often in job-embedded contexts.
4. **Uses models of effective practice:** Curricular models and modeling of instruction provide teachers with a clear vision of what best practices look like; examples include lesson plans, unit plans, sample student work, observations of peer teachers, and video or written cases of teaching.
5. **Provides coaching and expert support:** Coaching and expert support involve the sharing of expertise about content and evidence-based practices, focused directly on teachers' individual needs.
6. **Offers feedback and reflection:** High-quality professional learning frequently provides built-in time for teachers to think about, receive input on, and make changes to their practice by facilitating reflection and soliciting feedback.
7. **Is of sustained duration:** Effective PD provides teachers with adequate time to learn, practice, implement, and reflect upon new strategies that facilitate changes in their practice (Darling-Hammond et al., 2017, pp. v–vi).

From the literature on teacher professional development in crisis-affected contexts, Burns and Lawrie (2015) published a notable report about the needs of teachers working in these contexts. Continuous professional development, which they envisioned taking place as part of in-service training, was framed by the Organization for Economic Co-operation and Development's (2008) definition of professional development as a set of structured activities, including training, induction courses, in-service training, and continuous professional formation within school settings. The seven recommendations that emerged from consultations with national and international experts working within the field of Education in Emergencies entailed the following:

1. **Focus on teachers in fragile contexts—as professionals, learners, and individuals:** Regardless of the profiles and prior experiences of teachers recruited in crisis contexts, they must be recognized as professionals who need access to the same kinds of high-quality professional learning that other professionals receive.
2. **Develop, apply, measure, and institutionalize standards for teacher professional development:** Establish consensus on what constitutes quality teaching and implement standards for quality teaching; design standards for professional development providers in the competencies associated with quality teaching; rigorously evaluate professional development based on their successful transfer of learning to their classrooms.
3. **Create professional development opportunities that promote teacher collaboration:** Collaboratively based professional development allows teachers to move along a continuum from groups of individuals to communities of interest to communities of practice. It encourages adoption of agreed-upon best practice within the school itself and sustains the types of changes promoted by teacher training and professional development efforts. It allows teachers to reflect together on their own teaching and their performance as teachers.
4. **Provide teachers with ongoing support:** Teacher support was cited as the most important element of any professional development model or system. "Support" for teachers assumes a multitude of forms: place-based instruction, coaching, and even basic provisions of teaching materials (e.g., chalk).
5. **Invest in high-quality teacher educators:** Teachers need well-trained teacher educators who have actual classroom experience, can model the practices that teachers are supposed to implement and help teachers connect theory with practice.
6. **Build instructional leadership at all levels of the educational system:** Leaders (i.e., head teachers or principals) play a crucial role in ensuring that teachers continuously learn through systems, coaching, and classroom-based support.
7. **Use ICT (Information and Communication Technology) to provide access to content, professional development and professional learning communities:** While piloting ICTs is increasingly common within fragile settings, identifying, and scaling proven models of good practice remains rare. ICT can be used to support teacher development within fragile environments (Burns & Lawrie, 2015, pp. 146–148).

While these two lists differ, there are notable areas of overlap, particularly around the importance of teacher collaboration and the need for sustained support to help teachers apply new knowledge and skills to change their practices in the classroom. How these concepts are operationalized in stable versus crisis-affected contexts will inevitably vary given the different realities across these settings. Whereas experienced and veteran teachers may be best placed to provide coaching and mentoring support, the availability of teachers with these qualifications may be limited in most crisis-affected communities. Less experienced teachers can provide peer-to-peer support, but they require additional training to be able to play this role effectively (Burns & Lawrie, 2015).

Although there seems to be increasing clarity about the key components needed for effective professional development, disappointing results from rigorous studies in the United States that have included all or some of these criteria continue to create challenges for the provision of quality professional development (Hill, Beisiegel, & Jacob, 2013). The disappointing results may have arisen for a number of reasons, such as issues with implementation fidelity of the professional development activities being just one example, but it goes to show how challenging it is to design, implement, and measure the effects of teacher professional development. Other meta-studies (TNTP, 2015) show that teachers typically do not improve year after year, and that even when positive changes do occur, it is incredibly difficult to pinpoint a particular teacher development strategy that led to these positive changes. We must keep in mind these challenges as we work to better support teachers, and by extension improve student learning outcomes. It is also important to consider how teachers have been involved as active participants in the conceptualization, development, implementation, and evaluation of professional development approaches. It would be interesting to examine more closely the degree to which teachers were involved, if at all, in these processes and what that means for the overall effectiveness of efforts to improve teacher performance. While there may be agreement about the components of effective professional development, more evidence is needed about the unique experiences of teachers in crisis contexts. The Teachers for Teachers case study presented below is one attempt to elevate refugee teachers' perspectives and experiences about their own professional development needs as the field of education in emergencies struggles to adequately support teachers.

Kakuma Context

Teachers for Teachers was designed for the refugee and national teachers working in Kakuma Refugee Camp. The camp was established in 1992 in northwestern Kenya, and now serves 147,966 refugees fleeing war, famine, and persecution from across Africa, making it one of the largest camps in the world (UNHCR, 2018). The largest populations hail from Somalia and South Sudan, but there are also refugees from 18 other nations, including Burundi, the Democratic Republic of Congo, Ethiopia, Sudan, and Uganda (UNHCR, 2018). More than half of the refugees living in the camp are below the age of 18 with a total school-aged population (5–17 years) of 78,902 (UNHCR, 2017).

The Lutheran World Federation (LWF) is the lead implementing agency for the United Nations High Commissioner for Refugees (UNHCR) in basic education in Kakuma. The schools in the camp are recognized by the Kenyan Ministry of Education. The Kenyan curriculum is taught, and students are able to sit for the Kenya Certificate of Primary Education (KCPE). Yet for many children and youth in Kakuma, access to education remains a significant challenge. At the primary level, 35.7 % of children are out of school (UNHCR, 2017). At the secondary level, the out-of-school rate in Kakuma stands at 95% (UNHCR, 2017). There are numerous barriers to educational access, including inadequate infrastructure and resources, new and unfamiliar languages of instruction in English and Kiswahili, early marriage and pregnancy, financial barriers, and cultural barriers (LWF, 2015). Importantly, human resource barriers including unqualified and underqualified teachers, poor teacher retention, low teacher pay, low percentages of female teachers, and weak management structures have also been identified as having a significant impact on education quality, the security of learners at school, and student retention (LWF, 2015). Refugee teachers constitute the majority of the teaching population in Kakuma, representing 85% of the teacher cadre (UNHCR, 2017). Despite the large presence of unqualified and underqualified refugee teachers, there are limited training opportunities in the camp, and teachers face overwhelming challenges.

For refugees in Kakuma interested in teaching and teacher professional development, UNHCR and LWF partner with the Masinde Muliro University of Science and Technology (MMUST) to offer diploma and certificate programs. One of the academic programs entails a Diploma in Primary Education, which refugee students (mostly full-time primary school teachers) complete over the course of the year. The diploma consists of foundational courses (e.g., curriculum studies) and subject-specific courses (e.g., social studies, science, life skills, and peace education). The MMUST diploma provides teacher education to refugee teachers and a pathway toward certification. The hope is that the MMUST credential will prove useful when and if refugees are able to return to their country of origin. Currently, the credential is not recognized by the Kenyan Teachers Service Commission, and refugees do not have the right to work in Kenya. Jesuit Refugee Services (JRS) also provides distance learning opportunities to refugees, including a Primary Teacher Education certificate, offered by Jesuit universities around the world. Since we began Teachers for Teachers, there are even more actors working on teacher professional development initiatives at both the primary and secondary levels in Kakuma; however, it has proven challenging for UNHCR and its education partners to manage these diverse actors and to assess the effectiveness of these approaches.

The Teachers for Teachers Project

In May 2016 Teachers College, Columbia University, launched the Teachers for Teachers initiative in Kakuma Refugee Camp, Kenya, in collaboration with UNHCR and LWF and with financial support from IDEO.org and Safaricom Foundation. The goal of this new project was to support refugee and other primary school teachers in their efforts to improve their own teaching practice and student learning in the camp.

The Teachers for Teachers approach is based on the training model and materials developed through the Inter-agency Network for Education in Emergencies' (INEE) Teachers in Crisis Contexts Collaborative, a group of international non-governmental organizations, United Nations agencies, and academic partners who work together to better support teachers in crisis settings. The program built on the Training Pack for Primary School Teachers in Crisis Contexts, an open-source set of materials that builds basic teaching competencies for unqualified or underqualified teachers in emergency settings and seeks to provide the knowledge and skills necessary for teachers to make their classrooms protective, healing, and learning environments. The training model consists of two tracks: (1) short-term training conducted over four days consisting of 12 sessions of 23 hours; and (2) a long-term training that runs over several months, consisting of 18 sessions and 60 hours. The project in Kakuma served as the primary development and pilot site for both tracks of the Training Pack.

Drawing on the best evidence for developing the expertise, knowledge, and motivation of teachers, Teachers for Teachers integrates in-person teacher training, peer coaching, and mobile mentoring in support of the following core competencies: teacher's role and well-being; child protection, well-being and inclusion; pedagogy; and curriculum and planning. This model also actively aims to foster local and global communities of practice among teachers in the camp. Over the course of 2016–2017, 130 teachers participated in the Teachers for Teachers program. Of these participants 123 were refugee teachers and 7 were national Kenyan teachers. Due to the high percentage of male teachers in the camp, 113 male teachers participated versus only 17 female teachers. Teacher participants represented 20 out of the 21 primary schools in Kakuma and taught over 30,000 learners in the camp.

During the first year, the training component of this program utilized the short-term and long-term training approaches, with 100 and 30 teachers in the two tracks, respectively. During the training, international and local staff led in-person workshop sessions with cohorts of 25–30 teachers. Trainings were interactive, practical, and drew on local expertise in the Kakuma context.

The peer coaching component consisted of small groups of 4–6 teachers that were connected with a trained peer coach, another teacher from their training cohort, who facilitated continued opportunities for learning through Teacher Learning Circles (TLCs) and classroom visits. Peer coaches received additional training on how to be effective coaches through the Coaching Pack for Primary School Teachers in Crisis Contexts (also available as an open-source materials on the INEE website). These activities took place on a monthly basis for several months following the training. During TLCs, teachers discussed challenges faced by members of the group, shared experiences, brainstormed possible solutions, set individual goals for themselves based on the competencies they had developed in the teacher training workshops, and discussed successes and setbacks in achieving these goals.

All teachers who completed the training were invited to apply to be peer coaches, and the 25 selected (20 male, 5 female teachers) participated in an additional two- or three-day training (pending their short-term or long-term training cohort activities) on adult learning, positive leadership, supportive communication, and goal setting. Peer coaches were trained to create a supportive network, tap into the range of expertise and knowledge among local teachers, and develop collaborative learning opportunities among their peers as they worked to apply what they learned during the training in their own classrooms.

The mobile mentoring component assigned all participating teachers to a global mentor upon completion of the training, who provided online guidance and practical support for approximately six months. Global mentors were recruited and trained through online webinars to connect with groups of 4–5 refugee teachers over WhatsApp on a regular basis to share experiences, offer teaching tips directly connected to the training through a mobile mentoring curriculum, and problem solve in real-time with teachers on issues they faced in the classroom. All teachers were provided with phones, airtime, and data, making it possible for global mentors and teachers to communicate regularly. In addition to the small-group WhatsApp chats, teachers also participated in a WhatsApp group with all members from their training cohort, which served as a platform for teachers to exchange information and ideas with a larger group of approximately 30 teachers.

Methods

The approach we took to develop and implement the Teachers for Teachers initiative and related research study sought to prioritize the needs and ideas of the participating teachers. During pilot work in 2015, we interviewed teachers to better understand their experiences in the classroom (as both former learners and now teachers) and their teacher professional development needs. We used purposeful sampling to select 27 refugee teachers from diverse backgrounds, with particular attention focused on gender, nationality, and years of teaching. We conducted three semi-structured interviews with each of the 27 teachers on the following distinct themes, ultimately gathering 81 interviews during the pilot phase: (1) personal history and experience as students; (2) teacher identity; and (3) perceptions about their needs for teacher professional development. These same teachers also participated in the pilot training of the Training Pack for Primary School Teachers in Crisis Contexts, which allowed us to draw on observations and discussions about teaching in the training room and to compare and contrast them with the findings from the interviews. During the pilot training, we also partnered with a refugee head teacher in the camp to co-facilitate the training and to work with us each week in the lead-up to the training, which entailed four one-day sessions spread out over four weeks, to further contextualize the approach, the materials, and the examples to the needs of the teachers working in Kakuma.

During the implementation of the fully designed Teachers for Teachers program for the first cohort of teachers in 2016–2017, which entailed 130 participants, we collected data through training evaluations, training and classroom observations, peer coaching reflections, focus group discussions, and teacher interviews. In an effort to capture important changes that teachers noticed in their teaching practice, if any, as a result of their participation in our project, we employed a modified narrative inquiry technique. Narratives of Change, as conceived by Baú (2016), can be used as a tool to assess both the collective narrative of a community and the individual impact of a project. These narratives have the potential to identify the stories of significance, analyze the broader narrative that arises from different stories, and unveil formative and transformative experiences in a specific setting (Baú, 2016; Eastmond, 2007). Narratives created based on individual actions, description, and reflection can explain connections and attach meaning and significance, bringing out the dilemmas and challenges, and the ways refugee teachers use their knowledge, skills, and experiences in their environment. The narrative is therefore centered around the narrator, who ascribes meaning to experiences and interprets the contextual information. Narratives are not chronologies, but rather "retrospective meaning making" (Chase, 2011, p. 430); they are a "representation rather than documentation of reality" (Eastmond, 2007, p. 250). We gathered "narratives of change" from 33 teachers (one-quarter of all participating teachers in the first cohort of the program). In total, the findings presented in this case study represent the perspectives of 27 teachers interviewed between June and July 2015 and 33 stories of change that teachers narrated between January and June 2017.

Limitations

Our research efforts privileged teacher self-report data, which we value as critical to any research studies that are about or meant to benefit teachers. Nevertheless, we recognize the need for diverse research methods that provide more opportunities for triangulation and comparison. Given the use of "narratives of change" for this study, the examples provided below also favor the positive changes that teachers noticed through their participation in Teachers for Teachers.

Findings

Teachers working in Kakuma are largely untrained and unprepared. At the time we started our project, only 31% of teachers in Kakuma had received any form of teacher training (UNHCR, 2017), which may be as little as a one-day workshop. Teachers recognized their limited preparation and the paucity of opportunities to get the professional development they need. During the pilot research that laid the foundation for the development of the Teachers for Teachers initiative, all but two of the 27 teachers we interviewed requested more training.[1]

> The first thing's the training. [. . .] [T]hat is the main thing that can help teachers to improve their knowledge mostly, 'cause most of them sometimes they are Form 4 leavers [high school graduates], like maybe they don't know that, they don't have that experience of being a teacher, only the one that they were taught in high school mostly, so [. . .] through training it will improve [. . .] the knowledge and skills and how to teach.
>
> (Clinton, June 2015[2])

One teacher spoke of the inequity of training opportunities, commenting that some teachers in his school had attended multiple trainings while others had not attended any. He alluded to head teachers' unethical practices for teacher selection when explaining his concern (Majeed, June 2015). Though equity issues clearly need to be addressed, the teacher training programs offered by MMUST and JRS enroll approximately 25 teachers per year, leaving hundreds of other teachers each year without comprehensive training opportunities.

The limited opportunities to participate in professional development have larger implications on teachers' pedagogical and disciplinary practice, their motivation and well-being, and their professional identity as educators (described in more detail below). Taken together, these factors influence how teachers build relationships with their students and fellow teachers, and are key considerations for scholars and practitioners working to support learning in crisis contexts. Yet these factors often do not receive adequate attention, particularly from the perspective of the teacher, and may be deemed inferior to quantitative data including student achievement, retention, and completion, which are of great importance, but are insufficient on their own. The findings presented below, as well as the Teachers for Teachers methodology described above, work to expand the knowledge base of what it means to support student and teacher learning in crisis contexts. This section will explore the self-identified needs of teachers, the implications teachers acutely felt due to their lack of professional training, and the changes they identified as most meaningful in their role as teachers after participating in Teachers for Teachers.

Teachers Identify What They Need: More Training on Diverse Topics

Lesson Planning and Classroom Management

Teachers highlighted a range of topics and skills they would like to address through additional and expanded training opportunities. Their priorities for skills to learn included planning lessons and creating other "professional documents," managing the classroom and learners, and learning how to teach specific subjects using different pedagogical approaches. The trainings that teachers did receive and any school-based support that was provided in the camp schools once they were hired did seem to focus on lesson planning to some extent as well as the preparation of professional documents (e.g., schemes of work, individual lesson plans, etc.). Nevertheless, 11 teachers in the pilot group mentioned needing more help with lesson planning and the preparation of professional documents. Twenty teachers spoke about the urgency of learning classroom management skills given the sheer size of their classrooms, oftentimes with more than 100 students. Teachers were concerned about how to organize students in overcrowded classrooms and how to respond to disciplinary issues. One teacher commented that he wanted to learn to "deal with learners, different learners so that I'll not be annoyed when one of them misbehave[s]; you have to understand their habit and their behavior" (Issa, June 2015).

Content Knowledge and Pedagogical Support

Twenty-three (out of 27 teachers) cited the need to learn different pedagogical approaches, and felt that any existing trainings in the camp failed to cover these skills sufficiently, if at all. Suleyman commented that "the most thing that I wish to learn in teacher training, any teacher training, is methods—methods and how to teach subjects, different subjects" (June 2015). Twenty teachers felt that they needed more information about the specific subject they were asked to teach (content knowledge), while 16 teachers mentioned that they needed guidance on how to teach a specific subject (pedagogical content knowledge). In this discussion, several teachers pointed to the subject of science and the need for both lectures and practical applications in imparting this information to students, but other class subjects were also cited.

Additional Areas of Support

The priority topics that teachers proposed addressing included special needs education and counseling to better support learners experiencing psychological distress. Teachers were also keen to learn better time management and public speaking skills. Twenty-two teachers discussed the need for accessing and better utilizing technology, both in terms of classroom management (e.g., student attendance, grading), lesson planning (easier than writing everything in notebooks and for doing research for their lessons), and for delivery of content (e.g. projecting images and videos) that all learners can see. Additionally, some teachers were keen to raise awareness about the importance of school among families and communities so that they would send their children to school. As teachers reflected on these priorities and needs, they were acutely aware that any training they had received to date was condensed and inadequate for their professional development.

Teachers Understand How a Lack of Training Negatively Influences Their Work

The teachers continuously grappled with the consequences of a lack of training and the complex challenges they face in their classrooms. The 33 teachers who provided "narratives of change" about their participation in the first year of Teachers for Teachers (2016–2017) reflected on the consequences of not having had access to teacher professional development (TPD) opportunities. They reflected on the toll it takes on teacher well-being and confidence, which can be further compounded pending the setting of displacement, interactions with national teachers in these settings, as well as gender roles.

Effect of Lack of TPD on Teacher Well-Being

Teachers' stories illustrated that they felt self-conscious given their lack of professional preparation and identified how their lack of training negatively contributed to a wide range of factors that impacted their own well-being, student achievement, and their identity as a teacher. One teacher in Kakuma noted the connection between lack of teacher professional development, poor student learning, and teacher stress:

> Before [the Teachers for Teachers program] [the learners gave] me a hard time. Whenever I teach, the learners didn't understand . . . it was

even giving me stress. I was saying, "Is it that I don't know how to teach?" or "Is that what I am teaching is not clear?"

(Abdo, January 2017)

Teachers shared how a lack of training contributed to stress, exhaustion, and demotivation as they experienced difficulty managing their classrooms, poor basic lesson planning skills, and dissatisfaction with student achievement levels.

Effect of Lack of TPD on Teacher Confidence

Many teachers also noted how a lack of professional training and professional certificates contributed to a lack of confidence that negatively impacted their perception of themselves as professionals, their relationships with their students, as well as their relationships with other teachers. Teachers highlighted how this lack of confidence contributed to less trusting or open teacher-to-teacher relationships as untrained teachers felt they could not discuss their hardships and challenges for fear of being exposed as unprofessional or unqualified. As one teacher commented:

> before I entered in the Teachers for Teachers training, I was not having that confidence of grouping teachers together and [talking] to them. [. . .] I was fearing [. . .] if I say something these guys they are going to laugh at me.
>
> (Farhia, November 2016)

Lack of Teacher Confidence Compounded by Gender and Context

Teachers noted the confidence gap is exacerbated by being a refugee teacher in a context in which national Kenyan teachers have higher qualifications and salaries. One teacher shared:

> Those Kenyans, they feel they are professional teachers because they undergo training. And for us [. . .] they take us as incentive teachers, those that have not gone for training, school leavers, like Form 4, with the name of refugees. They do despise it. . . . The training, the certificates, give us some dignity. . . . [T]he knowledge we have gotten give[s] us professional techniques and professionalism. . . . At least I feel equal to them.
>
> (Sadiiq, April 2017)

It was also noted that a lack of confidence stemming from inadequate professional development is a particular challenge for female teachers given an environment that is largely dominated by male teachers (80.5%) (UNHCR, 2017).

Overcrowding and Diverse Student Needs in Kakuma

Kakuma's schools are hugely overcrowded with an average of 133 learners per classroom (UNICEF, 2018). As one teacher reported, "in lower classes you can find more than 200 [learners in one classroom]. You find that you don't even have space as you write on the chalkboard" (Idrissa, April 2017). In their stories, teachers related a wide range of difficulties they face due to overcrowded classrooms including disciplinary issues, classroom management challenges, and increased teacher stress. Compounding this challenge, classrooms in Kakuma include learners from a particularly wide range of educational backgrounds, ages, learning abilities, and language skills. Teachers noted that they are dealing with a population of learners, many of whom have been seriously affected by displacement, violent conflict, and other protection issues. Within this context, where teachers may be overwhelmed by huge class sizes contributing to disciplinary challenges, teachers are conscious of the adverse effects that their lack of skills and knowledge to resolve these cases might have on learners:

> Some learners are traumatized because they remember what had happened to their countries. Now when we become harsh to them again, when we punish them, when we do such things, you know they are traumatized and they can never learn. They can never learn because . . . they don't feel free to ask, they don't feel free to talk to you, they don't feel free to ask questions, they don't feel free to come and share with you if you are harsh to them.
>
> (Kwame, January 2017)

Teachers voiced that meeting the diverse academic and psychosocial needs of students within this context is a serious challenge.

Teachers Identify What Kind of Quality Professional Development They Need

In the face of these complex challenges, teachers continuously sought out the limited professional development opportunities available. Teachers for Teachers was a voluntary program and teachers applied to be participants on their own accord. Privileging teachers' perspectives was central to Teachers for Teachers; therefore, upon completion of the program, the 33 teachers who provided "narratives of change" reflected on what they thought worked well in the Teachers for Teachers approach. They cited that the program responded to their needs, provided longer-term support, and included opportunities for teacher collaboration through multimodal activities.

Responsive Approaches

Teachers emphasized how Teachers for Teachers provided contextually relevant pedagogical knowledge and core teaching competencies that could help them deal with daily challenges. Underscoring the low level of preparedness among teachers, some interviewees found the most basic teaching knowledge to dramatically improve their practice:

> In the training, the most I have learned is how to write the lesson plan [. . .] since the lesson plan is the most, the key to the teaching work. It means that once you don't have those teaching, you don't know how to write that lesson plan, it means you are doing nothing. [. . .] I should know it, so that at least when I go to class, I give what is there, and what is supposed to be taught. Before I never know it.
> (Sadiiq, April 2017)

This aligns with teachers' initial requests to receive more support on lesson planning, highlighting that teachers are well placed to identify their areas of professional development needs.

Self-reflection and awareness among teachers are also important aspects of the process in which relevant skills like lesson planning turned into practice:

> Before this training I was a "lazy teacher" simply because it was very hard for me to always make it to lesson plan. [. . .] At times I could even go to class without making lesson plans because maybe I think there is no inspection that will take place. But when I was taught about the consequence and effectiveness of lesson planning, then I came to realize that I was wrong. Today, it's not the case. Before I get to class I have to make sure that I am ready enough to present what I am supposed to.
> (Idrissa, April 2017)

While the training component covers a number of topics and skill sets, at its core it provides essential learning of the fundamental skills critical for new teachers.

Continuous Longer-Term Support and Peer-to-Peer Collaboration

Participation in training with relevant content does not automatically translate into changed practice in the classroom. Teachers identified continuous professional support as a key driver for the change process enabled by self-reflection and self-evaluation:

> At first the training seemed boring since I was not focus[ed], but when I [began] to reflect on some of the things I thought I was doing right I realized that I was doing them all wrong. [. . .] This change did not just happen suddenly but at first after doing self-evaluation on how I relate to my students and other teachers, it came to my mind that I was not always on the right track. Most of this change happened during the teacher learning circles.
>
> (Alghaliy, January 2017)

Alghaliy's comment supports the literature on teacher professional development being most effective when it provides sustained opportunities and supportive networks for teachers to make changes in their practice (Burns & Lawrie, 2015; Darling-Hammond et al., 2017).

Another teacher noted that long-term support served both to reinforce knowledge and skills gained during the training and to create a valuable sense of community among teachers who do not usually have the space or time to develop peer relationships. Teachers highlighted how peer-to-peer learning through monthly TLCs supported the development of reciprocal, mutually supportive professional and peer relationships that provided empathy and a sense of collegiality that reduced the feelings of professional isolation:

> In the coaching [. . .] what I learned most is teamwork. [. . .] We had our coach. [. . .] [H]e really motivated us to embrace teamwork. In our school, if I have a problem in a certain aspect or a lesson, I'll call one of the teachers to come and help me. And later the teacher will tell me where I went wrong, where I should improve, and what I needed to do to improve that lesson so that the learners will understand. So we are really helping each other in that team, in that coaching session. And also we used to visit each other in different schools, yeah, at least once in a week.
>
> (Hiba, June 2016)

Other teachers shared how the development of peer relationships and encouragement to discuss challenges with colleagues also builds confidence: "[Peer-coaching] has [encouraged me] to share out ideas with different people, so that when you meet with certain people [. . .] you are at least able to talk for yourself. It gives you courage" (Annitah, November 2016). Teachers also gain motivation and a sense of empowerment through the horizontal learning central to peer coaching and the Teachers for Teachers approach:

The name alone—Teachers for Teachers—sounds nice to me. It reinforces [. . .] that I can also have power, to other teachers, that I can also call another teacher. I can be like a coordinator also . . . because nowadays we are in the world of exchanging knowledge. [. . .] It also makes me feel happy, that I am important in this field. When I am given power, I can do better than before.

(Shaker, January 2017)

In addition to strengthening peer-to-peer relationships and a sense of community, teachers emphasized the importance of collaborative peer-to-peer problem solving in transferring learning from a professional development setting to the classroom. "[Changes happened] after the training when we were integrated and started [holding] teacher learning circles meeting discussing the challenges and experiences encountered in various school[s]" (Ibrahim, January 2017). Within TLCs, teachers reported sharing ideas, planning and practicing together, solving mutual school-based problems, and trying out different instructional approaches on key challenges including disciplinary issues, classroom management, absenteeism, and overcrowded classrooms. As one of the teachers reflected on their participation in the TLCs: "[Peer coaching] helped because we share ideas. We solve the same problem we are facing together. Because, if you are not able to solve the matter, maybe get ideas from your fellow teachers, whom you are together in that" (Raki, April 2018). Other teachers noted the benefits of peer-to-peer support are reinforced by other modes of professional development including the mentorship and training components.

Multimodal Support

The combination of face-to-face training, peer coaching, and mobile mentoring can enable self-reflection and awareness that become the starting point of a cyclical process of change in attitude and behavior. One teacher emphasized the fact that transfer and implementation of new skills are sustainable when the incremental change is supported through continuous multimodal support:

To me I believe all three [components of the program—i.e. training, coaching, and mentoring] are important because whatever knowledge you have learned in the training is what you apply in the classroom setting. And the challenges we face in the school is what we go and discuss in our coaching meetings, and that has really assisted us. And some of the issues that are still difficult we use to raise them to our global mentors and they provide solutions to them, but the three are all important because you cannot have coaching alone without training—all of the training.

(Farhia, June 2017)

Another teacher used the analogy of soccer team members playing together to describe the ways that different modes of learning harmonized to support his professional development:

> It's like players in a field who are playing for the same goal. [. . .] It's a team. Those three [. . .] different [components] of Teachers for Teachers, I think they work in collaboration to make me who I am. [. . .] [T]hey complement each other in a certain way that I cannot express.
> (Moise, April 2017)

Other teachers noted that from a practical perspective being able to access support through both in-person and virtual means is helpful given the daily challenges teachers face in their busy personal and professional lives.

Teachers Reflect on Changes in Teaching Practice Through Teachers for Teachers

In addition to recognizing their professional development needs and experiences in Teachers for Teachers, teachers meaningfully identified changes they saw in their teaching practice or in how they view their role as teachers. Through their own stories of change, participating teachers reflected on what changed most for them during the course of participating in the program.

Increased Confidence

When individuals try out and achieve success in activities, their self-efficacy—that is, their confidence and belief in their own abilities—is reinforced, resulting in behavioral changes (Bandura, 1998, 2002). According to the teachers' stories, gradual and recursive change in attitude can be detected in self-efficacy. Nine teachers noted that the most significant changes they experienced through the Teachers for Teachers program related to increased confidence in their role as a teacher, although they described the impact of increased confidence on their teaching practice in different ways. For example, one teacher explained the positive cyclical relationship he saw between increased confidence, greater learner engagement, and teacher motivation:

> The strategies have also given me a lot of confidence. I feel very, very confident whenever I go to class. I am totally confident. I have the feeling that I am doing the right thing all the time. It also give[s] me a bit of motivation. [. . .] [It] motivates me a lot. Apart from the fact that my learners are enjoying, it really motivates me

[. . .] when I see them smiling, participating, I feel better. I feel totally better.

(Malse, June 2017)

Another teacher shared how the enhanced perception of their ability as a teacher contributed to an overall improvement in their well-being and general approach to teaching challenges:

> The most significant change that I have experienced as a teacher is that I have acquired knowledge that has not only improved my skills, but also empowered me to always be positive minded in finding solution[s] in helping students and fellow teachers.
>
> (Alghaliy, January 2017)

Increased Self-Control and Stress Management

Teachers' improved confidence also pertains to their beliefs about where the locus of control lies. The stories teachers shared suggest that as teachers gradually feel more confident, they feel greater control over themselves, their classrooms, and desired educational and professional outcomes. One teacher noted how the increased control of his own emotions impacted his relationship with his students: "I learned [. . .] good ways of controlling temper in class when I am annoyed. This has really given me [a] chance to build trust and understanding with my learners" (NaNomi, January 2017). Another teacher shared how her increased capacity to manage stress positively impacts her students, their learning, as well as her own well-being:

> I came to realize the well-being of a teacher to learner is very important in the process of learning because when the teacher is not well, that [. . .] will affect the learners in the class. [. . .] It can affect the learner most because you find that if a teacher is not in that mood, then even the instruction will not be followed, the content will not be [delivered]. So I've tried very much wherever I have, I am able to manage my stress, I am able to manage my stress and think of the importance of the learners in school and not to bring my issues to the learners. [. . .] Whenever I have a problem, I know how to control and manage them because I've learned [. . .] how to manage stress.
>
> (Victoria, June 2017)

Reduction of Harmful Disciplinary Practices

Other teachers noted that increased self-control impacted the ability to approach disciplinary issues through more positive methods. Twenty-one of the 33 teachers shared that their most significant change related to the reduction or cessation of corporal punishment. Teachers explained the reasons for this change included increased knowledge of the negative effects of corporal punishment, the acquisition of new classroom management skills, and the proven effectiveness of positive discipline once they applied their new methods in class:

> The one thing is that before I was very harsh. But now [. . .] I am able to control my emotions. Even if learners can make noise, I can't go and beat them again. I usually call them and talk to them and they understand.
> (Mamadou, April 2017)

Importantly, eight teachers specifically pointed to the linkages they saw between reduction in corporal punishment and improved teacher-student relationships. For example, Ibrahim explained:

> I also developed good relationship with learners that really help[ed] me to make sure I had achieve[d] my objective at the end of the day through being open up in sharing their feeling[s] to me. At the beginning I was [a] fan of corporal punishment whereby learners were fearful to me. And I thought it was the best option of controlling [the] learner as [a] teacher. But after training, it is when I concluded that gap between teacher and learners doesn't lead to accomplishment of [the] goal because you will never get to know the learner['s] interest or need so that you can provide solution to it.
> (January 2017)

Other teachers further explained the relationship they saw between cessation of corporal punishment, improved teacher-student relationships, and increased student engagement and participation:

> So we discuss and we found that beating a child is not helping the child at all. If a child makes mistakes, there are so many alternatives that we can, that you can punish that child. We can correct a child in a way that he knows that he's wrong so that next time he cannot make mistake again. [. . .] When you beat that child, that child will never answer your question, that child will never feel free to talk to you, if he has any problem, he will not feel free to talk to you.
> (Kwame, January 2017)

For the teachers interviewed, the change toward positive disciplinary practices is significant, because it enables positive interaction with all students creating a safer learning environment where students are able to approach them openly with trust and honesty.

Improved Teacher-Student Relationships

The improvement in teacher-student relationships was cited by 15 teachers within their stories of change. Beyond the reduction or cessation of corporal punishment and how it improved student-teacher relationships, other teachers cited the benefits of a fundamental shift they experienced as they transitioned from a more authoritative role to a more nurturing role:

> Before you could see a teaching failing to find a solution to a certain problem, failing to handle a certain situation. [. . .] [Y]ou could find when a teacher is interrupted by a certain learner his will is to fight back, and it is not the right action to be taken by a teacher. Because a teacher is role model and a teacher is a parent. It's really not the right action that should be taken. Today, it is not the case among these trained teachers.
>
> (Idrissa, April 2017)

Another teacher explained that students now seek him out due to his efforts to create a more positive and nurturing learning environment:

> I feel like I'm the parent of the learner because a child always looks for a parent so for anytime. So once they come and look for me, I feel happy. I feel like that is my role as a teacher, a teacher can be a parent.
>
> (Kamal, November 2017)

Others noted that more positive teacher-student relationships also reinforce feelings of confidence and stronger teacher identity:

> I feel that now I'm a good teacher who is near my learners. [. . .] I feel that even sometimes they come and share their problems with me which are confidential because they have trust in me. Now, I feel I am a confident teacher because now the learners are able to share their problems with me.
>
> (Sahra, April 2017)

Improved Teacher Identity

Enhanced professional identity is also apparent as teachers begin to see themselves as role models to the students and advocates of education.

> Since [participating in Teachers for Teachers], my life in teaching has never been the same for I was equipped with not only teaching skills but also how to act as a teacher. [. . .] My profession being [a teacher]

states that I['d] be a role model so that my students should emulate me and so I should be well groomed and measure my steps.

(Mustafa, January 2017)

Another teacher emphasized that he now understands his role as a teacher is both in school and the community: "I mobilize the parents in [the] community on importance of girl child education, being also [the] role model in community and in the school [and] ensure tracking of absenteeism." Other teachers expressed that the training contributed to the way other teachers perceived their stature as professionals, reinforcing their teacher identity:

There was a time when one of my colleagues[. . .] told me that "I am always following you. Whatever you do is what I see always." And I did not tell that fellow teacher that I am happy about that. But inside me, I was feeling better. I was very very happy that a fellow teacher would actually follow me and observe me and try it [. . .] in her class. That was quite wonderful. And I also believe that came as a result of Teachers for Teachers program. That's why I am able to attract attention from others, from my colleagues, the teachers. And they want me to be with them always and share a lot of things, work together with them, and so on.

(Malse, June 2017)

Improved Learner Performance

Twenty of the 33 teachers claimed that a significant change they perceived after the Teachers for Teachers program was improvement in their learners' performance; they cited increased learner attention, greater participation, improved attendance, and higher test scores. While these claims are not substantiated by other evidence, teachers explained that the changes they perceived in their learners' performance serves to motivate them:

Concerning my teaching, I am able to apply more skills, strategies, and techniques in my teaching. And this has improved my learners' grade, they are able to get good marks during exams and even in the class level. [As a result of students' improvement], I feel motivated. I feel I am a good teacher. I feel that I am able to teach and they gain for it.

(Sahra, April 2017)

Another teacher explained how he perceived the causal relationships between improved classroom management, increased learning, and teacher well-being:

I also realized from this classroom management, I said the learners are attentive and from their attention, they improved in their performance. [. . .] It makes me feel happy because of the performance of the learners. The learners performed well; there's nothing good like when you see the learners performing because of you, because of the work you do.

(Kamal, November 2016)

Discussion and Conclusion

Teachers can clearly and vividly explain the challenges they face, how important it is for them to have meaningful opportunities for professional development, and how they can support one another in their collective efforts to improve the quality of education in Kakuma. The findings presented in this case study also show that change takes investment and time, which supports the literature that argues that effective teacher professional development is of sustained duration with multiple opportunities for learning and practice (Burns & Lawrie, 2015; Darling-Hammond et al., 2017). While the global education community, including donors, applies significant pressure on teachers and those supporting them to improve student learning outcomes, there are other elements to consider that arguably influence student achievement. While many of the initial changes in teaching practice may fall short of achieving measurable learning outcomes, improvements to lesson planning, classroom management, disciplinary practices, self-confidence, self-control, teacher well-being, and teacher identity are equally important. These changes also speak to the broader non-cognitive and social-emotional goals for learners in crisis contexts. Causal research may not be appropriate for examining many of these elements, such as teacher identity and well-being. Further, short-term funding cycles, prevalent in the field of Education in Emergencies, limit opportunities to better understand long-term outcomes of student learning and well-being, and their interactions with improved teaching practice. As a field, we must consider these factors and think reflectively about meaningful and methodologically diverse ways of understanding these concepts.

While we must continue to grapple with the challenges of measuring the effectiveness of teacher professional development and its relationship to student learning, research efforts that aim to prioritize teachers are equally important. The use of monitoring, evaluation, and research approaches that allow teachers to convey their own experiences and ideas related to professional development, such as the pseudo-narrative inquiry method applied in this study, are critical to developing a more robust understanding of what matters to teachers. Better support to teachers has enabling effects that can lead to ongoing improvements, first in teacher well-being, then teacher preparation and performance, and ultimately to student achievement. If we want to accelerate this process, then we need to ensure that teachers receive adequate and responsive training and sustained support through peer-to-peer learning and teacher collaboration. We need to further expand and strengthen the evidence base about what works for teachers in crisis contexts and how some of these key elements of quality professional development might take on different nuances in different settings. We can continue to draw inspiration from studies conducted in "stable" contexts, while finding ways to cross-fertilize and share findings from crisis-affected contexts.

The outcomes of teacher professional development are only one important element of the larger teacher management and support framework. We must also attend to the policy environment and make efforts to ensure fair recruitment and compensation, expand teacher education activities, and develop diverse pathways toward professional certification that will be recognized across the range of durable solutions (e.g., repatriation, local inclusion in host country, resettlement) (Mendenhall, 2018). The Global Education Monitoring Report recently pointed out that: "Recognition of qualifications and prior learning should be modernized to make the most of . . . refugees' skills, which contribute greatly to long-term prosperity" (UNESCO, 2018, p. 4). Until we pursue improvements in these policies and practices in earnest—and through meaningful partnerships with teachers—we will continue to seek gains in student learning outcomes in vain.

Notes

1. The 27 teachers who participated in the development phase of the Teachers for Teachers initiative (June–July 2015) shared during interviews that they needed more training and further specified the topics and skills that they would like to see in future projects. Their input informed the content and approach ultimately used in Teachers for Teachers.
2. Pseudonyms have been used for all teachers.

References

Bandura, A. (1998). Personal and collective efficacy in human adaptation and change. In J. G. Adair, D. Belanger, & K. L. Dion (Eds.), *Advances in Psychological Science: Vol. 1. Personal, Social, and Cultural Aspects*. Hove, UK: Psychology Press.

Bandura, A. (2002). Social cognitive theory in cultural context. *Applied Psychology: An International Review*, 52(2), 269–290.

Baú, V. (2016). A narrative approach in evaluation: "Narratives of change" method. *Qualitative Research Journal*, 16(4), 374–387.

Burde, D., Guven, O., Kelcey, J., Lahmann, H., & Al-Abbadi, K. (2015). *What works to promote children's educational access, quality of learning, and well-being in crisis-affected contexts* (Education Rigorous Literature Review). London, UK: Department for International Development.

Burns, M., & Lawrie, J. (Eds.). (2015). *Where it's needed most: Quality professional development for all teachers*. New York: Inter-agency Network for Education in Emergencies.

Chase, S. (2011). Still a field in the making. *The Sage Handbook of Qualitative Research*, 421–434.

Darling-Hammond, L., Hyler, M. E., & Gardner, M. (2017). *Effective teacher professional development*. Palo Alto, CA: Learning Policy Institute.

Dryden-Peterson, S. (2017). Refugee education: Education for an unknowable future. *Curriculum Inquiry, 47*(1), 14–24.

Eastmond, M. (2007). Stories as lived experience: Narratives in forced migration research. *Journal of Refugee Studies, 20*(2), 248–264.

Hill, H. C., Beisiegel, M., & Jacob, R. (2013). Professional development research: Consensus, crossroads, and challenges. *Educational Researcher, 42*(9), 476–487.

Kirk, J., & Winthrop, R. (2007). Promoting quality education in refugee contexts: Supporting teacher development in Northern Ethiopia. *International Review of Education, 53*, 715–723.

Kirk, J., & Winthrop, R. (2013). Teaching in contexts of emergency and state fragility. In J. Kirk, M. Dembélé, & S. Baxter (Eds.), *More and better teachers for quality education for all: Identity and motivation, systems and support* (pp. 121–139). Collaborative works. Retrieved from https://moreandbetterteachers.files.wordpress.com/2013/09/more-and-better-teaching_september-2013.pdf

Lutheran World Federation. (2015). *Rapid assessment of barriers to education in Kakuma refugee camp*. Kakuma, Kenya: Lutheran World Federation.

Mendenhall, M. (2018). Teachers for teachers: Advocating for stronger programs and policies for and with refugee teachers in Kakuma refugee camp, Kenya. *Studies in Social Justice, 12*(2).

Mendenhall, M., Dryden-Peterson, S., Bartlett, L., Ndirangu, C., Imonje, R., Gakunga, D., . . . Tangelder, M. (2015). Quality education for refugees in Kenya: Pedagogy in urban Nairobi and Kakuma refugee camp settings. *Journal on Education in Emergencies, 1*(1), 92–130.

Mendenhall, M., Gomez, S., & Varni, E. (2018). *Teaching amidst conflict and displacement: Persistent challenges and promising practices for refugee, internally displaced and national teachers*. Paper commissioned for the 2019 Global Education Monitoring Report; Migration, displacement and education: Building bridges, not walls. Retrieved from UNESCO Digital Library: https://unesdoc.unesco.org/ark:/48223/pf0000266060

Organization for Economic Co-operation and Development. (2008). TALIS 2008 technical report: Teaching and learning international survey. Retrieved from http://www.oecd.org/ dataoecd/16/14/44978960.pdf

Schwille, J., Dembélé, M., & Schubert, J. (2007). *Global perspectives on teacher learning: Improving policy and practice*. Paris, France: International Institute for Educational Planning (IIEP) UNESCO.

Sesnan, B., Ndugga, H., & Said, S. (2013). *Educators in exile: The role and status of refugee teachers*. London, UK: Commonwealth Secretariat.

Timperley, H. (2008). *Teacher professional learning and development* (Educational Practices Series 18). Brussels, Belgium: International Academy of Education.

TNTP. (2015). The mirage: Confronting the hard truth about our quest for teacher development. Retrieved from TNTP https://tntp.org/publications/view/the-mirage-confronting-the-truth-about-our-quest-for-teacher-development

UN General Assembly. (2015). *Transforming our world: The 2030 Agenda for Sustainable Development*. Retrieved from https://www.refworld.org/docid/57b6e3e44.html

UNESCO. (2018). *Global education monitoring report 2019: Migration, displacement and education: Building bridges, not walls*. Paris: UNESCO.

UNESCO IIEP. (2010). *Guidebook for planning education in emergencies and reconstruction, 2010*. International Institution for Educational Planning. Retrieved from http://unesdoc.unesco.org/images/0019/001902/190223E.pdf

UNHCR. (2017, March). *Kakuma camps and Kalobeyei settlement: Education note*.

UNHCR. (2018, June). *UNHCR Kakuma: Population statistics by country of origin, age, sex and age group*. Retrieved from https://data2.unhcr.org/en/documents/download/64364

UNICEF. (2018). *Refugee children get a fresh start at Kenya's Kakuma camp*. Retrieved from www.unicefusa.org/stories/refugee-children-get-fresh-start-kenyas-kakuma-camp/34455

10 "Whose Knowledge?" Putting Politics Back Into Curriculum Choices for Refugees[1]

Jo Kelcey

Introduction

> Behind Spencer's famous question about "What knowledge is of most worth?" there lies another even more contentious question, "Whose knowledge is of most worth?"
>
> (Apple & Christian-Smith, 1991, p. 1)

In 2012, the United Nations High Commissioner for Refugees (UNHCR) adapted its education strategy. Having previously advocated for teaching refugees their home state curriculum, the agency instead began to promote the integration of refugees into national systems and, by association, teaching host state curriculum to refugees. This policy shift was justified as better reflecting the realities of protracted displacement and facilitating access to education (UNHCR, 2018, 2015, 2012).[2] This chapter critically considers this policy shift through a historical analysis of the education provided to Palestinian refugees in the Middle East. Although UNHCR oversees education to refugee populations in most developing contexts, since 1950 the United Nations Relief and Works Agency for Palestine Refugees in the Near East (UNRWA) has provided education to Palestinian refugees in Gaza, Jordan, Lebanon, Syria, and the West Bank. Unlike UNHCR, UNRWA has consistently taught the refugees the curricula of their host governments, making the Palestinian case an important, although largely overlooked, case study for examining the use of host state curriculum in contexts of protracted displacement.[3]

Curriculum choices are never politically neutral (Apple, 2004). Politically sensitive in most societies, curriculum choices are especially complicated in contexts where large numbers of refugees are hosted owing to the multiple actors who share responsibility for refugees' education (UNGA, 2016). These complexities are well reflected in the Palestinian case. Some scholars have charged that the use of host state curricula weakens Palestinians' national identity, negates their history, and detracts from their right to self-determination and a culturally relevant education (Abu-Lughod, 1973; Sayigh, 2017). Others have claimed that the host state curricula used in UNRWA schools promote intolerance and anti-Israeli sentiments (Groiss & Shaked, 2017; Pardo & Jacobi, 2018). Finally, host state governments have historically resisted attempts to deviate from the use of their curriculum, arguing that the education content taught within their borders is a matter of sovereignty (see for example Lieber, 2017; Wells, 1987). A better understanding of these tensions may shed light on the implications of UNHCR's recent policy shift. Accordingly, this chapter asks the following question: What factors influence UNRWA's use of host state curricula, and what lessons does its experience of using host state curricula offer for other refugee contexts?

Drawing on King's analogy between curriculum choices and framing theory (King, 2017), I argue that while curriculum policies for refugees tend to focus on technical considerations related to access and efficiency, it is crucial to also understand curriculum choices as a political contest in which different power brokers vie for influence and control over the refugee narrative. Further, the failure to recognize the inherently political dimensions of curriculum choices can marginalize refugees' perspectives in policy making with potentially negative impacts for their education outcomes. To address this, I argue in favor of a more nuanced approach to curriculum in refugee settings. Such an approach would reflect both "the idea of return and the ongoing nature of exile" (Dryden-Peterson, 2017, p. 15). Accordingly, the next section reviews literature on curriculum choices for refugees. It charts the global shift from using home state curricula to host state curricula and positions the Palestinian case in relation to this shift. The third section describes my data and analytical approach. I then describe three contests that have taken place over the curricula used in UNRWA schools and consider what these contests reveal about the power dynamics that shape curriculum choices for refugees. The chapter ends by discussing the implications of the Palestinian case for UNHCR's more recent policy shift.

Curriculum Choices for Refugees

Formal, or official, curriculum "is a description of what, why, how, and how well students should learn in a systematic and intentional way" (UNESCO-IBE, 2013). Curriculum is also however, deeply political. It imparts a shared understanding of common identity and the responsibilities and obligations that accompany citizenship (Anderson, 1983; Bendix, 1964; Gellner, 1983; Marshall & Bottomore, 1992). Hence the centrality of curriculum to the creation and development of national identity and state building: choices about what to teach and how to teach it are embedded political statements about the nature of society and the roles, rights, and obligations of citizens therein (Waters & Leblanc, 2005). In this way curriculum helps to create and uphold the "national order of things" (Malkki, 1995), or the prevailing idea that the world is naturally divided into "sovereign, spatially discontinuous units" (Malkki, 1992, p. 26).

Often a politically sensitive topic, curriculum choices have a heightened importance in conflict-affected contexts, owing to their ability to shape the perceptions, attitudes, and actions that can contribute to conflict. "Negative curricula" refers to the structures and content of education that convey bias or hatred toward certain groups or to content that glorifies war or militancy (Burde, 2014). Studies on curriculum—and the textbooks that articulate curriculum choices—in Afghanistan, India and Pakistan, Israel, Palestine, and Rwanda, argue that curriculum content can increase normative support for violence or contribute to the inequities that fuel conflict (Burde, 2014; Lall, 2008; Peled-Elhanan, 2012; Berrebi, 2007; King, 2014). Scholars have paid particular attention to history education, owing to the influential role historical narratives play in forming national identity and socializing students (Cole, 2007; King, 2017; Paulson, 2015).

Research has also highlighted the importance of curriculum choices in refugee settings. Accredited curricula, curricula that support livelihoods opportunities, and the challenges posed by curricula that are taught in a second language all influence refugees' access to education and their future prospects (Dryden-Peterson, 2011a, 2011b; Kirk, 2009; Oh & Van der Stouwe, 2009). The political dimensions of curriculum choices in refugee settings have however, been less examined. This oversight is significant since the question of what to teach refugees is politically complex. Not only are decisions regarding refugees' education filtered through a host of local, national, and international stakeholders, including United Nations agencies, host states, home states, donor states, and the refugees themselves, but refugees are effectively caught in political limbo, waiting to be reinserted into the system of nation-states through repatriation, integration or resettlement. This makes the choice of which curriculum to teach them—or which country to socialize them into—particularly challenging (Waters & Leblanc, 2005).

To date, curriculum choices for refugees have comprised two options. Until 2011, UNHCR promoted the use of home state curriculum for refugees. This reflected the twin assumptions that displacement would be short-lived and that repatriation—the preferred durable solution—was around the corner. In this context, education, if provided at all, constituted a stopgap measure until return materialized and normal education trajectories resumed in refugees' countries of origin. In 2012, however, UNHCR began to promote the use of host state curriculum for refugees, a policy shift that it implemented in conjunction with efforts to better integrate refugees into host state public education systems. The agency argued that this approach better reflected the realities of protracted displacement and would facilitate the provision of education, and thus access to education for refugees in countries of asylum (UNHCR, 2015, 2012).

Protracted displacement does not, however, imply resettlement. Indicative of this is the slow uptake of durable solutions, defined as repatriation to home states, local integration within host states and, resettlement to third countries. The overall number of refugees to have been repatriated remains low and UNHCR reports that fewer than 1% of the 14.4 million refugees registered with the agency are in the process of resettlement. Host community integration is also a complex, demanding, and statistically unlikely outcome (UNHCR "solutions"). In short, to be a refugee means to be excluded from the very "national order of things" (Malkki, 1995) that curriculum helps uphold. What then are the implications of curricula that explicitly seek to socialize children into societies in which they cannot fully participate? Although it is too soon to ascertain the long-run implications of UNHCR's policy shift, the decision to teach host state curricula clearly merits critical examination. In the next section, I discuss how the case of UNRWA is well placed to shed light on this policy shift.

UNRWA and the "Palestine Refugees"[4]

Between 1947 and 1949, around 800,000 Palestinians fled conflict in Palestine for the relative safety of neighboring countries and territories (Pappe, 2006). Since this exodus preceded the drafting of the Refugee Convention and the creation of UNHCR in 1951, a different international framework emerged to support the Palestinian refugees. This framework included UNRWA, which was created in December 1949 as a temporary and operationally oriented organization to provide job opportunities and humanitarian relief for Palestinian refugees (Schiff, 1995). To avoid overlap, with UNHCR, Palestinians were then excluded from the provisions of the Refugee Convention and the associated mandate of UNHCR (Irfan, 2017).

Although designed as a temporary agency, the absence of a durable and just solution to the Palestinian refugee question means that UNRWA continues to operate. Today it serves 5 million "Palestine refugees" to whom it is mandated to provide relief, human development, and protection services. Education has emerged as UNRWA's largest and most important activity: the agency operates 711 elementary and preparatory schools for approximately 526,000 students across the Gaza Strip, Jordan, Lebanon, Syria, and the West Bank (UNRWA "what we do, education"). The persistence of UNRWA's separate institutional structure for Palestine refugees has contributed, however, to the exceptionalism, if not exclusion of the Palestinian case from scholarship and policy discussions related to forced migration (Kagan, 2009). Reflecting this, most literature on refugee education focuses on the policies and practices of UNHCR or populations falling under its mandate. Comparatively little has been written about UNRWA's Education Programme (Dryden-Peterson, 2017, p. 475).

The exclusion of UNRWA from scholarship on refugee education risks overlooking the lessons that the Palestinian case has to offer other refugee contexts. Of particular note are the many historical insights to be gleaned from UNRWA's curriculum policy. Unlike UNHCR, which only recently switched its policy, UNRWA has taught host state curricula in its schools since 1952. This policy has been, however a consistent source of tension between the agency, the refugee community, the host states within which the refugees reside, Israel, and, increasingly, donor states. This chapter argues that these tensions reveal a complex political landscape that needs to be accounted for, rather than ignored, when making curriculum policies for refugees.

Methods

A range of primary and secondary sources inform this chapter. I consulted archived documents held in the UNRWA archive in Amman, the United Nations Archives and Records Management Section (UNARMS) in New York, the UNESCO archive in Paris, the archives of the American Friends Service Committee (AFSC) in Philadelphia, and digitized sources such as those stored on the United Nations Information System on the Question of Palestine (UNISPAL) database to understand the emergence and development of UNRWA's curriculum policy. These documents ranged in form and content, from official decisions and policies adopted by UNRWA, to internal memos and restricted communications in which UN staff candidly reflect on events affecting the agency. Since archives are necessarily incomplete repositories of the past that privilege particular perspectives (in this case that of UNRWA's senior management and government representatives), I also draw on a range of secondary sources. These include oral history accounts and memoirs by Palestinian refugees (including former UNRWA students and teachers), which offer an important contrapuntal to the official United Nations' narratives.

Analytically, I draw on King's discussion of framing theory as a valuable but underutilized perspective for analyzing curriculum choices (2017). Frames are simplified constructions of reality that seek to convey social problems and social solutions and, ultimately, seek to influence how people process and act upon information. In this way, curriculum choices can be understood as a form of strategic communication that engages in the active and purposeful construction of reality "to shape shared understandings of the world . . . to produce cues upon which people act" (King, 2017, p. 24). King's analogy is useful precisely because it reorients our focus to the inherently and unavoidably political dimensions of curriculum. Specifically, it focuses attention on the ways in which "political entrepreneurs compete to frame events knowing that how events are understood will be important for building consensus, mobilizing action, and furthering interests" (Barnett, 1999; Ross, 2002)." This in turn leads to "framing contests . . . between movements, the state, and counter-movements" (McAdam, McCarthy, & Zald, 1996), whereby "frames of winning movements are translated into public policy and become representative of general culture" (Zald, 1996) (King, 2017, p. 25).

Whereas King uses framing theory to analyze textbook content, I focus instead on curriculum policy. Policy comprises both text (what is written down as policy) and discourse (or how policy statements are made possible) (Ball, 1993). Accordingly, I examine three points of tension (or framing contests) and critically reflect on the wider political implications of the choices that were made. I argue that these policy contests are indicative of the need to move beyond the technical discussions that have, until now, characterized decision making regarding what refugees should learn. Instead, it is crucial to acknowledge the deeply political dimensions, and implications, of curriculum policies for refugees. I further suggest that the humanitarian claim to neutrality may actually contribute to the marginalization of refugee perspectives in policy making, with negative impacts on refugees' education outcomes.

Curriculum Policies for Palestine Refugees

Establishing a Formal Curriculum Policy

Precisely when the decision to teach host state curriculum in UNRWA schools was made, is difficult to identify with complete certainty, since no written agreement has been located.[5] UNESCO documents suggest that the policy was arrived at verbally, during a conference held in 1951 or 1952 between representatives of UNESCO, UNRWA, and the host states.[6] That the policy was in place by 1952 is clear since it was explicitly referenced in a UNESCO Conference report dated May 1952. Under the heading "The Curriculum of the Primary School," the report states, "The Working Party was in agreement with the policy previously adopted of following the curriculum of the countries where the schools are located" (UNESCO, 1952).

Various reasons existed for using host state curricula. In the absence of a functioning Palestinian Ministry of Education, alignment to host state curricula facilitated the recognition and accreditation of the refugees' education. This meant that the refugees would be able to transfer more easily between schools run by UNRWA and public and private schools in the host states, especially at the level of secondary education, for which UNRWA did not operate schools.[7] The use of host state curricula was also financially expedient: it meant that UNRWA did not have to fund the development of an entirely new curriculum and maintain a separate accreditation scheme. Nor was the decision to use host state curricula a significant shift from existing practice. The first schools for the refugees emerged in a fragmented and ad hoc way, established by refugees, local communities, host states, and, later on, voluntary agencies that were contracted under the auspices of UNRWA's predecessor agency, the United Nations Relief for Palestine Refugees (UNRPR). There is evidence that an important number of these schools were using host state curricula and textbooks, suggesting that UNRWA's policy also followed and formalized precedent (see for example AFSC, 1950).[8]

Overshadowing these technical and administrative justifications, however, was a much larger political debate. UNRWA's main donors, the United States and United Kingdom, wanted the agency to promote the economic integration and ultimately, the resettlement of the refugees in host states (see for example USDOS, 1950).[9] Reflecting this, United Nations officials assumed that UNRWA's services, including its nascent school program, would be handed over to the host states and should thus be designed so as to facilitate their eventual transition. The host states and refugees however, wanted repatriation. These competing political visions were apparent in UNRWA's officially stated objective to "rehabilitate" (rather than resettle or repatriate) the refugees (Schiff, 1995). Curriculum policy reflected this equivocal stance. The same 1952 UNESCO report that articulated the policy of using host state curricula, qualified this decision with the strong recommendation that "the geography and history of Palestine be taught both in UNRWA-UNESCO and in Government and private schools accepting Palestinian children" (UNESCO, 1952).

Yet while UNRWA's official curriculum policy nominally sought to straddle the competing political visions of its stakeholders, in practice, agency officials actively avoided engaging with the political dimensions of education content. First, content related to Palestinian history and geography was not determined directly by UNRWA but was instead entrusted to host states. This both assumed that host state curricula were congruent with Palestinian narratives and overlooked the fact that host state security forces were actively seeking to suppress Palestinian nationalist politics within their borders. The following incident recorded in the memoirs of a Palestinian refugee in Nahr El Bared Camp, Lebanon, captures this phenomenon well:

> Once during the regular morning roll call, while we were standing in perfect rows and waiting for our teacher to lead us into the classroom, something unprecedented happened. The director, standing in his usual place, told us all to sing the Palestinian anthem! "Homeland, homeland, homeland, to you I give love even unto your heart. . . ." It was the first time that a Palestinian flag had flapped against the blue of the Lebanese sky on our school field. We finished singing and left class in wonder.

After several days' absence the same director reappeared at the school:

> They called us out to the school field at noon. . . . Policemen came out of the director's office and our director was with them. In the place where he usually stood, an empty table had been prepared. The policemen ordered the director to take off his shoes and socks and to place them on the table. . . . As he lay on his back, they bound his feet at the ankles; two policemen took positions at his head and held him firmly by the shoulders, while a third policeman on the other end began beating his bare soles with a stick. . . . He then stopped for a moment, turned to us, and in an official voice, announced that we found ourselves on the territory of the sovereign state of Lebanon, therefore we would learn only that which was taught in Lebanese schools.
>
> (Kotaishová, 2014, pp. 27–28)

Second, in cases where UNRWA teachers were found to be politicizing students and contravening host state curricula, they were dismissed. In Gaza for example, UNRWA teacher Mu'in Bseiso, "well-known as a communist," was fired after penning an "anti-Jordan and anti-King poem" entitled "Jordan on the Cross" that incited demonstrations in UNRWA schools in 1956/57 (see for example Labouisse, 1957; Lalive, 1957). A similar incident occurred in Lebanon in 1955 when UNRWA teacher Ahmed Al Yamani was fired for his active participation in political matters (Issa, 2015). These policies and the suppression of political discussions or activities in schools meant that very early on, curriculum content became a site of tension and a source of resistance for the refugee community (Basisu, 1980; Issa, 2015; Peteet, 2005; Sayigh, 2007; Turki, 1974). The centrality of curriculum to national identity also meant that the failure to properly account for refugees' narratives in official policies drove a wedge between formal curriculum policies, school-based practice, and the refugees' lived realities.

International Arbitration of Curriculum Content

By the early 1960s, education had emerged as UNRWA's most significant activity. Outwardly, senior UNRWA officials justified the expanding Education Programme in terms of the importance of education for refugees' self-support and employment possibilities within the growing markets of the Arab Gulf. In reality however, the agency's shift to education reflected the political possibilities of the environment within which it operated. By the late 1950s, it was clear that the works projects—UNRWA's original raison d'être—had failed because they were associated with resettlement, which was categorically rejected by the refugees and most of the host states. The agency's shift to education was however, accepted by the refugee population, which saw the expansion of schooling as a productive activity that did not compromise the right of return and by the host states and donor government who viewed education as a positive investment and way to control and securitize the refugee population (Al Husseini, 2017, p. 305). These divergent political perspectives on the purpose of education were thrown into even sharper relief in the wake of the 1967 Arab-Israeli conflict. Following its military occupation of the West Bank and Gaza, Israel announced plans to replace the Egyptian and Jordanian curricula used in Gaza and the West Bank with their own education content.[10] When this drew international criticism, Israeli authorities instead decided to edit and censor the existing Egyptian and Jordanian textbooks used in both government and UNRWA schools (see, for example, UNRWA, 1967a, 1967b). At the same time they complained to UNRWA and international media outlets that the agency was teaching hatred and intolerance in its schools, in violation of United Nations principles.

The Israeli complaint was referred to UNESCO for further deliberation. At its executive board meeting in November 1967, UNESCO decided to appoint an independent and neutral Commission of Experts to review all of the textbooks used in UNRWA's schools. The commission would make recommendations regarding the appropriateness of these textbooks to the Director-General of UNESCO, who would in turn work with UNRWA, the host states and Israel regarding their use in the schools. In reviewing the textbooks, the commission cited the need to deliberate content in light of three international standards: the UNESCO Constitution, UNESCO Resolutions on education, and article 26 of the Universal Declaration of Human Rights. To maintain neutrality however, the commission decided not to deliberate the substance of political problems or pronounce on whether a particular historical or geographical narrative was "true." The commission did, however, establish that any incitement to violence or calls for the destruction of a state or the expulsion or extermination of the nationals of that state was wholly unacceptable. Also unacceptable were disparaging remarks made about a community as whole. Finally, the commission recognized the importance of educational continuity for the refugees such that the curricula used in UNRWA schools should allow them to pursue higher levels of education outside of UNRWA's provision (Bertrand, 1967).

The review process was complicated from the start. On the one hand the commission maintained the importance of freely and sincerely discussing history and recognizing the right of displaced persons to express dismay or despair at their situation (UNESCO Expert Commission, 1969). Consequently, it did not consider content related to the forced displacement and exile of the refugees a mark of systematic hostility from one community to another as long as this content did not promote fanaticism or hostility to Judaism. Also acceptable were discussions of national emancipation and liberation. In this respect, the commission praised the overall moderate tone of the textbooks, especially when compared to "terms frequently used in the technically more developed countries when presenting their own history or judging their adversaries" (UNESCO Expert Commission, 1969). On the other hand, the commission was concerned with content that could engender frustration, despair, and revenge among refugee students and deliberated terms that could "lend themselves to oral commentaries in which violence may well be asserted explicitly" (UNESCO Expert Commission, 1969). On the right to a culturally relevant education, the commission was largely evasive. Host state historical narratives were deemed to sufficiently account for Palestinian identity, with the exception of Lebanon, where modern Arab history and geography was not part of the curriculum. To address this, UNRWA officials were tasked with developing a dedicated syllabus for their schools in Lebanon.

UNRWA officials were quick to recognize the potentially intractable political dimensions of the crisis, but equally keen to avoid implicating the agency in these debates. As UNRWA's acting Commissioner-General wrote to his Commissioner-General:

> Our expectation here is that UNESCO will, sooner rather than later, be confronted with having to choose between the contradictory principles involved in its resolutions and I believe that UNESCO must assume the responsibility for deciding on the educational propriety of these textbooks; UNRWA can regard this as a "technical" matter, even though the basic issues are really political.
>
> (Reddaway, 1967)

The political fallout was indeed swift. Syria, Jordan, and Egypt initially responded by accusing Israel of violating International Humanitarian Law and Human Rights Law and ignoring the principle of culturally relevant education (Al Khash, 1968). They argued that UNESCO and, by association, UNRWA were attempting to implement Israeli policies within their borders and accordingly refused to cooperate with the commission. The Syrian government adopted the most severe stance announcing publicly that the commission was a violation of Syrian sovereignty and hence the government would refuse to work with it (El Khani, 1968). Initially cooperative, Jordan and Egypt ultimately rejected the commission's recommendations, citing similar reasons as the Syrian government. Nor did the commission's recommendations please Israeli authorities who had initially supported the establishment of the commission. After learning of the commission's recommendations, Israeli authorities complained of leniency and conducted their own unilateral review. They implemented their review findings by refusing importation licenses for textbooks they deemed inappropriate. The overall lack of cooperation caused textbook shortages in Syria, Jordan, the West Bank, and, especially, Gaza.

Lebanon presented a different challenge. During 1969 and the early 1970s, UNRWA officials reached out to scholars of the Middle East in the United Kingdom to source material for a syllabus on Palestinian history and geography. Syllabus development did not happen quickly but eventually UNRWA, UNESCO, and Lebanese government officials agreed on content to be taught in UNRWA schools in Lebanon. Historical accounts of this period suggest that it had little influence, however. During the late 1960s and 1970s, the Palestine Liberation Organization (PLO) had built a considerable presence and authority in Lebanon.[11] This presence included support for the production and dissemination of children's books describing the refugees' plight and advocating for the return of Palestinians to their communities in historic Palestine (Sayigh, 2017). The PLO enjoyed especially strong support among UNRWA teachers in Lebanon, who were mobilized to teach Palestinian history both within UNRWA schools and through extracurricular activities. UNRWA's formal efforts were effectively dwarfed by the PLO's parallel education program in Lebanon during this time.

The shifting political structures created by the 1967 war thus transformed contests over curriculum content for the refugees. The host states continued to view curriculum content as a means by which to assert their sovereignty and authority over the refugees within their territories. These positions were entrenched following Israel's occupation of the West Bank and Gaza and its own efforts to use curriculum content to assert sovereignty over contested lands. Attempts to reconcile these perspectives through international arbitration were, however, largely ineffective since the prevailing discourses of neutrality meant that the commission did not actively engage with the outstanding political issues facing the region but rather sought to navigate the path of least resistance between competing perspectives. If anything, the experience of the commission highlighted the impossibility of determining neutral or politically innocuous curriculum content. Nor did the commission's attempts to consider the refugees' perspectives amount to much, since implementation of the commission's recommendations ultimately rested on the tacit acceptance of UNRWA and its schools by these same states. Only in Lebanon was the refugee community able to assert its influence over education content; however, these efforts bypassed rather than worked through the United Nations, further underscoring the absence of refugee perspectives from official curriculum policy.

Contests Over the Palestinian Authority Curriculum

UNRWA's policy environment underwent a major change in the 1990s. With it came a new curriculum contest. The signing of the Oslo Accords and the establishment of the Palestinian Authority (PA) resulted in the creation of a Palestinian Ministry of Education, and the development of a

Palestinian curriculum to replace the Jordanian and Egyptian curriculum used in schools in the West Bank and Gaza. The curriculum development process was a complex and highly political affair. It was marked in the first instance by significant domestic struggles over topics ranging from the role of religion within Palestinian society to which pedagogical practices were most appropriate (Brown, 2001; Mazawi, 2011). The curriculum also had to navigate the fact that key issues such as the final borders of a Palestinian state, the status of Jerusalem, and the Right of Return of the refugees had yet to be discussed at the time of curriculum development. Instead, the reality on the ground remained that of Israeli military occupation. Finally, the PA was not a sovereign entity: instead, the Palestinian Ministry of Education relied heavily on bilateral and multilateral donor funding to support the curriculum development process, which curtailed Palestinians' influence over curriculum content. Consequently, Palestinian textbooks had to maneuver between competing discourses of the nation, that came not only from within Palestinian society but also from powerful regional and international powers, sponsors, and stakeholders (Mazawi, 2011).

Political debates regarding the PA curriculum only intensified after its release. The new curriculum was widely lambasted in Israeli and Western media for inciting hatred and violence against Israel. The source for almost all of the accusations against the PA curriculum was however, a single Israeli organization, the Center for Monitoring the Impact of Peace (CMIP), which took it upon itself to review the new Palestinian curriculum and pronounce on its appropriateness (see for example Groiss, 2001). When reviewed by independent scholars, CMIP's work was found to contain unsubstantiated accusations and to misrepresent texts and translations from Arabic (Brown, 2001; Moughrabi, 2001). Nor did independent reviews of the PA curriculum corroborate the claims made by CMIP (Avenstrup, 2004). Although analysts found that the curriculum exhibited awkward silences regarding key topics such as the territory that actually constituted Palestine, what and whom constituted Israel, and even Palestinian refugees, it was not found to incite hatred, violence, or anti-Semitism (see for example Brown, 2001; Hovsepian, 2010). Nonetheless, the accusations made by CMIP were reiterated in the US Senate, the European Parliament, and even by President Bill Clinton himself (Moughrabi, 2001).

Although the official target of these accusations was the PA, UNRWA was also implicated since its policy to use host government curriculum meant that it used PA textbooks in its schools in the West Bank and Gaza. The US Congress asked UNRWA to stop using host state textbooks. In response, the agency stressed its policy to align to host state curricula but agreed to initiate an agency-wide policy on education for Human Rights, Conflict Resolution, and Tolerance (HRCRT). Content developed in line with this policy is now taught in UNRWA schools in addition to the host state curriculum. In the years since, and in response to demands by donor governments (primarily the United States and United Kingdom), UNRWA has increased its reporting and accountability to donor states and has even introduced an explicit policy that articulates its commitment to political neutrality (UNRWA, 2011). In the context of curriculum however, political neutrality can only ever be a misnomer that glosses over more embedded power dynamics.

In 2016, a revised Palestinian curriculum was launched, and the accusations that it incited hatred and violence against Israel resurfaced, spearheaded again by CMIP, which is now known as the Institute for Monitoring Peace and Cultural Tolerance in School Education (IMPACT-se) (see for example Groiss & Shaked, 2017; Pardo & Jacobi, 2018). This time around IMPACT-se took more direct aim at UNRWA's curriculum policy. These claims were again given substantial credence in US policy circles in spite of the previous and current concerns raised about their work and even though no independent review of the revised curriculum has taken place. In line with its neutrality policy however, UNRWA now initiates its own reviews of host state curriculum which include examining newly issued textbooks to ensure they convey a "neutral stance" and do not invoke bias. In cases where textbooks are found to violate these principles, UNRWA develops enrichment materials for students and teachers to be used alongside the textbooks, with the stated purpose of facilitating critical thinking and meaningful classroom discussions about controversial topics. Yet although this neutrality approach may placate donors, it created tensions with the Palestinian Authority, which viewed the review process as "an aggression against Palestine, targeting, muffling and endangering the national identity" (Wafa, 2017).

In this way, the ongoing debates regarding UNRWA's use of the Palestinian Authority curriculum demonstrate not only the unavoidably political dimensions of curriculum content but, as Mazawi notes, the differential political meanings that textbooks have for different actors engaged across the field of power (2011, p. 171). Furthermore, the idea that curriculum content can somehow be neutral or politically innocuous silences important discussion regarding the relevance of this curriculum (and other host state curriculum) for refugee students and their communities and the impact this has on student and teacher motivation. Like all curricula, the PA curriculum is imperfect. Scholars have argued for example that its focus on state building largely excludes the refugee narrative (Hovsepian, 2010; Sayigh, 2017). However, discussions regarding whether or not the PA curriculum meets the needs of refugee students in the West Bank and Gaza have been stifled by the practice of actively silencing politics through claims to humanitarianism (see also Murray, 2008; Sayigh, 2017). Seen in this way, the agency's curriculum policies do not transcend the power structures that determine whose knowledge is legitimate, but rather offer a vantage point to see how the humanitarian paradigm constitutes a political dynamic of its own that can actually reproduce unequal power structures.

Discussion

In his memoir, *The Disinherited*, Fawaz Turki, a former UNRWA student in Lebanon, writes:

> The schools that UNRWA sponsored were designed—unwittingly or not, no one can say—to raise Palestinian children on, and educate them in, accepting their plight in life as a preordained thing. They degraded the minds of Palestinian youngsters and trained, indeed pressured, them into viewing their reality as the norm of existence, never transcendable in its dimensions. They were taught about and given a model world where their destiny was left in the hands of others; a world and a society with directions that they did not understand and were growing up unable to reconcile to the order they saw around them. No attempt was made to explain the situation and the forces behind it that ruled their lives, or how they were to respond to them. They were thus made defenseless.
> (Turki, 1974, p. 58)

His reflections speak to the important role that curricula, and the education systems they are part of, play in instilling a sense of belonging and understanding of one's place in the world. This role may be especially important in refugee host contexts owing to the "complexity of the ways in which people construct, remember, and particular places as 'homelands' or 'nations'" (Malkki, 1992, p. 25). Curriculum policies for refugees have however, tended to overlook this, focusing instead on a narrower set of technical considerations: whether or not curriculum is accredited, which language curriculum is taught in, and how these factors affect refugees' access to education and job prospects (UNHCR, 2018, 2015, 2012). This technical orientation explicitly and implicitly reflects the generalized "national order" of education systems, which takes for granted state-citizen relations. It also reflects a particular claim among some humanitarians that aid, including education, can be provided in a neutral and apolitical way.

Contests over the curriculum used in UNRWA schools highlight the fallacy of these perspectives and point instead to the importance of understanding the highly political dimensions of curriculum choices for refugees and of accounting for this in policy making. Since its establishment, contests over the curriculum taught in UNRWA schools have reflected larger debates around state sovereignty, political legitimacy, and the politics of representation that have played out between the refugees, host states, Israel, and donor states. Palestinians have been nominally reflected in these debates through provisions to teach them about their national history, geography, heritage, and culture. In practice however, formal education content for Palestinian refugees has been subordinated to political narratives that serve the interests of various states from which the refugees are partially or wholly excluded. This has several important implications. As Sayigh (2017) has argued, it contributes to the acculturation of the refugee community and deprives refugees of self-knowledge, or the ability to see one's community reflected in formal education content. The history of the Palestinian case also suggests that refugee communities will pursue such self-knowledge regardless of official policies. Research has also found that a lack of congruence between curriculum and refugee realities has negative impacts on refugee students and teachers. In Lebanon, for example, studies have found that the use of the Lebanese curriculum combined with Palestinian's socioeconomic exclusion within this country (notably regarding their legal status and right to work) contributes to low student and teacher motivation for learning and even drop out among Palestinian students. In contrast, students requested educational content that deals with their own history and appeared more motivated to study when such content was available (Al Hroub, 2011; Shuayb, 2014).

UNRWA's experience thus draws attention to the wider ramifications of UNHCR's policy change. It raises the question of "whose knowledge" the decision to teach host state curriculum legitimates and how the resulting politics of representation may affect a wide range of education outcomes (Apple & Christian-Smith, 1991, p. 1). Answers to this question are not necessarily clear-cut. If anything, UNRWA's experience highlights the lack of independence multilateral organizations have in determining education policies for refugees. In navigating these complex political contests and contingencies, the analogy between curriculum and framing may prove, however, helpful. For frames to be effective they need to be compatible with the perspectives and experiences of recipients. This implies curriculum content that is both cognitively consistent, empirically credible, and responds to shifting dynamics experienced by refugee communities (King, 2017, p. 25). In cases where refugee integration is meaningfully, voluntarily, and holistically pursued across social, economic, and political sections, a lack of consistency may not be a severe problem. In many refugee host contexts, however, this is not the case. And, since children learn not only from formal curriculum content, but from their daily lived experiences, this means that for curriculum policies to be effective, then decisions about what to teach refugees need to be congruent with, rather than abstracted from, their historical and political context, however uncomfortable these realities may be to some stakeholders and power brokers. Curriculum content that allows students to process and understand their surroundings can better support their coping mechanisms and enhance their psychosocial well-being and resilience (see for example Abu-Amsha & Armstrong, 2018). Conversely the denial, repression, or avoidance of issues related to conflicts past and present can have negative long-term implications on both individual well-being and ultimately prospects for just and lasting peace (Burde, 2014).

Scholars have already highlighted the importance of education programs that reflect not only potential future solutions for refugees (repatriation, resettlement, or integration) but also their ongoing exile (Dryden-Peterson, 2017). The case of UNRWA highlights the particular importance of curriculum policies in this regard. Policymakers need to move beyond the technical discourses that have characterized curriculum choices for refugees and reflect on the ways in which education content may propagate power structures that can marginalize or negatively impact refugees' lives and future prospects. Practically, this requires a more holistic understanding of refugee education programs as a multi-facetted economic, social, cultural, and political endeavor. It also requires a more nuanced approach to curriculum in refugee settings than is reflected in the current dichotomous choice between home state or host state curriculum.

Notes

1. This chapter draws primarily on research conducted as part of my doctoral dissertation.
2. A protracted refugee situation is defined as a group of 25,000 refugees or more who have been in exile for a minimum of five years. However, this figure *excludes* the Palestine refugees under UNRWA's mandate (UNHCR, 2018).
3. UNRWA teaches the Lebanese curriculum in Lebanon, the Syrian curriculum in Syria, the Jordanian curriculum in Jordan, and the curriculum of the Palestinian authority in the West Bank and Gaza. Prior to 2000, UNRWA taught the Egyptian curriculum in Gaza and the Jordanian curriculum in the West Bank.
4. UNRWA defines its beneficiaries as "Palestine refugees" rather than the broader term, "Palestinian refugees." Palestine refugees are "persons whose normal place of residence was Palestine during the period 1 June 1946 to 15 May 1948, and who lost both home and means of livelihood as a result of the 1948 conflict" (UNRWA, "Palestine refugees").
5. The lack of an explicit policy document is understandable given that UNRWA's early years were overshadowed by considerable suspicion on the part of the host states and refugees, who rightly feared that the agency was an attempt by Western powers to forcibly resettle them. Nor was UNRWA intended as an institution that would engage in long-term planning and policy making. These factors likely favored decision making through verbal consensus over the pursuit of written agreements with governments.
6. UNESCO's engagement with education for Palestinian refugees began in 1948, when the agency funded schools for the newly displaced refugees. The Secretary-General of the United Nations then requested that UNESCO continue to support the newly created UNRWA through the provision of technical guidance.

7. Even today UNRWA does not comprehensively provide secondary education. Across its five fields it offers education of lower secondary level. In Lebanon it operates a limited number of schools that cover upper secondary education; however this provision is not comprehensive.
8. For example, in Gaza where schools were supported and administered by the American Friends Service Committee (AFSC) between 1949 and mid-1950, it was recommended policy to use Egyptian curriculum and textbooks.
9. The US Government originally conceived of UNRWA as a job creation scheme and assumed that once refugees were employed, they would more easily integrate into host state societies and large-scale repatriation, which was opposed by Israel, could be avoided. In this vision, subsidiary projects, such as the Education Programme, would be transferred to the host state governments: a process that would be easier if the schools were already aligned to the public systems in terms of their structure and content. See also Schiff (1995).
10. Between 1948 and 1967, Jordan administered the West Bank and Egypt administered Gaza. Thus the Jordanian and Egyptian curricula constituted the host state curriculum for the West Bank and Gaza, respectively.
11. The Cairo Agreement was negotiated in November 1969 between the PLO and the Lebanese army. The agreement provided for increased Palestinian control over Palestinian refugee camps in the country, including their use as bases for armed resistance activities.

References

Abu-Amsha, O., & Armstrong, J. (2018). Pathways to resilience in risk-laden environments: A case study of Syrian refugee education in Lebanon. *Journal of Education in Emergencies*, 4(1), 45–73.

Abu-Lughod, I. (1973). Educating a community in exile: The Palestinian experience. *Journal of Palestine Studies*, 2(3), 94–111.

Al Hroub, A. (2011). UNRWA school dropouts in Palestinian refugee camps in Lebanon: A qualitative study: Policy and governance in Palestinian refugee camps. *Issam Fares Institute for Public Policy and International Affairs*. Beirut, Lebanon: American University of Beirut.

Al Husseini, J. (2017). An agency for the Palestinians? In K. Makdisi & V. Prashad (Eds.), *Land of blue helmets: The United Nations and the Arab world* (pp. 301–317). Oakland, CA: University of California Press.

Al Khash, S. (1968, May 1). *Letter from Souleyman Al Khash, Minister of Education Syrian Arab Republic to Rene Maheu Director General of UNESCO* (File S-0169-0004-02) UNARMS archive, New York, US.

American Friends Service Committee (AFSC). (1950, February). *Operational report, February 1950, Appendix 1* (Foreign Service, Projects, School program 1950, File 132). AFSC archives, Philadelphia.

Anderson, B. (1983). *Imagined communities: Reflections on the origin and spread of nationalism*. London, UK: Verso.

Apple, M. (2004). *Ideology and curriculum* (3rd ed.). New York, NY: Routledge Falmer.

Apple, M., & Christian-Smith, L. (1991). The politics of the textbook. In M. Apple & L. Christian-Smith (Eds.), *The politics of the textbook* (pp. 1–19). New York, NY: Routledge.

Avenstrup, R. (2004, December 18). Palestinian textbooks: Where is all that incitement?. *New York Times*. Retrieved from October 1, 2018 from www.nytimes.com/2004/12/18/opinion/palestinian-textbooks-where-is-all-that-incitement.html?mtrref=www.google.com&gwh=601AB0E2C2F940D47C37CC626C143D49&gwt=pay&assetType=opinion

Ball, S. (1993). What is policy? Texts, trajectories and toolboxes. *Discourse*, *13*(2), 10–17.

Barnett, M. (1999). Culture, strategy, and foreign policy change: Israel's road to Oslo. *European Journal of International Relations*, *5*(1), 5–36.

Basisu, M. (1980). *Descent into the water: Palestinian notes from Arab exile*. Wilmette, IL: Medina Press.

Bendix, R. (1964). *Nation-building and citizenship: Studies of our changing social order*. New York, NY: John Wiley and Sons.

Berrebi, C. (2007). Evidence about the link between education, poverty and terrorism among Palestinians. *Peace Economics, Peace Science and Public Policy*, *13*(1), 1–36.

Bertrand, P. (1967, November 3). *Correspondence from Paul Bertrand to U Thant re: The UNESCO resolution* (File S-0169-0004-01). UNARMS, New York.

Brown, N. J. (2001). *Democracy, history and the contest over the Palestinian curriculum*. Paper presented at the Adam Institute Conference on Attitudes Toward the Past in Conflict Resolution. Retrieved from http://lllp.iugaza.edu.ps/Files_Uploads/635063694488064181.pdf

Burde, D. (2014). *Schools for conflict or for peace in Afghanistan*. New York: Columbia University Press.

Cole, E. (2007). Transitional justice and the reform of history education. *International Journal of Transitional Justice*, *1*(1), 115–137.

Dryden-Peterson, S. (2011a). *Refugee education: A global review*. Geneva: United Nations High Commissioner for Refugees.

Dryden-Peterson, S. (2011b). Refugee children aspiring toward the future: Linking education and livelihoods. In K. Mundy & S. Dryden-Peterson (Eds.), *Educating children in conflict zones: Research, policy and practice for systematic change* (pp. 85–99). New York, NY: Teachers College Press.

Dryden-Peterson, S. (2017). Refugee education: Education for an unknowable future. *Curriculum Inquiry*, *47*(1), 14–24.

El Khani, A. (1968, October 4). *A. El Khani, representative of the permanent delegation of the Arab Republic of Syria to UNESCO, correspondence to Rene Maheu, Director-General of UNESCO* (Box RE 26, RE230(1) Part 2). UNRWA archives, Amman, Jordan.

Gellner, E. (1983). *Nations and nationalism*. Ithaca, NY: Cornell University Press.

Groiss, A. (2001). *Jews, Israel and peace in Palestinian school textbooks: Survey of the textbooks published by the Palestinian national authority in the years 2000–2001*. Centre for Monitoring the Impact of Peace (CMIP). Retrieved from www.impact-se.org/wp-content/uploads/2016/04/PA2001.pdf

Groiss, A., & Shaked, R. (2017). *Schoolbooks of the Palestinian Authority: The attitude to Jews, to Israel and to Peace*. Simon Wiesenthal Center and the Middle East Forum for Promoting American Interests. Retrieved from www.terrorism-info.org.il/app/uploads/2017/12/E_259_17.pdf

Hovsepian, N. (2010). Palestinian education in a virtual state. In O. Abi-Mershed (Ed.), *Trajectories of education in the Arab world: Legacies and challenges* (pp. 125–156). London: Routledge.

Irfan, A. (2017). UNRWA and the Palestinian precedent: Lessons from the international response to the Palestinian refugee crisis. *IP Politics Review, 3*(1), 10–24.

Issa, P. (2015). *Abu Maher al Yamani and the unheralded Palestinian leadership in 1950s Lebanon* (Unpublished Masters Thesis). The University of Texas, Austin, TX.

Kagan, M. (2009). The (relative) decline of Palestinian exceptionalism and its consequences for refugee studies in the Middle East. *Journal of Refugee Studies, 22*(4), 417–438.

King, E. (2014). *From classrooms to conflict in Rwanda*. New York, NY: Cambridge University Press.

King, E. (2017). What framing analysis can teach us about history textbooks, peace, and conflict. In M. Bellino & J. H. Williams (Eds.), *(Re)constructing memory: Education, identity, and conflict* (pp. 23–48). Rotterdam: J. Sense Publishers.

Kirk, J. (Ed.). (2009). *Certification counts: Recognizing the learning attainments of displaced and refugee students*. Paris: UNESCO, IIEP.

Kotaishová, J. (2014). *Nahr Al-Bared (cold river)*. Self-published manuscript.

Labouisse, H. (1957, November 16). *Outgoing code cable number 429 from New York to Lalive in Beirut* (Folder S-0169-0010-07). UNARMS archives, New York.

Lalive, J. (1957, November 15). *Incoming code cable, Beico 122 to H. Labouisse in New York* (Folder S-0169-0011-01). UNARMS archives, New York.

Lall, M. (2008). Educate to hate: The use of education in the creation of antagonistic national identities in India and Pakistan. *Compare, 38*(1), 103–119.

Lieber, D. (2017, April 13). PA suspends ties with UNRWA over planned curriculum reform. *The Times of Israel*. Retrieved from www.timesofisrael.com/pa-suspends-ties-with-unwra-over-planned-curriculum-reform/

Malkki, L. (1992). National geographic: The rooting of peoples and the territorialization of national identity among scholars and refugees. *Cultural Anthropology, 7*(1), 24–44.

Malkki, L. (1995). *Purity and exile: Violence, memory, and national cosmology among Hutu refugees in Tanzania*. Chicago, IL: University of Chicago Press.

Marshall, T., & Bottomore, T. H. (1992). *Citizenship and social class*. London, UK: Pluto Classic.

Mazawi, A. (2011). "Which Palestine Should We Teach?" Signatures, palimpsests, and struggles over school textbooks. *Studies in Philosophy and Education, 30*, 169–183.

McAdam, D., McCarthy, J. D., & Zald, M. N. (1996). *Comparative perspectives on social movements: Political opportunities, mobilizing structures, and cultural framings*. Cambridge, UK: Cambridge University Press.

Moughrabi, F. (2001). The politics of Palestinian textbooks. *Journal of Palestine Studies, 31*(1), 5–19.

Murray, H. (2008). Curriculum wars: National identity in education. *London Review of Education, 6*(1), 39–45.

Oh, S., & Van der Stouwe, M. (2009). Towards the certification of learning achievements for Burmese refugees in Thailand: A nongovernmental organization perspective. In J. Kirk (Ed.), *Certification counts: Recognizing the learning attainments of displaced and refugee students* (pp. 149–159). Paris: IIEP-UNESCO.

Pappe, I. (2006). *A history of modern Palestine: One land, two peoples* (2nd ed.). Cambridge, UK: Cambridge University Press.

Pardo, E., & Jacobi, M. (2018). *Syrian national identity: Reformulating school textbooks during the civil war*. IMPACT-se. Retrieved from www.impact-se.org/wp-content/uploads/Syrian-National-Identity_IMPACT-se_July-2018-.pdf

Paulson, J. (2015). "Whether and how?" History education about recent and ongoing conflict: A review of research. *Journal on Education in Emergencies*, 1(1), 14–47.

Peled-Elhanan, N. (2012). *Palestine in Israeli school books: Ideology and propaganda in education*. New York: I. B. Tauris.

Peteet, J. (2005). *Landscape of Hope and Despair: Palestinian refugee camps*. Philadelphia: University of Pennsylvania Press.

Reddaway, A. F. J. (1967, November 14). *Correspondence from A. F. J Reddaway Acting Commissioner-General of UNRWA to Laurence Michelmore Commissioner-General of UNRWA* (Box OR70, Folder OR230(1) Part 4). UNRWA archive, Amman, Jordan.

Ross, M. H. (2002). The political psychology of competing narratives: September 11 and beyond. In C. Calhoun, P. Price, & A. Timmer (Eds.), *Understanding September 11* (pp. 303–320). New York, NY: New Press.

Sayigh, R. (2007). *The Palestinians: From peasants to revolutionaries*. New York: Zed Books.

Sayigh, R. (2017). Where are the history books for Palestinian children? *Journal of Holy Land and Palestine Studies*, 16(2), 145–175.

Schiff, B. (1995). *Refugees unto the third generation: UN aid to Palestinians*. New York: Syracuse University Press.

Shuayb, M. (2014). The art of inclusive exclusions: Educating the Palestinian refugee students in Lebanon. *Refugee Survey Quarterly*, 33(2), 20–37.

Turki, F. (1974). *The disinherited: Journal of a Palestinian Exile*. New York: Mr. Modern Reader.

UNESCO. (1952, May 26). *Report of the director general on the education of Arab refugees in the Middle East, execution of the programme for 1952, rehabilitation*. Resolution 7.15. Submitted to Executive Board 30 EX/42, UNESDOC.

UNESCO Expert Commission. (1969, January 23). *Commission on textbooks used in UNRWA/UNESCO schools: Second preliminary report* (Box RE 26, File RE230(1) Part 3). UNRWA archive, Amman, Jordan.

UNESCO-IBE. (2013). *Glossary of curriculum terminology*. Geneva: Author.

UNHCR. (2012). *Education strategy 2012–2016*. Geneva: Author. Retrieved from www.unhcr.org/protection/operations/5149ba349/unhcr-education-strategy-2012-2016.html

UNHCR. (2015). *Curriculum choices in refugee settings: Education: Issue brief 3*. Geneva: Author. Retrieved from www.unhcr.org/publications/education/560be1209/education-brief-3-curriculum-choices-refugee-settings.html

UNHCR. (2018). *Global trends: Forced displacement in 2017*. Geneva: Author. Retrieved from www.unhcr.org/globaltrends2017/

UNHCR. *Solutions*. Retrieved from www.unhcr.org/solutions.html
United Nations General Assembly (UNGA). (2016, September 19). *New York declaration for refugees and migrants*. A/Res/71/1. Retrieved from www.unhcr.org/new-york-declaration-for-refugees-and-migrants.html
United States Department of State (USDOS). (1950, February). *The Palestine refugee program*. Publication 3757. Near and Middle Eastern Series 3 (Foreign Service Reports, General, File 248). AFSC archives, Philadelphia, US.
UNRWA. (1967a, August 1). *Extract from a letter from the Director of Education to the Commissioner General* (Box RE26, Folder RE230(1) part 1). UNRWA archive, Amman, Jordan.
UNRWA. (1967b, August 17). *Memorandum from the Director of Education to the Commissioner General* (Box RE26, Folder RE230(1) part 1). UNRWA archive, Amman, Jordan.
UNRWA. (2011). *UNRWA and neutrality*. Retrieved from www.unrwa.org/userfiles/2011033075942.pdf
UNRWA. *Palestine refugees*. Retrieved from www.unrwa.org/palestine-refugees
UNRWA. *What we do*. Retrieved from www.unrwa.org/what-we-do/education
WAFA. (2017, March 25). *Ministry of Education warns UNRWA against making any changes to curriculum*. Palestinian News and Info Agency. Retrieved from http://english.wafa.ps/page.aspx?id=1M9GHEa66736920360a1M9GHE
Waters, T., & Leblanc, K. (2005). Refugees and education: Mass public schooling without a nation-state. *Comparative Education Review*, 49(2), 129–147.
Wells, C. (1987). *The UN, UNESCO and the politics of knowledge*. New York, NY: St. Martin's Press.
Zald, M. (1996). Culture, ideology and strategic framing. In D. McAdam, J. D. McCarthy, & M. Zald (Eds.), *Comparative perspectives on social movements: Political opportunities, mobilizing structures, and cultural framings* (pp. 261–274). Cambridge, UK: Cambridge University Press.

Contributors

About the Volume Editors

Lisa Damaschke-Deitrick is a professor of Comparative and International Education at Lehigh University, Pennsylvania. She holds a doctorate in Social Sciences from the University of Tübingen, Germany, a master's in International Relations from the Free University Amsterdam, The Netherlands, and a bachelor's from the University of Bielefeld, Germany. In her research, she focuses on how education is used as a solution or cure-all for societal issues. Her research areas include educational policies for poverty prevention primarily in education systems in Europe and other welfare states with the focus on early school leavers. She also conducts research on educational policies and practices designed to facilitate refugee youth's participation in their new host countries.

Ericka Galegher has a PhD in Comparative and International Education from Lehigh University. Using qualitative and quantitative methods, Dr. Galegher conducts research on international and private education, education in Egypt, and education and teacher preparation for the integration of refugees and marginalized groups. She has an MA in Middle East Studies from the American University in Cairo, graduate diploma in Secondary Education from the College of New Jersey, and a BA in International Affairs from the George Washington University. She has worked in the education sector in Egypt for over 10 years as a teacher, administrator, and researcher and on educational development projects in Cambodia and Egypt. Dr. Galegher resides in Egypt as an independent researcher.

Maureen F. Park is a doctoral student in Comparative and International Education at Lehigh University. Her research focuses on refugee and migrant education, mother tongue–based multilingual education, and gender and education. She has a BA in Political Science and an MEd in Multicultural Education. Maureen has experience in both international development and as an educator; she was a bilingual teacher in the United States as well as an international schoolteacher in Central Asia. She has also worked for the Peace Corps, World Vision, and the World Food Programme. Maureen serves as an editorial assistant for the *Annual Review of Comparative and International Education*. She is also co-founder of an NGO based in Kenya working to combat gender-based violence in schools and provide sexual and reproductive health education. She is currently based in Nepal.

Alexander W. Wiseman, PhD, is professor of Educational Leadership and Policy in the College of Education at Texas Tech University. Dr. Wiseman holds a dual-degree Ph.D. in Comparative and International Education and Educational Theory & Policy from Pennsylvania State University, an MA in International Comparative Education from Stanford University, an MA in Education from the University of Tulsa, and a BA in Letters from the University of Oklahoma. Dr. Wiseman conducts comparative educational research on educational policy and practice using large-scale education datasets on math and science education, information and communication technology (ICT), teacher preparation, professional development and curriculum, as well as school principals' instructional leadership activity and is the author of many research-to-practice articles and books. He serves as senior editor of the online journal *FIRE: Forum for International Research in Education*, series editor for the International Perspectives on Education and Society volume series (Emerald Publishing), and editor of the *Annual Review of Comparative and International Education* (Emerald Publishing).

About the Authors

Mariana Lima Becker is currently a doctoral student and graduate assistant in Curriculum and Instruction at Boston College, Massachusetts. Her research interests involve bilingual education, gender, and immigration, the educational experiences of Brazilian immigrant youth in the United States, and understanding second language and literacy development from a Vygotskian perspective. She taught English as a Foreign Language (EFL) for several years in Recife, Brazil, and is a licensed English as a Second Language teacher in the state of Massachusetts. Mariana completed a master's in Linguistics at the Federal University of Pernambuco, Brazil, focusing on Brazilian public school EFL teachers' understanding of the theoretical and methodological concepts that underlay the textbooks used in their instruction. She also completed a master's degree in Applied Linguistics at the University of Massachusetts Boston, where she focused on the inseparability of cognition and emotion in the foreign language classroom from a Vygotskian perspective.

Elizabeth R. Bruce holds a bachelor of science degree with honors in Textile Chemistry from Clemson University in Clemson, South Carolina, and a master of education degree in Globalization and Educational Change from Lehigh University in Bethlehem, Pennsylvania. She currently works as a nonresident researcher for the Sheikh Saud bin Saqr Al Qasimi Foundation for Policy Research, focusing on philanthropy and education. Her personal research centers on HIV/AIDS policies in education and health research partnerships, looking particularly at sub-Saharan Africa.

Elizabeth Buckner is an assistant professor at the Ontario Institute for Studies in Education (OISE) at the University in Toronto. Previously, she was a visiting assistant professor of International Comparative Education at Teachers College, Columbia University. At Teachers College, she led a case study of Lebanon's educational policies for Syrian refugees as part of the Urban Refugee Education project. She is currently a consultant with the Middle East Education Research, Training and Support (MEERS) project, a USAID-funded project that supports data collection and dissemination for Education in Emergencies. Her work has been published in the *Journal of Refugee Studies, Comparative Education Review, and Sociology of Education,* among others. She has a regional specialization in the Middle East and North Africa and has conducted fieldwork in Morocco, Tunisia, Jordan, Syria, Lebanon, and the UAE. Dr. Buckner holds a PhD in International and Comparative Education from Stanford University's Graduate School of Education.

Maihemuti Dilimulati (Dilmurat Mahmut) is a PhD candidate at the Faculty of Education, McGill University. His research interests include Muslim identity in the West, equity and education, education and violent extremism, and immigrant integration in Canada and beyond. Currently he is studying the Uyghur immigrants' identity reconstruction experiences in Canada. His recent publications include *The Radicalization of Youth in the West—How Can Canadian Teachers Effectively Approach this Issue in Their Classrooms?* (book chapter coauthored with Ghosh et al, forthcoming), "Revisiting Muslim Identity and Islamophobia in the Contemporary World" (book chapter, 2018), "Controlling Religious Knowledge and Education for Countering Violent Extremism: Case Study of the Uyghur Muslims in China Forum for International Research in Education" (forthcoming), "Can Education Counter Violent Religious Extremism?" *Canadian Foreign Policy Journal* (coauthored with Ghosh et al, 2016), and *Education and Security: A Global Literature Report on Countering Violent Religious Extremism* (coauthored with Ghosh et al, 2016).

Eileen Dombrowski is an early childhood education specialist with RTI International. She focuses on ensuring early childhood programming meaningfully includes children with disabilities and supports teachers to provide the differentiation of instruction these children need to be successful. Prior to joining RTI, Ms. Dombrowski was a policy and programs specialist at Easter Seals, where she advocated for increasing funding for programs that impact children with disabilities and their families. She started her career as an early childhood special education teacher and has taught in public schools in Washington, DC, and Baltimore City. While in DC, she served as director of an organization connecting volunteers with recently arrived refugee families. Ms. Dombrowski was a Peace Corps volunteer in Romania (2006–2008) and a Peace Corps Response volunteer in The Gambia (2010–2011).

Johanna Garnett works as a casual lecturer in Peace Studies and Political Science at the University of New England (UNE), Armidale. She has a PhD in peace studies (awarded the Chancellor's Medal for International Impact), a masters of environmental advocacy and bachelor of social science (sociology major), all from UNE. Her research focuses on social movements, youth, alternative development, and critical education for environmental peace building. Dr. Garnett works in Myanmar with agrarian youth from varying ethnic groups who are engaged in peace-building processes in their emerging democracy. She has presented her work in Australia and internationally, is well published, and currently coauthoring a book for Routledge—*Environmental Peace in the Anthropocene*. Dr. Garnett has a long history in political activism and education, working in a variety of capacities and contexts and teaching across all ages, from preschool to adults.

Ratna Ghosh is Distinguished James McGill Professor and William C. MacDonald Professor in the Department of Integrated Studies in Education at McGill University in Montreal, Canada. She was dean of education at McGill from 1998 to 2003, was appointed a member of the Order of Canada, officer of the Order of Quebec, officer of the Order of Montreal, and was elected a Fellow of the Royal Society of Canada and a Fellow of the World Academy for the advancement of science in developing countries, Social Sciences Division, in Trieste, Italy. Her publications, prestigious grants, and teaching reflect her varied research interests in comparative and international education. Her coauthored books *Education and the Politics of Difference* and *Redefining Multicultural Education* are based on several years of research in education and diversity. She is past president of the Comparative and International Education Society (CIES) (2011-2012).

Narjes Hashemi is a second-year master's student in the Department of Integrated Studies in Education at McGill University in Montreal, Canada. She has been working as a graduate research assistant on the SSHRC funded project Countering Religious Extremism Through Education n Multicultural Canada, under the direction of Dr. Ratna Ghosh. An

Afghan refugee herself who came to Canada as a teenager, she has experienced the problems associated with getting an education in a different culture and context. After finishing high school in Vancouver, British Columbia, she graduated with a BA degree in Sociology from the University of British Columbia. Now at McGill University, her MA thesis explores women's roles in preventing religious extremism in Afghanistan.

Shenshen Hu is currently a monitoring and evaluation manager at the LEGO Foundation, providing oversight on the design and implementation of monitoring, evaluation, and learning of programs centered around play-based learning. She earned her master of education degree in international educational development at Teachers College, Columbia University. She is also a graduate of Eötvös Loránd University of Science's double degree program in English Linguistics and Literature, as well as Communication Studies. Shenshen has a strong commitment to education coupled with diverse experiences in and out of the classroom. Born in China and raised in Hungary, she began her career as a secondary school teacher in Budapest. She has worked as a researcher and international development consultant.

Rachel Jordan is a monitoring and evaluation specialist at the RTI International–implemented USAID School Health and Reading Program in Uganda, where she led the development of teacher monitoring, coaching, and observation tools. Rachel supports data collection, analysis, and dissemination of the Early Grades Reading Assessment, as well as additional research on Primary 1 repetition, cost-effective alternatives for teacher training, refugee education, and community engagement in the Karamoja region. Before receiving her MS Ed in International Education Development from the University of Pennsylvania, Rachel taught English and history in Philadelphia's public high schools for five years.

Jo Kelcey is a doctoral candidate in International Development Education at New York University's Steinhardt School of Education, Culture, and Human Development and a senior researcher at the Centre for Lebanese Studies, affiliated with the Lebanese American University. Her research uses historical, qualitative, and quantitative methods to understand the effects of conflict on education and the relationship between forced displacement and education. Prior to her doctoral studies, Jo worked for aid agencies conducting research and managing education projects in the Middle East, Central America, South Asia and sub-Saharan Africa. She has an MSc in Violence, Conflict, and Development from the School of Oriental and African Studies, University of London and a BA (honors) in economics and French from the University of Sheffield. She is based in Beirut, Lebanon.

Contributors 297

Mary Mendenhall is an associate professor of practice and the director of the International and Comparative Education program at Teachers College, Columbia University. She designs and leads grant-funded implementation projects and research studies about the policies and practices of refugee education across camp, urban, and resettlement contexts as well as teacher support, collaboration, and professional development in crisis settings. Dr. Mendenhall leads the research workstream of the Teachers in Crisis Contexts Collaborative, under the auspices of the Inter-agency Network for Education in Emergencies. She also serves as an advisory council member for both the Carey Institute of Global Good's Center for Learning in Practice and the Right to Education.

Rehemah Nabacwa is the monitoring and evaluation manager at the RTI International–implemented USAID School Health and Reading Program in Uganda, where she oversees an RCT utilizing the Early Grades Reading Assessment in 13 languages, and has supported additional research on Primary 1 repetition, linguistic differences in reading performance, refugee education, and the uptake and use of technology for classroom coaching. Rehemah has been conducting research on education in Uganda for over 12 years, and has previously published articles on Early Grades Reading Achievement and the use and usefulness of school grants. She received her master of arts in Gender Studies from Makerere University in Uganda.

Mozynah Nofal is currently completing a PhD in Education Leadership and Policy at the Ontario Institute for Studies in Education (OISE) at the University of Toronto. Between September 2017 and June 2018, she took part in a research study at OISE focusing on refugee integration experiences in schools in Canada and Europe. In 2017 she completed her master's degree with a thesis titled "For Our Children: A Study of the Educational Experiences of Syrian Refugee Children in Ottawa" from the Department of Educationat the University of Ottawa. Mozynah completed her bachelor's degree in 2012 at Carleton University's Public Affairs and Policy Management Program with a specialization in development studies. She has previous work experience at the Canadian Bureau for International Education, the United Nations Human's Rights Council, and several local weekend education programs in Ottawa. She is also the founder of Ihyaa, an educational socio-psycho support program for children in the Alrahma refugee camp in Tripoli, Lebanon.

Gabrielle Oliveira is Assistant Professor of Education at the Lynch School of Education and Human Development at Boston College. She is also a National Academy of Education/Spencer Foundation Dissertation

(2013) and Postdoctoral (2019) Fellow. Her research focuses on immigration and mobility—on how people move, adapt, and parent across borders. Her expertise includes gender, anthropology, transnationalism, and bilingualism with a concentration on Latin America. Merging the fields of anthropology and education through ethnographic work in multiple countries, Oliveira also studies the educational trajectories of immigrant and first generation children. Oliveira received her bachelor's degree in her native Brazil and earned her master's and doctoral degrees from Columbia University, where she was also a National Academy of Education/Spencer Foundation Dissertation fellow. She is also the co-founder of the group Colectiva Infancias, which has received funding from the National Geographic Foundation to document the experiences of immigrant children across the Americas.

Arianna Pacifico is a doctoral student in International Comparative Education at Teachers College, Columbia University, whose research is focused on education in conflict and crisis contexts. Arianna previously coordinated the Standards and Practice Working Group at the Inter-agency Network for Education in Emergencies (INEE), which provides technical expertise and fosters inter-agency collaboration between 25+ working group member organizations. Areas of work included conflict sensitive education, the INEE Minimum Standards, social and emotional learning, early childhood development, and humanitarian capacity development. Arianna has over eight years' experience in international education and humanitarian aid and holds a master's degree in Global Affairs from New York University.

Mahbub Alam Prodip is an associate professor in Public Administration at the University of Rajshahi in Bangladesh. He is currently pursuing a doctor of philosophy in Peace Studies at the University of New England in Australia. He has a master of science in Gender and Development Studies from the Asian Institute of Technology in Thailand (with excellence in research work) as well as a master of social science in Public Administration from the University of Chittagong in Bangladesh (obtaining first position), and a bachelor of social science from the same discipline and institution. He was awarded a number of postgraduate scholarships from Italy, Thailand, and Australia. His research interests are gender and politics, gender and violence, and Rohingya refugee issues in Bangladesh.

Domenique Sherab is an independent researcher with a focus on forced migration, refugees, integration, and education issues. She has a master's of science in refugees and forced migration from Oxford University and a bachelors of international and global studies (honors) from Sydney University. She has worked and consulted for universities and NGOs in Australia, Canada, and the Middle East. She is currently conducting a FRQSC funded project with Dr. Ratna Ghosh focused on support services in adult education for young adult refugees in Quebec and working on a pan-Canadian longitudinal study focused on integration of Syrian refugees with Dr. Thomas Soehl and Dr. Dietlind Stolle at McGill University in Montreal, Canada.

Christin Spoolstra is an education development and management consultant based in Cambodia, focusing on improving the public school system and developing local staff capacity. She is currently pursuing her MEd in globalization and educational change at Lehigh University. Ms. Spoolstra moved to Cambodia in 2011, where she served as a Peace Corps volunteer in the education sector until 2014. Her main research interests are education equity and social capital.

Tshegofatso D. Thulare is a project management specialist and an education researcher, having recently completed her MEd in Globalization and Educational Change at Lehigh University. A Fulbright Foreign Scholar award recipient for 2016, Tshegofatso currently supports one of South Africa's largest Early Grade Reading Studies for the national Department of Basic Education and previously worked at a leading education management nonprofit in Johannesburg, where she worked collaboratively with teachers and school leaders in communities of effective practice. Passionate about the nexus of development and education on the African continent, Tshegofatso's research areas include issues of access and equity in public schooling, public-private partnerships in education, and large-scale systemic education reform.

Index

Note: Numbers in *italic* refer to a figure.

Afghanistan 5, 27, 72, 106, 114, 117, 121, 163, 166–167, 175–177, 179–180, 273
asylum 3, 16, 27, 33, 38, 163–164, 166, 175, 220–221, 274
asylum seekers/seeking 1, 3–6, 12–17, 33, 46, 75–81, 83–85, 89–90, 92, 95–98, 106–108, 111, 122, 142, 161–162, 164–166, 168, 197, 213, 221–222

Bangladesh 5, 10, 12, 16, 72, 191–193, 195–199, 204–206, 209–210, 213–215

Canada 4, 13, 15, 86, 102–115, 117, 119–120, 121
capabilities 10, 158, 162, 185
civil society 61, 67–68
classroom pedagogy 75
comprehensive refugee response framework 15, 131, 135, 137
conflict 2–3, 5–10, 17, 27, 39, 54–55, 58–61, 64–65, 67–69, 71, 75–77, 79–80, 85, 113–114, 117, 134, 140–141, 143, 157–159, 161, 163, 166, 176, 193–194, 196, 212–213, 245–246, 258, 273–274, 279, 282, 286
crisis contexts 245–249, 251–255, 267
curriculum 8–9, 11, 16, 31, 61, 109, 121, 144, 181, 195, 206, 223–226, 250–252, 272, 276

development 2, 28, 32, 54–57, 64, 106, 132, 135–136, 159, 192, 223, 245, 249, 258, 272

displacement 3–6, 9, 11–12, 16–17, 45, 53–56, 58–60, 64, 75, 110, 115, 134, 136, 142, 158–159, 175, 183, 195, 246, 256, 258, 271, 273–274, 279

education as a panacea 1, 5, 13–14, 16, 27, 31, 44–45
education in emergencies (eie) 10, 14, 56, 58–59, 66, 132, 192, 206, 245, 248, 251
education policy 6, 31, 37–38, 61, 239
Egypt 5, 13, 15, 157, 171, 280
emergency education 15, 64, 191–192, 197, 203
employment 28, 30, 35–36, 39, 42, 44, 110, 141, 147, 158–159, 164, 172, 177, 185, 278

female refugees 4, 15, 157–159, 162–163
forced displacement 4–5, 12, 279

Gaza 271, 274, 278–283, 286–287
gender 9, 12, 16, 28, 82, 92–93, 103, 118, 158, 174, 176, 194, 220, 228, 252
Germany 4–5, 13–15, 27, 33, 36, 76, 91, 97–98, 119, 157, 163

higher education 10, 15, 40–41, 62, 96, 118–119, 140, 157–158, 230
history 22, 28, 31–32, 37, 61, 102–105, 137, 165, 195, 279
host country/countries 8, 11, 15, 29, 31, 61, 68, 70, 77–78, 132–133, 135, 137, 139–140, 142, 144, 147–149,

Index   301

157–158, 161, 181, 183, 185, 223, 245, 268
human rights 3, 8, 14, 54, 56–58, 61, 68, 71, 131, 134, 162, 191–193, 213, 215, 279–280, 282

immigrant 3, 6, 13, 16, 29–30, 32–33, 35, 38, 40, 42, 44, 45, 76–81, 83, 85–88, 90, 93, 96–97, 104–106, 109, 111, 114, 116, 119, 122–123, 194
immigrant Latina youth 16, 220
inclusion 7–8, 11–13, 15–16, 61, 110, 113, 122, 140, 195, 251
inclusive society 13, 15, 103, 117, 123
information and communication technology (ICT) 248
integration 1, 4, 7, 11, 14–15, 27–33, 35–36, 38, 43–46, 62, 70, 107, 110–113, 120, 134, 139, 143, 145–147, 158, 164, 185, 223, 225, 271, 273–274, 277, 285–286
internally displaced, internal displacement 3, 55, 162–163, 222, 245
international development 10, 57
International Network for Education in Emergencies (INEE) 16, 60, 67–68, 194, 197, 199–200, 202–203, 214, 251–252
International Organization for Migration (IOM) 3
international organizations 27, 29, 31, 43, 59, 75, 180

Jordan 53, 55–57, 60, 238, 271, 278

Kakuma refugee camp 5, 16, 142, 245, 249
Kenya 4–5, 15–16, 119, 131, 142–146, 246
Kyrgyzstan 5, 13, 15, 157, 165, 175

Latinx 220–221, 225–227, 229–231, 240
Lebanon 53–57, 62–63, 271, 280
legislation 34, 103, 106–109, 164

Middle East 4, 14, 54, 105, 164, 181, 271, 280
migrants 2–3, 58, 132, 159, 162, 221
Millennium Development Goals (MDGs) 10, 57–58
Ministry of Education policies 62, 113, 116–117
Myanmar 72, 191, 195

narrative inquiry 253, 267
neoinstitutionalism 29–31, 43
No Lost Generation (NLG) 60, 64, 66
non-governmental organizations (NGOs) 62–63, 65, 67, 136, 140, 153–154, 169, 172–173, 192, 197–198, 202, 205, 208–209, 214

out-of-school children 16, 63, 65, 250

Palestinian refugees 5, 11, 53, 61, 271, 274
partnerships 14, 34, 107, 120, 161, 163, 268
PISA 14, 77, 80, 97
policy 2, 25, 29–32, 61, 103–108, 115, 131–133, 135, 137, 148, 165, 198, 271
post-conflict 2, 6–7, 9–10, 75, 77, 79, 141, 157–159, 161–162, 194
primary education 10, 57, 75, 197
professional development 13–16, 56, 83, 90–91, 96, 116, 122, 230

refugee: education 1, 6, 13, 15–16, 29, 31, 43, 45, 54, 56–59, 69, 76–77, 109, 112–114, 135–138, 246, 274; education policy teachers 5, 76, 118, 144, 249–253; integration 14, 27, 29, 30–32, 43–44, 111–112, 271, 273–274; transitions 16, 185
Regional Refugee and Resilience Framework (3RP) 14, 60, 64–66, 70
resettlement 3, 6, 10, 12, 17, 27, 29, 34, 76, 105–107, 118–119, 131, 134, 141–142, 145–146, 148, 159, 165, 174, 222–223, 268, 273–274, 277–278, 286
Rohingya 5, 10, 12, 15–16, 71, 191, 195–197

schooling 5, 37–38, 40, 61, 109–111, 138–139, 146, 175, 220, 278
secondary education 65, 140, 157, 160, 163, 176, 184, 239, 276
student learning 16, 62, 77, 79, 111, 116, 246–247, 267
supra-national 10, 54, 56, 58–60, 71
Syria 5, 7, 14, 27, 32, 53, 60, 63, 76, 91, 102, 105, 160, 271, 280

teacher education 250
teacher preparation 14–15, 75–76, 112

teacher professional development *81*, 90, 245–246
teacher training 14, 75, 81, 97, 117–118, 158, 248, 254
tertiary education 10, 113, 120, 132, 136, 139, 141, 157–160
Turkey 55–56, 58–66, 70–72, 86

Uganda 4, 15, 131, 137
unauthorized 3, 222, 227
undocumented 3–5, 13, 16, 108, 122, 220–223, 225–228, 235, 238–240

UNESCO 43, 160
UNHCR 2–5, 10–11, 14, 16, 28, 30, 34, 53, 55–56, 63, 66, 75–76, 131, 143, 157, 164, 196, 250, 271, 273–274
UNICEF 53, 56, 63–64, 66, 193
United States 3–5, 14, 16, 27, 33, 39, 54, 77, 102, 106, 160, 220–221, 276
UNRWA 53, 55, 271, 274

West Bank 271, 281
world society theory 54, 56, 69, 71